A Social History of Christianity

To Elizabeth and Marilyn,
who shared some of this history with me,
and to Penny,
who helped me write about it

A Social History of Christianity
North-west India Since 1800

John C.B. Webster

OXFORD
UNIVERSITY PRESS

OXFORD

UNIVERSITY PRESS

YMCA Library Building, Jai Singh Road, New Delhi 110 001

Oxford University Press is a department of the University of Oxford. It furthers the
University's objective of excellence in research, scholarship, and education
by publishing worldwide in

Oxford   New York

Auckland   Cape Town   Dar es Salaam   Hong Kong   Karachi   Kuala Lumpur
Madrid   Melbourne   Mexico City   Nairobi   New Delhi   Shanghai   Taipei   Toronto

With offices in

Argentina   Austria   Brazil   Chile   Czech Republic   France   Greece   Guatemala
Hungary   Italy   Japan   Poland   Portugal   Singapore   South Korea   Switzerland
Thailand   Turkey   Ukraine   Vietnam

Oxford is a registered trademark of Oxford University Press
in the UK and in certain other countries

Published in India
by Oxford University Press, New Delhi

© Oxford University Press 2007

The moral rights of the author have been asserted
Database right Oxford University Press (maker)

First published 2007

ISBN-13: 978-019-569045-3
ISBN-10: 019-569045-1

Typeset in DanteMT Regular 11/13.3
by Sai Graphic Design, New Delhi 110 055
Printed in India at De Unique, New Delhi 110 018
Published by Oxford University Press
YMCA Library Building, Jai Singh Road, New Delhi 110 001

Contents

Tables and Maps

Tables

Maps

Preface

Some time ago, the editorial board of the Church History Association of India invited me to write a 200-page book on north-west India during the nineteenth and twentieth centuries for its multi-volume *History of Christianity in India*. What has emerged in response to that invitation has been a much larger volume than they wanted. Since the history of Christianity in the north-west, as in the rest of India, is complex, ambivalent, and a subject of recent controversy, the fuller, more detailed history I have sought to present here seems warranted. I want to thank the Oxford University Press for publishing it and the Church History Association of India's editorial board, with whom I intend to keep faith, for allowing me to publish this volume independently of their series.

Since I have been deeply involved with this project for many years, it seems appropriate to say a few words about myself and about my relationship to the subject matter. I came to India first as a tourist (1958), next as an MA student (1960–62), and then as a missionary of the United Presbyterian Church in the USA (1963–81), teaching history first at Baring Union Christian College in Batala, Punjab, and then at United Theological College in Bangalore. At Baring College, my own 'discovery of India' coincided with both my initiation into the academic discipline of historical research under the guidance of some outstanding Indian scholars and with my growing association with the north Indian Christian community. Since then, although a foreigner and in recent years no longer resident in India, I have sought to write about the history of Christianity from within that Indian social and intellectual context. This accounts in good measure for my continuing focus upon the social history of the Christian community as a whole, not just upon the foreign missionaries, and for setting that history primarily within a 'social history of India' rather than a 'history of Christian missions', 'history of the East-West encounter', or a 'history of colonialism' framework. It is my hope that this history will contribute not only to a better understanding of the Christian community in India but also to a greater appreciation, within wider academic circles, of the part it has played in modern Indian history.

Two technical problems that have arisen during the writing of this book need a brief explanation. A history of this kind requires the use of some Indian terms, which may not be familiar to many western readers, and of some Christian terms, which may be unfamiliar to many Indian readers. I have defined a few of these in the text or footnotes; others I considered likely to be unclear I have put in the glossary at the end. The other problem has been the English spelling of Indian place names, as quite a few spellings have changed over time and on a few there is still disagreement today (for example, Punjab or Panjab). I have tended to use those spellings which were current when I lived in north-west India and trust that the reader will be able to make the necessary phonetic connections when alternative spellings appear in quotations or footnote references.

The research for this book has taken me to many libraries in different parts of the world. In India they are the National Archives of India, the Brotherhood of the Ascended Christ, Vidyajoyti, and St. Stephen's College in Delhi; Panjab University in Chandigarh; Baring Union Christian College in Batala; Leonard Theological College in Jabalpur, and United Theological College in Bangalore. In Pakistan, I used the library of Forman Christian College before it was nationalized and of Gujranwala Theological Seminary. In the United Kingdom, I spent considerable time in the British Library, the School of Oriental and African Studies Library (University of London), the Church Missionary Society Library, the Salvation Army International Heritage Centre, the University of Birmingham Library, the New College Library at the University of Edinburgh, as well as the Rhodes House Library and Angus Library of Regents Park College at Oxford University. In the United States, I have consulted the libraries of Union Theological Seminary in New York City, Columbia University, Yale Divinity School in New Haven, the Presbyterian Historical Society in Philadelphia, Princeton Theological Seminary, Pittsburgh Theological Seminary, Boston University School of Theology, the Mary Immaculate Friary in Garrison, New York, and, close to home, Connecticut College. I also made very fruitful visits to the Archives of the Presbyterian Church of New Zealand in

Dunedin and the General Synod Archives of the Anglican Church of Canada in Toronto. I wish to thank the staff in all of them for their assistance.

The individuals who have helped me in the research for this history are simply too numerous to mention by name. Many people have given me hospitality, interviews, access to relevant materials in their possession, and references to other people who would be of further help to me. All of them deserve my thanks for sharing their time, knowledge, and resources. I must, however, mention just a few whose help has been quite indispensable and out of the ordinary. The Brotherhood of the Ascended Christ has provided me with a home in Delhi more times than I can count. The Roman Catholic portion of this history has been greatly enhanced by the help of Fr Leonard Fernando SJ and Fr Julius in Delhi as well as Bishop Peter Celestine in Jammu. Freddi Joseph set aside several days on two separate occasions to introduce me to Pentecostal pastors in and around Jullundur. Nazir Masih and his family convened the meeting of Christian activists at their home in Shahpur. Itty Benjamin at Baring Union Christian College took me on several research expeditions within Gurdaspur district. Dr Frederick S. Downs, Rev. W.W. Jones, and Penny Webster have read through draft chapters offering their reassurance, comments, and suggestions. I have also discussed several smaller segments of my draft chapters with others who were either directly affected or who had special expertise on the subject. To them my thanks are due as well. However, the end product is mine and I alone am responsible for any errors of fact or interpretation that have distorted the story I have sought to tell in these pages.

As other authors have testified in their prefaces, writing a book is something of a family affair. Dedicating this book to my daughters, Elizabeth and Marilyn, who grew up in India, and to my wife, Penny, is perhaps the best way to express publicly my gratitude to them for all that they have contributed to it and to me personally during the years I have been working on it.

Abbreviations

BCISS	Bulletin of the Christian Institute of Sikh Studies
BJP	Bharatiya Janata Party
BM	The Baptist Magazine
CEZMS	The Church of England Zenana Missionary Society
CHA	The Church at Home and Abroad
CMI	Church Missionary Intelligencer
CMO	Church Missionary Outlook
CMR	Church Missionary Review
CMS	Church Missionary Society
DMN	Delhi Mission News
EW	The East and the West
FM	The Foreign Missionary
FMC	Foreign Missionary Chronicle
HFR	Home and Foreign Record
HFMR	The Home and Foreign Missionary Record of the Church of Scotland
ICHR	Indian Church History Review
IFE	The Indian Female Evangelist
IS	The Indian Standard
ISPCK	Indian Society for Promoting Christian Knowledge
IW	India's Women
IWCD	India's Women and China's Daughters
LDM	Lahore Diocesan Magazine
LDR	Lahore Diocesan Record
LW	Life and Work
MF	The Mission Field
MH	The Missionary Herald
MMQ	CMS Mass Movement Quarterly
NCCR	National Christian Council Review
NIC	North India Churchman
OL	Other Lands
SPG	Society for the Propagation of the Gospel

UCNI   United Church of Northern India
UCR   United Church Review
UP   The United Presbyterian
WMM   Women's Missionary Magazine

1 Introduction

This study in regional social history deals with what the British census referred to as 'The Punjab and its Dependencies'. Since that time the region has been subdivided several times, most importantly in 1947 when the partition line separating India and Pakistan went right through the middle of the region. Today it encompasses the Indian states of Jammu and Kashmir, Himachal Pradesh, Punjab, Haryana, the Union Territories of Delhi and Chandigarh, as well as the Pakistani states of Punjab and the North-West Frontier Province. While ecclesiastical and civil boundaries rarely coincided, ties among Christians within this area have been strong enough to make the north-west a workable and meaningful unit for studying the history of Christianity. This history will cover the entire north-west up to 1947. The chapter on the post-Independence period is confined to developments within India and deals only indirectly with Pakistan.

Regional history offers particular advantages to a social historian of Christianity in India. Christianity functions primarily at the local and regional levels, and national developments, whether originating inside or outside the churches, have had different regional impacts and responses. Thus, regional history offers the best opportunity to explore in some depth the particular and distinctive dynamics of Christianity's changing internal life and interactions with the immediate society of which it has been a part. At the same time, regional history forces the historian to move beyond the history of a particular Christian mission, institution, or type of work (for example, education), in order to gain a vision of Christianity as a whole within a specific locale. Depth and comprehensiveness are often incompatible goals. Regional history may offer the best way of achieving a good measure of both at the same time.

The Study of Christianity in North-west India
So far, Christianity has received only passing glances in histories of the north-west. References to it have been confined mostly to

discussions of the 1857 revolt and to histories of nineteenth-century religious reform and revival movements, generally as background.[1] This historical attention has been directed to the foreign missionaries, while virtually none has been paid to the Indian Christian community. Moreover, with rare exceptions, in histories of the years following World War I, the missionaries have also been ignored and Christianity drops out of sight.

There has been a similar pattern of neglect in general histories of Christianity in India. James Hough completed his history while Christianity was establishing itself in the north-west. John Kaye's history, written in 1859 as a rebuttal to the Evangelical post-mutiny 'Christian Policy' for India, which based much of its justification on the experience of Evangelical missionaries and administrators in the Punjab, virtually ignored the north-west and concentrated instead upon Bengal.[2] In 1875, M.A. Sherring took a region-by-region approach to the history of Protestant missions and so devoted a chapter to a narrative of the work which missionaries had been doing in Delhi and the Punjab. Sherring's main concern was with the plans, operations, and achievements of the various missions, noting that 'in the main, with a few important exceptions, the missionaries of the Punjab are following out the same diverse and multitudinous methods and plans of labour in their limited tract as are being prosecuted over the whole of the remaining country'.[3] Julius Richter's *A History of Missions in India* (1908) was not arranged regionally; it provides a broad historical overview of mostly Protestant missions with an emphasis upon strategies, patterns, and issues. There are many references to missions, organizations, institutions, and events in the north-west, but no connected history of them.

---

[1] Kenneth W. Jones and Spencer Lavan included religious controversy and competition between Christians on the one hand and Arya Samajis or Ahmadiyahs on the other. Kenneth W. Jones, *Arya Dharm*, pp. 139–45; Spencer Lavan, *The Ahmadiyah Movement*, pp. 66–74.

[2] For a fuller analysis of these and other general works on the history of Christianity in India, see John C.B. Webster, 'The History of Christianity in India: Aims and Methods', pp. 87–122.

[3] M.A. Sherring, *The History of Protestant Missions in India*, p. 220.

Prior to Independence, the only histories dealing specifically with Christianity in north-west India were denominational mission histories written by missionary members or their admirers for a Western readership.[4] Their focus was upon the missionary, the mission, and 'the work'. The emerging Christian community was largely ignored, while north-west India was treated simply as a stage on which the Christian missionary drama was played out; the people there had no significant roles within that drama and little influence in shaping its outcomes. Robert Clark wrote about 'the work of God by means of the Church Missionary Society'.[5] He described the founding of the mission, its missionaries, statistics, geographical and human setting before presenting a mission station by mission station account of important developments involving the personalities, structures, and institutions of the Church Missionary Society (CMS) through which God worked. He concluded with a discussion of needs and challenges before the mission. Forty years later, E. Morris Wherry wrote a similar history of the Punjab and other missions in India of the Presbyterian Church in the USA, arranging his material topically rather than on a station-by-station basis.[6] Only Andrew Gordon, in *Our India Mission*, devoted considerable attention to the lives, trials, and contributions of Indian converts and workers.

What was true of mission histories was also true of missionary biographies. Maconachie's biography of Rowland Bateman, a CMS missionary in the Punjab from 1868 to 1902, was written to inspire. Its 'account of the work which God had done through him'[7] largely follows Bateman's journal of his India years, and gives special attention to Bateman's 'character'. In an important sense, therefore, the Punjab became the scene on which his character unfolded, revealed itself, and thus could inspire. J.C.R. Ewing set his biography of the Rev. Kali Charan Chatterjee within the context of Christian education in India, through which Chatterjee had been converted

---

[4] For a complete list with some analysis, see John C.B. Webster, 'Mission Sources of Nineteenth-Century Punjab History'.

[5] Robert Clark, *The Punjab and Sindh Missions of the Church Missionary Society*, p. vii.

[6] E.M. Wherry, *Our Missions in India 1834–1924*.

[7] R. Maconachie, *Rowland Bateman*, p. vii.

before migrating to the Punjab. While providing a sketch of Chatterjee's life and work, most of which was spent as the Presbyterian Mission's resident missionary in Hoshiarpur, Ewing also stressed the quality of Chatterjee's Christian life and the recognized leadership he gave to the Church, a powerful vindication of Presbyterian mission work there. [8]

Since Independence, two important shifts away from that mission perspective have taken place. Christian historians writing in India have tended to focus upon the Christian Church and community. Three impulses seem to have been behind this shift: a desire to understand how the Indian Church came into being in its existing state; a nationalist reaction to the almost exclusive emphasis upon foreign actors that affected Indian historiography in general; and a later emphasis upon social history that might enhance the self-understanding of Christian communities within India. In 1974, the editorial board appointed by the Church History Association of India to develop a multi-volume history of Christianity in India, sought to set this history within the context of Indian rather than of mission history by focusing upon the sociocultural, the regional, the national, and the ecumenical. The first two, it thought, would 'provide insight into the changing identity of the Christian people of India through the centuries'.[9] Meanwhile, academic historians writing outside India for a largely Western readership became interested primarily in those aspects of the history of Christianity in India which highlight the religio-cultural encounter of East and West in the interaction between foreign missionaries and Indians.[10]

The general histories of Christianity in India written since Independence have, like their predecessors, tended to overlook the north-west. John N. Hollister's *The Centenary of the Methodist Church in Southern Asia* and M.E. Gibbs's *The Anglican Church in India 1600–1970*, utilized a region-by-region approach, which included the north-

---

[8] J.C.R. Ewing, *A Prince of the Church in India.*

[9] A Scheme for a Comprehensive History of Christianity in India (mimeographed), p. 2.

[10] This categorization of historians may be a bit too neat, but does get at some general tendencies.

west, but remained similar to the mission histories of pre-Independence times. Some recent Roman Catholic[11] histories also provide brief accounts of their history in the north-west. Like the earlier Protestant histories, they tend to be 'missionary' and 'denominational' in that they confine themselves to 'the work' of members of one religious order.[12] However, there have also been some important research monographs which have departed from the denominational mission pattern of the earlier period, a survey of which will help to place the present study in its historiographical context.

Two studies on the life and growth of the Church in India, published around 1960, dealt with the north-west: *The Church in the Punjab* by Ernest Y. Campbell and *The Church in Delhi* by James P. Alter and Herbert Jai Singh. Campbell, a sociologist, had an historical background chapter that was devoted primarily to the Chuhra conversion movement from which the vast majority of Punjabi Christians are descended and to its impact upon the churches. Alter and Jai Singh's sixty-page history begins with the Jesuits at the Mughal Court. They treated the period from 1803 to 1910 in standard mission history fashion with historical narratives of pioneering missionaries, converts, types of mission work, and a concluding section on mission–church relations. The next chapter brought the separate histories of several Christian denominations up to 1950 and then discussed the Christians' response to the nationalist movement, Independence, the partition riots, and the Constituent Assembly. The remainder of the book, like Campbell's, provides a descriptive analysis of current congregations and the (Protestant) Christian community.

---

[11] The terms 'Roman Catholic' and 'Catholic' are used interchangeably throughout this history. The choice of terms has historical roots in differing understandings of the Church produced by the Reformation, but see Leonard Fernando and G. Gispert-Sauch, *Christianity in India: Two Thousand Years of Faith*, p. 56.

[12] Daniel D'Souza, *Capuchin Missions in India*; Peter Celestine, *North Indian Capuchin Missions 1972–1992, Capuchins in India 1972–1997*; Alicia Mitra, *A History of the Congregation of The Religious of Jesus and Mary in India (1842–1993)*.

In 1971, two doctoral dissertations were the first written on Christianity in the north-west by academic historians for an academic rather than a Church readership. Both looked into the role of Christianity in processes of social change but approached the subject differently. Stanley Brush was interested primarily in the clash of religious systems following the introduction of British rule, and especially in the impact which 'institutional Protestant Christianity as conceptualized in terms of the structure and dynamics of its organization rather than as a system of belief alone'[13] had upon patterns of religious organization already prevalent in the Punjab. This process of change he called 'Protestantization'. He juxtaposed the Punjabi religious sect or *sampradaya* (whether Hindu, Sikh, or Muslim) with the Protestant mission society, with its voluntarism, autonomy, purposefulness, and pragmatic rational manner of operating. In tracing the history of the mission societies in the Punjab through the 1860s, he saw an 'Evangelical Entente' forged between missionaries and those administrators who were Evangelicals, especially in the field of education where the missions used their virtual monopoly of private, government-aided education to evangelize and indoctrinate several generations of students. The unintended result was the creation of a group of 'New Protestants' in the Punjab 'motivated by a resentment of Christian missionary Evangelicalism, a distaste for paternalism, whether British or of the conservative Indian variety, and by a passionate devotion to their visions of a reformed society' who were 'anxious simultaneously to defend the essence of their cultural heritages and reform their communities'.[14] To further their respective aims they created religious reform bodies based on the mission model. Brush concluded,

From the historical perspective, the appearance of an articulate, politicized and anti-missionary class of Protestantized Punjabis and the religious, literary, educational, humanitarian and political enterprises they created represented the fulfillment—unanticipated at the outset and only dimly perceived later—of Protestant mission work and the reformation era in the Punjab.[15]

[13] Stanley Elwood Brush, 'Protestants in the Punjab', pp. 4–5.
[14] Ibid., p. 287.
[15] Ibid., p. 324.

My own doctoral thesis was published in revised form as *The Christian Community and Change in Nineteenth Century North India* in 1976. It covered the period from 1834 to 1914 topically, using the Lodiana (later Punjab) and Farrukhabad (later North India) Missions of the Presbyterian Church in the USA as a case study for detailed analysis, and was based on three premises: (1) the Christians of the nineteenth-century Punjab and United Provinces were a community; (2) this Christian community interacted with other communities in the Punjab and United Provinces; and (3) such interaction brought about numerous changes both within and beyond the Christian community.[16] Two chapters analyse the Christian community itself: one on the missionaries' backgrounds, motivations, theological outlook, and conditions of service; the other on the converts' backgrounds and motivations, the screening process they were put through prior to baptism, their post-baptismal identities and social life, their relationships with the missionaries, and the contributions to interaction and change they made. The chapters on interaction deal with religious controversy, evangelism, education, famine relief, and politics (including politics within the Christian community). The concluding chapter seeks to generalize from the Presbyterian case to the north Indian Christian community as a whole, to show how the Christians became a community, and to assess their role in the changes which took place in north India during the nineteenth century.

There were four major differences between the two theses that perhaps account for all the others. First, I limited myself for the most part to one Protestant denomination and covered an eighty-year time span, whereas Brush studied more missions over a shorter time span. Second, Brush highlighted the strength of the 'Evangelical Entente', while I tended to emphasize the competition and tensions between the missions and the government. Third, Brush equated Protestantism with the missionaries and missions, while I not only included the converts as a distinct element in the Christian community but also assigned to them, and to the threat their conversion posed, the central role in social change. Finally, my book

[16] John C.B. Webster, *The Christian Community and Change*, pp. 7–8.

investigated a broader range of social and cultural changes among a broader range of north Indian society than did Brush's thesis, which remained focused upon the 'Protestantization' of the western-educated elites.

The other history written during the 1970s was Frederick and Margaret Stock's *People Movements in the Punjab*, the first large-scale history of the mass conversion movements that so altered the course of the history of Christianity in north-west India. It concentrates on a 'small arrested' conversion movement among the Meghs (1854–84) and a 'large well-developed' one among the Chuhras (1873–1973) in order to discover the principles that might serve as guidelines for fruitful evangelistic work in the future.[17] The result is more a missiological reflection on historical events from the church growth perspective developed by Donald McGavran than a history per se. It concludes with ten essential principles for Church planting today.

Daniel O'Connor's biography of C.F. Andrews's 'missionary years' (1904–14) was set within the context not only of the broader events in which Andrews became so deeply involved but also of the Cambridge Mission to Delhi, of which he was a member, and its particular theology of mission. Andrews considered writing for educated Indians to be his main missionary work. Because he arrived in Delhi just as the partition of Bengal gave new energy to the nationalist movement, 'His emerging theology of mission told him that, because this was pre-eminently the issue which engaged people in their thoughts and feelings, it was an important area of mission, and one in which new formulations of Christian faith would be required'.[18] Thus in and through Andrews the historian can see in microcosm the Christian Church, especially in north-west India, engaging itself internally and externally with the full range of British imperialism and Indian nationalism during ten very important years.

Jeffrey Cox's *Imperial Fault Lines: Christianity and Colonial Power in India, 1818–1940* 'is not a comprehensive history of missionary work in Punjab. It is a study of how [Protestant] missionaries in the most

---

[17] Frederick and Margaret Stock, *People Movements in the Punjab*, p. xxi.
[18] Daniel O'Connor, *Gospel, Raj and Swaraj*, p. 64.

important mission societies, and those with whom they associated, Indian Christians and non-Christians, struggled with the conflict between universalist Christian religious values and the imperial context of those values.'[19] It also seeks to undermine 'a providentialist master narrative of progress toward a multiracial Christian community'[20] built into many mission studies of Christianity in India and elsewhere. What mars this master narrative in Cox's view are the major imperial fault lines running through the full range of missionary work and relationships, produced by '(1) the cultural gap—racial, religious, political, and academic—between foreigner and Indian; (2) the association of the mission presence with foreign rule; (3) the disproportionate material resources and professional status accorded to foreigners in mission institutions.'[21] Cox organized his material thematically within a loose chronological framework and provided a series of probes into the various aspects of each theme. In 'The Ecclesiastical Invasion of Punjab 1818–1890', Cox examined missionary relationships with the imperial state and their institutional presence, arguing that the missionaries were 'not primarily evangelists, but institution-builders—compulsive, inveterate institution-builders'.[22] The next section looked at the contradictions or fault lines of race, culture, gender, and class/caste within the churches and institutions through which the missions sought to exercise influence between 1870 and 1930. The final section described various missionary attempts to overcome those contradictions between 1900 and 1940 as well as their failures, in the face of the national movement of that period, to achieve their main objectives of 'shaping the course of Indian history' through their elite institutions and creating a 'self-governing, self-supporting, and self-extending Indian church'.[23]

The latest historical study of Christianity in north-west India is Christopher Harding's doctoral thesis 'The Dynamics of Low-Caste

---

[19] Jeffrey Cox, *Imperial Fault Lines*, p. 6.
[20] Ibid., p. 12.
[21] Ibid., p. 221.
[22] Ibid., p. 27.
[23] Ibid., p. 252.

Conversion Movements: Rural Punjab, c.1880–1935'. Harding focused on 'the "dynamics" of these conversion movements in rural Punjab: the ways in which the backgrounds, aspirations and behaviour of converts and mission personnel shaped an unpredictable, many-sided encounter'[24] of 'different individuals and socio-cultural worlds',[25] which he analysed in terms of 'presentation and perception'.[26] The result is not a history of the conversion movements per se; instead, Harding treated them as locations of the presentations, perceptions, and encounters which provided their dynamics during a fifty-five-year period. He used the CMS and Belgian Capuchins as case studies, comparing the two as they brought different structures, understandings (especially of 'uplift'), methods, and strategic priorities to their encounters within the Punjab. He then examined the roles played by local leaders and formal mission agents as communicators of Christianity, the Christian communities created from the conversion movements, and finally some of the Christian villages the two missions established. These dynamics, the assumptions and relationships undergirding them, as well as the tensions, fissures, disconnects, and forms of resistance they reveal, all informed the direction these conversion movements took during the late nineteenth and early twentieth centuries.

These histories do not encompass the full range of approaches employed thus far to study Christianity as an Indian phenomenon. There is a growing body of conversion studies on what led individuals or groups to convert, what the conversion process entailed for the converts themselves, and how conversion changed (or did not change) their religious beliefs and practices as well as their social status and economic conditions.[27] Other historians have drawn upon cultural

[24] Christopher Harding, 'The Dynamics of Low-Caste Conversion Movements', p. 1.

[25] Ibid., p. 2.

[26] Ibid., p. 8.

[27] See, e.g. G.A. Oddie (ed.), *Religion in South Asia*; Geoffrey A. Oddie (ed.), *Religious Conversion Movements in South Asia*; Rowena Robinson, *Conversion, Continuity and Change*; Rowena Robinson and Sathianathan Clarke, (eds), *Religious Conversion in India*; Eliza F. Kent, *Converting Women*.

anthropology to look at 'popular Christianity' and shown how untenable simple foreign/Indian dichotomies in Christianity are.[28] Finally, some important histories have given primacy to caste and caste conflict in the history of Christianity and thus have opened up yet other ways of viewing it as an Indian phenomenon.[29]

The Present Study

As the preceding section indicates, this is the first attempt to write a connected and comprehensive history of Christianity in north-west India. Regional history has built into it a presumption of regional distinctiveness. Christianity is itself an extremely complex phenomenon, involving diverse and changing belief systems and ethical norms, rituals, and styles of worship, patterns of leadership and organization, borrowings from surrounding cultures, social compositions, modes of expansion, and encounters with those of other persuasions and traditions. Any attempt to combine comprehensiveness with depth is going to emphasize some of these dimensions at the expense of others. Those choices are made here not according to some predetermined theological or theoretical criteria, but according to observed relative significance within the north-west. If, because of this more inductive approach, Christianity in north-west India comes out looking different from Christianity elsewhere, that in itself is an important finding.

Since the history of Christianity in the north-west has been more socially than theologically or missiologically driven, and marked more by social than by spiritual or cultural developments of significance, this will be primarily a social history of the Christian people there. In that respect there is considerable continuity between this and my earlier work, *The Christian Community and Change in Nineteenth Century North India*, as well as the Church History Association of India's 'new

---

[28] See, for example, Judith M. Brown and Robert Eric Frykenberg (eds), *Christians, Cultural Interactions, and India's Religious Traditions*; Robert Eric Frykenberg (ed.), *Christians and Missionaries in India*.

[29] For example, Duncan B. Forrester, *Caste and Christianity: Attitudes and Policies on Caste of Anglo-Saxon Protestant Missions in India*; Susan Bayly, *Saints, Goddesses and Kings*; John C.B. Webster, *The Dalit Christians: A History*.

perspective'. The most obvious differences are that this covers a longer time span, is arranged chronologically rather than topically, and abandons the case study in favour of a more inclusive and synthetic approach to the subject. Because its focus remains upon the Christian community rather than upon just the missionaries, it cannot be subsumed under the 'master narratives' described by Cox.[30] The Christian community, unlike the missionary enterprise, emerged from the Indian rather than a foreign or imperial context, and its basic internal dynamics have been shaped far more by Indian realities than by missionary designs. The major clues to understanding it, therefore, lie in Indian social history rather than in the history of either Christian missions or British imperialism.

Its story must, therefore, not only begin with a description of the early nineteenth-century north-west Indian society out of which the Christian community emerged, but also continue to trace the kinds of social changes the region has undergone since then, as these have shaped the history of Christianity there throughout the past two centuries. This is not to argue for a kind of social determinism, but rather to recognize the extent to which interaction with the rest of society has shaped both the changing social identity of and the historical possibilities for Christianity in north-west India. It is also to differentiate an important assumption underlying this history from those of most of the earlier histories of Christianity in the region.

Specifically, while north-west Indian society cannot be characterized as uniform throughout the region, it was nonetheless based on hierarchies of ascribed status of caste or lineage, of age and gender, as well as upon patron–client relationships between individuals or families differently placed within those hierarchies. The hierarchies did vary considerably in their degree of stability as patterns of domination, acquiescence, and resistance fluctuated and

---

[30] Cox names and rejects two other master narratives at the outset: the 'imperialist/nationalist' which renders the missionaries irrelevant or marginal, and the Saidian narrative which unmasks their complicity with empire. Why he considered my *The Christian Community and Change in Nineteenth Century North India* to be illustrative of the 'providentialist' master narrative is unclear to me. *Imperial Fault Lines*, pp. 12, 87–8, 276.

adjusted to political and administrative innovations imposed from above. Yet, even before the arrival of foreign missionaries, and quite independently of their evangelistic work in the region, there were people who were already individually or collectively alienated from the local societies in which they were immersed. It is from the ranks of the socially and culturally alienated that Christianity drew its support and membership, while the socially and culturally dominant placed major constraints upon what Christianity might accomplish and become within those societies, whether urban or rural, in the hills or on the plains, at the frontiers or in the heartland of the north-west.

Thus, Christianity began its history in the region as a social anomaly which did not fit easily into existing social paradigms. It attracted people from a wide range of social, religious, and occupational backgrounds and represented a form of deviance or dissent, the legitimacy of which the culturally dominant emphatically denied. Conversion to Christianity had to be prevented because it upset the prevailing sociocultural order and brought disgrace upon those affected. An important part of the history of Christianity in north-west India is the story of how this social anomaly came to find a 'place' as both movement and community within the society from which its members had been alienated.

A second working assumption built into this social history approach is that the basic demographics of the Christian community itself are of crucial importance for understanding its history. The community was neither homogeneous nor unchanging in its social composition, denominational affiliations, or geographic distribution. Much attention has been paid to the missionaries in previous histories and they are given their due here. What has not received proper attention is the caste composition of the Christian community as well as the positions or places its members occupied within the wider urban and rural society. Caste status, occupation, and social mobility not only affected relationships and interaction with others within north-west Indian society, but also created opportunities for, or imposed constraints upon, the realization of the community's ambitions, whether religious, social, cultural, economic, or political.

Religious diversity within Christianity is another important variable. Unlike in most other parts of India, Christianity in the north-west has been overwhelmingly Protestant. Protestant missionaries were the first to establish permanent churches in the region; by 1857 there were seven different mission societies working there. Other Protestant groups and Roman Catholic religious orders came later, thus creating a variety of Christianities in the north-west whose relationships ranged from cooperation and union on the one hand to rivalry and even conflict on the other. Denominational pluralism within Christianity suggests both that unity/community among Christians cannot be assumed but must be investigated and that the question of who the authentic Christian voice is in the public arena cannot be avoided.[31]

The other defining demographic feature of Christianity in the north-west is that Christians have been distributed very unevenly throughout the region. By far the heaviest concentration has been in the central Punjab, although a large number did migrate to the canal colonies in western Punjab when those opened up. Elsewhere, except in Delhi itself, the Christian population has been very small. The varying concentration and dispersion of the Christian population not only affected the viability of sustained corporate Christian religious and social life, especially in rural areas, but also had a direct bearing upon the degree of local influence Christians might exercise.

Given this social, religious, and geographic diversity, writing a unified social history of the Christian community in north-west India faces the obvious challenges of selectivity and weightage. Each area within the region has its own churches, institutions, and saints, all of which might well be included here. Moreover, with the proliferation of Christian mission societies and organizations,

---

[31] By using internal diversity rather than homogeneity as its point of departure; by making the possibility of shared social, political, and economic interests a matter to be investigated rather than a presupposition; and by integrating its history into the wider social history of which it is a part, a social history of a religious community such as this one can avoid the trap of communal history. For a succinct statement on the basic premises of the communal view, see Bipin Chandra, *Communalism in Modern India*, pp. 1–3.

especially in the years following Independence, it is simply not possible to keep track of and do justice to them all. The choices made here reflect a certain majoritarian bias. Those areas with the largest concentrations of Christians receive more attention than those where Christians are few; the 'historic missions' that came early and grew over time receive more attention than relative latecomers. An effort has also been made to discern patterns and trends cutting across denominational boundaries on the assumption that the Christian community as a whole may well be a more important social entity than the distinct denominations represented within it.

This history covers approximately two centuries so that the transitions and transformations which Christianity and the Christian community have experienced under changing circumstances may become more fully apparent. The history of Christianity in the region has been locked into a nineteenth-century mould and thus been forced to bear a basically nineteenth-century and foreign missionary image for too long.[32] The chapters are arranged chronologically and set off from one another by important events in regional rather than Christian history. The year 1800 is a convenient starting point not only as the beginning of a new century but also as the approximate time when two important new regimes came to power in the north-west: Maharaja Ranjit Singh in Lahore (1799) and the British in Delhi (1803). In keeping with the social history approach outlined above, Chapter 2 begins with an extended treatment of the volatile political situation, the more stable social structure, and the religious milieu of the north-west into which Christianity entered in the early nineteenth century. After describing the beginnings of each mission society there, it examines both the nature of their early interaction with the people they evangelized and the early converts. The chapter ends with the events of 1857 that had such a traumatic effect upon Christians, especially in Delhi.

---

[32] Shourie even locates the 'essence' of Christianity in nineteenth-century India; he sees changes since then only as tactical and/or cosmetic adjustments made in order to fulfil or disguise its true 'essence'. Arun Shourie, *Missionaries in India: Continuities, Changes, Dilemmas.*

The aftermath of the 1857 revolt ushered in a period of virtually unchallenged British domination in the north-west, described in Chapter 3. In this period, Christian relations with the government, especially in the field of education, receive special attention. While their closeness at that time is a matter of some debate, they were never as close again. An examination of both education and the continuing religious encounter, as well as of the Christian population itself, suggests that Christianity was by this time taking on the characteristics of both a community and a movement.

By 1881, some new developments that were affecting the course of Christian history had taken in the north-west. The most obvious of these was the rise of a wide range of Hindu, Muslim, and Sikh religious reform and revivalist organizations in the urban centres and the emergence of a large-scale conversion movement to Christianity among rural Dalits in central Punjab. It also marked the beginning of extensive Christian 'women's work' throughout the region. It was in this period, described in Chapter 4, that Christianity could best be described as a movement with a significant religious and socio-cultural impact upon both the urban and the rural north-west. It was also when many of those ties that made it a community were consolidated.

At the close of World War I, north-west India entered a new phase of its history characterized by constitutional change and unprecedented agitation against British rule, culminating in both Independence and Partition in 1947. Politics took precedence over religious and socio-cultural change and the small Christian community was left on the sidelines while other larger communities contended for power. At the same time, it had to make major internal adjustments in order meet the challenge of Indian nationalist aspirations both outside and within its own membership. The result was a major transfer of power within the churches from foreign missionary to Indian hands. These changes provide the substance of Chapter 5.

Chapter 6 focuses upon the reorganization and proliferation of churches following Independence and Partition, the Church's institutional complex, and the Christian community itself. All three, taken together, show the transformations that Christianity has undergone both as a movement and as a community during a period of profound change in north-west India. The final chapter seeks to set the history of Christianity in the north-west within the wider context of its history in India as a whole. It then concludes with an analysis of some key concepts used in this particular social history of Christianity that might prove useful in studying its history in other parts of the country.

The Nature and Use of the Missionary Archive

Most of what we know about the history of Christianity in north-west India comes to us after passing through missionary filters. The use of the missionary archive raises two critical issues. The first is that the missionaries who produced our source materials were not very interested in the social history of the Christian community; they were preoccupied with their own work, its progress, problems, and challenges. Our inquiry thus operates at cross purposes with most of the source material upon which it is dependent. Moreover, the missionaries who produced them were foreigners who, like the British rulers, were seeking to understand the people among whom they lived so as to carry out their mission more effectively. Thus, missionary perceptions and reporting, like that of administrators, could well have been infected by 'colonial forms of knowledge', distorting and even manipulating the social realities they sought to grasp.[33]

Does this critique also apply to the missionaries and to the sources of knowledge they produced? Few missionaries were Orientalists or administrators, except within their own small domain of the Church and its institutions. Their aim was not to control but to 'win' the people of north-west India. Nevertheless, as foreigners they were exterior to India even though they lived there; they were there on a mission for which 'knowledge' was essential; and they were part of the changing colonial ethos for most of this history. However, rather

---

[33] See Edward W. Said, *Orientalism* and Bernard S. Cohn, *Colonialism and Its Forms of Knowledge*.

than prejudge the issue simply on the basis of their position vis-à-vis the people and events about which they wrote, it is best to look at the kinds of materials and thus at the kinds of 'knowledge' they actually produced.

Mission sources may be divided into several categories. The first are the missions' official records, usually minutes of meetings and their more informative annual reports that were circulated to mission boards at home as well as to supporters in India. A second consisted of correspondence with home mission boards. This included letters, personal journals, and short articles that were then published or excerpted in missionary magazines in the United Kingdom and the United States. Both reports and correspondence were usually narrative, at times anecdotal, in form and descriptive of mission or personal activities, of important encounters or external developments, and of personal reflections and assessments. While often full of implicit and explicit value judgements, they were written primarily to inform and educate; the editors who published them also sought to justify and solidify support at home for overseas missions as well. Their content reveals a reliance upon (British) 'conventional wisdom' concerning the local population, especially in the early years when the missionaries had only very limited experience of their own to draw upon. Later, they made ample use of census data and other official documents to assess the situations they were facing.

A third category of mission sources consisted of publications intended primarily for other missionaries and Christians within India itself. This category includes conference reports, articles in periodicals published in India, catalogues, pamphlets, books, and later some weekly or monthly newspapers. Through these, the wider Christian community within India sought to share information and reflections on developments affecting the missionary enterprise and Christian Church as a whole. This body of literature not only grew in size and importance over time, but it was also the one type that gave Indians a larger voice until, in the post-Independence period, their voice came to dominate. The fourth category is made up of mostly translations, tracts, booklets, and even a newspaper intended primarily for a general Indian readership. These were most often evangelistic in purpose and written in Urdu, Hindi, Hindustani, or Punjabi. Unfortunately, little of this material remains today.[34]

It is fairly easy to detect stereotypes, value judgements, and theological/ideological commitments in missionary writings, as most are quite explicit. The more problematic issue is whether these so distort both the selection and the presentation of the merely descriptive, 'factual' representations in these sources as to render that 'information' virtually useless to the historian. At this point, generalization about all missionaries becomes impossible; they were not all alike and their styles of communicating not only differed but also varied from subject to subject. Thus, this issue must, in the last analysis, be resolved pragmatically on a case-by-case basis, so as to move through missionary perceptions to the Indian realities they perceived as responsibly as possible.[35]

This brings us back to the first critical issue raised at the outset of this section. As indicated earlier, the missionaries' primary concern was not the social history of the Christian people and so the Indian 'voice' in the sources they produced is relatively silent. Voice is very important in social history; at the very least it is indicative of what people wanted, of what aims and purposes lay behind their actions. The voices that do come through are those selected by the missionary writer for that missionary's own reasons; one does not get to hear most of the other voices. It is in this 'preselection of voices' that the issue of representation once again becomes acute. Who speaks for the community or for the varying sections of it? Does the missionary's anecdote or illustrative example speak only for the individual whose voice is conveyed or for a significant number of others as well? These questions can only be answered on a case-by-case basis.

Social history of this kind, which goes against the grain of the sources themselves, requires piecing together bits of information

---

[34] An earlier discussion of these sources is John C.B. Webster, 'Mission Sources of Nineteenth-Century Punjab History'.

[35] I have attempted to address these methodological issues directly in 'The Women of Amritsar through Missionary Eyes'.

from here and there in a vast archive in order to get specific questions answered. Some of those questions cannot be answered; there are gaps that cannot be filled and voices that cannot be heard. Nonetheless, a great deal can and has been discovered through an examination of these sources. The missionary writers were not totally blind to all that was going on around them and, in several instances, were quite sensitive to social needs, aspirations, and changes of which administrators, Indian elites, and other producers of 'knowledge' were relatively ignorant. Mission sources, for all their inadequacies, do provide windows through which to look at the missionary observer, the social history of Christianity in the north-west, and the wider society of which they were a part over the course of the past two centuries.

2 The Beginnings: 1800–57

Christianity began to take root in north-west India at a time when the region was making the transition from Mughal India to British India. The Mughal emperor lived on in Delhi until 1858 and much that was Mughal remained in the institutions as well as in the general ethos of the period. The military and diplomatic impact of the British was certainly felt, but the full cultural impact of the Raj still lay in the future. For Christianity these were times of only small beginnings. An examination of its context in transition provides an important clue to why those beginnings were so small and why, in later periods, Christian history in the north-west took the course it did.

North-west India

The peculiar geography of north-west India has contributed to its diversity and its history. It is bounded on the east by the river Yamuna and on the south by the great Indian desert. As one moves from the city of Delhi near the south-eastern corner on the Yamuna towards the western boundary provided by the Sulaiman Range and the mountains leading up to the Hindu Kush west of the Indus river, the southern half of the region is a very low and flat plain watered by the five rivers of the Punjab: the Jhelum, Chenab, Ravi, Beas, and Sutlej. This plain, with the cities of Lahore and Amritsar near its centre, includes some of the finest agricultural land in India. On the other hand, the northern half of the region is entirely mountainous. It is divided between the lesser Himalayan range or shivaliks bordering on the plains and, behind it, the Great Himalayas in northern Himachal Pradesh as well as virtually all of Jammu and Kashmir. Not only are the plains far more heavily populated than are the mountains, but the mountains have often cut the people there off from much of what has been happening on the plains, giving them a somewhat different kind of society and history.

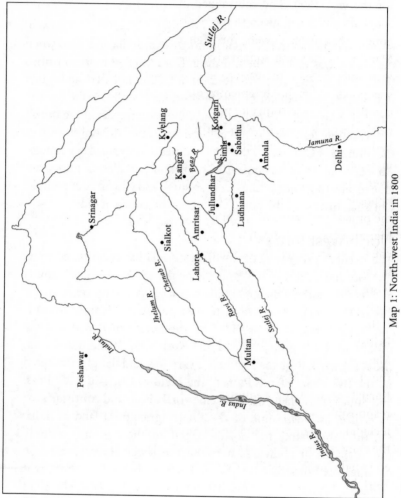

Map 1: North-west India in 1800

THE CHANGING POLITICAL MAP

It is virtually impossible to draw a political map of north-west India for the year 1800. The centralized political authority which the Mughal empire had given to the region a century earlier was now gone. Two outside powers, the Afghans to the north-west and the Marathas to the south, sought to control the region, while the British were appearing on the eastern horizon. Internally, the north-west was politically highly fragmented and very volatile, as local chiefs competed with each other for power, territory, and revenue. Of these chiefs the most powerful was clearly Ranjit Singh Shukerchakia who had led a coalition of Sikh *misldars* in preventing a final Afghan invasion of the Punjab in 1799 and then began consolidating his rule over Lahore, the provincial capital city of the Mughals. At the opposite end of the region, the Mughal emperor made the Marathas the official protectors of the empire in 1785. The land between the Marathas and Ranjit Singh was in the hands of vassal or autonomous chiefs. On the plains of the Punjab most of these were Sikh misldars; in the hill areas of Himachal Pradesh they were Rajput rajas. Many were no more than leaders of robber bands and one was an Irish adventurer.

In August 1803, war broke out between the Marathas and the British. The British captured Delhi in September, succeeded the Marathas as official protector of the Mughal empire, and received the 'Delhi Territory' (Delhi, Gurgaon, Rohtak, Hisar, Sirsa, and Karnal) west of the Yamuna. The British resident at Delhi was responsible for diplomatic relations with the regional powers, including the emperor, and for administering the Delhi territory in the emperor's name. Meanwhile, Ranjit Singh was rapidly expanding and solidifying his rule over the areas adjacent to Lahore. On 12 April 1801 he was declared maharaja, following which he claimed sovereignty over the Punjab, and demanded that the revenues previously paid to the Lahore governor now be paid to him. He soon brought rival misldars into alliance or subordination and took control of Amritsar, the largest city and commercial centre of the Punjab.

On 25 April 1809, Ranjit Singh and the British signed a treaty making the river Sutlej the basic boundary between them.

Afterwards, the British posted an agent and built a military cantonment near the Sutlej at Ludhiana, while Ranjit Singh built one opposite it at Phillaur and then turned his attention to filling out his territories in the west and north. By the time of his death in 1839, his sovereignty over the territory from the Indus river in the west, to Kashmir and Ladakh in the north, to the Sutlej river in the south and east was undisputed. Meanwhile, the British, after staving off a Maratha attack on Delhi in 1804, devoted themselves to bringing law and order to the Delhi territory. They posted armies in Delhi, Karnal (1805), and Ambala (1842–43), as well as in Ludhiana, to assert their authority in the region, but administered most of the territory indirectly through subordinate local chiefs. Those tracts they administered directly they changed as little as possible, working along Mughal lines, through existing village leadership and institutions according to customary practice. In addition, they acquired territory in the hill states between the Yamuna and Sutlej rivers not only by defeating the Gurkhas of Nepal, who had occupied and fortified them, but also through treaties and land purchases from the hill rajas who had joined them against the Gurkhas. Thus, like Ranjit Singh, the British very quickly gained control over the territory of the north-west on their side of the Sutlej. In 1832, they ceased administering the Delhi territory on behalf of the Mughal emperor and simply merged it into their new Agra Presidency (in 1834, the North-Western Provinces) as its Delhi Division.

There were two wars between the British and the successors of Ranjit Singh, the first in 1845 and the second in 1849. The British won both with great difficulty and imposed stiff terms. At the end of the first one, the British annexed the territory between the Beas and Sutlej rivers. When the Lahore government proved unable to pay the fine the British also imposed, Raja Gulab Singh of Jammu offered to pay it in exchange for recognition as maharaja of Jammu and Kashmir. This the British agreed to in a separate treaty. After the second war, the British annexed the rest of Maharaja Ranjit Singh's Punjab. No further significant territorial changes occurred until 1858 when the Delhi Division was transferred from the North-Western Provinces to the Punjab. Thus north-west India under the British

Raj became 'The Greater Punjab' or, as it was called in the later British census, 'The Punjab and its Dependencies'.

The British used a pattern of government in the Punjab very similar to the one they had used earlier in Delhi. They first administered it as guardians of Maharaja Dalip Singh and then, after annexation, ruled it in their own right first through a three-member Board of Control and then from 1853 through a single chief commissioner. They disarmed the population, eliminated open violence, established a judicial system that relied heavily on local panchayats and local custom, and made land revenue settlements directly with village communities. They vested enormous power, unhampered by detailed regulations, in their own officials, urging them to come into close contact with the people and make decisions on the spot, so as to bring the Punjab under control and win its loyalty.

THE SOCIAL STRUCTURE

Despite frequent warfare and political change, the social structure of north-west India remained quite stable during the first half of the nineteenth century.[1] The region was overwhelmingly rural and its largest cities had become depopulated. Delhi was estimated to have only 100,000 inhabitants at the turn of the century and 120,000 in 1833.[2] Lahore was said to have a mere 72,500 in 1844 and 94,143 in 1854, while Amritsar grew from 60,000 to 112,188 during the same decade.[3] The population of Srinagar, the largest city in the region during the first quarter of the nineteenth century, dropped dramatically from an estimated 240,000 in 1823 to about 65,000 in 1846 due to the decline of its shawl industry.[4]

Our present understanding of the prevailing social structure in the rural north-west has been strongly influenced by the writing of

[1] Indu Banga found social mobility but no structural change in Ranjit Singh's Punjab. 'Social Mobility in the Punjab under Maharajah Ranjit Singh', in J.S. Grewal and Indu Banga (eds), *Maharajah Ranjit Singh and His Times*, p. 135.

[2] Percival Spear, *Twilight of the Mughals*, p. 194.

[3] Bikrama Jit Hasrat, *Life and Times of Ranjit Singh*, p. 375.

[4] Dewan Chand Sharma, *Kashmir under the Sikhs*, pp. 30–1.

government officials who viewed the village as a revenue-producing economic unit and its social structure as a product almost solely of economic relationships among its inhabitants. Land ownership was central to their view of the village. They found small landholdings of ten to twenty acres, cultivated by the owner, to be the norm. Tenant cultivators either held long-term hereditary tenancies or were simply tenants-at-will. Each village had its artisan and service castes, who received fixed shares of the harvest for their services or an agreed price for their goods. Throughout most of the plains the Jats and Rajputs were the major landowners. The most important artisan castes were the Lohars (blacksmiths), Tarkhans (carpenters, bricklayers, and masons), and Kumhars (potters and brick-makers). The predominant menial castes were the Chamars (leather workers) and Chuhras (sweepers) who also provided the bulk of the landless agricultural labour. J.S. Grewal has estimated that all these non-cultivators combined received a mere fifteen per cent of the harvest, which offered them only a subsistence standard of living.[5]

Tom Kessinger has provided a picture of one Punjabi village in 1848. Vilyatpur had 565 people belonging to fifteen different castes, living in 123 houses clustered together on a slight mound near the centre of the village's 500 acres of agricultural land. Sahotas, a Jat clan who had founded the village, owned all the land; other cultivators included non-Sahota Jats, some Brahmins, *faqirs*, barbers, and sweepers. Leather workers, weavers, carpenters, water-carriers, barbers, dyers, a drummer, and a goldsmith also lived in the village. The Sahotas lived in large houses on the height of land; the menial castes were clustered together in small houses lower down at one end of the village. The Sahotas comprised 44 per cent of the village

---

[5] These paragraphs are based upon Indu Banga, *Agrarian System of the Sikhs*; J.S. Grewal, *The Reign of Maharaja Ranjit Singh*; Daljinder Singh Johal, 'Literary Evidence on Social Structure in the Punjab (1750–1850)'; B.S. Hira, 'Social Structure in the Upper Bari Doab Towards the End of Sikh Rule', in J.S. Grewal and Indu Banga (eds), *Maharajah Ranjit Singh and His Times*, pp. 158–68; Harish Chander Sharma, 'Artisans in the Punjab under Maharaja Ranjit Singh', in ibid., pp. 177–86; and Radha Sharma, 'Agrarian Structure in the Districts of Amritsar and Lahore in the early Nineteenth Century', in ibid., pp. 169–76.

population and dominated the village politically as well as economically; there was no outside check on their use of force and no alternative to the justice they dispensed.[6] Families in the village were connected to each other by caste and by patron–client relationships. Families of the artisan and menial castes were attached to families of the landholding castes, providing them with various forms of service determined by their caste occupations, and in many instances agricultural labour as well, in exchange for a fixed proportion of the harvest or a fixed amount of grain according to long-standing custom. According to Kessinger:

The tie between families of the cultivators and the servants was often long-term and personal, though a clearly dependent one from the *sepidars'* point of view. They played a role in rituals conducted at celebrations in their patron's house. At a marriage, for example, the Barber in particular, but also the Water-carrier, Chamar, and Sweeper, had specific duties for which they were rewarded. Also, work outside the customary services was paid for separately.[7]

Vilyatpur appears to have been fairly representative of a pattern of rural society which prevailed throughout the north-west, albeit with sub-regional variations. In some villages, Rajputs or (near Delhi) Gujjars rather than Jats were the dominant caste. In the Muslim-dominated areas along the north-western frontier, the villages were organized along tribal rather than caste lines.[8] The same may well have been true of the villages in present-day Himachal Pradesh, except that the landowners were almost always Hindu Rajputs, the Brahmins were more prominent, while the menial castes were much fewer than on the plains, and an important section of the population were nomads engaged in grazing their herds rather than in agriculture.[9] The picture in rural Kashmir is not at all clear; the rural population was overwhelmingly Muslim, but the villages appear to have been controlled by *jagirdars* or absentee landlords in the city

[6] Tom G. Kessinger, *Vilyatpur 1848–1968*, pp. 46–83.

[7] Ibid., pp. 56–7.

[8] Ian Talbot, *Punjab and the Raj 1849–1947*, p. 17.

[9] Sukhdev Singh Charak, *History and Culture of Himalayan States, Vol. III: Himachal Pradesh, Part Three*, pp. 4–5, 41–70.

who either belonged to eminent lineage groups or converted from high castes.[10] There the major social cleavage was between the landowners and *taifadars* (market gardeners, herdsmen, shepherds, boatmen, leather workers, and menial servants).[11] In Ladakh, on the other hand, everyone was of 'one race or caste', eating together and intermarrying, with all eligible to be monks.[12]

The towns and cities were centres of government, commerce, industry, and culture. Their social structure was thus more complex than that of the villages. In the capital cities the Mughal emperor, the maharaja of the Punjab, and their respective courts formed the aristocracy. While the emperor's court and family were forced to live within the very narrow political and economic constraints set by their British protectors, they still functioned as a significant cultural influence as patrons of the arts and learning, especially Islamic learning, in the 'Urdu culture' of Delhi. On the other hand, in Lahore, Maharaja Ranjit Singh and his aristocracy had real power and wealth along with cultural influence. Like the emperor and the maharaja, the hill rajas and many courtiers were patrons of the arts, learning, and religion.

It was the Khatris—whether Hindu, Sikh, or Muslim (Khojas)—who dominated urban commercial life and were prominent in government service. Next in importance were the Aroras and the Banias. Every town also had its skilled artisans, both in textiles and in more specialized industries, as well as those engaged in marketing agricultural produce. Traditional learning was for the most part in the hands of Brahmins, Sikh *bhais*, and Muslims who either held important religious offices or were from prominent lineages. Education above the level of basic literacy and arithmetic was primarily religious in nature and given in *dharmshalas* and mosques.

Three things of great importance made this social structure highly functional and cohesive. One was that all males, whether urban or rural, tended to stay within their traditional occupations as defined

---

[10] Dewan Chand Sharma, *Kashmir under the Sikhs*, pp. 109–16.

[11] *Imperial Gazetteer of India. Provincial Series: Kashmir and Jammu*, p. 37.

[12] Alexander Cunningham, *Ladakh, Physical, Statistical and Historical*, p. 291.

by caste or clan. Individual mobility was possible and did occur, but it was relatively rare. New occupations which were not caste specific had not yet opened up to any significant degree. Secondly, people married within their castes and lineage groups. Kinship ties thus reinforced this social structure based on caste and occupation. Each caste and clan had its own hereditary local leaders who mediated disputes (often over marriage arrangements) and enforced traditional group norms of behaviour. Finally, in the towns and cities, as well as in the villages, people belonging to the same caste or clan tended to live together in the same neighbourhoods. Social life and social standing were thus deeply communal rather than individual in nature, in what was a profoundly hierarchical social structure.[13]

THE RELIGIOUS MILIEU

The first systematic study of religion in north-west India was carried out in conjunction with the 1881 Census. Historians have used that data in order to understand this period on the assumption that at least the religious demographics and broad patterns of religious belief and practice did not change very much between 1800 and 1881, even if some aspects of religious life did change. The same assumption is made here. The census provides an invaluable source for the 'big picture', but it must be supplemented by other studies that can fill in some of the most important details.

Two broad features of the religious milieu are quite apparent from that census. The first is that it was not uniform throughout the north-west. The 1881 census reported that 51.35 per cent of the population was Muslim, 40.74 per cent was Hindu, 7.56 per cent was Sikh and

---

[13] These paragraphs are based upon Christopher Bayly, 'Delhi and Other Cities of North India during the "Twilight"', in R.E. Frykenberg (ed), *Delhi Through the Ages*, pp. 121–36; Anand Gauba, 'Amritsar in the Early Nineteenth Century', in J.S. Grewal and Indu Banga (eds), *Maharaja Ranjit Singh and His Times*, pp. 187–200; J.S. Grewal, *The Reign of Maharaja Ranjit Singh*, pp. 12–37; J.S. Grewal, *In the By-Lanes of History*, pp. 3–32; Narayani Gupta, *Delhi Between Two Empires 1803–1931*, pp. 1–38; Daljinder Singh Johal, 'Literary Evidence on the Social Structure of the Punjab'; Kanchan Jyoti, 'The City of Jullundur', pp. 35–64; and Percival Spear, *Twilight of the Mughals*.

0.01 per cent was Buddhist.[14] Buddhism was limited to the sparsely populated mountain regions near the Tibetan border where it was an isolated but dominant religion. Islam was clearly the religion of the north-west frontier, western Punjab, and Kashmir. Hinduism was equally dominant in Jammu, Himachal Pradesh, and Haryana. Sikhism was strongest in the central Punjab, where there were also significant numbers of Hindus and Muslims as well. The other feature of this milieu was that the boundaries between the religious traditions and communities of faith were not always rigid or even clear.[15] The census commissioner noted a kind of pervasive popular religion shared by Hindus, Muslims, and Sikhs alike, especially in rural areas where people had similar beliefs, worshipped at the same shrines, and joined in different religious festivals together.[16] At the same time, reformers sought to 'purify' the religious life of their people by drawing clearer boundary lines of belief and practice. The religious milieu in the north-west during the first half of the nineteenth century was therefore quite complex, as can be seen in brief descriptions of the major traditions represented there.

Islam When the Mughals ruled the north-west, Islam enjoyed a privileged position. The region attracted a Muslim professional elite and Muslim interests were protected. Policy was set and patronage granted to foster Muslim learning as well as a Muslim way of life. However, Maharaja Ranjit Singh and the British changed that. Neither set out to destroy Islam. Both sought the loyalty of the Muslim population within their territories and did provide some patronage to Muslims, but neither granted to Islam the privileged position it had previously enjoyed. Muslims, therefore, had to adjust to a new

---

[14] These figures do not include Jammu and Kashmir. Denzil Charles Jelf Ibbetson, *Report on the Census of the Panjab Taken on the 17th of February 1881. Part I: Text* (Calcutta, 1883), 101. (Hereafter the census will be referred to simply as *Punjab Census* with the year of the census attached.)

[15] Ibid., p. 101. This is a major theme of Harjot Oberoi, *The Construction of Religious Boundaries*.

[16] *Punjab Census, 1881*, p. 101.

political situation and practice their faith within a changing milieu. Two Muslim groups adopted differing approaches to this challenge.

The first of these were the Sufi *pirs*, most of whose major centres had developed over time at the tombs and shrines of a founding Sufi saint whose spiritual attainments, it was believed, enabled him to intercede with God on behalf of others. The pir, an heir of the original saint and custodian of his shrine, was a figure of considerable influence. Pirs had disciples to whom they gave advice and blessing, and from whom they received gifts and obedience. These pir–*murid* relationships, and the popular religious festivals held around the original saint's death anniversary, provided the pir with land, wealth, and political influence.

The other important group was the *ulama*, or religious scholars, especially those in Delhi. The most influential of these was Shah Waliullah (1703–1762), a scholar and a reformer who 'sought to stem the tide of decline by consolidating and clarifying the entire body of the Islamic tradition'.[17] While somewhat eclectic and flexible, he nevertheless wanted Muslims to be guided by the Quran and the *hadith*, or authentic sayings of the Prophet, in their individual and collective lives. His successors in Delhi issued judicial opinions (*fatwas*) for the guidance of Muslim believers in the areas of law, ethics, trade, inheritance, family relationships, and other matters of everyday life so that they might persevere in a life of religious obedience under the conditions of alien rule. These ulama popularized their scholarly views through preaching, debates, and the use of the Urdu press. They also participated in what became known as the 'Delhi Renaissance', the focal point of which was Delhi College. Developed from a former *madrassa* (school of religious learning) under both Muslim and British patronage, in 1825 it became an Oriental College and in 1827 an English department was added. This meeting of Western and Muslim learning there attracted Muslim teachers and students, and proved to be more invigorating than threatening to Delhi's long-prevailing patterns of scholarship, cultural activity, and religious reform.

[17] Barbara Daly Metcalf, *Islamic Revival in British India*, p. 36.

Between the reforming Delhi ulama, who sought to define the boundaries of Islam with some precision, and the Sufi pirs who tended to blur them, were millions of Muslims who affirmed that 'There is no God but God and Muhammad is the Prophet of God' and engaged, with varying degrees of faithfulness, in the basic religious disciplines of Islam. Muslim mosques were in all the towns and cities, but not in all the villages, where Muslims lived. The same was true of Muslim *maktabs* (primary schools) and, to a lesser extent, madrassas. *Maulvies* and *mullahs* were the 'clergy' at the mosques; faqirs could be found either wandering about or connected with Muslim shrines. The 1881 census stated that over 98 per cent of all the Muslims in the region were Sunnis, but allowed that the Shia total may have been higher than reported. Beyond that, it is difficult to generalize because of the variety and complexity of belief and practice among Muslims in the north-west during this period.[18]

Sikhism While the political fortunes of Islam were on the decline at the outset of the nineteenth century, those of Sikhism appeared to be on the rise. A Sikh maharaja, Ranjit Singh, ruled the central Punjab in the name of the Khalsa[19] and was a generous patron of the Sikh elite as well as of Sikh institutions. J.S. Grewal has estimated that half of his ruling class was Sikh and that sixty per cent of the religious grants Ranjit Singh made were to Sikhs.[20] He not only took responsibility for the management of the Golden Temple in Amritsar but also visited it many times. His own religious beliefs, however, seem to have been quite eclectic.

[18] In addition to ibid., pp. 3–86, this section is based upon the *Punjab Census 1881*; Peter Hardy, *The Muslims of British India*, pp. 1–60; David Paul Gilmartin, 'Tribe, Land and Religion in the Punjab', pp. 1–113; Ian Talbot, *Punjab and the Raj*, pp. 1–37; Gail Minault, 'Sayyid Ahmad Dehlavi and the "Delhi Renaissance",' in R.E. Frykenberg (ed.), *Delhi Through the Ages*, pp. 174–85; M. Mujeeb, *The Indian Muslims*, passim; Narayani Gupta, *Delhi Between Two Empires*, pp. 1–37; and Avril A. Powell, *Muslims and Missionaries in Pre-Mutiny India*.

[19] A militant Sikh order with a rigorous discipline, membership of which became a mark of true Sikh orthodoxy. See. W.H. McLeod, *Historical Dictionary of Sikhism*, pp. 121–2.

[20] J.S. Grewal, *The New Cambridge History of India. I.3: The Sikhs of the Punjab*, pp. 114, 116.

In analysing Sikh religious life during this period scholars have drawn an important distinction between Khalsa Sikhs and Sahajdhari Sikhs. Guru Gobind Singh, the tenth and final Sikh Guru, created the Khalsa in 1699. A century later the Khalsa had not just an initiation ceremony but also a developing code of conduct which set them apart from other Sikhs. This included keeping one's hair uncut as well as prohibitions against eating meat slaughtered in the Muslim way, intercourse with Muslim women, and the use of tobacco. Khalsa Sikhs 'believed in the indistinguishability and the unity of Guruship from Guru Nanak to Guru Gobind Singh and in the end of personal Guruship after Guru Gobind Singh'.[21] The Guru's presence, however, continued in the Guru Granth (the Sikh scripture) and the Guru Panth (the Guru's community of followers). In the presence of the Guru Granth, in the worshipping congregation, and in community meals at the *gurdwara*, social distinctions prevalent elsewhere were to be set aside and all Sikhs considered equal.

Sahajdhari Sikhs are less easily described. Often they are presented as simply a miscellaneous category of 'non-Khalsa Sikhs' who did not undergo the Khalsa rite of initiation or adhere to the Khalsa discipline. What Sahajdharis had in common, and what made them Sikhs, were their respect for Guru Nanak and their acceptance of his teachings. Harjot Oberoi has suggested that there was, alongside the Khalsa Sikh tradition, an alternative 'Sanatan Sikh tradition' in which ancient custom, including *varnashramadharma*, provided the norm in belief as well as practice, and for which 'religious intermediaries' (not unlike the Muslim pirs) not only played an important role in religious life but also controlled a wide variety of religious institutions.[22] Clearly, such tendencies were present among Sikhs in the first half of the nineteenth century, but whether they had in fact coalesced into an alternative tradition at that time is less clear.

Sikhs had no special religious festivals which were exclusively their own, but they did have their own special places of pilgrimage where they often congregated at festival time. The Golden Temple in Amritsar was the most important of these. Sikhs were also involved

---

[21] J.S. Grewal, *The Sikhs of the Punjab*, p. 118.
[22] Harjot Oberoi, *The Construction of Religious Boundaries*, pp. 92–138.

in some of the same forms of popular religion, and seeking the same kinds of blessing from them, as were other Punjabis. In short, the Sikh religious milieu, like that of the Muslims, was varied and complex in the first half of the nineteenth century, showing some of the same patterns, but lacking that dynamic which the reforming ulama provided.[23]

Hindu Religion   Denzil Ibbetson, the Punjab census commissioner in 1881, was hard pressed to determine who should be classified as a Hindu. He found not only an enormous range of religious belief and practice among Hindus but also strong similarities between their belief and practice on the one hand, and that of their non-Hindu neighbours on the other. There were, in short, no clear boundaries to determine who was by religion a Hindu and who was not. Ibbetson solved the practical problem of census enumeration simply by making 'Hindu' a residual category in which to place any Indian who did not belong to 'some other recognized faith'.[24] He saw neither shared belief nor a common code of conduct but Brahminism as the distinguishing feature of Hinduism and described the Hinduism of his day as

... a hereditary sacerdotalism, with Brahmans as its Levites, the vitality of which is preserved by the social institution of caste, and which may include all shades and diversities of religion native to India, as distinct from the foreign importations of Christianity and Islam, and from later outgrowths of Buddhism, more doubtfully of Sikhism, and still more doubtfully of Jainism.[25]

[23] This section is based upon ibid., pp. 1–203; J.S. Grewal, *The Sikhs of the Punjab*, pp. 82–127; W.H. McLeod, *The Evolution of the Sikh Community: Five Essays*, pp. 37–58; W.H. McLeod, *Who is a Sikh? The Problem of Sikh Identity*, pp. 43–70; Khushwant Singh, *Ranjit Singh: Maharajah of the Punjab*; Madanjit Kaur, 'The Harmandir and Maharaja Ranjit Singh', in J.S. Grewal and Indu Banga (eds), *Maharaja Ranjit Singh and His Times*, pp. 117–24.

[24] *Punjab Census 1881*, pp. 101, 113. See also Romila Thapar, 'Syndicated Moksa'; Robert Eric Frykenberg, 'The Emergence of Modern "Hinduism" as a Concept and as an Institution'; Vasudha Dalmia and Heinrich von Stietencron, 'Introduction', in Vasudha Dalmia and Heinrich von Stietencron (eds), *Representing Hinduism*, pp. 17–32.

[25] *Punjab Census, 1881*, p. 112. 'The Jain I take to be little more than a Hindu sect.' Ibid.

Ibbetson focused primarily upon the religion of the Hindu peasant in what is now Haryana, but did make note of variations from that 'norm' both in what is now Himachal Pradesh and on the north-west frontier. While Hindu peasants acknowledged that there was only one God, knew the names of Vishnu and Shiva, and might enter their temples once or twice a year, their religious life centred around honouring pure and appeasing impure village deities, primarily through making offerings at their local shrines. They also built shrines in honour of deceased saints and ancestors whose blessings they invoked. Belief in the evil eye, as well as in good and bad omens, was also quite common. Cows were venerated, monkeys and peacocks were considered sacred, and the Brahmins played a central role in their religious life. Some Brahmins were ascetics, more functioned as family priests performing life-cycle and other occasional rituals for their clients, while many had no religious responsibilities at all but were nonetheless fed on special occasions.[26] In addition to these features of what might be called routine religious life were some special events: the great annual Hindu festivals of Dusserah, Diwali, and Holi; the lesser ones of Lohri and Raksha Bandhan; and annual festivals associated with particular deities and saints. Hindus also undertook pilgrimages to Hardwar, Kurukshetra, the Amarnath cave in Kashmir, or other points of pilgrimage as the occasion might warrant.

Also to be included in Hindu religion were a number of *bhakti* 'cults' (*panths*) which used the local languages rather than Sanskrit, dispensed with the use of a Brahminical priesthood, and sought to overcome the division between the pure and impure that lay at the basis of the caste system. Among these were the Kabir Panthis and Raidasis who were particularly popular among the lower castes.

Buddhism The brief and sketchy description of Buddhism in Ladakh, Lahaul, and Spiti in the 1881 Census gives the impression that it was really popular religion with a veneer of Tibetan Lamaism

---

[26] Ibid., p. 120. Brahmins were major beneficiaries of Maharaja Ranjit Singh's generosity. See Indu Banga, *Agrarian System of the Sikhs*, pp. 161–5.

on the surface. The people made offerings to mountain, forest, river, field, and family divinities; Shakta religion was also engrafted on to Buddhism so that its symbolism was prominent in Buddhist places of worship. Prayer wheels and flags did not replace but supplemented local shrines and served the same religious purposes. Almost every village had a monastery with anywhere from one or two to more than a hundred monks[27] who played roles in the religious life of the Buddhist population analogous to those of the Brahmins among Hindus: foretelling events, determining auspicious and inauspicious times, and exorcising evil spirits. On the other hand, caste was not so prominent a feature of their society and there is no indication it received any religious sanction from Buddhist sources.[28]

Conclusions   In 1849, Ganesh Das described some of the shrines in the city of Lahore honouring past figures of spiritual accomplishment and/or miracle working power—Muslims, Hindus, and Sikhs—all of which had become places of pilgrimage or of regular visitation.[29] His brief description reveals several features of the religious milieu, which need to be highlighted by way of conclusion. The first and most obvious is the pervasiveness and importance of religion in north-west India during this period. It was everywhere and undergirded, albeit in different ways, virtually all aspects of life; neither politics nor economics nor social relationships were exempt from its influence. Another is not only the rich diversity and complexity brought about by the coming together in one place of several religious traditions but also common religious impulses, senses of the divine, and patterns of religious behaviour regardless of tradition. Among the more striking commonalities were a common desire to enjoy *barakat* or blessing and avoid misfortune;

[27] Frederic Drew, *The Northern Barrier of India*, p. 266.

[28] See also Alexander Cunningham, *Ladakh, Physical, Statistical and Historical*, pp. 363–84 on which most of the census material is based.

[29] J.S. Grewal and Indu Banga (editors and translators), *Early Nineteenth Century Panjab*, pp. 121–2. J. Stuart Jackson reported that prior to 1857 there were, in Delhi, 261 mosques and 188 temples for a population of 150,000 people. *The Delhi Mission of the Society for the Propagation of the Gospel*, p. 11.

the use of offerings and the like to gain the former and escape the latter; and the prevalence of patron–client (pir–murid, *guru–chela*) relationships in religious as in socio-economic or political life. While Islam seemed to exhibit the most intellectual vitality and social activism during this particular period, the influence of Hindu religion seemed to be more pervasive, shaping religious life and social practices across all boundaries defined by distinctive traditions, and giving to life an integrated interconnectedness which, in the ensuing decades, would begin to fall apart.

1857

On 9 May 1857, eighty-five Indian sepoys in the British army, found guilty of refusing to handle the new Enfield rifle cartridges they believed to be greased with cow and pig fat, were publicly shackled and imprisoned in front of their comrades on the parade ground at Meerut. The next evening, while British soldiers were attending church services, the other sepoys mutinied, set the prisoners free, killed as many Europeans as they could, and plundered their homes. The mutineers then left, arriving in Delhi the following morning. Delhi was caught completely by surprise. While some sepoys went directly to the Red Fort to urge the Mughal emperor, Bahadur Shah, to lead the revolt against the British, others moved into the city to take control of it. In this process they killed Europeans, Christians, and others considered sympathetic to the British. Delhi thus became the centre of revolt and Bahadur Shah its reluctant head. Success in Delhi led to mutinies elsewhere and Delhi became a magnet, drawing the disaffected to join in bringing British rule to an end.

Just before being killed, a British telegraph operator in Delhi sent a message to Lahore telling John Lawrence, chief commissioner of the Punjab, what had happened. This gave Lawrence the advantage of surprise in disarming disaffected sepoys in Lahore and in seizing the key forts, arsenals, and strategic positions throughout the Punjab before the sepoys there could mutiny. Despite prompt action and notable success, however, there were successful mutinies in a dozen cities of the Punjab. Lawrence also organized efforts within the Punjab to recapture Delhi. Within a month there was a British force on the ridge overlooking the city and in September the British retook Delhi.

The major area of revolt in the north-west, outside of Delhi itself, was the district of Haryana which the British themselves administered. The sepoys stationed at Ambala were among the earliest required to use the greased cartridges. They set a number of fires in protest and even planned to mutiny on 10 May.[30] Immediately after Delhi fell to the sepoys from Meerut, the peasantry in the surrounding districts, already alienated by the inflexibly high land revenues and intrusive judicial system introduced by the British, rose in revolt and, within three weeks, eliminated all signs of British rule. However, by the time the British had retaken Delhi, they had also retaken most of Haryana. The Punjab remained relatively quiet. Punjabis had little interest in making common cause either with the outsiders whom the British had employed to defeat them or with the Mughal emperor. In fact, Punjabis helped the British recapture Delhi and return the surrounding area to British control. Only on the north-west frontier were there a few minor outbreaks and these were quickly put down. Himachal Pradesh and Jammu and Kashmir were quiet, while the major chiefs between the Sutlej and Delhi promptly offered assistance to their British protectors.

There was at the time considerable debate over the nature and causes of the 1857 revolt. Bahadur Shah in his proclamations and sepoys in their reported conversations appealed for support from Hindus and Muslims alike on the grounds that their religion was in danger. Within Delhi itself there were people on both sides of the conflict, but all the people of Delhi suffered together the privations of siege and reconquest. Outside Delhi the villages seem to have been more disaffected than the towns. Even though their primary concerns may have differed, there was not only communication as well as some mutual support between Bahadur Shah and local leaders in the nearby districts but also some effort to establish a new

---

[30] Like the Meerut sepoys, they intended to attack while the European troops were in church, but the time of the church service was changed and so the mutiny could not develop. K.C. Yadav, *The Revolt of 1857 in Haryana*, pp. 40–50.

administration in areas under rebel control. This, however, did not have time to take definite shape because the British were so quick to reestablish their authority. Clearly, a whole way of life, sanctioned by religion and supported by long-standing social custom, had been threatened by the changes which the British had introduced. For the most part the threat was political and economic in nature, but Christianity was also seen to be playing a role as well.

The Coming of Christianity

There were very few Christians in north-west India in 1800. The Jesuits' Mughal Mission had not left a continuing Christian community behind. The two Roman Catholic churches built in Delhi were in ruins. The Christians attached to the armies of the Marathas and European adventurers were transients. Christianity had yet to sink any roots in the region. Following the papal suppression of the Jesuit order in 1773, the northern portion of their Vicariate of the Great Mughal was entrusted to another religious order, the Discalced Carmelites, one of whose priests, Fr Gregory, moved to Delhi where Emperor Shah Alam gave him a village in Palam for his support. When he died in 1807, there was no priest to replace him. Meanwhile, in 1784, because the Carmelites could not supply more missionaries, Rome entrusted the region to the Capuchin Fathers, who incorporated it into their Tibet–Hindustan Mission. After Fr Gregory's death, one of their priests at Sardhana visited Delhi periodically. Only in 1856 was there another priest resident in Delhi and he was killed in the revolt not long after he arrived.[31]

Roman Catholic activity in the north-west during this period was confined to fellow Catholics in the East India Company's services and churches were built for them in Karnal (1834), Ambala (1843), Kasauli (1844), Sabathu (1844), Simla (1850), and Delhi (1856). In 1829, Fr Adeodatus was sent to Lahore to officiate at the weddings of two of Ranjit Singh's European generals. He stayed on for two years to look after the Catholics in Ranjit Singh's armies.[32] Thus, the

[31] Daniel Anthony D'Souza, *The Growth and Activities of the Catholic Church in North India*, p. 43.

[32] Fulgentius Vannini, *Hindustan–Tibet Mission*, p. 276.

Roman Catholic presence was throughout this period really only a chaplaincy to Christian outsiders in the region. Instead, it was the Protestants who planted and nurtured congregations drawn from the local population.

THE EARLY PROTESTANT MISSIONS

Between 1800 and 1857, seven different Protestant mission societies established permanent 'mission stations', or centres of missionary work, in north-west India. The first of these was the Baptist Missionary Society which sent a missionary to settle in Delhi in 1818. When the East India Company's 1833 charter allowed non-British missionaries into the Company's territories, the Western Foreign Missionary Society, which in 1837 became the Board of Foreign Missions of the Presbyterian Church in the USA, immediately sent out its first missionaries, one of whom arrived in Ludhiana in 1834. The next, in 1844, was the CMS formed in 1799 by the Evangelical wing of the Church of England, followed by the Society for the Propagation of the Gospel (SPG), which, after the creation of the CMS, became the mission society of the bishops of the Church of England. Then, at the very close of this period, in quick succession, three societies established their first mission stations in the north-west. The Associate Presbyterian Synod of North America and Church of Scotland chose Sialkot. The Moravian Brethren in Germany, after failing to start a mission in Tibet, established one in Ladakh in 1856 instead. Each of these will be described briefly in turn.

The Baptist Missionary Society   After some exploratory visits, the Baptists made Delhi one of their mission stations and in 1818 posted the Rev. James Thompson there. Thompson used Delhi as a home base from which he itinerated throughout the surrounding area, preaching and distributing Christian literature. He found the people west of the Yamuna more receptive than those east of it,[33] and was

---

[33] *The Annual Report of the Committee of the Baptist Missionary Society, Addressed to the General Meeting, held at Cambridge On Thursday, June 20th, 1822; Being a Continuation of the Periodical Accounts Relative to the Said Society*, p. 11. (Hereafter

fully convinced that the long-term effects of this kind of evangelism would be great.[34] He did the same thing in Delhi itself, but also held Sunday worship services at his own home and among the army's Christian drummers in the cantonments.[35] He also did a lot of translation work and wrote Hindustani tracts and hymns.

Thompson was an unusual missionary. He was a Eurasian, was very fluent in Hindustani, and, in contrast to later missionaries in the region, almost totally avoided developing mission institutions. He worked alone and spent much of his time itinerating. In the Society's 1842 report, there is reference to a school in the cantonment attended mostly by the wives and children of soldiers,[36] but that was all. He acquired some land for a chapel only in 1846.[37] Thompson died in 1850 and his successor, J. Mackay, arrived in Delhi in 1856 with two 'native assistants'. In 1857, the Baptists were running two schools with an enrollment of 130 children. Clearly, they had adopted a very different approach to missionary outreach, even though they continued to preach and itinerate.[38]

The Presbyterian Church in the USA The second mission in the north-west during this period began when the Lowries and the Reeds, arrived in Calcutta in October 1833 with instructions to start mission work in northern India. There they consulted Alexander Duff and Charles Trevelyan among others, before deciding on the Punjab, partly because of the Sikhs, who were 'described as more free from prejudice, from the Brahmins, and from caste, than any other people

---

this source will be referred to as *Baptist Annual Report* followed by the year of the report.)

[34] Referring to the distribution of tracts, Thompson said 'Experience justifies our waiting with long patience for these fruits, and we shall assuredly reap.' *Baptist Annual Report 1843*, p. 26. See also *Baptist Annual Report 1841*, p. 16.

[35] *Baptist Annual Report 1827*, p. 41. The drummers were not local people but came with the army from outside the region.

[36] *Baptist Annual Report 1842*, p. 12.

[37] Only sixty people, not all of them Indians, had joined Thompson's church during his thirty-two years in Delhi. *Baptist Annual Report 1852*, p. 31.

[38] *Baptist Annual Report 1857*, p. 48.

in India' and eager to learn English, and who were thus considered to be open to missionary influence.[39] Captain Wade, the British Political Agent in Ludhiana, also invited these missionaries to take charge of the school he had started there. However, before they could proceed to the Punjab, Mrs Lowrie died and William Reed became so ill that he and his wife had to return to the USA. John C. Lowrie went on alone and reached Ludhiana on 5 November 1834.

Lowrie's stay in the Punjab was brief but significant. He took over superintendence of Captain Wade's school and, after getting Wade's approval, introduced religious instruction into the curriculum. He toured the area, considered locations for future mission stations, and even visited Maharaja Ranjit Singh's court in Lahore. He conducted Sunday services and opened a school for Christian drummers in the army. He was allotted 50 acres of land for the mission one quarter of a mile outside Ludhiana and purchased a house in Sabathu within the Protected Hill States. Lowrie welcomed the support he received from Wade and other Europeans. He believed that the people he encountered held Europeans, for the most part, in high regard. He chose to live in the fort rather than the city because he believed that the 'circumstance of my dwelling in the government Fort will most probably increase my influence among the natives'.[40] He gave priority to the English department of Wade's school because he saw the demand for English and sought to turn it to good advantage.[41] He thought that future mission stations should be located in territories under British rather than Indian rulers because problems with government interference were apt to be fewer.[42] After two years, his health broken, the twenty-eight-year-old Lowrie left the Punjab, but not before welcoming three missionary couples to Ludhiana.

---

[39] 'Mission to Northern India', *FMC* (April 1834), p. 201.

[40] 'Journal of Rev. J.C. Lowrie at Lodiana', *FMC* (October 1835), p. 148.

[41] 'Mission to Northern India', *FMC* (November 1836), pp. 181–2. Lowrie believed that those who learned English would be in time become an influential group in Indian society and wanted them to exercise their influence in ways favourable to Christianity.

[42] Ibid., p. 183.

Lowrie's successors began by organizing themselves to carry on the work that he had started. In 1836, they created a presbytery, made up of all clergy and lay representatives of (thus far non-existent) member congregations, which was responsible for such ecclesiastical matters as the ordination and discipline of clergy. The following year, all the male missionaries formed a mission, which was responsible for policy and its implementation, including the allocation of money and personnel.[43] In 1840, they decided to divide themselves into the Lodiana (later Punjab) and the Farrukhabad (later North India) Missions. The former had stations in the Punjab and north-western section of the North-Western Provinces, while the latter was concentrated in the central and eastern portions of the North-Western Provinces.

In 1836, Presbyterian missionary activity expanded to include Sabathu and Saharanpur. Following the first Anglo-Sikh war, the Presbyterians sent Rev. Golaknath, one of their first converts and their first ordained Indian clergyman, to start a new mission station in Jullundur (1846). In 1848, they opened another station in Ambala and in 1849, after the British annexed the rest of the Punjab, in Lahore. Their other major mission stations begun prior to 1857 were in Dehra Dun (1853), Rawalpindi (1856), and a Mission to the Afghans in Peshawar (1856). In each case a school was promptly either taken over or started, but preaching/itinerating was slower in getting started because of the time required to learn the language properly. They also set up the Lodiana Mission Press, thus increasing the number of tracts, scriptures, religious books, and school books the missionaries could make available to meet the growing demand. In 1838, its first year, the press printed 57,743 tracts and 500 portions of the Bible for distribution at *melas*, fairs, evangelistic gatherings or in response to individual requests.[44] In 1840, they published a Persian newspaper, *Lodiana Akhbar*,[45] *Pilgrim's Progress* in Hindustani, as well

---

[43] A fuller discussion of this is found in John C.B. Webster, *The Christian Community and Change*, pp. 208–9.

[44] 'India Missions', *FMC* (June 1839), pp. 184–5.

[45] Brush saw a link between the government and this newspaper. 'Protestants in the Punjab', pp. 78–9.

as Matthew's Gospel in Punjabi.[46] By 1844, they had *Pilgrim's Progress* and a 128-page *Brief Bible History* in Punjabi as well.[47] Clearly, translation and writing were major components of Presbyterian missionary work. John Newton, who arrived in Ludhiana in 1836, wrote the first comprehensive grammar of the Punjabi language in 1851, the first Punjabi vocabulary book, and (with Levi Janvier) the first Punjabi dictionary in 1854. While intended primarily to help fellow missionaries with language study, these books as well as some of their translations, such as Newton's Punjabi New Testament (1868), came to mark a transition from traditional to modern Punjabi and Newton is today considered one of the fathers of the modern Punjabi language.[48]

The Church Missionary Society (CMS) Unlike its predecessors in the north-west whose presence arose from overseas missionary impulses, the work of the CMS was begun at the initiative of British residents committed to evangelizing the local population. In 1840, a group of British civil and military officers met in Simla to establish a Christian mission to the Pahari (hill) people, which they decided to call the Himalayan Mission, and to raise money to support two German missionaries at Kotgarh.[49] In order to give their mission permanence and stability, this committee entered into correspondence with the CMS and transferred the Himalayan Mission to it in 1844. Three years later, the Himalayan Mission was placed under the Calcutta Corresponding Committee of the CMS. British families in northern India also started the Punjab Mission 'as a Thanksgiving to Almighty God for His late mercies towards the Governments of England and India, in the past signal victory [in the

---

[46] '1840 Report of the Lodiana Station', *FMC* (August 1841), p. 244.

[47] *The Seventh Annual Report of the Board of Foreign Missions of the Presbyterian Church in the United States of America, May 1844*, p. 21. (Hereafter referred to as *BFM PC in USA Annual Report* with the year added.)

[48] James Massey, 'Presbyterian Missionaries and the Development of Punjabi Language and Literature', pp. 258–9.

[49] K.N. Thakur Das, 'Himalayan Mission of C.M.S. And Spiritual Movements in Simla Hills 1840–1947', pp. 1–4.

second Anglo-Sikh War] and the present promised blessing of peace'.[50] The CMS selected Amritsar as its first Punjab mission station in order to be 'in the midst of the Sikhs'[51] and two missionaries began work there in 1852.

Both the Himalayan and Punjab Missions began expanding beyond their original mission stations prior to 1857. The former had started at Kotgarh, included Simla for only a few years, but began work in Kangra in 1854. The latter expanded from Amritsar to Peshawar (in response to a local initiative led by Major Herbert Edwardes) in 1854, and to Multan in 1856. Like the Presbyterians, they quickly opened up a school at each station. The CMS missionaries were also active in itinerating throughout the areas around their respective stations. The CMS organizational structure differed from the Presbyterians'. Their congregations became part of the diocesan structure of the Church of England in India, but their missionaries reported to the Calcutta Corresponding Committee of the CMS, which dealt directly with the CMS in London.[52] Local committees of European supporters were also formed in Lahore and Peshawar. The missionaries do not appear to have had a formal organization of their own by the close of this period and it would seem that, while assured of greater financial support from within the resident European community, they did not have the same degree of autonomy which their Presbyterian counterparts enjoyed.

---

[50] *Proceedings of the Church Missionary Society for Africa and the East. Fifty-first Year, 1849–50*, p. cxxxviii. (Hereafter referred to as *CMS Proceedings*, with the year added.) John Newton brought news of a British army officer's anonymous gift of Rs 10,000 to the CMS and invited them to join the Presbyterians in evangelizing the province. Ibid., *1850–51*, p. clvii.

[51] Like the Presbyterians, the CMS saw the Sikhs as receptive to Christian preaching and had found elsewhere that they made excellent converts. Ibid., p. clv.

[52] These Corresponding Committees usually had the bishop as chairman and an ordained CMS missionary as secretary. The other members were generally British chaplains, and civil and military officers. CMS missionaries generally had their own Missionary Conferences, but they were only to advise the Corresponding Committee. See M.E. Gibbs, 'The Anglican Church in India and Independence', pp. 48–9.

The Society for the Propagation of the Gospel (SPG) Like the Himalayan and Punjab Missions of the CMS, the Delhi Mission of the SPG was begun at the initiative of British residents 'on the spot'. The prime movers in Delhi were Mrs J.P. Gubbins, the wife of a judge there, and the Rev. M.J. Jennings, a Company chaplain in northern India. The mission also received the backing of James Thomason, lieutenant governor of the North-Western Provinces. Their efforts were greatly helped by the baptisms of Professor Ram Chandra of Delhi College and Dr Chaman Lal, assistant surgeon of Delhi, on 11 July 1852. In December 1852, the SPG decided to establish a mission in Delhi, 'the great object' of which was 'to propagate the Gospel among the native inhabitants of Delhi, and afford the youth, especially those who are engaged in acquiring secular education at Government Schools, an opportunity of obtaining a knowledge of Christianity'.[53] Its first two missionaries arrived in Delhi on 11 February 1854.

Since the evangelistic opportunities in Delhi were perceived to be among the Western educated, as the baptisms of Ram Chandra and Chaman Lal had indicated, the Delhi Mission was to be 'of a superior kind; the Missionaries were to be learned as well as devout'.[54] The SPG planned to 'establish a Missionary and Collegiate Institution at Delhi' and appointed the Rev. John S. Jackson, a Fellow of Caius College, Cambridge, as 'Senior Missionary and Professor' as well as the Rev. Alfred R. Hubbard, also of Caius College, as 'Junior Missionary Professor'.[55] When Jackson and Hubbard arrived, they started a school in the city and placed Daniel Sandys, a Bishop's College student, in charge of it. Since the Europeans already had a chaplain to look after them, Jackson and Hubbard were able to concentrate on occasional tutoring and especially language study, the former specializing in Urdu/Persian and the latter in Hindi/

[53] Quoted in F.J. Western, 'The Early History of the Cambridge Mission to Delhi', pp. 25–6.

[54] Society for the Propagation of the Gospel, 'Delhi', *Quarterly Paper No. CIV* (April 1858), p. 3.

[55] F.J. Western, 'The Early History of the Cambridge Mission to Delhi', pp. 24–5.

Sanskrit. Within the year, Jackson was conducting Urdu services at St. James Church.[56] Supporters of the mission in Delhi organized a committee that had oversight of and raised money for the mission's work. At the end of 1856 it received a serious setback when Jackson had to leave owing to his wife's failing health.

The Associate Presbyterian Synod of North America On 13 February 1855 the Rev. Andrew Gordon, his wife, daughter, and sister arrived in Calcutta with instructions to start a mission in north India. After consulting with missionaries they met in Calcutta and visited on their way to the north-west, Gordon chose Sialkot. On reaching his destination in August, Gordon was given hospitality and assistance in getting started by Captain John Mill, an artillery officer and member of the Free Church of Scotland. In 1856, the Gordons were joined by two more missionary families as well as by two Indian catechists from the Lodiana Mission and their families. The three male missionaries formed a mission in November, as well as a congregation with one of the catechists as an elder, and a presbytery in December. Most of their time prior to May 1857 was devoted to building houses on a plot of land about three-quarters of a mile from the city and to learning the language. By May 1857, they had begun preaching in the city, in surrounding villages, and at two melas. They had also taken over a school in the city begun by a CMS Missionary in Amritsar and had started a small orphanage with three children in it.[57] In 1858, this became a United Presbyterian mission when the Associate Presbyterian Synod of North America joined with the Associate Reformed Presbyterian Synod to form the United Presbyterian Church of North America.

The Moravian Church The Himalayan Mission of the Moravian Church was the result of a failed effort to maintain a mission to the Mongols. In 1850, the Moravian Mission Board in Germany appointed

---

[56] Built in 1836 by Colonel James Skinner, St. James Church, located near Kashmiri Gate, was the Anglican church where the British in Delhi worshipped.

[57] Andrew Gordon, *Our India Mission*, pp. 17–127.

August Wilhelm Heyde and Eduard Pagell to start a mission to Inner Mongolia in the Chinese empire. After studying Mongolian and some medicine in Germany, they sailed for India in July 1853. In April 1854, they reached Kotgarh where they stayed with Dr Prochnow, a German CMS missionary, to study Mongolian, Tibetan, and Hindustani. In the spring of 1855 they set out for Leh. They made three unsuccessful attempts to enter Tibet, but were turned back at the border each time. They then requested permission to establish a mission at Kyelang in Lahaul instead. This was granted and they began work there on 16 May 1856.[58]

The Church of Scotland In 1855, the Church of Scotland received from the estate of a Captain Murray, who had served in the Punjab, a bequest of £1500 with instructions to use the money to establish a mission to the Sikhs. The Rev. Thomas Hunter and his family were sent out to start a mission 'at Lahore or in its neighbourhood',[59] but were detained in Bombay. The Hunters and Mahommad Ismael, an Indian convert, left Bombay in October 1856 and arrived in Sialkot at the end of the year, surprised to find three missionary families already in residence. A letter dated 2 February 1857 indicates that within a month the Hunters had started two vernacular schools, one for girls and one for boys, and were conducting a Presbyterian service for the resident Europeans as well as a Hindustani service for their servants.[60]

THE RELIGIOUS ENCOUNTER
The encounter between Christianity and the other religions of north-west India during the first half of the nineteenth century may be viewed as a product of, and hence in good part patterned on, the Evangelical revival in the United Kingdom and the Second Great

[58] This is based on John Bray, 'A History of the Moravian Church in India', pp. 28–33.
[59] *Report to the General Assembly of the Church of Scotland by the Committee for the Propagation of the Gospel, Especially in India, 29th May 1855*, p. 14. (Hereafter referred to as *Report to the Church of Scotland General Assembly* with the year added.)
[60] 'Punjab', *HFMR* (June 1857), pp. 132–3.

Awakening in the United States. The former had begun in the mid-eighteenth century with the preaching of John Wesley and George Whitefield. By the end of the century it had not only affected the inner life of all of the British Protestant denominations for a long time to come but also led them to form missionary societies as well as such interdenominational bodies as The Religious Tract Society (1799) and the British and Foreign Bible Society (1804). The Second Great Awakening began at the very end of the eighteenth century, soon after the United States had become independent, and continued in full force into the middle of the next century. As in the United Kingdom, this revival resulted in considerable effort to evangelize the nation's large 'unconverted' population, to establish churches among them, and to recruit them in a massive effort to create a Christian nation through a variety of reform, benevolent, educational, and missionary societies. Both movements laid special emphasis upon the experience of individual conversion, an inner piety based upon a vital personal relationship to God mediated through Jesus Christ, and a passion for mission to those who had not yet received the Christian message, whether at home or abroad.[61] Both used such methods of evangelism as outdoor preaching as well as the distribution of tracts and scriptures to share the Christian gospel with people where they were.

In north-west India, the religious encounter that is documented for us was the result of persistent initiatives from some highly educated representatives of these religious movements in the West. Virtually every foreign missionary who went there during this period was an ordained clergyman.[62] Of the twelve Presbyterian missionaries from the United States for whom data is available, all

---

[61] These have been considered defining characteristics of Evangelicalism, along with an implicit individualism, a concern for moral transformation and disciplined living, and a belief in the centrality and authority of the Bible for Christian life.

[62] Those who were still laymen upon arrival were ordained soon afterwards. Adolph Rudolph, whom the Anglicans would not ordain, joined the Lodiana Mission and the Lodiana Presbytery ordained him. Missionary wives were not considered missionaries in their own right until much later, even though some were involved in starting girls' schools and in other forms of missionary work among women.

were college graduates, at least seven had earned their theological degrees as well, while another three had partially completed theirs.[63] The CMS, SPG, and Church of Scotland missionaries in the Punjab and Delhi were also university graduates; the German missionaries in the hill areas were differently but nonetheless well educated.[64] James Thompson, the lone Baptist missionary in Delhi for so many years, who was recruited from within India before the university system had been established there, had been an East India Company clerk and became an outstanding linguist, translating the New Testament and authoring a Hindustani dictionary.[65] The education of these missionaries, and especially their professional training, profoundly influenced the outlook of all of them, with the possible exception of Thompson.

This is not immediately apparent. The missionaries had brought from home no grand visions, theories, or strategies to guide their labours; instead, they simply responded to perceived opportunities and needs around them. Even though three of the mission societies had been attracted to the Punjab by the presence there of the Sikhs, neither they nor any other social group, including 'the educated', were specifically 'targeted' to the relative exclusion of others, for concentrated evangelistic effort. The missionaries were young generalists rather than seasoned specialists. Their reports and journals indicate that, for them, this was a period of exploration and of basically personal, face-to-face interaction with the people of north-west India. The 'great debates' of the period were held elsewhere and the press had not yet come to play the major role in shaping the encounter it would later. Missionary reflection upon their task was confined primarily to practical details of evangelistic method. Where the impact of their education becomes most apparent is in the

[63] Biographical data provided in theological seminary alumni directories supplemented by obituaries and other biographical sketches presented in mission histories or contemporary missionary magazines.

[64] Stuart Piggin has argued, in addition, that these missionaries were drawn from the most restless, dynamic, and self-confident classes in British society. *Making Evangelical Missionaries 1789–1858*, pp. 40–1, 47.

[65] 'Delhi', *MH* (November 1850), p. 167.

important assumptions behind their evangelistic initiatives as well as in the content of their message, both of which shaped the religious encounter throughout this and the subsequent period. These come out quite clearly in a paragraph from the journal of Robert Clark, written home in the face of opposition to his preaching when on a tour to Kashmir.

We have endeavoured here, as throughout the whole journey, to avoid as much as possible all mention of the existing religions; and have only stated our opinions when expressly called upon to do so. We have also abstained from argument and controversy as much as possible. Our simple object has been to make plain *statements* of the gospel, and to set before the people the fundamental doctrines of our religion in a manner as would be most likely to inform their understandings, and then call upon them to use every effort to investigate the truth, and to attain to everlasting life according to the revealed will of God. The uncertainty of life and the certainty of death, the contrast between heaven and hell, between realities and vanities, between eternity and time, constitute the stimulating arguments which make this all-important duty imperative on all men. As messengers of God, it would seem that our simple duty is to deliver our message faithfully, and even authoritatively, as a direct communication and command of God to them, and then leave all results and consequences of whatever kind, in the hands of Him whose work it is we are endeavouring to perform. We do not, therefore, state at once why it is so, or how it is so, but simply that it is so. Its truth rests upon the truth of the word of God. If the latter be true, then is the former true also, however difficult or incomprehensible it may seem to men. When this is stated, the proofs, the credentials of its truth, the reasons why we know the Bible to be the word of God, must then be forthcoming when we are called upon to declare them, and these we trust we are prepared to give.[66]

Clark's starting point, as of all Evangelicals, was divine revelation. This revelation, given fully and definitively in Jesus Christ, was attested to by the Bible, which was written under 'such a divine influence upon the sacred writers as rendered them exempt from

[66] 'Kashmir', *CMI* (March 1855), pp. 69–70. See also, 'The Punjab Mission', *CMI* (May 1853), p. 103.

error, both in regard to the ideas and words'.[67] This was the everlasting truth upon which Clark and the other missionaries took their stand and in the light of which they initiated religious encounters throughout north-west India during most of the nineteenth century. To them, the God-given truth in Jesus Christ stood in marked contrast to false and/or merely human systems of truth, whether based on Western rationalism or Indian religions. When called upon to defend this revealed truth against competing claims, they drew upon the theological texts which they had studied in their theological courses back home: William Paley's highly influential *Evidences of Christianity* or the similar arguments from prophecy and miracle of the Princeton theologians, Archibald Alexander and Charles Hodge, in the USA.[68]

James Thompson defined the 'two distinguishing features of the gospel' in good Evangelical fashion as 'the insufficiency of all human righteousness and the all-sufficiency of the Saviour',[69] while in Srinagar, Robert Clark responded to the maharaja's question about the 'principle doctrines of the gospel' by saying that they were 'the sinfulness of fallen man and his restitution to the favour of God by the merits of Christ'.[70] John Newton spelled this out somewhat more fully in providing these 'five elements of religion':

1. God is Lord of us all; 2. All men are sinners against God; 3. Hell has been prepared for the punishment of sinners; 4. God's only Son, Jesus, is the Saviour from hell; 5. Those, and those only, who believe in Jesus will be saved.[71]

[67] Archibald Alexander, *Evidences of the Authenticity, Inspiration and Canonical Authority of the Holy Scriptures*, p. 230.

[68] Piggin attests to the popularity of Paley among the British missionaries. Stuart Piggin, *Making Evangelical Missionaries*, pp. 63, 245. The Presbyterian Church in the USA and its missionaries, the largest contingent in north-west India at this time, were under the influence of the Princeton Theology which used a similar 'Christian Evidences' apologetic throughout this period and the next. See John C.B. Webster, *The Christian Community and Change*, pp. 30–4.

[69] 'Delhi', *MH* (January 1826), p. 4.

[70] 'Kashmir', *CMI* (April 1855), p. 93.

[71] 'The Gospel Preached in a Hindu Monastery: Sketch No. IV', *FM* (March 1852), p. 164.

Two aspects of this gospel are particularly noteworthy. The first is its strong individualism. Both judgment and salvation were individual; both called for individual response. While the missionaries were well aware of the socio-economic networks (particularly that of caste) within which members of their audiences lived, the gospel they preached was about the individual and intended for the individual. The other was that its primary focus was on eternity rather than on the present; their message looked beyond the present life to the life after death, as the former, where decisions with consequences for life in eternity were made, was considered to be a preparation for the latter. Thus, in Thompson's terms, the question of sufficiency or insufficiency related to the reward of heaven and the punishment of hell rather than to coping with the difficulties of this present life.

The 'stimulating arguments' missionaries employed to evoke a 'spirit of inquiry' among individuals in their audiences were based upon neither a systematic study of the religions they encountered nor an empathetic effort to enter into the mindset of the people they were addressing. Instead, they assumed that human nature and human reason were the same everywhere, regardless of culture or religion. In this they followed Joseph Butler's *Analogy of Religion*, whose apologetic they greatly admired and recommended to inquirers. Butler's work is divided into two parts. The first deals with natural religion, 'that system of things and dispensation of Providence which experience, together with reason, informs us of'.[72] Butler and the missionaries considered this generic religion universal unless corrupted, and thus a common reference point for religious discussion. For example, Butler began this section of the *Analogy* with a chapter on the future life, not only the subject which Clark and other missionaries used as their most 'stimulating argument' when presenting the case for the Christian message of salvation through Jesus Christ, but also an assumption which Thompson was surprised to have a Brahmin in his audience question.[73] From this

---

[72] Joseph Butler, *The Analogy of Religion*, p. 37. This was first published in 1736.

[73] Specifically, he opposed the 'universally received truth' that 'there is a heaven and a hell'. 'Delhi', *MH* (January 1826), p. 4.

and other features of natural religion which offered more 'stimulating arguments',[74] Butler moved on in the second part of his book to revealed religion (Christianity) which, he considered to be 'a republication and external institution of essential religion, adapted to the present circumstances of mankind, and intended to promote natural piety and virtue' as well as containing 'an account of a dispensation of things not discoverable by reason'.[75] This was, in essence, the way in which one missionary apologetic proceeded. Another common, and somewhat similar apologetic proceeded simply from sin to salvation from the eternally damning consequences of sin only through belief in Jesus Christ. This apologetic provoked many 'stimulating arguments' when Evangelical views both of sin and then of salvation were contested.[76]

While the desired outcome of this apologetic was 'conviction of truth', that alone was not enough. The heart had to be changed. This was central to Evangelicalism, central to the personal experience of those who went to India as missionaries,[77] and central to the missionary presentation of Christianity. Whereas the religions of the north-west were at times treated as religions of external observances only, Christianity led to inner transformation. Among the external signs of this inner transformation were sincere repentance for past sin, a genuine commitment to following a strict moral code in conformity with God's commandments, and a life of faithful piety. For converts, repentance included a total break from one's Muslim, Hindu, or Sikh past which had been lived (by definition, even if unknowingly) in denial of or rebellion against God.

Where missionaries disagreed was on the issue of whether or not to criticize the existing religions of their audiences. Clark chose not to criticize unless pressed to comment. He also discovered that using Old Testament prophecies to prove the divinity of Christ was very provocative to Muslims because they accepted the prophets but not

[74] See Joseph Butler, *The Analogy of Religion*, pp. 42–3, 194.

[75] Butler concluded that 'though natural religion is the foundation and principal part of Christianity, it is not in any sense the whole of it'. Ibid., p. 194.

[76] See John C.B. Webster, *The Christian Community and Change*, pp. 93–6.

[77] Stuart Piggin, *Making Evangelical Missionaries*, pp. 55, 64.

the inferences Clark was drawing from the prophets.[78] Other missionaries were often quite critical of specific religious beliefs or practices because this suited their particular apologetic for Christianity. For example, when these were presented as legitimate alternative ways of salvation, missionary preachers often pointed out that these totally failed to address the human predicament as defined by Evangelical theology. Christ and only Christ could save.[79]

This Evangelical view of God and reality, of the consequent nature and means of salvation, as well as of appropriate religious impulses and patterns of behaviour stood in marked contrast to what was already present in the religious milieu of north-west India. The journals of James Thompson, the first and only missionary there for fifteen years, attest to the sense of novelty his message evoked. While there was criticism and opposition to his preaching,[80] the most common response was curiosity. There was considerable demand for the books, tracts, and scripture portions he always had with him;[81] some people read and kept them for long periods of time. Many Hindus in particular listened with interest to what he had to say,

[78] 'The Punjab Mission', *CMI* (May 1853), p. 104.

[79] Brush cites several instances in which missionaries were quite provocative in their criticisms of other religions and at times incurred near violent opposition. 'Protestants in the Punjab', pp. 85–9. Cox has observed that missionaries were more critical of other religions in their reports back home than they were in addressing Indian audiences and readers. *Imperial Fault Lines*, p. 25. I have found in my review of the sources that some missionaries, like John Morrison, were more confrontational and critical than others, thus making generalization difficult.

[80] It was reported much later that Thompson was frequently persecuted and openly beaten in the streets of Delhi. 'Progress of the Gospel in Delhi', *BM* (April 1866), p. 219.

[81] See, e.g., 'Delhi', *MH* (January 1823), pp. 4–6; 'Delhi', ibid. (August 1841), pp. 120–4; 'India', ibid. (October 1850), pp. 146–9. The response was not always positive. Thompson reported one of his hearers saying to others, 'The instant any one reads the book, he is sure to lose his holiness and cast and become a Feringhee', while another reported, 'I once took a book of yours home, and shortly after fell ill. My family and friends told me it was in consequence of having brought your books into the house.' 'Delhi', ibid. (January 1823), p. 5 and 'Delhi', ibid. (August 1841), p. 122.

asked questions about, for example, the cross and divinity of Christ,[82] and demonstrated considerable openness to his message. At one religious fair, he reported that he drew larger audiences than 'the reader and expounder of the shastras'. This difference he attributed to 'a deep interest in the new, strange, and sometimes unwelcome truths advanced [by the missionary], and as if there was something at stake'.[83] Among those who joined him in public or private conversation were people of all religions including Brahmins, ascetics, faqirs, Udasis, maulvies, and leaders of diverse religious sects.[84] When Thompson died in Delhi in 1850, about 500 Indians attended his funeral, a number over twenty times larger than the membership of his tiny congregation.[85]

After Thompson's death the scene of the religious encounter in Delhi shifted from the bazars to Delhi College and the central figure was not a missionary but Ram Chandra, a Hindu teaching in the Oriental department who had translated a number of European scientific works into Urdu and introduced Copernican astronomy into his classes and publications. Ram Chandra's baptism in 1852, as well as his links with William Muir and the CMS missionaries at Agra who were deeply engaged in 'the Mohammedan Controversy', posed a more serious threat than did Western learning per se. Ram Chandra was responsible for circulating in Delhi Carl Pfander's *Mizan-ul-Haq* (Balance of Truth) and other Christian works challenging the very bases of Islam. Through classroom teaching and personal conversations, he had a good number of Delhi College students seriously questioning their inherited religions and even leaning towards Christianity. This resulted in a Muslim counter-attack led by Maulana Rahmat Allah Kairanawi of Delhi and, in 1854, to the 'Great Debate' at Agra in which Rahmat Allah and his colleague, Dr Muhammad Wazir Khan, drew upon Christian scholarship to

---

[82] 'Delhi', ibid. (December 1840), p. 291; 'Delhi', ibid., (October 1841), p. 156.

[83] 'Delhi', ibid. (August 1841), p. 122.

[84] In 1847, Thompson estimated that between 50 and 100 people heard him daily in 'conspicuous parts' of Delhi. 'Delhi', ibid. (February 1848), p. 20.

[85] 'Delhi', ibid. (November 1850), p. 166.

challenge some basic Evangelical premises accepted by their CMS opponents, Carl Pfander and Thomas Valpy French.[86]

The religious encounter in the rest of north-west India was not a debate between scholars. Missionaries introduced Western learning and textbooks into the schools they established, using it as an ally of specifically Christian teaching but, as Clark's statement indicates, the main evangelistic emphasis was placed upon Christian proclamation, to which others responded. The reports, journals, and correspondence which the missionaries wrote did not and could not describe all of these in detail. It is, therefore, difficult to speak of typical or representative encounters during this period. However, four of the more graphic descriptions do provide important insights.

An early one was John C. Lowrie's conversation with Maharaja Ranjit Singh in the Lahore darbar. At his initial interview, Lowrie presented Ranjit Singh with an English Bible and a Punjabi Pentateuch. Ranjit Singh then posed a series of questions that Lowrie interpreted as tests: 'where is God?' and 'what precepts has God given in His word?' However, Lowrie's answer to the question, 'what will be done to those who disobey his commandments?' seems to have captured the maharaja's interest.

'God will punish them with eternal suffering in the next world.' 'If so, why do rulers punish men who commit murder, for instance, in this world?' 'Rulers are appointed by God to punish in this world many kinds of wickedness; but all will have to give an account, in the next world, to God, both rulers and subjects.' He inquired if that was so written in our Scriptures. I took occasion then to mention that 'Christians believe that they may avoid the suffering in the next world which is due to all men for sin, by trusting in the Lord Jesus Christ.' 'Why, then, if Christians think they can avoid suffering in the next world by trusting in Christ, do Christian rulers inflict punishment on any of their people?' 'God requires the sin which is in the world to be visited with suffering in this life also as a punishment, even though there may be deliverance from suffering in the next.'[87]

[86] This paragraph is based on Avril Ann Powell, *Muslims and Missionaries*, pp. 192–262.

[87] 'Journal of Mr. Lowrie's Trip to Lahor', *FMC* (December 1835), p. 187.

Lowrie's was something of a 'command performance'. Ranjit Singh asked Lowrie not only about his religious beliefs but about a number of other subjects as well. The nature and content of the religious discussion was dictated not by the missionary but by the maharaja. Ranjit Singh's responses demonstrated understanding and perhaps appreciation of the views expressed rather than approval or commitment. The more common form of interaction took place in the bazars at missionary initiative but not totally on missionary terms, as this excellent description by the Rev. Adolph Rudolph indicates.

The missionary has taken his stand in that part of the town which appears to be pretty crowded, and yet not too noisy. He places himself on a platform before an empty shop, or on the edge of a wall, a piece of timber, or any other thing which raises him about a foot or two higher than his audience. He thus is better heard and understood, and finds it easier to address a large crowd, than if he stood on a level with them. He finds it easier to breathe, and is less oppressed by the heat. His texts are such as may easily be understood by persons who have never before heard the Gospel. His discourse is more a familiar address, than a sermon in grave style. It almost always contains the two great doctrines, 'the fall of mankind,' and 'salvation by Christ,' although his text may not refer to them directly. The missionary endeavors to convince his hearers of the great truth, that all are under sin; that there is none righteous, none that does good, not one. He points out particular sins, and such as he knows, in general, all are guilty of, and shows the great sinfulness of these sins. To this truth every one assents. But the second, redemption by Christ, salvation by grace, justification by faith in a crucified Redeemer, is in a great measure new to them. To a few only it appears acceptable; others manifest their doubts about it; others seem disappointed; some are indifferent; and some ridicule it. Questions and objections raised by the people, lead the preacher away from his text. He has to correct errors, to contend with false doctrines, and show where the consciences of his hearers are misguided. He thus loses the thread of his discourse, and often speaks on certain subjects much against his will, but perhaps to the real advantage of his audience.[88]

---

[88] 'Journal of the Rev. A. Rudolph', ibid. (June 1848), p. 175.

Rudolph's description may explain why there are so few detailed descriptions of sermons or the ensuing discussions which took place in the bazars of north-west India. There was an ad hoc quality to each one and few seemed to lead anywhere specific. To many in the audience they could well have been, as Rudolph suggested later in the same description, an unexpected form of entertainment. The hope was that they would stimulate further inquiry, which could occur in more private, less distracting settings. An instructive example of an exception, because it reveals some of the major themes of 'The Mohammedan Controversy' being dealt with at the popular level, is this summary of a public conversation which took place in Ludhiana between Rev. Levi Janvier and a young Muslim who asked about Christ. Janvier told him that Christ was the Son of God and that 'we preach salvation through him.'

'No, call Christ a prophet, but don't call him the Son of God.' 'But what God has declared, ought we to believe it or not?' 'Certainly we ought to believe it.' 'But He has declared that Jesus Christ is his Son.' 'God has no Son. Men have wives, and children, and brothers, and sisters, but this cannot be with God.' 'Still it is declared in the Gospel that Christ is the Son of God, and you are quarreling now not with me, but with the Holy Scriptures?' 'But in the Koran it is written that the Gospel is no longer in force; it is done away.' 'No, in the Gospel it is written that the word of God can never pass away; and Christ said, I have not come to destroy the law and the prophets, but to fulfill.' 'That book which you have we do not mind; it is not the true gospel.' 'But you believe the law, and psalms, and prophets to be the word of God, do you not?' 'Yes certainly.' 'Well, there are abundant evidences of Christ's Sonship in these also.' ' You have not the true psalms and prophets; they have been changed.' 'It becomes now my duty plainly to tell you that the book on which you rely is misleading you. The Koran is not the word of God.' 'The Koran not the word of God? You are just saying this for spite. Then the law and the prophets are not the word.' 'But you have already acknowledged them to be His word; and I am not speaking from spite, but from a desire to save your soul. If you should see a man about to eat poison instead of bread, how could you refrain from crying out and preventing him? Thus I am warning you that the Koran, which you esteem the bread of Life, is only poison to your soul. I am a poor, helpless, unworthy sinner, but God has been pleased to make known to me the way of Life, and I wish now to tell you.' 'Well, if I show you a prophecy recorded in the psalms, that Mohammed will come, a prophet of God, and that all must obey him, will you become a follower of Mohammed?' 'Yes.' 'Very well, I will come to your house for the purpose.' 'No, let it be shown before all these people. Bring it to-morrow evening. I wish to see it, and to let them see it too; and I speak without fear, because I have the psalms in the original Hebrew, and I know what is written in them.'[89]

Here, a theological discussion moves from the divine sonship of Christ to a discussion of the relationship between three sets of holy scripture—the Old and New Testaments and the Quran—where it comes to a stalemate. The young Muslim did not return the following evening, perhaps because his somewhat reckless challenge could not be sustained under the conditions which Janvier had set, but that really did not resolve the outstanding issue between them.

The final account is a description not of a verbal interchange but of a Hindu response to the preaching of Jesse Jamieson near Sabathu. At this time it was rare and unusual (later a more refined version of it would become frequent and even 'standard'), but it probably articulated some of the deep sentiments Evangelical preaching aroused during this period.

At one place we were told by a Brahman, that as neither his ancestors nor he had ever heard of Jesus Christ before, he could not be a true Saviour, and was not worthy of their worship—that we need not preach the gospel to the people of this country, for they would not leave their own gods, to worship Christ of whom their fathers had never heard. Others said, Christ is a true Saviour for the English, but not for them,—that God had given every nation a peculiar faith, as well as customs, and that it was his will that each should serve him in its own religion and customs, whether they are good or bad—that a man who forsakes his own religion, can never be trusted in any thing, and is equal to a woman who forsakes her husband, and associates with another man.[90]

[89] 'India: Lodiana Mission: Journal of the Rev. L. Janvier', ibid. (January 1846), pp. 7–8. The formatting but not the words of this conversation has been slightly altered, so that it reads more easily.

[90] 'Journal of J.M. Jamieson—Sabathu', *FMC* (March 1841), p. 60.

As in the case of the young Muslim, this interchange also resulted in a stalemate; in fact, the underlying assumptions about God and truth were so totally at odds with those of the Evangelicals that Jamieson considered the man seriously deluded.

Seen within the context of the religious milieu described earlier in this chapter, these missionary accounts of interaction illustrate how far apart these Evangelical missionaries and their Muslim, Hindu, and Sikh audiences were. What the missionaries were preaching was quite new and unfamiliar; it could often be quite challenging when, in the course of discussion or debate, missionaries chose to question or attack the basic beliefs of those in their audiences, but novelty was the chief characteristic of their message. It is equally clear that the missionaries had not yet made a serious attempt to enter the Indian mindset and to present the Christian message in terms of the traditions or specific needs which shaped the Indian religious quest, whether Muslim, Hindu, or Sikh. Instead, they presented their message in terms of their own Evangelical world view and the human priorities it established, and attempted to draw their Indian audiences into that way of thinking. This is most apparent in some of their early tracts, which simply are translations into Hindi, Punjabi, or Urdu of basic Western Evangelical preaching.[91] The missionaries' knowledge of India, while broadening all of the time, did not seem to go very deep. One finds in their writings repetitions of rather than challenges to common European stereotypes of Muslims, Sikhs, Hindus, hill people, plains people, frontier people, Kashmiris, and of their respective religious outlooks, but no fresh or deep insights which were then put to evangelistic use.[92] At times the resulting encounter was combative, as in the case

[91] There are three Hindi tracts by Jesse Jamieson on Reel 31 of the Correspondence of the Missionaries in India with the Board of Foreign Missions of the Presbyterian Church in the USA which are of this type: 'The Way to Obtain Salvation' (No. 782), 'Religious Counsel' (No. 775), and 'Conversation between a Missionary and a Pilgrim' (No. 770).

[92] See *CMS Proceedings 1852–1853*, p. 108; Jesse Jamieson, 'The Present State and Prospects of the Missionary Work in India', *FMC* (November 1847), p. 321, and 'Presbyterian Board of Foreign Missions', ibid., (March 1839), p. 80. An exception would be John Newton and William Rogers', observation that 'the Mohammedans

of Janvier and the young Muslim; otherwise it was a more polite stand-off, as between Lowrie and Ranjit Singh.

There were a couple of exceptions in which the two sides seem to be moving closer together. One was John Newton's attempt to present Christ as the tenth incarnation of Vishnu.

He is spoken of as the *Nihkalank avatar*, that is, the spotless incarnation, a thing which cannot be affirmed of any of the nine who have come and gone. The object of his coming will be to destroy or take away the sin of the world. This incarnation, we aver, is in truth no other than Jesus of Nazareth; who was holy, harmless, undefiled, and separate from sinners, and whose great work is to save men from sin.

Newton assumed that Hindus must have acquired this belief from Jewish or Christian sources and introduced minor distortions; 'yet the Saviour foretold in the Shasters is, in his main features, so much like the Saviour whose history is recorded in the Bible, that we hesitate not to declare, that he whom the Hindus look for has already come into the world'.[93] The other examples were some new 'Christian' sects which grew up outside the missionary structure but in response to their teaching. One was a group south of Ludhiana who worshipped 'The Father Jesus' and was reportedly spreading far and wide, but it was not the only one.[94]

THE CONVERTS
Conversion to Christianity was an extraordinarily difficult thing for the people of north-west India to go through during the first half of

---

who speak the Punjabi language, so far as we have been able to form an acquaintance with them, are not so bigoted as their brethren in other places are represented to be'. 'Lodiana. Journal of the Rev. Messrs. Newton and Rogers', ibid., (March 1840), p. 89.

[93] 'The Gospel Preached in a Hindu Monastery: Sketch No. IV', *FM* (March 1852), p. 164.

[94] 'India: Lodiana Mission. Communication from the Rev. Joseph Warren', *HFR* (January 1854), p. 19; 'India: Lodiana Mission: Appeal for More Laborers', ibid. (July 1854), p. 212.

the nineteenth century. As has already been pointed out, its doctrines were new and strange to them, very much at odds with everything that was already present in their religious milieu. However, the difficulties extended well beyond matters of belief. To convert meant to join an alternative community based on religion. This involved not only leaving behind one's former community of caste or tribe, but also being accepted into the Christian community on the missionaries' terms. On the one hand, those who were baptized were outcasted and cut off from their families—including spouses and children—as well as from their friends. This constituted such a total break with the past that few were willing to take the step. On the other hand, the missionaries had a strict screening process through which inquirers had to pass before they were baptized. Their knowledge of Christian doctrine, their motives for wanting to become Christians, the nature of their Christian experience, and their character were all examined—at times for as long as two or three years—to determine whether all of these measured up to Evangelical standards. This screening process was not considered foolproof but it was considered necessary.[95] The result was that the number of converts by 1857 was extremely small. The total Indian Christian community in the entire north-west did not exceed 200 members in May 1857.

It is very difficult to get a clear picture of who the converts were. References to them in the missionary accounts were usually very brief and biographical details are hard to come by. Of the seventy-two people baptized in the north-west during this period for whom some biographical data is available, fourteen were Muslims, twelve were Brahmins, fourteen were described as high-caste Hindus, two were low-caste Hindus, seven were Hindus of unspecified caste background, eleven were Sikhs, five were orphans of unknown background given to the missions for care, and seven were drummers

---

[95] For a more detailed discussion of this screening process, common to all Protestant missions during this period, see John C.B. Webster, *The Christian Community and Change*, pp. 53–7.

in the army who came from Christian backgrounds.[96] The vast majority were men. There were eleven married couples, although both spouses were not often baptized together, and only three were single women. They ranged in age from the elderly and infirm to the young.

However, what is striking about the group as a whole was their uprootedness, transience, and/or their occupational links with the European presence in the north-west. Some had been orphans whom the government had placed in the care of the missionaries at Ludhiana during and following the 1837–8 famine. Several were in the army of the East India Company; Ram Chandra taught at Delhi College and Chaman Lal was an assistant surgeon there; two converts in Jullundur were a doctor in government service and his wife; two were munshis engaged by missionaries for language study; and one had been the servant of a British couple for many years. The itinerants included not only some Bengalis and people from what is today Uttar Pradesh, but also several Hindu pilgrims, a Muslim faqir, an Afghan political refugee, a young Kashmiri woman who had been bought or stolen and then turned over to the mission for care by a magistrate, as well as the orphans. There were also two Muslim maulvies and a Sikh granthi. In other words, most seemed to have already begun to move out of their own traditional society, either for economic or for spiritual reasons, prior to conversion. Only in rare cases did those already well and happily integrated into their own communities seek baptism; for them, either Christianity had no appeal or, if it did, the social cost of conversion was simply too high.

There is even less detailed evidence available about what happened to the converts after baptism. They were organized into congregations which met on Sunday, and often also during the week, for worship. Some of the converts became officers in the congregation. Many more were employed by the missions as teachers, scripture readers, catechists, and even as ordained clergymen. There were also instances of discipline, excommunication, and

---

[96] These were tabulated from references in the missionary reports and magazines already cited in previous footnotes.

desertion either because the converts did not live up to the missionaries' expectations of Christian conduct or because the converts themselves decided to return to their former communities.

Two converts became outstanding leaders of the infant Christian community during this period. Golaknath grew up near Calcutta and attended Alexander Duff's school until his parents called him home against his will. He then ran away, became a *sanyasi* and eventually a clerk for the East India Company in Allahabad and Karnal. During this time he read the Bible and other Christian literature his British employers had given him. When he learned that some missionaries had arrived in Ludhiana, he resigned and in 1836, placed himself under John Newton's instruction. He took up residence in the mission compound, was baptized in 1837, married in 1838, and worked as a catechist. He was ordained in 1845 and in 1846 was placed in charge of the newly opened Presbyterian mission station in Jullundur, where he spent the rest of his life.[97] Ram Chandra's leadership has already been referred to. He was born into a Kayasth family in Panipat in 1821, studied in the English department of Delhi College, and was appointed a senior lecturer in the Oriental department. There he gained a reputation as a free thinker, actively engaged in religious disputes. A chance visit to St. James Church, where he saw several Englishmen whom he respected praying devoutly, led him to make an intensive study of the New Testament, largely on his own. His baptism in 1852 did not change his public life very much; he continued to work at Delhi College and remained active in the religious controversies of this day, only now as the leading spokesperson for Christianity in Delhi.[98]

A clearer insight into the nature of the Christian community can perhaps be gained from the brief biographical sketches of the small congregation in Ambala which the Rev. Jesse Jamieson happened to

[97] This account has been based on the broad outlines of the often hagiographic *Golak, The Hero* by his son, Henry Golaknath. See also the earlier work by S.S. Hewlett, *Daughters of the King*, pp. 219–23.

[98] Of the many biographies of Ram Chandra the most recent and most careful is in Avril A. Powell, 'Processes of Conversion to Christianity in Nineteenth Century North-Western India', pp. 24–31.

provide in May 1854. This congregation had been formed in October 1848 and at the time of writing had grown to fourteen members, excluding the missionaries and their families. Nathu, a shopkeeper in Sabathu, who was outcasted and his shop boycotted when he started attending Christian worship, had tried to become a Christian without losing caste (even proposing to bring his own bread and wine for holy communion), but after several years of inner struggle had chosen to be baptized. He followed Jamieson to Ambala where he learned to read, was suspended briefly for equivocation, and was employed supervising workmen and keeping accounts. His son, Saudagar, was baptized prior to his father and became a catechist, was suspended from office and church membership for falsehood and deception, and was at the time of writing, penitent and seeking restoration. Since his wife had refused to become a Christian with him and had returned to her father's house, he was eventually married again to the daughter of a Christian. Abraham Davis, born of Portuguese parents and baptized by them, joined the church in Ambala and worked as a tutor in a private home. Kulin, an elderly man of low caste, who had been a servant to British military officers, was employed as a watchman. His wife had died before his baptism and all but one of his children had left him; his remaining son, Thomas, had been baptized and sent to Ludhiana to become a printer at the Mission Press. William Basten was, like his wife, born of Christian parents. He had been a drummer in the army but was now a catechist and church officer. Two couples were raised in Christian orphanages; one of the men served as headmaster of the mission school while the other was a scripture reader and teacher. Matthew, a Brahmin sepoy, had converted to Christianity and had recently gone with his regiment to Burma. Finally, Gutab Singh and his wife had been baptized in Ludhiana and were currently employed as servants by one of the missionary families in Ambala.[99]

Clearly, this was not a homogeneous group but a very diverse collection of individuals and nuclear families. They came not only from different places inside and outside the region, but also from a

---

[99] 'Native Church Members at Ambala', *FM* (September 1854), pp. 97–100.

variety of social backgrounds. Each seemed totally cut off from his or her own individual past associations; as a community they had no common past but only a shared religious faith and life to hold them together as a congregation. Some had obviously faced serious persecution either before or as a result of baptism. Nathu had had to undergo a change of occupation upon becoming a Christian whereas Matthew had not. Most, but not all, were employed by the mission which desperately needed Christians to help carry on its work of evangelism and education. Some had changed their names to Biblical or Western names upon baptism to symbolize their new identity; others had kept their former names. What influenced these particular choices is not known, but most were changed either to get rid of names with religious connotations (e.g., Muhammad or Krishna) or, especially in the case of orphans, to honour a benefactor.[100] Whatever their backgrounds, they were now urban rather than rural and exhibited as a group an unusually high level of literacy and education. They were also, by the very nature of the mission's work, a highly visible group but, as popular derisive references to Saudagar as 'the black padri' indicate, not one which was held in high public regard.

1857

The infant Christian community in Delhi was decimated by the events of 1857. Among the Baptists, Mrs Thompson and her daughters were killed (the mother and eldest daughter decapitated) in their home. Rev. Mackay fled to the Skinner house where he and the other Europeans who took shelter there were killed. Walayat Ali, Mackay's assistant from Agra, was at home when neighbours informed sepoys of his presence. He was put to death, after refusing to return to Islam, with bystanders taunting him, 'Now preach to us, now preach to us'. His house was then looted and burned down. His wife, Fatima,

---

[100] Although Ram Chandra and Chaman Lal were given the Christian names of Yesudas ('servant of Jesus') and Masih Sahai ('Christ's helper') respectively at the time of their baptism, they continued to be known by their earlier names. For a discussion of names and name changes, see John C.B. Webster, *The Christian Community and Change*, pp. 66–8.

and their seven children were given refuge for three days by Mirza Haji, a Muslim prince who knew them and was partial to Christianity. When he could no longer protect them, they left and wandered about for weeks before ending up in Sonepat. They returned to Delhi only after the British had retaken the city, but one child had died of fever during the ordeal. Thakur, a Baptist preacher, was killed but Silas Curtis, a teacher who escaped with his family to Agra, as well as Ganesh and his family, survived.[101]

The Anglicans fared no better. The Rev. M.J. Jennings, the chaplain, and his daughter were killed in their home. The Rev. Alfred Hubbard, the SPG missionary, was killed in the bank, as was Louis Koch, a European assistant recently arrived from Bishop's College in Calcutta. The other European assistant, Daniel Sandys, was shot in the street. Dr Chaman Lal was killed at home, but his family was spared; his widow was urged by her family to return to Hinduism but refused to do so. Ram Chandra was concealed by his brothers in the female quarters of the family home and was not betrayed by the neighbours. On the night of 13 May, he and two servants fled to the village of Mataula ten miles away where they remained for a month under the protection of a zamindar, until villagers antagonistic to his protector revealed his presence to some passing sepoys. The three refugees managed to escape and two days later reached a British camp where Ram Chandra served as a translator of daily news from Delhi until the city was retaken. There he found his family had been living in constant danger, but it was the European troops who plundered his home and mistreated his family when sacking the city. Hira Lal, a catechist, and Miss Sales, the headmistress of a school for European and Eurasian children, also survived. St. James Church was badly defaced but not destroyed.[102] Out in the cantonment, Fr Zachery,

---

[101] 'India', *MH* (August 1857), pp. 510–11; 'The Martyred Walayat Ali', ibid. (October 1857), pp. 643–4; 'The Martyrs and Confessors of Delhi', ibid. (May 1858), pp. 325–8.

[102] *SPG Report, 1857*, pp. xciii–xcvi; J. Stuart Jackson, *The Delhi Mission of the Society for the Propagation of the Gospel*; F.J. Western, 'The Early History of the Cambridge Mission to Delhi', pp. 29–31; E. Jennings, 'Memoir of My Father, The

the newly arrived Catholic priest, was dismembered in the church he had built the previous year and the church itself was destroyed.[103]

Nowhere else in the north-west did Christians face such devastation as in Delhi. In Peshawar, Multan, and Amritsar (where they did spend some time in the fort) the missionaries experienced some anxiety but no real danger; Carl Pfander continued to preach in the bazars of Peshawar throughout the crisis except for a few days when it was considered unwise.[104] The United Presbyterians in Sialkot decided to take refuge in the Lahore fort. However, the Church of Scotland missionaries, the Hunters, waited too long and were killed by mutinying sepoys while trying to leave, but Mahommad Ismael survived.[105] The Catholics in the cantonment remained unharmed.[106] In Lahore, the Presbyterians' preaching tent in the city was destroyed the day after the sepoys there were disarmed; the missionaries spent some anxious nights in the fort but Charles Forman continued to preach in bazars to good audiences virtually as before. The sepoys in Jullundur mutinied on 8 June and, after giving the mission there a brief scare, marched on to Ludhiana where a local group of Kashmiri Muslims led them to the mission compound. There they looted and set fire to the residences, school house, library, book depot, depository, and bindery. While the property loss was serious, nobody was hurt; the missionaries took refuge with other Europeans in a fortified area and the Indian converts were given shelter on the premises of one of the Afghan princes who lived nearby. When the British restored order, they hanged twenty Kashmiri Muslims considered responsible for sacking the compound and recovered much of the stolen property. They then levied a tax on the city to

---

Rev. M.J. Jennings, M.A.', p. 66; Edwin Jacob, *A Memoir of Professor Yesudas Ramchandra of Delhi*, pp. 102–7.

[103] 'Mission History of Delhi', p. 2; Daniel D'Souza, *Capuchin Missions in India*, p. 148.

[104] 'Recent Intelligence', CMI (September 1857).

[105] Andrew Gordon, *Our India Mission*, pp. 128–49.

[106] Fr Leo, *The Capuchin Mission in the Punjab*, p. 109.

compensate the victims for the losses they had incurred. The missionaries there moved to Ambala, taking the orphan girls and some of the converts with them. When the local authorities in Ambala informed the missionaries that they could no longer protect them, the whole band moved to the hill station of Kasauli on 1 July and returned only in mid-August.[107] The mission stations in the hills were unaffected and by the end of September, Christians throughout the north-west were out of danger.

Clearly, Christians, whether foreign missionaries or Indian converts, were targets in 1857. However, this account indicates that in those urban centres where they lived, Christians were victims primarily of the sepoys, to whom they were strangers, and not of the local residents among whom they lived. The sepoys treated Christians as automatic enemies solely because of their religion. Some they killed in such brutal ways that the intensity of their passion stood in marked contrast to the more mixed attitudes of the Christians' actual neighbours. A few Muslim faqirs pointed out Walayat Ali to the sepoys and some neighbours taunted him as he died, but another neighbour protected his family at great personal risk. Ram Chandra was saved by the silence of his neighbours. In Ludhiana, one group of local people directed the sepoys to the mission compound and joined in looting it, while other neighbours protected the converts living there from harm. Such contrasting patterns of behaviour, while open to exaggeration, are nonetheless noteworthy. The tiny Christian community of, at most, two dozen foreign missionaries and two hundred converts scattered throughout the entire region, while highly visible and unusually assertive in proclaiming its faith, was hardly a threat to the prevailing social and religious order. Far more threatening, especially to the sepoys, was the mandatory use of greased cartridges as well as the harsh and humiliating punishment of those who refused to bite them. Thus, Christians were probably less the victims of a generalized Muslim fanaticism (which was the common perception in the missionary literature of 1857 and 1858) than of sepoy rage at a Christian

[107] See John C.B. Webster, *The Christian Community and Change*, pp. 190–1.

government's offences against what they held to be sacred. This rage they ventilated against all whom they identified by race or religion with that government.

On a tour from Amritsar to Peshawar at the end of 1853 or beginning of 1854, Robert Clark commented that in one place the people had responded to his message with nothing 'more apparent than respect for a Sahib; and I dare say that they took me for an officer of government, and that one of its measures was to make Christians of them all'.[108] Whether this was a fanciful conjecture or an astute observation on Clark's part, the perception he pointed to cannot be dismissed out of hand. To Clark himself it was foolish, the product of simple ignorance. But Clark's own mission had close ties with important government officials and regularly received from them considerable support, which, while personal, was also publicly known. The same was not only equally, and very conspicuously, true of the SPG Mission in Delhi, but also, to lesser degrees, true of the other missions as well. Moreover, the missionaries, with the possible exception of Thompson, were at this stage both rather uncritical westernizers and strong supporters of British rule in India. Thus, if the sepoys perceived them, and the Indians who had chosen to identify with them through baptism, as part of a general government effort to undermine a long-standing Hindu and Muslim way of life, this perception is at least understandable, even if it was not totally accurate.

Conclusions

For Christianity in north-west India, the period from 1800 to 1857 was a period of small beginnings. In 1800, there were few if any local Christians in the region. In 1857, there were still less than two hundred. James Thompson, the pioneer missionary in the region, had seen his own role with the eyes of faith as sowing seed which would be harvested later on. Other missionaries had established an institutional base of churches, schools, orphanages, and a printing press which gave Christianity the permanent presence in the region

[108] 'The Punjab', CMI (April 1854), p. 88.

it had previously lacked. It is, therefore, quite correct to consider this to be the period which marks the beginning of a continuing Christian community in north-west India.

It was also a period of cautious exploration. Missionaries left their (generally middle-class) homes in the West and travelled long distances by ship, by boat up the river Ganga, and then by overland caravan to reach their final destinations in the north-west. Once there, they explored the region, on foot and on horseback, as they engaged in itinerant preaching or looked for places to expand their work. They studied the languages of the region, some of them more than one language, and engaged the people there in earnest religious discussion. They faced up to some of the intellectual, social, and spiritual challenges inherent in their preaching, education, publishing, and distribution work.

Yet, at the same time, they maintained a certain social and intellectual distance from the people they had come to evangelize. Their homes were located on the edge of the city where land was cheaper and the air considered healthier. When they toured through the countryside, they took their own tents and pitched them outside the villages. Nevertheless, their homes and tents were places where people could and did come for conversation, study, and worship, even if caste restrictions and dietary laws placed limits on the hospitality that would be accepted. The missionaries were also dependent upon British presence. Not only did it give missionaries the freedom to preach without molestation, but the missions also received moral and financial support from British officials. Moreover, in trying to understand the people of the north-west, the missionaries drew heavily upon the conventional wisdom among the British officers who had preceded them there; they had only begun to develop their own insights based upon their own studies and observations. The evangelistic methods they used were those considered tried and true in the revivals in their home countries. At a deeper level, the missionaries remained very much wedded to the world view, based on Western knowledge and ways of knowing, which they had brought to India; there is little indication that they had begun to modify it in the light of their Indian experience. In this sense, despite their many initiatives, missionaries and the general Indian population still stood apart from one another and viewed each other from a great enough distance to be out of touch with the deeper religious impulses, senses of the divine, and religious behaviour patterns of each other.

It is this gulf between them which perhaps best accounts for not only the smallness of the beginnings the missionaries made during this period but also some of the reaction in 1857. The missionaries preached a highly individualistic gospel to a highly integrated, caste-based society and presented it in such a way that only those who were already socially or spiritually alienated could be in a position to understand, appreciate, or fully accept it. For the rest, it seems that the missionaries had been offering some very interesting answers to questions about personal guilt and the life after death which nobody was really asking. The result was that the Christian gospel had begun to touch north-western Indian society only at its periphery and, to an even lesser degree, among those few who had absorbed some of the spirit as well as the substance of Western learning. The converts were very few, most often uprooted, widely scattered in little clusters, highly heterogeneous, and generally looked down upon for having converted, despite the excellent attainments, commitment, and character of more than a few of them. In 1857, the courage they exhibited when converting in the first place was tested once again; some died but most lived to enter a very different era in the history of Christianity in north-west India.

3 The High Imperial Era: 1858–80

The British put down the 1857 revolt with great severity. In Delhi their troops launched a reign of terror, ransacking and plundering its buildings. The city was placed under a military governor and a special commission tried 3306 persons of whom 2025 were convicted, 392 hanged, and 57 given life imprisonment. Early in 1858, the emperor himself was put on trial for conspiracy, rebellion, and the murder of forty-nine Europeans. His life had already been spared and in October he was sent into exile to Rangoon.[1] Order was restored throughout the region and Christians were compensated for losses suffered during the revolt.[2] By the Government of India Act of 1858, the British Parliament did away with the East India Company and assumed direct control of the administration of the country. In September 1858, it took the Delhi territories from the North-West Provinces and attached them to the Punjab, which on 1 January 1859 was raised to the status of a lieutenant governorship with its capital in Lahore. This completed the consolidation of north-west India as 'the Punjab and its Dependencies'. The British military became involved in the second Afghan War along the frontier in 1878–81, but in general peace prevailed and no further territory was annexed. British rule in the region during this period was firm, more direct, and more British than in the preceding period. However, neither the social structures nor the religious milieu underwent immediate or significant change.

For the Christian missions in the north-west, this was a period of recovery, expansion, some innovation, and major cultural influence, especially through their dominant position in the field of education. The Baptist and SPG missions in Delhi as well as the Church of Scotland mission in Sialkot had to begin again because their losses

---

[1] Percival Spear, *Twilight of the Mughals*, pp. 218–28.
[2] General Report on the Administration of the Punjab Territories, from 1856–57 to 1857–58, pp. 50–1.

had been so severe. They and the other missions also expanded their activities not only by establishing new mission stations but also by adding medical and women's work to their existing evangelistic, educational, and literary work. There was some experimentation in mission work, but the basic theology and strategy of mission developed prior to 1857 remained the same. What was more apparent, however, among missionaries and administrators alike, was not only an inner sense of security and confidence about their place and role in the divine scheme of things, but also a certain unquestioned cultural dominance within the region which characterized the period from 1858 until about 1880 when Christianity in north-west India had to face a new set of serious challenges, both external and internal.

The Imperial Ethos

The first three lieutenant governors of the Punjab—Sir John Lawrence (1859), Sir Robert Montgomery (1859–65), and Sir Donald McLeod (1865–70)—as well as many other important officials in the Punjab government, were staunch Evangelicals. Along with the missionaries there they interpreted the events of 1857 theologically. God had rescued the British and given them the responsibility of ruling India for the benefit of their Indian subjects. In this they were to be guided not by the voices of those over whom God had placed them as guardians but by their own Christian consciences. That it was God who had delivered them they were quite convinced; they had experienced too many 'miracles' first in their extremity and then in their recapture of Delhi to believe otherwise.[3] Deliverance was also seen as divine vindication of the policies and procedures of the Punjab government, as opposed to those of the Calcutta government,

[3] Sir John Lawrence told a public meeting in London on 24 June 1859 that 'Nothing but a series of miracles saved us'. Sir Herbert Edwardes, when addressing the Conference on Missions at Liverpool in 1860, listed a series of 'interpositions of God' that had saved the British. 'Recent Intelligence', *CMI* (1 August 1859) and *Conference on Missions Held in 1860 at Liverpool*, London: James Nisbet & Co., 1860, pp. 348–52. See also Richard Temple in General Report on the Administration of the Punjab Territories, from 1856–57 to 1857–58 Inclusive, p. 55.

especially in religious matters.[4] Their past accomplishments, their hard work, and now this conviction that divine providence enveloped and guided their work gave them that extraordinary self-confidence and sense of purpose which became the hallmark of the 'Punjab School' of administration.

The Biblical text that was frequently cited to express their core convictions was 'Those who honour me I will honour'.[5] Since annexing the Punjab in 1849 these Evangelical officials had not only made an open profession of faith at appropriate public events but also supported Christian missions in their personal capacities. Now, they believed, England must abandon the East India Company's policy of 'religious neutrality', which had been impossible to implement and brought on the 1857 revolt by the misunderstandings it had created. Instead, the government should openly acknowledge its Christian faith, take all legitimate means to promote it in India, and at the same time grant religious liberty to all the Queen's Indian subjects. Charles Forman, an American missionary in Lahore, put this 'Christian policy' in the context of 'the lessons of 1857'.

In these heavy judgments God speaks, in an unmistakable voice, to the Government of India. A policy has too long been pursued which was entirely unworthy of a Christian government. It is necessary only to mention a few of the most glaring instances. They had been guilty of supporting idolatry by making grants to temples and religious devotees; by allowing native soldiers to worship their colors; by favoring men of high caste. They discouraged and discountenanced Christianity by excluding the Bible from their schools, and allowing the Koran and Shasters to be read; by refusing positions of responsibility to native Christians, and turning converts out of positions which they had previously occupied.[6]

---

[4] 'The Administration of the Punjab', *CMI* (November 1859), p. 242.

[5] I Samuel 2:30. 'Administration of the Punjab—Crisis of 1857', *CMI* (December 1859), p. 270; it was used in the Lord Bishop of London's address to Sir John Lawrence ['Recent Intelligence', *CMI* (1 August 1859)] and at the Punjab Missionary Conference by William Butler, a Methodist missionary. *Report of the Punjab Missionary Conference*, p. 337.

[6] 'Ends to be Answered by the Sepoy Mutiny', *FM* (May 1858), p. 388.

It was primarily the mission societies and church leaders in England who fought the battle for a 'Christian policy' for India.[7] The government, however, was committed to a policy of caution and conciliation in the wake of the tumultuous events of 1857–8. The Queen's Proclamation in November 1858 set the parameters within which the Government of India had to work in religious matters.

Firmly relying ourselves on the truth of Christianity, and acknowledging with gratitude the solace of religion, we disclaim alike the right and the desire to impose our convictions on any of our subjects. We declare it to be our royal will and pleasure that none be in anywise favoured, none molested or disquieted, by reason of their religious faith or observances, but that all shall alike enjoy the equal and impartial protection of the law; and we do strictly charge and enjoin all those who may be in authority under us that they abstain from all interference with the religious belief or worship of any of our subjects on pain of our highest displeasure.[8]

While this proclamation ruled out the more aggressive Christian policy advocated by Herbert Edwardes and accommodated the more moderate attitudes of toleration and forbearance of John Lawrence and Donald McLeod, it still left room for significant disagreement. The issue that served as a litmus test in determining how far the government was prepared to go was the proposed introduction of Bible teaching in government schools. Edwardes wanted this to be compulsory; Lawrence and McLeod wanted it to be voluntary; the government in Calcutta and London did not want it at all.[9] The Secretary of State for India decided that 'the Bible should be lodged in every Government Library, and free access allowed to it'. The Punjab government, therefore, supplied it to all school libraries,

---

[7] See 'Recent Intelligence: Memorial to the Queen on the Indian Crisis', *CMI* (January 1858) and 'Recent Intelligence: Christianity in India. Important Deputation to Lord Stanley', ibid. (September 1858).

[8] C.H. Philips, H.L. Singh, and B.N. Pandey (eds), *The Evolution of India and Pakistan 1858 to 1947*, p. 11.

[9] On this 'Christian Policy' see Thomas R. Metcalf, *Aftermath of Revolt*, pp. 92–110.

stipulating that students could read it outside school hours.[10] Another Evangelical grievance was addressed in October 1857 when Sir Robert Montgomery issued a circular opening the government services to Indian Christians and inviting missionaries to submit the names of suitable applicants.[11]

While these debates were going on, three incidents occurred in the Punjab which tested the interpretation of the Queen's proclamation because all concerned Punjab officialdom's association with the conversion of the Indian people. The first of these was a request in November 1858 from United Presbyterian missionaries to preach to prisoners in the Sialkot jail. Permission was granted by the district officer and supported by his superiors in the Punjab government, including Lawrence and McLeod, but rejected by the viceroy, Canning.[12] A second occurred in April 1859 when four Punjab officials attended the baptism of six converts in Amritsar. When the Government of India questioned the Punjab government about this, Robert Cust, the commissioner and one of the officials present, replied that while he understood his duty 'to be entire abstinence in my public capacity from the affairs of any sect or religion, directly or indirectly, and my convictions coincide with my duty', he also asserted that 'as a private individual, I have as much right to religious views as the Mahomedan and Hindoo employees of Government'. Obviously, the government was finding it difficult to know where exactly to draw the line between the public and the private.[13]

A third incident requires more detailed explanation. During the sack of Delhi, some Mazhabi[14] Sikh sepoys found some Christian

[10] *Report on Popular Education in the Punjab and Its Dependencies for the Year 1860–61; by Captain A. R. Fuller, Director of Public Instruction, Punjab*, p. 11. [Hereafter referred to as *DPI Report* with the year added.] Colonel Edward Lake established a Scripture Knowledge Prize to encourage students to take Bible reading seriously. Stanley Elwood Brush, 'Protestants in the Punjab', pp. 215–20.

[11] *CMS Proceedings, 1857–58*, pp. 122–3.

[12] Ibid., pp. 106–7.

[13] 'East India (Baptisms at Umritsar)' IOL: Parliamentary Papers, 1860, Volume 52.

[14] A Mazhabi is a Sikh belonging to the Chuhra caste.

tracts and books, became interested in Christianity, and approached their Christian officers for instruction early in 1859. This the officers provided and invited in a CMS missionary who formed an inquiry class. A few sepoys were baptized. When the regiment transferred to Peshawar where there were no missionaries, the officers led the converts and inquirers in worship together, answering their questions, and encouraging them in their study of the Bible. As interest increased within the regiment, its commanding officer, Major Hovenden, informed General Birch who wrote back telling Hovenden that 'it will be advisable to warn the officers commanding the troops at Peshawar against using their authority in any way for the furtherance of conversion'. Hovenden then verbally ordered his officers not to attend religious meetings with their men.[15] The sepoys understood this order to mean that the government did not want them to become Christians. The CMS was outraged and agitated to get the order reversed. The Bishop of Calcutta intervened with the Government of India. While the government procrastinated in clarifying the intention of General Birch's order, Robert Clark consulted Sir Robert Montgomery, whose personal and private view was that 'an officer of a Regiment should *not* read the service to the Native Christians. The soldiers cannot separate the commanding officer from the Christian gentleman and I feel sure the Government would not approve.'[16] More than a year after supporting Birch's order, the Government of India issued a dispatch saying that it did not wish to interfere 'with the private action of its officers in countenancing the movement'.[17] The conversion movement revived for a short time and the CMS sent Robert Clark to nurture it along, but it had lost most of its early momentum and the total number of converts was fifty, including sixteen sepoys.[18]

There were obviously serious constraints preventing what Brush has called the 'Evangelical Entente' of officers and

[15] Bishop of Calcutta, Letter to Rev. R. Clark, dated Simla, 2 June 1860.

[16] R. Montgomery, Letter to R. Clark, 16 November 1859.

[17] *CMS Proceedings*, 1860–1861, p. 117.

[18] Ibid., *1859–1860*, pp. 117–8; *1860–1861*, pp. 117–9; Personal Correspondence File of Robert Clark CI 10 69/15.

missionaries[19] from pursuing the 'Christian Policy' they had advocated. This is reflected in the most important consensus document produced by Evangelical missionaries and officials during this period, the report of the Punjab Missionary Conference held at Lahore from 26 December 1862 to 2 January 1863 to strengthen 'the hands of those who are engaged in carrying on the details of God's work, in this portion of His vineyard'[20] through a process of mutual consultation. Modelled on the 1860 Conference on Mission in Liverpool and presided over by Sir Donald McLeod, it was attended by thirty-one missionaries (three of them Indian), three chaplains, and thirty-seven others including some very prominent members of the Punjab Government. Sessions were devoted to preaching, schools, itineration, religious controversy, dealing with inquirers, and the need for starting up medical and women's work in the region. The closing papers were on Inter-Mission discipline and on overcoming denominational differences by creating one Church in India. The only subjects on which there was serious disagreement concerned whether 'heathen schoolmasters' should be allowed to teach Bible and religion classes, whether prior to baptism polygamists had to divorce all wives but their first one, and the nature of existing relations between missionaries and their converts. For the rest, there was remarkable unanimity. On the all-important question of cooperation between missionaries and government officials, Col. Edward Lake saw lay people (which in his usage referred to Europeans) helping missionaries through prayer, witnessing to their own domestic servants, assisting in specific benevolent projects during their off-duty hours, and helping converts find employment, while Robert Cust summed up their role as providing money, offering advice and support, engaging in writing and translation work, and setting a positive personal example.[21]

Because the conference deliberations were remarkably free of imperial ideology and racial stereotyping, the ideological

[19] Stanley Elwood Brush, 'Protestants in the Punjab', pp. 155–80.

[20] The words are McLeod's in his opening remarks. *Report of the Punjab Missionary Conference*, pp. 2–3.

[21] Ibid., pp. 97–100, 107.

commitments of the participants were more implicit than explicit. Evangelism and conversion were taken for granted as good in their own right, requiring no further justification than the Biblical injunction itself. So, too, was British rule in India as well as the freedom to preach and convert which it made possible. However, in the closing reflections on the conference there were references to divine providence that sought to place the conference in theological and historical perspective. Lake referred to the conference as seeking to establish the eternal kingdom of Christ upon the ruins of the perishable glories of the Sikh empire and Edwardes saw the conference promoting 'the truest welfare of the people, and the glory of God'. 'We have not come to conquer [the Punjab] for ourselves: our mission here is to conquer it for God.'[22] For the rest, the presentations and discussions were very Biblical, very pragmatic, and at times very technical. Major emphasis was given to the importance of humility and to moving out of exclusively Western ways of living, of association, and of expression so as to move closer to the Indian people.[23]

Nonetheless, a basic assumption of the conference—at times articulated[24] but most often simply assumed—was profoundly ideological. Just as civil officers in the Punjab combined the functions of magistrate, judge, police officer, and revenue collector so as to deal promptly, personally and on the spot with situations as they arose, so too did the missionary within his own domain. His authority was unchallengeable. He was the father and the guardian of the infant Christian community; he held the purse strings and supervised all aspects of mission work at the station to which he was posted. He decided what was best for whom and there was really no court of appeal above him. He was, of course, subject to the policy decisions and discipline of the mission society to which he belonged, but it was far away and gave him broad discretionary powers within his own jurisdiction. This put the missionary in a position of widely accepted political and cultural strength.

[22] Ibid., pp. 322, 343, 344.
[23] For example, ibid., pp. 72, 78, 91, 164, 269.
[24] For example, ibid., pp. 13, 160, 176, 181, 277.

While all the missions and their missionaries were immersed in this imperial ethos, not all of them had equally close relations with the government and none equated the interests of empire with those of Christianity in India. The CMS had the closest ties with the Raj. It was a society of the established church; their structures brought missionaries and officials closely together on local mission committees; and they used the progress of empire as an opportunity for the progress of Christianity in ways other missions did not. The most obvious example of this was the creation of CMS mission stations along the north-west frontier. The commissioner, Col. Reynell Taylor, who considered such a mission to be an act of friendship towards the people there, offered a gift of £1000 to get a mission started. His plan had the support of the lieutenant governor, Sir Robert Montgomery, as well as of Sir Herbert Edwardes.[25] The CMS, which saw this as an opportunity to spread the Christian message along the frontier and even into Afghanistan, accepted the offer.[26] After war broke out with Afghanistan in 1878, the Rev. G.M. Gordon, an itinerant missionary on the frontier, accompanied the army from Quetta to Kandahar, ministering to the troops and scouting out evangelistic possibilities in the land he was passing through. He was killed during a British sortie in Kandahar in August 1880 and became a hero.[27] For other missions the link between Christian duty and patriotic duty was neither so close nor so adventurous.

Education

Education was one area of public life in which Evangelical missionaries and British officials worked together closely during this period, even though their aims were different. Schools had become a standard feature of mission work throughout the north-west. Lowrie took over the school in Ludhiana which Captain Wade had started in anticipation of his arrival in 1834. For the next twenty

---

[25] Herbert Edwardes, Letter to Mr. Venn, 15 October 1861.
[26] Robert Clark, *The Punjab and Sindh Missions*, p. 195.
[27] 'The Late Rev. George Maxwell Gordon', *CMI* (October 1880), pp. 612–3.

years the mission schools in Ludhiana, Jullundur, Ambala, Lahore, Amritsar, and Kotgarh, like other schools, functioned as completely autonomous units with their own purposes, methods, policies, curricula, and standards. There was at that time no educational 'system' of which they were a part, no required uniformity or standardization. What set the mission schools apart from the others were their evangelistic aims carried out through compulsory classes on Christianity and participation in Christian worship, a basically Western curriculum, the Christian perspective from which it was taught, and classes in English.

The Education Despatch of 1854 from the East India Company's Board of Control created an educational system. It set up education departments under Directors of Public Instruction (DPIs) in each of the provinces, envisioned a network of graded schools from universities down to primary schools, and established a programme of government grants-in-aid to encourage private initiative in education. To be eligible for grants-in-aid, a school had to '(i) impart a good secular education, any religious instruction which they may impart being simply ignored; (ii) possess good local management; (iii) agree to submit to inspection by Government officers and to abide by such other conditions as may be prescribed; and (iv) levy a fee, however small, from the pupils.'[28] The Despatch also looked forward to the time when the government could close its schools and turn them over to 'the management of local bodies under the control of, and aided by, the State'.[29] The Punjab DPI's annual reports indicate that this educational system was slow in evolving. During the period between the Despatch and the Education Commission in 1882, which reviewed its workings, there was growth, experimentation, instability, as well as both competition and cooperation between government education officials and missionary educators. Only near the end of this period was there something of

[28] Syed Nurullah and J.P. Naik, *A Students' History of Education in India*, pp. 118–9.

[29] Quoted from the Wood Despatch in ibid., p. 119.

a standardized system within which all government and aided educational institutions functioned.

The Punjab government's first objective following the Wood Despatch was to establish a government school to provide a basic education in every tehsil headquarters town. This it accomplished quickly either by co-opting existing indigenous schools or by creating new schools of its own. It made Urdu in the Persian script, which with English was the official language of the province, the medium of instruction and introduced a curriculum consisting of the rudiments of history, geography, arithmetic, and grammar. It recruited the best teachers available from the indigenous schools and placed government schools under the district magistrate's supervision. The government also established in the major cities its own 'higher' or 'superior' schools which offered an education that went beyond the elementary level.[30] In his report for 1860–1 the DPI noted that 37,280 students, or 0.25 per cent of the population, were being educated in government or aided schools. Of these, 3912 attended 'superior' schools, while the rest were in elementary schools. During that year the government had increased the number of its superior (*zillah* or district) schools from six to twenty; these schools had 2066 boys whereas the eight comparable mission schools had 1897.[31] Thus, as far as the education of the urban elites was concerned, the two major educators were of roughly equal strength at the outset of this period. What ensued was expansion of Western (as opposed to indigenous) education as well as considerable competition between the government and the missions, not for the education of province as a whole (which was totally beyond the capacity of the missions) so much as for the education of its major urban centres.

---

[30] General Report on the Administration of the Punjab Territories, from 1856–57 to 1857–58, pp. 20–2; General Report on the Administration of the Punjab and its Dependencies for 1859–60, pp. 15–7; Education Commission, *Report by the Punjab Provincial Committee*, pp. 1–8. [Hereafter this is referred to as *1882 Education Commission Report.*]

[31] *DPI Report 1860–61*, pp. i, v.

In 1860, only three cities had both government and mission schools: Amritsar, where the government school opened in 1851 and the CMS school followed in 1853; Delhi, where both the government and the SPG opened schools in 1858; and Lahore, where Charles Forman had started a school right after annexation in 1849 and the government opened its school in March 1860. In four cities the missions had a monopoly on superior-level education: Peshawar, Jullundur, Ludhiana, and Ambala. In 1860, the government closed its school in Rawalpindi to make room for a Presbyterian school, thus giving the missions a monopoly there as well.[32] Throughout this period no other private bodies maintained aided schools, except for a brief duration in Lahore and Ludhiana. Thus, aided or private education in fact meant mission education.

In October 1863, Sir Robert Montgomery indicated in a minute to the education department that the government should use its resources not to maintain its own institutions so much as to provide aid and encouragement to private bodies that wished to enter the educational field.[33] Two months later, at a meeting of an educational committee appointed by the lieutenant governor, Charles Forman put this to the test by asking the DPI, Captain Fuller, to close the government school in Lahore. This Fuller refused to do, arguing that there was room in Lahore for both schools. Then,

Captain Fuller stated that he was about to open branch schools in the city of Lahore, and suggested that Mr. Forman should do the same. Mr. Forman proposed that the opening of the branch schools be left entirely in his hands, but the proposition was strongly opposed by Captain Fuller, and it was shewn that there was ample room for both Government and private schools.[34]

This was not an isolated case. In 1861, when the government school in Lahore had started night classes in English for adults,

[32] *DPI Report 1860–61*, pp. 41, 51, Appendices A and B.

[33] Minute by His Honour the Lieutenant Governor to the Education Department under the date 21 October 1863.

[34] Abstract of Proceedings of the Education Committee appointed by His Honour the Lieutenant Governor in his minute of 21 October. Second meeting, 28 December 1863.

Forman did the same and, by charging no fees, got most of the students.[35] In 1863, when the government school in Amritsar took students from the mission school, the missionaries brought this to the attention of the civil authorities and that ended the matter.[36] In 1864, when the government added post-matriculation college classes to its schools in Delhi and Lahore, the SPG in Delhi and the Presbyterians in Lahore followed suit.[37] However, the SPG could continue its classes for only one year and then transferred its students to the government college,[38] which was in turn closed down in 1876. In Lahore, the Presbyterian school continued its college classes until 1869 when the missionary in charge of them died.[39] In 1868 the government closed its school in Peshawar, sending its students to the CMS school, and handed over its school in Sialkot to the Church of Scotland mission.[40]

That, however, was as far as the government was prepared to go. It was quite obvious that the DPIs did not wish to lose control of the educational system, particularly at its apex. Moreover, officials in the education department had some serious reservations about

---

[35] *DPI Report 1861–62*, p. 17. Forman felt threatened by the government school in Lahore and took steps to counter any perceived advantage students there were given in scholarships, awards, and jobs. Charles Forman, Letter to the Board of Foreign Missions, 16 April 1861; Charles Forman, Letter to the Board of Foreign Missions, 16 March 1864; From the Manager of the Lahore Mission School to the Director of Public Instruction Punjab, dated 30 August 1864. Education Proceedings of the Government of Punjab for the month of October 1864, No. 17.

[36] Annual Letter of Rev. J.M. Brown of the CMS for 1863.

[37] *DPI Report 1863–64*, p. 7.

[38] January 1864 to January 1865. *DPI Report 1864–65*, pp. 26, xxxiii.

[39] *DPI Report 1869–70*, p. 33 and p. 23 in the report from the Lahore Circle.

[40] *DPI Report, 1867–68*, p. 32. The United Presbyterians had found it impossible to compete with the large, well-appointed government school in Sialkot and closed theirs. The Church of Scotland mission then opened a school in the city and eventually took over the government school without loss of students. 'Missionary Statement for the Monthly Concert', *UP* (1 October 1862), p. 158; 'Monthly Missionary Statement', ibid. (29 August 1868), p. 2; *Report by the Committee for the Propagation of the Gospel in Foreign Parts Especially in India to the General Assembly of the Church of Scotland May 1869*, p. 113. [Hereafter this is referred to as *Church of Scotland Annual Report* with the year added.]

missionary education. The most important and most frequently cited was basically political. It was their view that 'the influential classes' were unwilling to send their children to mission schools where Christian religious instruction and worship were mandatory.[41] Since the government wanted to spread Western education among those classes, it took their perceived wishes very seriously. Another reason was educational. Education officials did not believe that mission schools could recruit the same quality teachers and sustain high educational standards because of the religious influence they sought to exercise and the responses, including 'religious panics', which that evoked.[42] Moreover, both at the beginning and at the very end of this period, education officials argued that the missions, by offering good secular education to the people 'gratuitously, or almost gratuitously' themselves, had stifled rather than stimulated private local initiatives in establishing and supporting schools.[43] The DPI concluded in 1881–82, as his predecessor had in earlier arguments with Charles Forman, that there was room for and value in having both government and mission schools.[44]

Two things kept the mission schools competitive. One was the quality of education they provided, although this did not go unquestioned by the government inspectors. Apart from minor disagreements over curricular differences,[45] two major criticisms appear in the DPI reports. One was that the quality of mission education at the primary level, where teachers were pretty much left on their own, was not as good as at the higher levels where they were more closely supervised.[46] The other was that even at the higher levels the mission schools did not have as good results in the university entrance examinations as did the government schools,[47] a judgement

[41] *DPI Report 1867–68*, p. 33; *1872–73*, p. 33; *1876–77*, p. 57; *1879–80*, p. 36.

[42] *DPI Report 1867–68*, p. 33; *1876–77*, p. 62.

[43] Government of the Punjab, Education Proceedings, December 1863, no. 21. and *DPI Report 1879–80*, p. 10.

[44] *DPI Report 1881–82*, pp. 57–58.

[45] For example, *DPI Report 1860–61*, p. 23.

[46] *DPI Report 1873–74*, p. 73; *1876–77*, pp. 56–7; *1881–82*, p. 60.

[47] *DPI Report 1881–82*, p. 59.

based on highly selective evidence.[48] The mission schools also charged lower fees than did the government schools. Fuller had wanted but failed to get aided schools to charge at least one quarter, or one half, the rate government schools charged.[49] Lower fees meant higher enrolments.[50] Lower fees also enabled the missions to open up the possibility of Western education to those who could not afford to pay the fees the government schools charged.[51] The missions were thus creating opportunities for individual and family mobility to a somewhat lower economic strata than was the government.

The missions made an enormous investment in education. Every mission had at least one school.[52] Their major purpose remained evangelistic and most of their students were either Hindus, Muslims, or Sikhs. Throughout this period the schools retained their own distinctive ethos, but they did have to bring their own individual practices into conformity with the requirements of the education department. For example, there were mission schools that introduced English right from the youngest classes whereas the government schools did not; some missions did not require Persian whereas the government schools did;[53] some mission schools promoted students

---

[48] All the DPI reports except for 1865–66, 1866–67, 1869–70, 1871–72, 1872–73, and 1877–78 were consulted. In 1874, Charles Forman reported that from 1861 through 1873 the government schools sent up 114 students for the Calcutta University entrance examination of whom 43 or 36.3 per cent passed. The comparable figures for the mission schools were 71 sent and 34 or 47.8 per cent passed. He also pointed out that mission school students often left school before finishing in order to get jobs, even at a lower salary. Charles Forman, Letter to David Irving, 5 June 1874.

[49] *DPI Report 1863–64*, p. 75. See also *DPI Report 1866–67*, p. 43; *1868–69*, p. 34; *1874–75*, p. 55.

[50] See John C.B. Webster, *The Christian Community and Change*, pp.155–7.

[51] See *DPI Report 1879–80*, p. 36.

[52] Even the Moravians had one at Kyelang in Lahaul. Government officials there were eager that boys from the area learn Urdu as well as Tibetan and preferred that the school be under the supervision of a missionary on the spot rather than of a government official far away. *DPI Report 1867–68*, p. 46.

[53] *DPI Report 1872–73*, p. 34. The government schools required Persian because they believed it helped students learn Urdu, the official language of the Punjab.

from primary to middle school classes without requiring them to pass the primary examination first.[54] During 1879–80, the education department instituted a system of standardized class gradation with an external examination (and thus a somewhat standardized curriculum) at the end of each stage. This was three years of lower primary school followed by two years of upper primary, three years of middle school, and two years of high school.[55] The mission schools had no choice but to conform to this pattern.

Although there were schools for girls and government support for female education during this period, there was no regular educational 'system' for girls.[56] Even as late as 1880–81, no girl had as yet passed the upper primary examination and only five had passed the lower primary examination.[57] Whereas schools for boys were oriented towards qualifying students for employment outside their homes and traditional occupations, those for women and girls were aimed at basic literacy and 'useful knowledge' for their domestic responsibilities. By 1880, there were 4000 girls in schools being run by the government itself and another 5000 in aided schools, most of whom were in mission schools. That was about one-tenth of the number enrolled in schools for boys.[58]

The missionary effort in women's education began when Mrs Newton established the Orphan Girls School at Ludhiana in 1836. Its curriculum included reading, writing, arithmetic, geography,

---

The missions tried to give students the languages that they wanted. See the testimony of the Rev. C.W. Forman in *1882 Education Commission Report*, p. 214.

[54] *DPI Report 1870–71*, p. 18 of the report from the Lahore Circle. Forman considered this 'unfair to the pupils, as it placed each one on trial not less than four times before he entered college, at each of which, by coming a few marks below the prescribed number in one subject, he might be put back a year; while if he were only allowed to go on, having been informed of his weak point, he might take a good stand at the next examination'. *1882 Education Commission Report*, p. 216.

[55] *DPI Report 1879–80*, p. 3.

[56] *DPI Report 1872–73*, p. 36.

[57] *DPI Report 1880–81*, p. 50. At the time of the Education Commission inquiry no girl in the Punjab had yet passed her middle school examination. *1882 Education Commission Report*, p. 62.

[58] *DPI Report 1879–80*, p. 5.

religious instruction, as well as 'some kind of useful work, such as cooking, knitting and sewing'.[59] The CMS also began its work in women's education in Amritsar with a school for orphan girls; in 1861, they also had girls schools in Kangra, Jandiala, and Narowal.[60] However, the largest effort in women's education during this period, that of the SPG in Delhi, began in 1859 with day schools for girls. In 1864, they opened a female normal school with eight Hindu and fifteen Muslim students.[61] The students seem to have been widows who were being trained to serve as teachers in zenanas and in government schools.[62] When the demand for trained zenana teachers exceeded the supply, the mission made up the difference by using some of the better educated Christian orphan girls or additional zenana missionaries from England. By 1872 there were

...five Zenana Missionaries who manage the two Normal Schools for Hindu, Mussulman and Christian women; four day schools for Mahomedan girls; one Industrial school; and classes in Bengali, up-country Hindu, and Mussulman zenanas. A sixth Missionary gives her whole time to training English and Eurasian girls as teachers; a seventh is a female Medical Missionary, visits patients in zenanas and has a dispensary and hospital for women only. There are also three branch Zenana Mission out-stations. The numbers under instruction have increased ten-fold in ten years.[63]

In 1876, there were a total of thirty mission schools educating a total of 1254 women and girls, up from four schools with 154 students fifteen years earlier.[64] Miss Rose Greenfield, who was working in Ludhiana, testified before the Education Commission that 'a large number of our pupils belong to the families of government officials,

---

[59] *A Brief Account of the Lodiana Mission from its Commencement in November 1834 to the Beginning of November, 1844*, p. 23.

[60] *DPI Report 1860–61*, p. 36.

[61] *DPI Report 1864–65*, p. xlvii.

[62] This is the implication of Mrs Winter's remarks in her address on 'Missions to Women' in the *Report of the General Missionary Conference held at Allahabad, 1872–73*, p. 157.

[63] Ibid., p. 159.

[64] See Table 12 drawn from DPI Reports in John C.B. Webster, *The Christian Community and Change*, p. 143.

native doctors, etc. And a large proportion of the boys educated in mission schools seek instruction for their wives and daughters. We have also a very large number of pupils among the lower classes.'[65]

The missions were also pioneers in the education of Dalits in north-west India. In Delhi, the Rev. James Smith, a Baptist missionary, not only admitted Dalits to the Baptist Central School[66] but also began establishing schools in the Chamar *bastis* where his converts resided. These used the Bible as a text to teach students how to read. From that starting point the curriculum gradually expanded to include the subjects in the standardized government curriculum. During the 1870s, Smith increased the number of these basti schools and used his position as secretary of the Delhi Municipal Committee to get municipal grants for them, arguing that because low-caste students were not being allowed to study in the government schools, the government should pay for their education. In 1877, the Baptists closed their Central School and concentrated their educational work exclusively upon those 'low caste schools'. The DPI Report for 1875–76, the first to report on these schools, stated that the Baptists ran a total of thirty-five schools in and around Delhi with 558 pupils enrolled and an average daily attendance of 397. 'The course usually consists of a little preliminary reading and spelling, and then a Gospel or a Bible history, with a very little lettering and figuring.'[67] Three years later they reported an additional nine schools for low-caste women with 192 students.[68] The education of Dalits was quite a radical step. In 1874, the DPI had stated that 'caste is not formally recognized, but in both Mission and Government schools sweepers and chumars are virtually excluded'.[69] During the 1876–77 school year, the American Presbyterians admitted a Dalit boy into their school in Lahore and the immediate effect was a large but temporary drop in attendance.[70] Like conversions, the inclusion of Dalits posed

---

[65] *1882 Education Commission Report*, p. 231.

[66] *Baptist Annual Report, 1870*, p. 54.

[67] *DPI Report 1875–76*, p. 62.

[68] *DPI Report 1878–79*, p. 68.

[69] *DPI Report 1873–74*, p. 7.

[70] 'Monthly Concert. India', *FM* (April 1877), p. 377.

a serious threat to the socio-cultural order and, as such, was a risk to institutional stability, but a risk the missions considered worth taking.

Brief mention should be made of the missions' education of European and Anglo-Indian children to round out this picture. In 1859, in gratitude for deliverance in 1857, George Cotton, the Anglican Bishop of Calcutta, proposed building an English public school for boys in India. This school was opened in Simla in 1863 and was renamed Bishop Cotton School in 1867 following the bishop's death.[71] Auckland House School was opened at Simla in 1866 as The Punjab Girls' School, but in 1869 moved into the house previously owned by Lord Auckland and changed its name accordingly. Initially managed by the local governors of Bishop Cotton School, it soon formed its own constitution and managing committee.[72] In 1863, the Vicar Apostolic of Hindustan in Agra transferred their orphanage for the children of Roman Catholic European soldiers in India from Agra to Simla.[73] The boys were moved to Mussoorie in December 1866 and the orphanage at Chelsea in Simla remained an exclusively girls' school run by the Congregation of Jesus and Mary.[74] The following year the school was opened up to Catholic girls who were not orphans so that in 1870 only a quarter of the students were orphans; just over a half were the daughters of soldiers, and the rest were the daughters of civilians who paid fees.[75] In 1876–77, the Catholics opened another orphanage in Muree with thirty-six girls and five nuns.[76]

In 1882, the Government of India appointed an Education Commission under the chairmanship of Sir William Hunter to make a comprehensive review of the development of education since the

[71] 'A Brief History: Bishop Cotton School, Shimla (1859)', *Overcome Evil with Good. Bishop Cotton School Shimla: An Introduction* (n.d.), pp. 3–4; Edward J. Buck, *Simla Past and Present*, pp. 131–2.

[72] 'A School with a History', *Prospectus Auckland House School* (n.d.).

[73] *DPI Report 1862–63*, p. 37.

[74] *DPI Report 1866–67*, pp. iii–iv; 'Brief History of the School', *Convent of Jesus and Mary Chelsea Shimla Calendar 2001*, p. 11.

[75] *DPI Report 1867–68*, p. iv; 'Report on Roman Catholic Orphanage, Simla', *DPI Report 1870–71*.

[76] *DPI Report 1876–77*, p. 53.

Wood Dispatch. The report of the Punjab Provincial Committee, with the testimony and memorials it received, provides important perspectives on where education in general and the mission contribution to it stood at the end of this period. There seems to have been a general consensus among those testifying that it was the urban middle classes and castes—Kayasths, Khatris, and Banias—who were seeking a Western education in order to enter government service and the professions. Thus the system as a whole catered primarily to their needs.[77] Views among Indian respondents differed on whether they preferred government or mission schools. Government schools had more prestige, while mission schools had more English and lower fees. Government schools were criticized by some for teaching no religion, while Christian schools were criticized for making Christian religious education compulsory. Some thought Christian schools would be less objectionable to the public if a conscience clause were introduced, especially in those places where there was no alternative school available.[78] None of the Indians testifying showed any awareness of the rivalry between government and mission educators, but some saw them working closely together, often in rather devious ways, to spread Christianity through the school system.[79] The most commonly expressed sentiments were that the government follow the path of strict religious neutrality, that students should be taught the religion of their parents, and that other religious communities should establish aided schools on the mission school model.[80]

A good number of missionary and Indian Christian educators also testified before the Commission, sharing their expertise on a wide variety of policy issues. Not even Charles Forman now advocated

[77] *1882 Education Commission Report*, pp. 129, 197, 236, 249, 288, 438, 500.

[78] Ibid., pp. 134–6, 238, 255, 308, 473, 493.

[79] For example, Dr Rahim Khan reported that people generally believe the government has lowered the standard of English, made the middle-school examination overly strict, and raised fees in order to allow the missionaries to do just the reverse and in that way attract students to their schools. Ibid., p. 417. See also p. 321.

[80] Ibid., pp. 134, 238, 255, 308, 321, 473, 485, 512.

government withdrawal from direct educational work, while James Smith in Delhi said that the government would be doing the missions a favour by forcing them out of educating the general public.[81] Missionary evidence also indicated greater diversity and flexibility than earlier in their views about compulsory religious instruction. Forman testified that it was still required of all students; Worthington Jukes said it was voluntary in the CMS school at Peshawar, while in Delhi, Robert Winter of the SPG was 'increasingly in favour' of making it voluntary and James Smith was known to oppose mandatory instruction in Christianity.[82] Forman thought concessions would be made in schools handed over by the government[83] and that schools established by other religious communities on the missionary model should be entitled to grants-in-aid.[84] On the language question, the most controversial issue to come before the Commission, the testimony of Christian educators was (unlike the government view) flexible and pragmatic, adjusting to the needs and wishes of the students in their particular locales. Perhaps their most forceful and provocative statements, however, were made on behalf of educating both women and Dalits because they found in Indian society little interest in educating women and strong opposition to educating Dalits. James Smith saw municipal committees playing a positive role in promoting education, but feared giving them full responsibility for it; he thought the low castes would suffer because local prejudices against them were so strong.[85]

[81] Ibid., p. 447.

[82] Ibid., pp. 218, 300, & 456. In 1872, Smith had told the General Missionary Conference at Allahabad that 'Parents, whether Heathen or Christian, are the appointed guardians of their children, and I doubt the propriety or advantage of opposing their real wishes in imparting Christian instruction to their children in Mission schools.' *Report of the General Missionary Conference held at Allahabad*, p. 119.

[83] So did the Anglican Bishop of Lahore, T.V. French. *1882 Education Commission Report*, p. 222.

[84] Ibid., pp. 218 and 217. .

[85] This comes out in the testimony of Rev. Kali Charan Chatterjee (pp. 168 and 174), Mrs Mary Chatterjee (p. 175), Charles Forman (p. 212), Rev. Golaknath (pp. 224 and 226), James Smith (p. 445), and Robert Winter (pp. 452 and 455) in ibid.

In 1880, the DPI reported that there were 100,402 students on the rolls of government and aided schools, almost three times the number twenty years earlier.[86] During that period the missions had retained their position as the pre-eminent (often sole) private educators in the province and a prominent one at the middle- and high-school levels. They had also been pioneers in the education of women and Dalits, being the sole advocates and providers for the latter. By the end of the period they had given up any ambitions they once entertained of taking over the educational system; some, most notably the Baptists and United Presbyterians, had come to question the evangelistic effectiveness of their schools, and were, therefore, directing their limited resources to what they considered to be more productive uses. Nonetheless, at the end of this period, as at its outset, the mission school was a central feature and powerful symbol of the Christian presence and Christian cultural influence in the region.

The Religious Challenge

Evangelism remained the central aim and main justification of all the work done by the Christian missions in north-west India throughout this period. There is no indication in the Punjab Missionary Conference deliberations that the basic evangelistic message had changed from the previous period. Such Evangelical themes as the character of God, human sinfulness, the atoning death and resurrection of Christ, as well as the doctrine of eternal rewards and punishments were to remain at the heart of Christian preaching.[87] While the conference did not discuss the nature of the specific apologetic through which to convey the Christian message, the missionaries were enjoined to familiarize themselves thoroughly with the religious 'systems' of the region. In like manner, no 'grand strategy' for the evangelization of the region (beyond making current methods more efficient and effective) was put forth, but a very significant discussion on religious controversy indicated a general consensus on the approach to be adopted. Controversy was

[86] *DPI Report 1879–80*, p. 1.
[87] *Report of the Punjab Missionary Conference*, pp. 5–7.

considered counterproductive, because it made people defensive rather than receptive, and yet unavoidable, not only because preachers could not control the responses of their audiences but also because contrasts with prevailing beliefs helped to clarify central Christian teachings.[88]

During the years from 1858 to 1880, the missions expanded their work both geographically and socially. In Delhi not only did the Baptists and SPG revive their missions after the near-death blows of 1857 and then spread into the surrounding suburbs, villages, and towns, but the Baptists also established a mission station in Simla. The American Presbyterians started a new station at Hoshiarpur, while the United Presbyterians added Gujranwala, Gurdaspur, Jhelum, and Zaffarwal to their existing station at Sialkot. The Church of Scotland had first to re-establish itself at Sialkot and then it opened stations at Gujrat, Wazirabad, and Chamba. However, the most expansive mission during this period was the CMS, which spread out from Amritsar into Batala, Narowal, and Lahore in central Punjab; from Peshawar on the north-west frontier into Dera Ismail Khan and Dera Ghazi Khan; and also into Kashmir. New orphanages were opened in Amritsar (later moved to Clarkabad), Sialkot, and Delhi to accommodate children orphaned usually by famine, especially in 1877–78; many of these children were subsequently baptized. The missions also sought to gain access and be of service to sections of Indian society that had been virtually closed to them before. A concerted effort was begun in working among women during this period and from about 1870 onwards single women missionaries came to north-west India in increasingly large numbers because men could not reach secluded Indian women. Medical missions were also set up to demonstrate Christ's healing love and power to men and women unaffected by mission schools, printed literature, or direct preaching. As the following survey indicates, both Christianity's religious challenges and the responses to it varied considerably from place to place throughout the region during this period.

[88] Ibid., pp. 13–30.

DELHI

The Christian community in Delhi had been devastated by the events of 1857. The Baptist Missionary Society sent out the Rev. James Smith, who already had considerable missionary experience in Agra and who was to be one of the most radical and innovative missionaries of this period. When Smith reached Delhi from his furlough in England in March 1859, he found only one Indian Baptist there.[89] The SPG mission was revived initially by Professor Ram Chandra who gathered the surviving converts together. Another convert, Theophilus Qasim Ali, reopened the school and only then, in February 1859, did the first missionary arrive. There he found a congregation of only six Christians.[90] The Delhi Mission of the SPG retained its elite focus throughout this period. The Baptist mission, on the other hand, had never 'targeted' any one particular section of society but had sought to reach out to any and all who were interested. Despite this difference in emphasis there were two categories of people within Delhi society with whom their direct evangelistic work brought them into constant contact: Muslims and Chamars.

The most frequent and persistent contact between representatives of Christianity and Islam in Delhi came through public preaching in the city's streets and bazars. Initially, the encounter was very confrontational. James Smith reported

The Mahommedans are very much excited just now, and nightly come to our preaching-stands for controversy. We have been weekly answering their questions for years. Lately I have turned the tables on them, and told them that it is now our turn to question them; and hence we demand proofs of the Inspiration of the Koran and the Divine character of Mahommed's mission. This course has quite startled the people, especially as I have closed all controversy with them until our reasonable demands are complied with.[91]

[89] *Annual Report of the Delhi Mission, Branch of the Baptist Missionary Society* (Benares 1860), p. 4. [Hereafter this is referred to as *Delhi Baptist Annual Report* with the year added.]

[90] *SPG Report, 1859*, p. 103.

[91] 'Delhi', *BM* (September 1867), p. 618.

However, it was not long before Smith found controversy of this type to be 'perfectly useless' because Muslims were not in the least open-minded.[92] Between 1867 and 1871 the SPG mission published a newspaper, *Mowaiz-i-ookba* (Admonitions Related to the Other World), with a circulation of 150 copies in the hope of 'exciting a spirit of inquiry among the Mahometans'.[93] Muslims responded by publishing a newspaper of their own. For a short time in 1869, the Rev. Tara Chand, who had earlier questioned the wisdom of street preaching 'as not suited to the condition and circumstances of the people of this country',[94] held some meetings devoted to religious discussion in his home with about seventeen Muslims. The atmosphere was very different from that in the bazar and 'nothing was ever said on one side or the other which might irritate the opposite party'.[95]

However, the group with whom the Delhi missions interacted most was the Chamars. Almost from the start of this period, they were the ones who responded most positively and in the largest numbers to Christian evangelism. This both the Baptists and the SPG attributed to certain affinities between Christianity and the Chamars' prior religion, as many had been Kabir Panthis and Raidasis who rejected idolatry, ritualism, and caste hierarchy.[96] In fact, James Smith considered the faqirs of these *panths* to be examples of how to make Christianity take root and spread in north India.[97] His good friend, Seetal Das, a Christian faqir who was proving to be an effective rural evangelist, was a case in point. 'Seetal Das is not paid by us, but goes over hundreds of miles of country, sowing broadcast the seed of the Kingdom, and the people everywhere feed him; he is an evangelist

[92] *Delhi Baptist Annual Report, 1869*, pp. 6–7.

[93] Ibid., 1867, p. 106 and 1868, p. 87; 'Delhi and Kurnaul Mission', *MF* (May 1871), p. 143.

[94] *SPG Annual Report, 1866*, p. 120.

[95] 'Progress of the Gospel in Delhi', *MF* (April 1869), p. 112.

[96] Ibid., p. 583; *Delhi Baptist Annual Report*, p. 5; 'The Good Fight in the Diocese of Calcutta', *MF* (May 1875), p. 151.

[97] See his remarks in *Report of the General Missionary Conference held at Allahabad, 1872–73*, p. 242.

of the most primitive kind.'[98] Smith became so convinced that India would never be effectively won by evangelists paid by foreign religious bodies, that on 5 November 1868 he persuaded the evangelists in Baptist mission employ to give up their mission salaries and do evangelism as they were able on a voluntary basis.[99] A year later, four of them were itinerating and preaching in the villages around Delhi.[100]

The Baptists also attempted to bring worship closer to the people by 'the establishing of small assemblies in the middle of the houses of the converts, wherever they exist, thus bringing our instruction, as far as practicable, within hearing of the women and children, with a view of reverting to the old apostolic plan of the church in the house'.[101] Often, more than a hundred neighbours would be present for these evening prayer meetings, which became the focal points of the community's devotional life and an effective means of evangelizing the people in the bastis. The SPG was less radical in its approach to the Chamars. They continued to use paid evangelists and conduct services in the bastis, but whereas the Baptists were trying to develop independent, congregations led by their members free from mission control (but not guidance) as a means of spreading Christianity, the SPG was seeking to incorporate the Chamars into congregations dominated by the clergy and mission. Moreover, by the 1870s Smith had come to focus his mission almost exclusively on the low castes, whereas the SPG continued to retain its elite priority even though the vast majority of their converts were also Chamars.[102]

Both women's and medical missions in Delhi were developed to complement existing evangelistic work. Mrs Priscilla Winter's zenana work was in keeping with the SPG emphasis upon the elites in Delhi; her first invitation to open up zenana classes came from Bengalis

[98] J. Smith, 'Delhi', *BM* (September 1866), p. 593. By 'primitive' Smith obviously meant close to the New Testament model.

[99] *Delhi Baptist Annual Report, 1868*, p. 5.

[100] Ibid., 1869, p. 5.

[101] *Baptist Annual Report, 1872*, p. 8.

[102] This story is told in much greater detail in John C.B. Webster, 'Missionary Strategy and the Development of the Christian Community: Delhi 1859–1884'.

and then from Muslims. However, the SPG also had Bible women doing systematic, house-by-house visitation among Chamar women,[103] which the understaffed Baptists did not. The earliest SPG medical work was part of the zenana mission to secluded elite women, whereas the first Baptist doctor came to Delhi to meet the needs of the Chamars who were not being given proper medical attention at government clinics and dispensaries.[104]

The Punjab Plains

The rest of the Punjab was not as badly affected by the events of 1857 as Delhi had been. The Christians in Ludhiana were compensated for the loss of their homes, printing press, book depot, and personal property.[105] The Church of Scotland decided to continue their mission at Sialkot; Muhammad Ismael, the Muslim convert who had accompanied the Hunters from Bombay, reopened the school and two new missionaries arrived in March 1860.[106] All the Punjab missions increased the number of their mission stations in order to 'fill out' the area they already 'occupied' and continued to use the same methods as before to evangelize the population. Unlike in Delhi, no one section of society was specifically targeted for special evangelistic attention and no one group's response was markedly greater than the others'. However, the missions did begin to develop an experientially based knowledge and scholarship of their own about the religions of the Punjabi people, and so were less dependent upon stereotypes found in travellers' or official accounts.

While virtually no scholarly interest was shown in Hindu religion during this period, even though most of the converts came from Hindu backgrounds, the Rev. William Keene from Amritsar presented

---

[103] 'Delhi and Kurnaul Missions', *MF* (August 1869), p. 236; 'Diocese of Calcutta–Delhi—Tounghoo', ibid. (November 1876), p. 326.

[104] 'Missions to Women', *Report of the General Missionary Conference held at Allahabad, 1872–73*, p. 159; *Baptist Annual Report, 1875*, p. 73

[105] *Lodiana Mission Annual Report, 1857*, pp. 5–6; 'George O. Barnes, Letter to the Board of Foreign Missions, 15 June 1857', *FM* (October 1857), pp. 129–31.

[106] 'Punjaub', *HFMR* (September 1858), p. 225; *Church of Scotland Annual Report, 1860*, p. 7.

a paper to the Punjab Missionary Conference on the Sikhs. Keene saw Guru Nanak freeing the mind 'from the gross errors of the popular Hindu belief' and reverting to 'the simplicity of natural religion', believing in one God and rejecting idolatry as well as caste.[107] Keene noted that in recent years Sikhs were departing from the pure teachings of Nanak and the other Sikh gurus, particularly in the matters of idolatry, caste practices, and the immolation of widows. While acknowledging that 'the influence of Nanak's teaching was for good', he was noncommittal about whether his teaching prepared Sikhs to receive Christianity.[108]

However, the most significant Christian scholarship in the Punjab was carried out with reference to Islam. The key figure was the Rev. Imad-ud-din, a well-trained maulvie from an eminent family who converted to Christianity in 1866 after a long spiritual struggle. He spent the rest of his long life in Amritsar as a pastor, evangelist, and prolific writer. Avril Powell sees his early Christian tracts as modelled on Pfander's *Mizan ul Haqq* (Balance of Truth).[109] Pfander had argued that human beings cannot know God by reason alone but only by divine revelation. He set up five criteria for a true revelation of God and then showed how the Bible and its teaching met those criteria whereas the Quran and its teachings did not.[110] At the General Missionary Conference in Allahabad at the end of 1872, Imad-ud-din saw 'the sonship of Christ, his divinity, and the doctrine of the Trinity' as 'great obstacles' to Muslims becoming Christians. Yet their salvation depended on those truths. What was, therefore, needed above all else was a book 'filled with arguments conclusive and silencing' built upon evidence not from the Quran but from the Church 'generation after generation' that the Bible is the Word of God.[111] Soon after the conference, according to Powell, Imad-ud-din shifted from controversial writing to writing on the uniqueness

[107] *Report of the Punjab Missionary Conference*, pp. 262–3.

[108] Ibid., pp. 265–6.

[109] Avril A. Powell, '"Pillar of a New Faith"', pp. 223–55.

[110] C.G. Pfander, *The Mizan ul Haqq: or, Balance of Truth*, 1867.

[111] 'Preaching to Muhammadans', *Report of the General Missionary Conference held at Allahabad, 1872–73*, pp. 52–3.

of Christ.[112] By March 1875, he considered the period of controversy over and the Muslims in total defeat.[113] By way of contrast, T.V. French, who as a young missionary had been Pfander's partner in the 'great debate' with Muslim ulama at Agra in 1853, told the Conference that Christians should make their appeal to the Muslims' quest for a fuller spirituality rather than to arguments and proofs, as Imad-ud-din continued to do.[114] However, French was finding this at times difficult in the face of fierce and, in his view, unscrupulous opposition in Lahore.[115]

A survey of the generalized impressions and anecdotal evidence in the missionary records suggests that during this period Imad-ud-din's approach was the more characteristic of the public religious encounters of Christian preachers with the Punjabi people, no matter who initiated them, and French's preferred method was at best confined to more private conversation. Missionaries reported varied responses to their preaching in the bazars of the Punjab; some audiences were attentive, some rowdy, and some insulting.[116] Arguments with Muslims seemed to focus on such questions as the superiority of Christ to Muhammad, the supersession of the dispensation of Christ by that of Muhammad, and the genuineness of the Christian scriptures as the Word of God.[117] However, with

[112] Avril A. Powell, '"Pillar of a New Faith"', p. 244.

[113] Imad-ud-din, 'The Results of the Controversy in North India with Mohammedans', *CMI* (September 1875), pp. 276–80.

[114] 'Preaching to Muhammadans', *Report of the General Missionary Conference held at Allahabad, 1872–73*, pp. 58–64. A decade earlier, upon arriving on the north-west frontier, French had been very critical of a missionary colleague there for his use of invective and denunciation. 'I am for thoroughly following the apostles, who (except under *peculiar* opposition) treated their hearers not only as reasonable beings & able to judge, but as *gentlemen* likewise.' T.V. French, Letter to Mr. Stuart, 21 April 1862.

[115] 'Missionary Work in the Punjab', *CMI* (September 1872), p. 272 and 'Annual Letter of the Rev. T.V. French', ibid. (May 1873), p. 160.

[116] Thomas Henry Fitzpatrick, Letter to Mr. Venn dated 19 February 1864; Rowland Bateman, Annual Letter dated 15 November 1872; T.P. Hughes, Letter to Col. Dawes dated 3 May 1865; 'India Mission', *HFMR* (1 January 1872), p. 555.

[117] The Annual Report of Rev. Imam Shah, Native Pastor of Peshawar, 1874; T.R. Wade, Letter to General Lake dated 31 January 1873; *Church of Scotland Annual Report,1866*, pp. 52–3; 'India Mission', *HFMR* (1 January 1872), p. 555.

Hindus as with Muslims, the key issue presented by the evangelists in one way or another was whether one is saved by faith in the grace of God mediated in the atoning work of Jesus Christ or by a prescribed discipline of ritual and ceremonial activity. For their audiences the key question seemed to be why one should give up the religion of one's ancestors and caste fellows. While there was some engagement between these two positions, largely focusing upon the nature of sin and of God, the results were almost always a stand-off.[118]

Although the religious challenge, embodied in street preaching and the controversial literature that supported it, could be set aside as merely entertaining, annoying, or provocative,[119] an actual or immanent conversion was a far more serious matter. One missionary commented that the conversion of a high-caste person aroused far more public commotion than did that of a low-caste person.[120] The conversion case that probably produced the strongest public reaction and had the most significant public ramifications involved three students at the Lahore Mission School in August 1866. Each of the students had decided to become a Christian and each knew that in order to do so they had to leave home. The first was Dina Nath whose parents, knowing of his desire, had kept him closely watched at home and had even threatened to kill him if he converted. Dina Nath took refuge with Rev. John Newton in the mission compound. He was followed first by Sant Ram and then by Puran Chand. The families of all three were given access to the boys and used combinations of flattery, threats, and entreaties to get them to return

---

[118] 'Letter from Rev. R. A. Hill', *UP* (7 July 1858), p. 1; The Annual Report of the Rev. Imam Shah, 1874; Rev. E. P. Swift, 'Missionary Travels in India', *UP* (12 September 1868), p. 2, ibid. (26 September 1868), p. 2 , ibid. (2 January 1869), p. 2; 'The People Only Admire the Gospel', *FM* (November 1863), pp. 153–4; 'Missionary Work at Jalandar, 1863', *HFR* (December 1864), pp. 276–7.

[119] For example, the *Punjabi Akhbar* of 26 July 1873 accused the missionary preachers in Lahore of treating their audiences uncivilly, 'a practice dangerous in a political point of view, besides being prejudicial to the spread of Christianity'. *Selections from the Vernacular Newspapers in the Punjab, North-Western Provinces, Oudh, and the Central Provinces, 1873*, p. 512.

[120] *Church of Scotland Annual Report, 1877*, p. 121.

home, but to no avail. The family of Dina Nath, the youngest of the three, took the matter to court arguing that their son was too young (reports of his age varied from thirteen to sixteen years) to make such a decision. The district judge decided to examine Dina Nath in order to determine whether he knew enough to choose which religion to follow. Dina Nath's answers satisfied him and the judge allowed him to be baptized. All three boys were baptized together in the Naulaka Church on 13 August 1866.

This rather bare account omits the public commotion created by these boys' decision to leave home in order to be baptized and the severe pressures to which they were subjected both before and after baptism. Writing almost forty years later, Puran Chand, who became a distinguished pastor, said, 'I can not describe the condition of Lahore in those days. Hundreds of men, women and boys kept continually going from morning till late at night to the Naulaka Mission Compound, to have a chance of seeing these two high caste school boys, whom they believed, to be under the wizard charm of the Padri Sahib.'[121] There were also the parental pleas and manoeuvrings to regain custody of their errant boys. Sant Ram's widowed mother, in the presence of her son, 'tore her hair, and beat her breast till it was all red and sore, and put earth on her head, and wailed just as Hindoo women always do when their children die'.[122] Public meetings were held in protest. The Punjabi press, reporting on events, urged appropriate government action to prevent such things from recurring. A petition was sent to the lieutenant governor (which was denied), and parents withdrew their children from the mission school. Attendance dropped from about 400 to 100 and a Hindu School was started as an alternative. A year later, attendance at the mission school was about back to normal and one of the students was Dina Nath's brother![123]

[121] Puran Chand Uppal, *The Conversion of Puran Chand Uppal*, pp. 9–10.
[122] John Newton, 'Three Boys Baptized in Lahore', *FM* (January 1867), p. 219.
[123] Education Proceedings of the Government of the Punjab for the Month of January 1867, nos. 12 and 13; *DPI Report, 1866–67*, p. 43; *DPI. Report, 1867–68*, p. 30. For an Indian perspective on these events, see the abstracts from the *Koh-i-Noor*, the oldest Indian newspaper in the Punjab, in *Selections from the Vernacular Newspapers*

This was not an isolated case.[124] Although few conversions were filled with as much high drama as this one, it does provide a very vivid illustration of what many people considered to be at stake when members of the elite chose to convert. Both the missionaries and the converts were well aware of the sacrifices involved and often quoted Jesus' words, 'Whoever loves father or mother more than me is not worthy of me' (Matthew 10:37) as a reminder. Conversion required enormous courage and commitment; many who were so inclined for religious reasons simply could not take the step for social reasons. On the other side, the families experienced conversion as a death in the family; they felt rejected and disgraced. Dina Nath returned to his family for some time after his baptism and his family sought to get him restored to caste. In the end he left them.[125] Puran Chand's father never forgave him, but his mother and sisters did.[126] It also posed a serious threat to the very organic nature of Punjabi society itself, which is why it aroused such a public clamour. The courts in their turn came down on the side of individual religious liberty and fourteen was considered the minimum age of discretion in such matters.[127]

Although the missions retained their solidly urban base throughout this period, they did pay greater attention to rural evangelism than they had previously. An example of this was John Taylor, a Church of Scotland missionary, who reported on a tour of over 200 villages between November 1865 and March 1866. He would go to the centre of each village and try to attract an audience.

Published in the Punjaub, North-Western Provinces, Oudh and the Central Provinces, From the 8th to the 16th of September, 1866, pp. 217–20.

[124] For other examples of cases that ended up in court, see 'Discretionary Age of Youthful Converts in India', *CMI* (March 1865), pp. 94–5; *CMS Proceedings, 1873–1874*, p. 105.

[125] J.H. Morrison, 'Dina Nath', *FM* (September 1867), pp. 96–7.

[126] Puran Chand Uppal, *The Conversion of Puran Chand Uppal: The Story Told By Himself*.

[127] See J.E. Howard, 'Is the Baptism of a Minor Legal?', *The Indian Evangelical Review*, XVII (July 1890), pp. 56–77.

I avoid as much as possible anything controversial, and give a plain outline of the Gospel, showing its adaptation to the wants of sinners. In most places the people listen attentively, make no objections, and even promise seriously to consider the claims of Christianity. In other places where the Mohammedan element prevails, if there be a moolvie in the village he is generally summoned to confront the padre with a few old but oft-repeated objections.[128]

Taylor saw himself 'sowing the seed' and during that lengthy tour found only two people, a Brahmin and a Sikh faqir, among whom it might take root.[129] The problem was that such itinerating could not and did not produce the kind of sustained contact necessary for the Christian message to have a lasting effect, even if its initial presentation in a village did produce constructive discussion and the evangelist left some Christian literature behind for the literate to ponder. In 1866, Taylor proposed a 'district scheme' according to which catechists and scripture readers would be placed in villages about ten or twelve miles apart. 'The people would have more frequent opportunities of hearing and above all of *seeing* the truth in the character and conduct of native Christians. With itinerations of five months in the year we can only overtake the whole district in three or four seasons.'[130] Taylor died a few years later at the age of thirty and his scheme was implemented soon afterwards with money from a fund established in his memory.[131]

As the description of Taylor's tour indicates, no special groups in rural Punjab were 'targeted' for special attention and none proved to be unusually 'receptive'. The Church of Scotland mission did some work among the Sansis, a very low-caste gipsy tribe that the government was trying to rehabilitate.[132] The United Presbyterians found some response among the Meghs, a weaver caste, in some villages near Zafarwal in Sialkot district.[133] The Rev. Kali Charan

---

[128] *Church of Scotland Annual Report,* 1866, p. 52.

[129] Ibid., p. 53.

[130] *Church of Scotland Annual Report,* 1866, p. 54.

[131] Ibid., *May 1868,* p. 110 and *May 1869,* pp. 116, 125.

[132] Ibid., *May 1862,* p. 12.

[133] Andrew Gordon, *Our India Mission,* pp. 191–378.

Chatterjee, the Presbyterian missionary in Hoshiarpur, baptized thirteen out of about thirty faqirs, including the leader, who were residing near a village eighteen miles from Hoshiarpur as well as a dozen Rajput zamindars in the village of Ghorawaha, also near Hoshiarpur. As in the case of the Megh converts, severe sanctions were applied to these converts, including social boycotts and loss of services. The converts in Ghorawaha were denied the use of the village well and the government had to intervene.[134] The villages, it would seem, were more open to Christian preaching than were the towns and cities, but less open to conversion to Christianity and certainly more capable of applying overwhelming social pressure against those who attempted to convert.

Courteous indifference, baptism, and hostility were not the only responses to Christian evangelism in rural Punjab during this period. Hakim Singh of Rampur village in Patiala state was much influenced by a tract on the second coming of Christ as well as by conversations with Rev. Adolph Rudolph. These led him to conclude that Jesus was the *nishkalank avatar* (immaculate incarnation) of God who would come again to manifest his power and glory in Hakim Singh himself. Until Christ did so, Hakim Singh was the true guru, in fact Christ himself not fully manifested. His followers, called *Nishkalankis*, ate with Christians and were persecuted as Christians, but never accepted Christian baptism. They felt that they did not need it since that had received the baptism of the Holy Spirit.[135] Chet Ram's direct contacts with Christian evangelists are less clear. In the early 1860s he had a vision of Christ who told him to build a church in his village of Buchhoke and place a Bible in it. His creed and that of his followers was 'Help, O Jesus, Son of Mary, Holy Spirit, Lord God Shepherd. Read the Bible and the Gospels for Salvation', but his followers tended to identify Chet Ram himself with Christ and suffered persecution

---

[134] 'Ghorawaha', *FM* (April 1875), pp. 336–7. For a fuller description of the faqirs and of the Ghorawaha zamindars, see John C.B. Webster, *The Christian Community and Change*, pp. 124–5, 138–9.

[135] A fuller description of these faqirs is given in John C.B. Webster, *The Christian Community and Change*, pp. 122–3. See also 'A Sect of Sikh Christians', *UP* (27 June 1872), p. 1.

as Christians even though they too never received Christian baptism.[136]

THE PUNJAB HILLS AND KASHMIR

The 1857 revolt did not spread into the Punjab Hills and so the missions there were unaffected by what had happened on the plains. The Moravians expanded their work in Lahaul near Tibet. The CMS added to its mission stations at Kotgarh, Kangra, and Simla a new substation at Dharmsala. Three new missions were also established that deserve special mention. In the early 1860s, the Baptists began evangelistic work in and around Simla. In 1863, the Rev. William Ferguson, a military chaplain in the Punjab, resigned his position in order to start a mission in Chamba, which he handed over to the Church of Scotland ten years later. Finally, the CMS, after gathering private support from a number of prominent Evangelical officials in 1862, established a mission to Kashmir. Since each of these endeavours was quite distinctive, they will be treated separately.

The three Moravian missionaries in Kyelang began by learning Tibetan and studying the religious texts preserved by the lamas. Once they started preaching, the villagers listened attentively but lost interest when the novelty wore off. Heinrich August Jeaschke devoted himself to translating basic Christian works into Tibetan and these were printed at a press the missionaries had brought to Kyelang in 1858. This led in turn to starting a school that had an industrial department in addition to regular primary classes.[137]

The general pattern of CMS evangelistic work in the hills was much the same as on the plains. Evangelists preached daily in the town bazars and spent the cool season itinerating through the hill villages and visiting melas. What did differ was the response which their preaching evoked. Not only were the hill town populations small and thus easily overexposed to street preaching, but there was little opposition. In his report for 1866–67, Rev. Merk in Kangra stated

[136] H.D. Griswold, *The Chet Rami Sect*, 1904, p. 13.
[137] John Barton, 'Report of Missionary Work in Thibet', *CMI* (August 1862), pp. 183–8.

that all opposition had ceased.[138] Twelve years later, the report from Kangra was that there was neither opposition nor interest and this applied to religion in general, not just to Christianity.[139] What evangelistic success these missions did have seemed due more to their schools and literature than to their public preaching.

The Rev. Gulzar Shah, a Baptist pastor employed by the Public Works Department in Calcutta, began evangelistic work in and around Simla when he was posted there during the summer months. He gathered Indian Christians for Sunday worship and prayer meetings as well as engaged his fellow government employees in religious discussions as opportunity arose. Finally, like the CMS workers, he toured some of the adjacent villages as time permitted.[140] By 1869, the Baptists had built a chapel in Simla and employed two workers there.[141] Their converts, though few, came from among both migrants working in the hills and the hill people themselves.

Another individual initiative was that of the Rev. William Ferguson in Chamba. Ferguson, a Church of Scotland chaplain, attended the Punjab Missionary Conference. A few months later he resigned and, because of difficulties in joining the Church of Scotland mission, started an independent mission in Chamba which the local raja seemed pleased to welcome.[142] Ferguson gave priority to evangelistic preaching and used a simple, conversational style aimed more at the heart than at the head. 'Do you pray?' 'To whom?' 'To any others?' 'To the one great God; so do I.' 'And how do you come before this great God?' He then presented Jesus Christ as the necessary mediator to that God similar to a *vakil* who can take one's petition to the raja and plead your case.[143] Ferguson used schools only for nurturing Christians, although others were allowed to attend on those terms. When Ferguson's health broke down and he turned

---

[138] *CMS Proceedings, 1866–1867,* p. 92.

[139] *CMS Proceedings, 1878–1879,* p. 62.

[140] 'The Native Pastor at Simlah', *MH* (January 1867), pp. 56–8.

[141] 'A Native Missionary's Work at Simla', ibid. (October 1869), p. 680.

[142] 'The Chumba Mission, Punjab', *HFMR* (September 1863), pp. 151–3.

[143] 'Missionary Meeting at Meerut', ibid. (June 1870), pp. 55–8.

over the mission to the Church of Scotland in 1873, 130 baptisms had been performed.[144]

While touring Kashmir in 1854, Robert Clark was given an audience by Maharaja Gulab Singh who consented to have a mission in his territories.[145] In 1862, an appeal signed by Sir Robert Montgomery, Sir Donald McLeod, and other prominent Evangelical officials in the Punjab raised Rs. 14,000 for the mission.[146] In 1863, two missionaries visited Kashmir to begin work there and the following year the mission was officially established. However, it faced two major obstacles right from the outset. The first was an agreement between the maharaja and the British government that prevented Europeans from spending the winter months in Kashmir without the maharaja's permission. Since the maharaja applied this to missionaries as well as to government officials, the missionaries could be there only from April through September.[147] The other was the very serious opposition from the governor in Srinagar, almost certainly with the maharaja's backing, to evangelistic work of any kind. While the European missionaries were rarely touched, their preaching and preachers were spied upon and harassed, their inquirers arrested, the names of those using their medical or educational facilities noted down, and baptisms prohibited.[148] One of the chief aims of the medical mission was to overcome this suspicion and opposition by demonstrating genuine concern for the people's well being.

In the spring of 1865, Dr William Elmslie made his way slowly into the vale of Kashmir, stopping to offer free medical attention in the villages en route to Srinagar. At each place on the way, as in Srinagar itself, he gathered the patients together for a short service of prayer and preaching before treating them individually.[149] At that time he was the only doctor in Kashmir trained in the West, and

[144] *Church of Scotland Annual Report, 1874*, p. 130.

[145] Robert Clark, *The Punjab and Sindh Missions*, p. 147.

[146] Ibid., pp. 148–9 and *CMS Proceedings, 1862–63*, pp. 128–9.

[147] *CMS Proceedings, 1863–64*, pp. 446–7.

[148] See, for example, *CMS Proceedings, 1865–66*, pp. 124–5.

[149] *CMS Proceedings, 1866–67*, p. 100.

people came to him in large numbers despite the obstacles the local authorities put in their way. Elmslie protested frequently and bitterly that the British government, as a Christian government and paramount power, should intervene to insist upon greater religious liberty, but it refused to do more than put his requests before the maharaja's government.[150] Elmslie returned each year until his death in 1872. Subsequently, the maharaja built (and later enlarged) a hospital for the medical mission's use and during 1877–8 finally gave permission for the missionaries to remain in Kashmir during the winter months.[151] It thus became a year-round mission and could establish continuity of work and relationships with the Kashmiri people.

The Christian Community

The period between 1858 and 1880 was one of significant growth for the Christian community in north-west India. The Punjab government's 1855 census made no mention of Indian Christians.[152] In 1868, its next census reported a total of 2675 Indian Christians.[153] Either this figure is inflated or there were many Christians in the Delhi and Jullundur cantonments who were unaccounted for by mission statistics.[154] The 1881 census, the first comprehensive and reliable Census of India, listed a total of 3912 'Native Christians' in the Punjab and its dependencies. This figure is probably reliable, although the denominational breakdowns it offered do pose awkward questions. There were 299 Catholics recorded, even though Roman Catholic activity among Indians in the region was confined to their

[150] This can be seen quite clearly in his personal correspondence, file C I 1 0 102 / 1–15.

[151] *CMS Proceedings, 1877–78*, pp. 126–7.

[152] *Selections from the Records of the Government of India (Foreign Department) No. XI Report on the Census Taken on the 1st January 1855 of the Population of the Punjab Territories* (Calcutta 1856).

[153] *Report on the Census of the Punjab Taken on 10th January 1868* (Calcutta 1870), p. 24.

[154] Ibid., General Statement No. III : Population According to the Great Divisions of Castes and Tribes. The census reported 1475 Indian Christians in Delhi and 101 in Jullundur.

chaplaincies in military cantonments. The 191 Baptists reported in Lahore district were probably baptized Presbyterians (whose total of twenty-five was much too low). The Ambala total of 224 suggests that there were Christians in the cantonments unattached to the churches.[155]

The increase of the Christian community from about two hundred to almost four thousand during this period had two important consequences. One was the emergence of important structures of ecclesiastical and community life. In the beginning there had been only the missions and their employees. However, as more and more converts were added, congregations emerged as entities distinct from the missions, requiring their own lay and clerical leadership. At the same time the missions continued to provide the structures through which Christians throughout the region might become more interconnected as a community. Missionaries and their employees scattered at various mission stations got together at least annually for meetings at which decisions concerning postings, policies, and finances were taken. The Punjab Missionary Conference was a very visible expression of the informal friendships and networks that existed between members of different missions. All the missions made use of the Mission Press at Ludhiana and the Teacher Training School at Amritsar. Together they created the Vernacular Education Society to publish educational materials for all their schools. Following the General Missionary Conference held at Allahabad over the new year of 1872–3, there were some conversations about a greater union among the churches in the north-west, but these produced no concrete results during this period.

The other consequence of numerical growth was the possibility of cultural and even religious change within the Christian community itself. This was bound to occur as Indian Christians greatly outnumbered the missionaries and their congregations grew beyond missionary control. The question is thus how far this process had advanced by the end of this period and what the Christian community

---

[155] *Punjab Census Report 1881 Volume II Appendix A*, Table IIIA, 'Subsidiary Table Showing Christians by Race and Sect.'

looked like as a result. The simple answer is that it did not have a uniform look about it because converts in the major areas within the region came from different backgrounds and thus brought different kinds of 'Indianness' into the churches and Christian community. This can be seen most clearly by examining each major area within the region separately.

Delhi

The social composition of the Christian community in Delhi proved to be quite distinctive. The Rev. James Smith began preaching in Delhi in March 1859 and by the end of 1860 the Baptists there had increased from virtually nothing to at least ninety-four. Of the sixty-five he baptized in 1860, nineteen were Muslims, thirty-three were Chamars, six were Hindus of other castes, and seven were Christians formerly belonging to other churches.[156] In 1862, he baptized Mirza Feroze Shah, a nephew of the Mughal emperor who had been a good friend of Thompson and had written a tract on the divinity of Christ.[157] However, while converts from other castes and communities continued to trickle in, the vast majority of the Baptist converts were Chamars. As Smith's colleague, Parsons, had noted back in December 1859, 'A spirit of inquiry prevails amongst the whole community of [Chamars] in and about this city, and a considerable number of them have already come forward and made an open profession of Christianity.'[158] Although the SPG was intended to be a mission to Delhi's educated elite, it had the same experience. While it had a few converts from among the elites, most notably some high-caste students or former students, the vast majority of the converts were Chamars. In his 1873–4 report, Rev. Robert Winter stated that twenty-seven were high-caste Hindus, thirteen were Muslims, eighty-two were weavers and Chamars, and the rest were children of Christian

---

[156] 'The Work of God in Delhi', *MH* (September 1861), p. 584. Never again would the number, or even proportion, of Muslim converts in Delhi be as high as this.

[157] 'The Progress of the Mission in Delhi', *BM* (August 1862), p. 525.

[158] J. Parsons, 'Northern India', ibid. (January 1861), p. 49.

parents.[159] In subsequent reports the number and proportion of Chamars increased dramatically.[160]

The development of the Christian community in Delhi was shaped by its distinct social composition as well as by the divergent strategies of the Baptist and SPG missionaries. James Smith began by organizing Baptist converts into congregations where they already lived, but he also had a central church and a central school. He sought to develop independent, self-sustaining churches and to that end began entrusting the panchayats of local congregations with more and more responsibility for worship, nurture, discipline, and development. By the end of the 1860s, as converts who entered and left churches with great frequency, he became convinced that Christianity was an exotic thing which would not take root or spread in north India as long as converts and churches were dependent upon foreign patronage.[161] As previously noted, in 1868, he persuaded all the paid evangelists to resign and in 1872 he made 'public worship subservient to family religion'[162] by setting up Sunday and weekday evening prayer meetings in the bastis where their people lived. These meetings were led by Christian residents and addressed by school teachers, evangelists or missionaries. Over time, Smith made the Chamars the focus of all his evangelistic, pastoral, educational, and medical work.

In 1878, the Baptists sent a delegation to Delhi to investigate Smith's work. There they visited a good number of basti prayer meetings that were very well attended not only by the converts but

[159] F.J. Western, 'The Early History of the Cambridge Mission to Delhi', p. 52.

[160] For example, twenty-two of the twenty-three adult men baptized in 1875 were Chamars; in 1878, between three and four hundred Chamars were baptized; and in 1879, forty-three of the fifty-three adult baptisms were Chamars. See *SPG Annual Report, 1875*, p. 15; Edward Bickersteth, Letter to Mr. Bullock, 16 October 1878; *SPG Annual Report, 1879*, pp. 24–5.

[161] See 'An Independent Native Church in Delhi', *MH* (February 1869), p. 593 and Smith's remarks in the *Report of the General Missionary Conference held at Allahabad, 1872–73*, p. 242.

[162] *Baptist Annual Report, 1877*, p. 8. Moreover, Smith had found basti people to be so irregular in attending formal worship at the central church that he decided to bring Christian worship to them where they lived.

by their neighbours as well. Prayers were led by local residents and the singing of 'thoroughly Evangelical' songs to 'native tunes' was, in the deputation's words, 'as a rule, loud, sometimes boisterous, and accompanied by much bodily exercise'.[163] Clearly these meetings were at the very heart and centre of the community's devotional life. The deputation also found that some of the church panchayats had raised money and received volunteer labour to purchase land and build or repair simple school and chapel buildings. These panchayats were connected with a central panchayat that met weekly. The deputation was impressed with the independence, vitality, and growth they witnessed.[164] What Smith's strategy and the predominantly Chamar converts had created over the previous twenty years was a highly decentralized church which was lay led and dependent upon congregational initiative. In form as well as in devotional style it resembled the Kabir Panthis, but it was Christian.

As has already been noted, the social composition of the Anglican community created by the SPG in and around Delhi was very similar to that of the Baptists, but with one very significant exception. The SPG had begun work among Chamar women at the end of the 1860s, so that they had more women converts and thus more Christian families than did the Baptists. Like their Baptist counterparts, the SPG missionaries urged their converts to remain in their own neighbourhoods among their own people so as to exercise a Christian influence among them. However, there were two important differences between the Anglicans and the Baptists. The Anglicans had two important Indian leaders during this period. One was Professor Ram Chandra who, after surviving the trials of 1857, had gathered the surviving community together and, despite postings outside Delhi, remained a community patriarch until his death in 1880. The other was Lala Tara Chand, a protégé of Ram Chandra and convert who studied at Bishop's College in Calcutta prior to his ordination in 1864. Rev. Tara Chand had major pastoral and

[163] Report on Mission Work in Delhi: Report of Revs. John Aldis and Wm. Sampson, p. 23.
[164] Ibid., pp. 23, 24, 49.

evangelistic responsibilities throughout this period and was the only Indian to serve on the Mission Council which was formed after the arrival of the Cambridge Mission to Delhi in 1877.

In addition to prominent Indian leadership, the Anglican community was characterized by a caste cleavage between the Chamar and other Anglicans which was religious rather than social in nature. In order to become a communicant member of the church and thus receive holy communion, a convert had to give up joining with friends and relatives in feasts that involved idolatry.[165] This posed no obstacles for the socially boycotted Muslim and caste Hindu converts to overcome because they were not invited to such feasts. However, the Chamars did not boycott converts, but invited their Christian friends and relatives to join them in their marriage celebrations and other festivities. The result was that Chamar converts who retained these ties with their caste fellows were ineligible for communicant membership and were thus second-class members of the Church, even though they were included without discrimination in the social events of the community.[166] This religious distinction continued throughout this period and was only partially resolved in the 1880s when the Chamar converts had to choose between their caste and religious loyalties.

The post-1857 resurrection and expansion of the Anglican community in Delhi began with only five or six people. In May 1867, almost ten years to the day after so many Delhi Christians had been martyred, the Delhi Memorial Church was consecrated. In 1869, a Native Pastorate Fund was instituted to which all church members were expected to contribute on a regular basis and the practice of bi-monthly meetings at which communicant members could express their views on matters of concern to them was begun.[167] In the 1870s,

---

[165] *SPG Annual Report, 1863*, p. 93.

[166] For example, in 1869, Professor Ram Chandra sponsored a community meal to which all Christians, including the Chamar converts, were invited and ate together, much to the amazement of the onlookers. 'Delhi and Kurnaul Mission', *MF* (May 1871), pp. 141–2.

[167] Ibid.

a more formal church organization was created as the mission became more committed to 'native agency' and employed more 'native agents' in order to expand its work. In 1875, the mission divided Delhi into eight parishes and placed each under a head catechist who was accountable to the mission. Each parish also had a panchayat consisting of two locally elected members and one appointed by the mission. Its responsibilities were to 'advise the local catechists, make arrangements for the services, settle petty disputes and exercise a useful influence upon the unconverted neighbours'.[168] In 1880, all of the pastoral and outreach work, which up to that time had been the responsibility of Robert Winter as senior missionary, was placed under a mission council comprising all the male missionaries plus Rev. Tara Chand.[169] Thus, power in the SPG church and mission structures was not only highly centralized but also dependent upon clergy initiative and leadership.

This brings out the sharp contrasts between the two sections of the Christian community in Delhi. Whereas the Baptists became more and more committed to the Chamars and sought to create among them a church which would take root and be independent of the mission, the SPG retained throughout the period a focus upon the elites (despite obvious success among the Chamars), a socially hierarchical outlook on their work (separating the high from the low castes),[170] and a centralized, hierarchical ecclesiastical structure. Descriptions of Christian worship in Delhi highlight the contrast. The Baptists had their basti meetings; the SPG normally conducted 'simple and short services' in the bastis, adapted to the requirements of the people there.[171] The Baptist delegation from England

[168] 'Calcutta', *MF* (June 1877), p. 184 and 'Organization of the Delhi Mission', ibid. (September 1877), pp. 381–2.

[169] R.R. Winter, Letter to Mr. Tucker, 9 June 1880.

[170] Both the work in general and the schools in particular were divided into elite and low-caste categories. 'Organization of the Delhi Mission', *MF* (September 1877), pp. 381, 383.

[171] 'Organization of the Delhi Mission', *MF* (September 1877), p. 385. When mission staff could not be present, the people did conduct (probably read) their own services. *SPG Annual Report, 1875*, p. 16.

commented upon the vitality of worship in the bastis; the Bishop of Lahore was impressed by the solemnity of worship during his visit. It would seem that whereas Smith wanted converts to develop their own ways of being Christian, Winter wanted to bring them into conformity with churchly ways. One thing is clear from the correspondence and occasional printed comments: the Baptist and SPG missionaries did not like or approve of each other very much. Whether this disapproval and sense of competition was shared by the Indian Baptists and Anglicans is not clear.

THE PUNJAB PLAINS

The Christian community on the plains to the north and west of Delhi was socially more diverse than that within and around Delhi itself. For example, of the 132 baptisms mentioned in the printed records of the Lodiana Mission between 1858 and 1880, fifty-seven (43 per cent) were Muslims, eleven (8 per cent) were Brahmins, fourteen (11 per cent) were high-caste Hindus, twenty-nine (22 per cent) were Hindus of unspecified caste, twelve (9 per cent) were low-caste Hindus, and nine (7 per cent) were Sikhs.[172] The CMS reports of conversions indicate a similar diversity, except for the higher proportion of Muslims, due to the mission's location in the Muslim-majority western portion of the Punjab, and of Sikhs, due to the conversion of Mazhabis in the 24th Punjab Native Infantry. The CMS report for 1863–4 described its Amritsar congregation as 'composed of the most heterogeneous materials': Muslims, Sikhs of the highest class, a Rajput, several sweeper families, a few Bengalis, and Madras Eurasians.[173] A similar description in 1870–1 indicates that it also included a large number of orphan girls and boys.[174] A

---

[172] The differences between these figures and those found on page 49 of *The Christian Community and Change* are due to three things: that table covers a longer time span, 1858–86; it includes converts at the Dehra Dun and Saharanpur stations of the mission which are outside the geographic area covered in this history; and I now have a better understanding of caste names and so am able to move some of the Hindu converts out of the 'unspecified caste' category.

[173] *CMS Proceedings, 1863–1864*, p. 137.

[174] Ibid., *1870–1871*, p. 112.

year later, their Peshawar congregation was portrayed as comprised of Afghans from Kabul, Pathans from Peshawar district, Punjabis, Hindustanis, and Armenians.[175] Virtually all the missions reported some of their students or former students among their converts.

There were several prominent individuals who became part of the Punjabi Christian community during this period. One was Maulvi Imad-ud-din, baptized in 1866 and ordained in 1868, who has already been referred to as a leading CMS pastor, evangelist, and author of Christian literature for Muslims. Another was Kanwar (later Raja Sir) Harnam Singh, the second son of Maharaja Randhir Singh of Kapurthala, who had been very pro-Christian in sympathy (even attending the Punjab Missionary Conference) and was married to a Christian wife. Harnam Singh moved to Jullundur when his father died and his elder brother, Kharak Singh, succeeded to the throne. After some time, he was baptized there by Rev. Golaknath on 1 February 1874.[176] He subsequently married Golaknath's daughter, Pauline, and became an important leader of the entire Christian community, serving in the Punjab and Imperial Legislative Councils. Their children included two doctors, two administrative officers, a high court judge, Sir Maharaj Singh who was governor of Bombay 1948–52, and Rajkumari Amrit Kaur who was a personal secretary of M.K. Gandhi and the first health minister of independent India. A third prominent Christian was the Rev. Kali Charan Chatterjee, a native of Calcutta who had attended Alexander Duff's college and was baptized there in 1854. In 1861, he became headmaster of the mission school in Jullundur and a year later married Golaknath's daughter, Mary. He taught mathematics at the Mission College in Lahore from 1865 to 1868 and then was made missionary in charge of the newly established station at Hoshiarpur where he spent the rest of his life. He was an outstanding evangelist, served as president of the Hoshiarpur Municipal Committee, chaired the Forman Christian College Board of Directors for thirty years, became the first Moderator of the Presbyterian Church in India, and was one of

---

[175] Ibid., *1871–1872*, p. 114.
[176] 'Baptism of a Hindu Prince', HFMR (April 1874), p. 15.

the very few non-European delegates to the World Missionary Conference at Edinburgh in 1910.[177]

For virtually everyone who accepted it, baptism marked a decisive break from the past. Not only did the converts take on a new religious identity and way of life, but their social and economic lives were altered as well. Most were cut off from caste, clan, and family; some even had to leave their spouses and children behind. All had to bear the additional stigma of having joined the religion of foreigners who had little sympathy or respect for them.[178] Many lost property and/or work and thus either became destitute or had to find new employment upon conversion. For some, harassment and even persecution continued after conversion. For rural converts, the social boycott was often so severe that they were forced to migrate to the towns or cities to begin life anew. Some of the mission stations owned urban compounds where converts could live and create a new community life.

In one well-publicized case, converts faced prejudice and harassment not just as individuals but also as a community. When some Muslim Rajputs in the village of Ghorawaha converted, they were denied the use of the public wells they had always used until the lieutenant governor intervened to restore this right to them. The controversy then spread to Hoshiarpur where not only did two Muslim maulvies pass a sentence of excommunication and interdiction against any Muslim who drew water from wells used by Christians, but the Muslims also got the Hindus to cooperate. The Christians decided to stand firm on their right to use public wells, but other people stopped using them. In the end, some Muslim and Hindu leaders took the initiative to resolve the dispute. The matter was settled when some Hindu leaders signed a statement in favour of using the wells and then three leading maulvies issued fatwas stating that it was lawful for Muslims to eat and drink with Christians.[179]

---

[177] J.C.R. Ewing, *A Prince of the Church in India*.

[178] *CMS Proceedings, 1871–1872*, p. 108; ibid., *1875–1876*, p. 123.

[179] 'Monthly Concert—India', *FM* (April 1875), pp. 335–8; Ahmud Shah, *Risala Ezhar al-Haqq*, 1–4; *Koh-I-Nur*, 8 August 1874 in *Selections from the Vernacular*

The economic transition at baptism seems to have been as difficult as the social transition. Data is lacking on how many converts lost their sources of income upon conversion and how they managed to support themselves afterwards. In the early years when the missions were new and converts were few, almost all could be employed by the missions or missionaries. By 1857, this was more difficult, but when Sir Robert Montgomery asked the missionaries to recommend Christians for government employment, at least one regretted that none had the necessary qualifications.[180] That soon began to change[181] and as the community grew so too did the number of occupations in which Christians were engaged. In 1871, the CMS reported that of the forty-one men in their Amritsar congregation there were two agriculturalists, one contractor, one language teacher, eight domestic or mission servants, six students, three in government employ, and twenty agents in religious societies.[182] In 1880, they described their Lahore congregation as consisting 'chiefly of Government clerks and pensioners, tradesmen and others who have collected by the gravitation which draws people towards the capital of the province'.[183] In 1876, the Lodiana Mission made a study of the number and income of converts employed by the mission relative to the entire communicant membership. At their seven mission

---

Newspapers 1874, p. 315; *Rohilkhand Akhbar*, 9 September 1874 in ibid., 400–2. This was not the first time Christians had been denied water rights. In 1868 the Punjab CMS Conference had recommended 'that in any special case in which it can be clearly proved that Native Christians have been forbidden to draw water from public wells be brought to the notice of the Magistrate'. *Selections from the Proceedings of the Punjab C. M. S. Conferences 1855 to 1872 Inclusive* (Lahore 1872). See also *Church of Scotland Annual Report, 1873*, p. 126.

[180] Thomas Henry Fitzpatrick, Letter to Mr. Montgomery, 12 October 1857.

[181] In its Proceedings for 1858–9, p. 116, the CMS reported that following Montgomery's circular many Christians joined the army and some had become writers in government offices. Employment was still considered a problem at the time of the Punjab Missionary Conference and a special committee, with the lieutenant governor as patron, was set up to address this as one of its issues. *Report of the Punjab Missionary Conference*, p. 346.

[182] *CMS Proceedings, 1870–1871*, p. 112.

[183] Ibid., *1879–1880*, p. 65.

stations on the Punjab plains, there were a total of fifty-nine mission employees as compared to 144 otherwise employed, but the average income of the mission employees was slightly higher.[184] Ten years later, when writing a history of the mission, John Newton placed their converts into forty occupational categories ranging from superintendent of a large royal estate and a barrister at one end to day labourers and paupers at the other. Of these, eight to ten were in what might be described as the modern as opposed to the traditional sector of the economy.[185] All social classes from a member of the 'native aristocracy' to the very poor were represented, but the small community as a whole seemed to be predominantly urban, literate, and socially diverse.

The major enterprise begun during this period to help converts earn a living was the Christian village. The first was Scottgarh near Zafarwal in Sialkot district which the United Presbyterians began in 1867 with some relocated Christians from Sialkot. That experiment proved to be a failure; the seven families did not work and soon left. However, some rural Megh converts, who had agricultural experience and later settled there, made it a success.[186] In 1869, four prominent Indian Christians founded Clarkabad on 2000 acres of land near a canal between Lahore and Multan. They promised to settle any Christians willing to work there and to pay teachers for a school. They got the land from the government on a ten-year lease with the assurance that they could then gain title to it if they had brought it under cultivation and paid the land revenue on it. This they failed to do and after seven years the CMS took it over. They made a success of it, but Christians were a minority within the village.[187] The other was Santokh Majra, about thirty-eight miles from Karnal, which the Rev. M.M. Carlton of the Lodiana Mission bought in the 1870s and

[184] The table of station by station statistics is found in John C.B. Webster, *The Christian Community and Change*, p. 76.

[185] *Historical Sketches of the India Missions of the Presbyterian Church in the United States of America*, pp. 59–60.

[186] Andrew Gordon, *Our India Mission*, pp. 163–6, 377.

[187] Report of the Amritsar Mission 1865–68; *CMS Proceedings, 1879–1880*, p. 61; Robert Clark, *The Punjab and Sindh Missions*, pp. 84–7.

the mission took over in 1902. Initially, the land was waste and unsuitable for anything but grazing cattle. Only when canal water was provided did it become a more attractive and economically viable settlement.[188]

Even though the Christian community was thus somewhat set apart from the others by the social and economic consequences of conversion, there are several indicators which suggest that it did not immediately become an obviously westernized community. Extant photographs of students, mission workers, and prominent Christians from this period indicate that they wore Indian rather than Western clothes. Men and women tended to sit on separate sides of the church rather than together as families during public worship.[189] In fact, screens were installed in the Amritsar and Peshawar churches so that women who had observed *purdah* all their lives could still attend church services.[190] Controversy raged over whether or not men should remove their turbans during worship.[191] On the complex question of caste, caste practice was rejected in principle and the community was far too small and diverse for converts to practise caste endogamy. While no distinction was observed at the Lord's Supper, there seems to have been little social mixing or intermarriage between high- and low-caste converts.[192]

It was the missionaries who formed a caste and class apart, at least in the eyes of the English-speaking elite. This came out most forcefully during the session on 'Sympathy and Confidence of Native

[188] John C.B. Webster, *The Christian Community and Change*, p. 73.

[189] *Selections from the Proceedings of the Punjab C.M.S. Conferences 1855 to 1872 Inclusive*, (from 1871).

[190] Report of Amritsar Mission 1865–68 [in the correspondence file of Robert Clark]; *CMS Proceedings, 1876–1877*, p. 112.

[191] *Selections from the Proceedings of the Punjab C.M.S. Conferences 1855 to 1872 Inclusive*, (from 1871); William Keene, Annual Letter, 19 December 1870.

[192] This is based on a discussion among elite converts about whether inquirers who wished to practise caste should be baptized or not. Their statements reveal a certain pride in the Christian rejection of caste combined with compassion towards those who had great difficulty in giving it up. *Report of the Second Meeting of the Punjab Presbyterian Conference, held at Lahore in December 1879* (Ludhiana 1880), pp. 22–5.

Christians' at the Punjab Missionary Conference. In a presentation that was courteous, deferential, and frank, Rev. Golaknath pointed out that the missionary was in a social position and had cultural attainments so far superior to those of the native Christians that the latter could not be expected to excite much fellow feeling from the former. Converts, in turn, tended to look upon the missionary not only as a 'paid agent of a religious company' but also as a patron who is to look after their temporal well-being as well as their moral and spiritual development. He, therefore, recommended that missionaries treat converts as friends and mix with them as much as possible, that they never get angry with converts but treat them with due deliberation and impartiality. In the discussion which followed, the other converts concurred. The parent–child, or patron–client, relationship was taken for granted and was to be made friendlier. To Golaknath's mind what was at stake was the progress of Christianity itself.

...if the heathen see piety, prosperity and enterprise springing up among the despised converts, and hear them testifying, that these are the results of the teaching and care of their foreign gurus (teachers), they will at once begin to look upon the missionaries, as the real benefactors of the people and the country.[193]

The point was an important one. What attracted or repelled Punjabis about Christianity was not so much 'the message' or 'the work', which were missionary obsessions, but the quality of life they saw in the new Christian community emerging in their midst.

In fact, the power relationship between foreign missionaries and Indian converts built into the very structures through which they worked became a major issue during this period. All four missions on the Punjab plains functioned independently of, and so were not accountable to, the churches they had created. The missions made all the important policy decisions concerning the work, including the deployment of personnel and financial resources; they also recruited, trained, paid, supervised, evaluated, promoted, fired or

[193] *Report of the Punjab Missionary Conference*, pp. 171–2.

retired all mission personnel. In this they were accountable to God and to their parent mission organizations in the West.[194] Congregations had their own governing bodies, which usually included a missionary, and which could 'call' clergy to serve as their pastors only if they were able to support them financially, which only a very few could during this period. Congregations were organized into presbyteries or, in the case of the CMS, were part of the diocese of Calcutta of the Church of England, and then, in 1877, of its newly created Lahore diocese. In the dioceses, both missionaries and converts alike were completely overshadowed by the chaplains of the ecclesiastical establishment. The presbyteries in which Indian clergy and congregational representatives had voices and votes along with the missionaries, had very limited powers, usually not much more than the ordination and discipline of clergy. In the two largest missions, steps were taken to rectify this situation.

The first to do so was the Lodiana Mission. In November 1857, it invited the Rev. Golaknath to become a consultative member of the mission and then a permanent consultative member. In 1866, it voted to make him and Rev. Guru Das Maitra full members of the mission so as to remove racial distinctions between foreign and Indian missionaries, and to enhance Indian interest in and responsibility for the work of the mission.[195] However, the Board of Foreign Missions in New York turned this down. Indians then refused to attend as non-voting members.[196] Between 1870 and 1872 the mission tried again. One missionary explained that this was a grievance of the Indian Christians generally who 'look upon it as an invidious distinction due solely to the difference of colour and dictated exclusively by European pride'.[197] In 1878, it tried once more to make Indians full members of the mission and so close the widening

---

[194] The Church of Scotland had a Corresponding Board at each mission station, while the CMS had a Corresponding Committee in Calcutta (through 1877) as well as a bishop in Calcutta (after 1877 in Lahore). These served as intermediaries with their respective home boards.

[195] *Minutes of the Lodiana Mission, 1866*, p. 13.

[196] C.B. Newton, Letter to David Irving, 12 February 1870.

[197] John Newton Jr., Letter to David Irving, 24 April 1871.

gap between Indian Presbyterians and foreign missionaries, but this too failed.

The CMS took a different approach. Instead of seeking to incorporate Indians into their Mission Conference and thus share power with them, they set up a separate body to which they could transfer some of the Mission Conference's power and responsibility. This was the Native Church Council established in 1877 at the same time as the Lahore diocese. The idea first came up in 1870–1.[198] At the Mission Conference in December 1873, four Indian pastors requested the Corresponding Committee in Calcutta to state the principle according to which they were excluded from voting at Mission Conference meetings.[199] When it next met in January 1875, the Mission Conference recommended the formation of a Native Church Council and the CMS in London approved.[200] The Native Church Council included all the Indian clergy and at least two lay delegates from each recognized congregation. Robert Clark was its first chairman. Its initial responsibilities included appointing, paying, and transferring clergy connected with it as well as recommending individuals for ordination to the Mission Conference. It also discussed subjects related to the future development of the Church.[201] Initial enthusiasm for this council was high and remained so for several years. However, as with the Presbyterians, the underlying problems of subordination within the Christian community remained unresolved by these efforts at structural change.

THE PUNJAB HILLS

The picture of the Christian community in the hills is even more sketchy than that of the community on the plains. In Simla there were two congregations. The earlier one was Anglican and related

---

[198] *CMS Proceedings, 1869–1870*, p. 126 and *1870–1871*, p. 111.

[199] Proceedings of the Twelfth Conference of Church Missionaries in the Punjab at Lahore, December 13th, 14th, 15th, 16th and 17th, 1873.

[200] Eugene Stock, *The History of the Church Missionary Society. Volume III*, p. 148; Proceedings of the Thirteenth Conference of Church Missionaries in the Punjab at Umritsar, January 4th, 5th, 6th, 7th 1875.

[201] 'A Native Church for the Natives of India', pp. 3–13.

to the CMS. In 1875, it had forty-six members and was still lay led.[202] Its size fluctuated during the year, as it was greatly dependent upon the comings and goings of the European population.[203] The later congregation was Baptist, organized by the Rev. Gulzar Shah who, as a government employee, also arrived in and then left Simla when the government did. His first baptisms were a Brahmin from the hills and a young Roman Catholic.[204] His later baptisms included a few families from the plains, a widow who worked as a day labourer and her daughter who had been thrown out of her home when her husband married a second wife. In 1879, he reported that he had baptized twenty-eight people since beginning his work; of these only five were hill people and the rest were migrants. The congregation at that point had nineteen members; four recent Sikh converts who were cultivators had returned to their villages to face persecution.[205] The CMS presence in Kotgarh presented a marked contrast to the Simla congregations in that it was composed entirely of hill people, from Rajputs to Kolis, all of whom had been baptized locally. The only outsiders were the catechist and the schoolmaster.[206]

The hill congregation for which the most information is available was in Chamba. Two principles of its founder, Rev. Ferguson, made this section of the Christian community somewhat distinctive. The first was that converts had to rely on their own resources and not those of the missionaries for a livelihood, to build self-respect among the members as much as to promote self-support among the congregations. The other was that as Christianity was a religion of the heart and caste was a matter of social standing, it was not necessary to break caste upon conversion.[207] This second principle

[202] *CMS Proceedings, 1874–1875*, p. 96.

[203] Ibid., *1878–1879*, p. 63.

[204] 'A Native Missionary's Work at Simla', *BM* (October 1869), p. 682.

[205] 'Address at the Baptism of Five Converts at Simla, August 7th 1870', *MH* (September 1871), pp. 148–9; 'A Baptismal Scene in the Himalayas', ibid. (December 1875), p. 236; 'Baptism at Simla', ibid. (September 1878), p. 222; 'Baptism at Simla NWP', ibid. (January 1879), pp. 23–4; *Baptist Annual Report, 1879*, p. 77.

[206] *CMS Proceedings, 1873–1874*, p. 95.

[207] 'Missionary Meeting at Meerut', *HFMR* (June 1870), pp. 56–7.

had almost immediate repercussions. Virtually all the converts in Chamba were Chamars and Duminas (basket weavers), whose caste fellows were not of one mind about allowing them to share in the Lord's Supper with Christians of other castes, but did forbid interdining with Christians from castes considered inferior to their own.[208] On their side the church elders tried to solve the problem by allowing 'individual communion', but in 1876 returned to using common bread and a common cup.[209] That same year one of the elders 'participated in heathen ceremonies' at his daughter's wedding; while he was not excommunicated for this, he was removed from office.[210] In 1880, one of the elders, Sohun Lal, was ordained as pastor.[211]

There were as yet only a very few Christians in either Lahaul or Kashmir. The Moravians had baptized only six Ladakhis at Kyelang by 1868[212] and their congregation remained small. In Kashmir, baptism was almost impossible. Two Kashmiri Muslim shawl-makers were baptized secretly in 1868[213] but there was no resident Christian community to speak of. The mission's Kashmiri assistants, who had been baptized elsewhere, came and went with the missionaries each spring and autumn.[214]

Conclusions

Christianity in north-west India had a tentative, exploritory quality about it in the years prior to 1857. It then emerged very quickly from that crisis with a profound sense of divine vindication and vocation. The earlier insecurities seemed to vanish, to be replaced by a sense of self-confidence and even 'masterfulness'. This was the period *par*

[208] Ibid. See also, 'Chumba Mission', ibid. (August 1873), p. 446.

[209] 'Foreign Missions', ibid. (May 1876), pp. 26–7; *Church of Scotland Annual Report, 1876*, p. 135.

[210] Ibid., *1876*, p. 135 and *1877*, p. 127.

[211] Ibid., *May 1880*, p. 79.

[212] 'Mission Work in Kunawar, Lahul, &c.', *CMI* (September 1868), p. 286.

[213] 'The Wrongs of Cashmere', ibid. (December 1868), p. 371.

[214] They were borrowed from the Lodiana Mission which did not do work in Kashmir. The Fifth Annual Report of the Kashmir Medical Mission Established 1865, Extract for 1869.

excellence of the white male Evangelical. Whether in the service of the state or of the church, he dominated the scene with his energy, competence, and self-assurance. His authority was unquestioned and he had convinced himself that he not only knew what was best for the people but had also won their confidence. Whether he had actually engaged the religious spirit of his age any better than his pre-1857 predecessors had is an open question, but he believed that he represented the wave of the future, most obviously in educating the new generation of leadership, but even in religion as well. By the end of the period he considered the religions of the north-west to be no longer viable options, kept alive only by the force of prejudice and habit.[215] This aura of invincibility, undoubtedly due in good part to the internalization of the colonial guardian mentality, was most obvious in such conspicuous carry-overs from the earlier period as James Smith in Delhi, Charles Forman in Lahore, Robert Clark in Amritsar, and T.V. French on the frontier and then in Lahore, but seemed to characterize the mission enterprise as a whole. It even rubbed off on some of the leading Indian protagonists of Christianity in the north-west: Ram Chandra, Imad-ud-Din, Golaknath, K.C. Chatterjee, Muhammad Ishmael in Gujarat, and Elisha Swift in Sialkot.

It is less easy to generalize about the Indian Christian community during this period. It was diverse and was no longer drawing its members solely from the various margins of society. While still very small, it had grown twenty-fold in just over twenty years. The sources indicate that by the very act of conversion, converts were treated as scoundrels by their caste and clan fellow. These sources also testify to the extraordinary courage required to become a Christian in those days. Not only did one stand to lose all of one's family and economic

---

[215] Robert Clark put it this way in 1878: 'Mohammedan and Hindu objections to Christianity have been fully answered; and Christianity (instead of Mohammedanism) now stands forward in the eyes of many learned, earnest, thoughtful Natives as being unassailable. The arguments of Christianity against Mohammedanism and Hinduism are those which now remain unanswered. India's own sons and daughters have laid hold on Truth with a grasp, which they will not quit.' *CMS Proceedings, 1877–1878*, p. 113.

resources, but one had to meet and continue to live up to the expectations of foreign missionaries as well.

Three particularly vivid glimpses of the self-presentation of Indian Christians during this period perhaps offer the best insights into the subjectivity of the community. The first is in the Indian contributions to the discussions of missionary–convert relationships at the Punjab Missionary Conference at the end of 1862. In these the convert is portrayed as subordinate and even dependent not only for salary (if a mission employee) but especially for respect, kindness, friendship, and help from 'superiors' very different from themselves. They were thus very sensitive to the good and bad opinions missionaries held of them as well as to the kind of treatment they received from the missionaries.[216] A second glimpse is offered by the address that the Native Christians of the Punjab presented to the Prince of Wales during a reception for him at the Mission House in Amritsar on 24 January 1876. There they presented a public image of themselves as a very diverse group, grateful for the blessings received from missionaries and a government committed to religious liberty, and desirous of spreading the Word of God throughout the region.[217] The third is a brief recitation, written in 1880, of his own and his wife's pastoral duties to thirty-one Christian families in Clarkabad by the Rev. Daud Singh, an early convert but now an old man.

The work of me, Daud Singh, is this: to hold daily service with the people, and to take two services on Sundays; to care for the sick and needy, and comfort and help them as much as I can; to settle disputes, and make peace again; and to give instruction to inquirers. And my wife's work is this: every day to collect the women, and teach them the Bible and hymns; to settle and heal every sort of quarrel which occurs among the women; to visit house by house; and to help and comfort the poor families as far as she can; to tend the sick; and to teach female inquirers.[218]

[216] *Report of the Punjab Missionary Conference*, pp. 166–83.
[217] A Translation from the Urdu Language of a Humble Address Presented to His Royal Highness Albert Edward Prince of Wales at Umritsar, Punjab 24th January 1876 from the Native Christians of the Punjab.
[218] 'Punjab and Sindh Mission', *CMI* (October 1880), p. 637.

While quite ordinary and routine, this simple statement of 'duty' does suggest that by the end of this period Indian Christians in the north-west had a pattern of community life of their own.

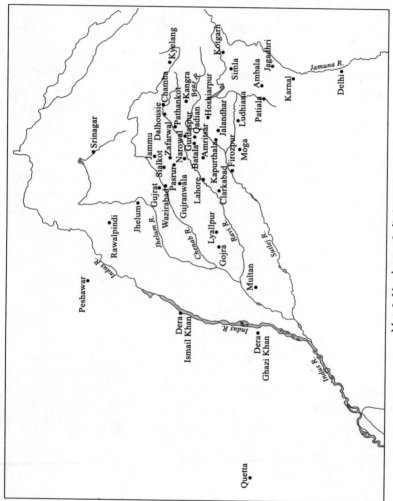

Map 2: North-west India in 1900

Source: Author.

4 The North-west in Ferment: 1881–1918

Beginning in the early 1880s, Christianity entered a new phase of its history in north-west India. This was due in part to developments internal to Christianity itself. New missionary societies entered the region and began work alongside those who had been there for decades. The Church of England Zenana Missionary Society (CEZMS), the Zenana Bible and Medical Mission,[1] the Methodist Episcopal Church, the Salvation Army, and the Seventh Day Adventists were fellow Protestants. The Roman Catholics, who had not been engaged with the Indian population of the north-west since the century began,[2] now directed some of their attention towards them following the establishment of the hierarchy in 1886. In addition, there was such a huge influx of single women missionaries into the north-west for 'women's work for women' that by the end of this period they greatly outnumbered the men. Finally, this was for Christianity in the north-west a period of unprecedented growth and expansion that has not been equalled since then.

Perhaps even more important to the future history of Christianity were the developments taking place within north-west Indian society itself. Some of the long-term effects of earlier British innovations were now becoming visible and producing a ferment in the region's urban and rural areas. In the cities there was a critical mass of men who had received a Western education and were beginning both to shape and to organize Indian public opinion. In the villages the unanticipated consequences of the early British land revenue

[1] In 1880, the non-denominational Indian Female Normal School Society, which was already in the Punjab, split into the Anglican CEZMS and non-denominational Zenana Bible and Medical Mission.

[2] Fr Emmerich Blondeel, *A Short History of the Catholic Diocese of Lahore*, pp. 4, 6. Christopher Harding has provided extensive details on the deployment of mission personnel within the diocese. 'The Dynamics of Low-Caste Conversion Movements', pp. 124–30.

settlements as well as the creation of new canal colonies in the western Punjab generated a degree of mobility and unrest not witnessed earlier in the century. Christians and Christianity had helped to produce some of this ferment and were now to be profoundly affected by it. They were challenged and even put on the defensive in the cities by the very Western-educated elite they had helped to create, while in the villages they faced unprecedented opportunities that pushed them beyond their urban bias and urban base. In this new context whatever 'Evangelical Entente' between officials and missionaries had existed earlier vanished from sight. Evangelical officials were far less conspicuous than previously[3] and the religious problems with which the government was now confronted made such an entente inexpedient. In the emerging religio-political situation Christians had to make their way on their own. Because this changing context is so important to the history of Christianity during this period, it requires further description.

The Changing Context

At the outset of this period the entire north-west was under the jurisdiction of the Government of the Punjab. The Punjab had been created as a non-regulation province run entirely by officialdom, and that continued to be the case even after it became a regulation province in 1866. Its government co-opted key figures in the towns and countryside whom it appointed as local officials or to district and municipal committees. Only in 1883–4 were elections to these committees held, but their powers remained very limited. The Punjab Legislative Council, established in 1897, had no elected members and very limited advisory influence. The Government of India Act of 1909 introduced the elective principle (five of the twenty-five members of the Punjab Legislative Council were to be elected) and allowed more scope for discussing and moving resolutions, but retained the lieutenant governor's autocratic powers. The Act also

---

[3] Only two of the lieutenant governors of the Punjab from 1870 through 1918 were staunch Evangelicals: Sir Charles Aitchison (1882–7) and Sir William Mackworth Young (1897–1902).

granted separate electorates to Muslims as a distinct political 'interest', an action that would have a profound effect upon not only the political but also the religious life of the region. In addition, the Government of India divided up the region's unified administrative structure. In 1901, it created the North-West Frontier Province out of the settled districts and the tribal belt on the frontier. After the viceroy announced that Delhi would become the new capital of India in 1911, the 'Delhi Enclave' was separated from the Punjab and made into a distinct political and administrative unit.

The most conspicuous sign of ferment in the region during this period was the proliferation of activist religious organizations throughout its major urban centres. The religious controversies of the previous decades had done much to heighten the sense of religious identity, especially among the urban elites.[4] In apparent imitation of the Christian missions, Hindus, Muslims, and Sikhs created *samaj*s, *anjuman*s, and *sabha*s to articulate, redefine, defend, inculcate, and spread their respective faiths through preaching, the dissemination of religious literature, and the creation of schools.[5] In seeking to win the religious and ideological loyalties of the population, these new religious associations came into direct competition and even conflict not just with the Christian missions but also, and even more importantly, with each other. They also gave shape to the emerging politics of the region during this and the subsequent periods of its history.

Four associations played pioneering roles, were imitated, and then superceded by other, more dynamic bodies. These were the Brahmo Samaj (1863), the Anjuman-i-Punjab (1865), the Anjuman-i-Islamia (1869), and the Amritsar Singh Sabha (1873).[6] However, with the

---

[4] See John C.B. Webster, *The Christian Community and Change*, pp. 121–2.

[5] This organizational revolution in Punjabi religious life is what Brush called 'Protestantization'.

[6] Historians have attributed the Singh Sabha's formation to a 'Christian threat', which Barrier described as the persistent challenge, posed by Western and more specifically Christian learning, to traditional Sikh theology and custom. Oberoi saw this in terms of an immediate crisis—four Sikh students in Amritsar were planning to convert—which provoked the Sikh leadership to form the Sabha. I

founding of the Arya Samaj by Swami Dayanand Saraswati at Lahore in 1877 religio-cultural change entered a new, more assertive and combative phase. What Swami Dayanand and the Arya Samaj set forth was a monotheistic faith, based on the Vedas as an authoritative scripture, that laid emphasis upon the active moral life as a means of salvation which, as Lala Lajpat Rai, one of its earliest and most famous members, pointed out, appealed to a budding religious nationalism among educated middle-class Hindus.[7] The Arya Samaj took upon itself the twin responsibilities of reforming Hinduism from within and defending it from Christian and Muslim inroads. It not only engaged in religious controversy but also took steps to reconvert those who had left Hinduism and to raise the status of the low castes through *shuddhi* (purification) ceremonies. In addition, the Arya Samaj played an active role in opening schools and in providing a distinctly Hindu nationalist ideology for the struggle against British rule.

This more assertive, militant spirit became characteristic of some other religious associations as well. The Lahore Singh Sabha, founded in 1879, unlike its predecessor in Amritsar, argued that Sikhism was a distinct religion and emphasized the difference between the teachings of the Sikh gurus and current Sikh religiosity. It soon won the support of almost all the other Singh Sabhas and, in 1902, united with the Amritsar Singh Sabha to form the Chief Khalsa Diwan. The Singh Sabhas concentrated their energies primarily upon publication and education, and the Lahore or *Tat Khalsa* (True Khalsa) view of Sikhism came to prevail within the community. In like

---

have not found any reference to these four boys in the printed records or correspondence of the missionaries at Amritsar. Had they in fact converted, this would surely have been mentioned. N. Gerald Barrier, 'The Singh Sabha Movement 1875–1925', in Harish K. Puri and Paramjit S. Judge (eds), *Social and Political Movements: Readings on Punjab*, p. 61; Harjot Oberoi, *The Construction of Religious Boundaries*, p. 218.

[7] Lajpat Rai, *The Arya Samaj*, p. 258. Kenneth Jones saw the appeal of the Arya Samaj in its capacity to address the cultural alienation of middle-caste Punjabi Hindus, *Arya Dharm*, pp. xii–xiii, 3–6, 29, 40–50, and Jordens in the justification for Khatri religious leadership it provided. J.T.F. Jordens, *Dayanand Saraswati*, pp. 181–2.

manner, the Anjuman-i-Himayat-i-Islam formed at Lahore in 1884, with units established elsewhere soon afterwards, defended Muslim interests, published tracts in defence of Islam against its rivals, and established a number of educational institutions for Muslim youth. A Muslim anjuman with roots in the north-west was Mirza Ghulam Ahmad's Sadr Anjuman Ahmadiyya. In 1891 he claimed that he was the *mahdi* and messiah foretold in the Jewish, Christian, and Muslim scriptures. In 1904, he claimed to be also an *avatar* of Krishna, thus fulfilling the hopes of Hindus as well as of Muslims and Christians. These claims attracted both followers and severe opposition from Christians, Hindus, and especially Muslims.[8]

As this description indicates, these new revitalization and defence organizations did not agree on what authentic Hinduism, Islam, or Sikhism was, and none had won all its own co-religionists to their respective visions. Each was at best a 'community-in-the-making', seeking to redefine its own religious tradition vis-à-vis the others. This gave to the newly organized religious activism of the period a distinctly competitive, at times hostile and combative, thrust,[9] which carried over into in the political arena when the Punjab government increased opportunities for Indian involvement in decision-making beyond mere petitions and public outcries. Political organization in the north-west throughout this period tended to be communally based. The Indian National Congress, which sought to be the voice of Indians of all religions, remained largely ineffectual there. In 1906, when the viceroy gave his support to the principle of separate electorates for Muslims, members of the urban Hindu elite formed the Punjab Hindu Sabha to protect their political interests. In 1907, Muslims formed the Punjab Muslim League. The Chief Khalsa Diwan led the Sikh agitation for separate electorates until 1919 when the Central Sikh League was formed. In the face of pervasive

[8] Spencer Lavan, *The Ahmadiyah Movement*.

[9] This can be seen in the treatment of other religions in Swami Dayanand's *Satyarth Prakash*, in Mirza Ghulam Ahmad's debates with Pandit Lekh Ram, and in the Arya Samaj's decision to perform shuddhi on thirty low-caste Sikhs in 1900. Durga Prasad, *Light of Truth*, pp. 355–8, 460–562; Spencer Lavan, *The Ahmadiyah Movement*, pp. 64–6, 74–87; Kenneth W. Jones, *Arya Dharm*, pp. 207–10.

communal competition for power and advantage during the late 1880s, the Punjab government abandoned its earlier policy of hiring, co-opting or otherwise rewarding people without regard to religion, and sought instead to balance the competing claims made on behalf of the Hindu, Sikh, and Muslim communities.[10] This led in 1909 to granting Muslims separate electorates and in 1919 to giving them to Sikhs as well.

The ferment in the countryside was of a different sort. When the British annexed the Punjab, they sought to make lenient land settlements with the cultivators, but these proved over time to be both too high and too inflexible to prevent cultivators from falling into debt and losing their land to urban moneylenders. As the number and size of alienated landholdings increased to crisis proportions, the government enacted the Punjab Land Alienation Act of 1900 to prohibit the transfer of landownership from 'agricultural' to 'non-agricultural' castes. This did not solve the problem of rural indebtedness but it did enhance the insecurity of village menials who were already being forced out of traditional patron–client relationships into short-term contractual employment.[11] The Land Alienation Act did not classify menials as 'agricultural castes', even though they provided much of the agricultural labour and in some cases were tenants or small landholders, and so prevented them from acquiring agricultural land. Thus, their interests, like those of the urban Hindu moneylenders, were sacrificed to the interests of the 'agricultural castes' whose loyalty the British were eager to maintain.

The other major source of rural ferment was the opening up of canal colonies on vast tracts of wasteland in western Punjab, which the government had taken over and then sold off under carefully prescribed conditions. The government gave preference to the peasant cultivator castes of the central Punjab for purchasing land in these newly irrigated tracts and declared the menial castes ineligible to acquire such land. Of course, menials could move to the canal

---

[10] N. Gerald Barrier, 'The Punjab Government and Communal Politics, 1870–1908', pp. 523–39.

[11] On the menials see Himadri Bannerjee, *Agrarian Society of the Punjab 1849–1901*, pp. 175–200.

colonies either with their landowner patrons or on their own to take advantage of the higher wages being offered there.[12]

In 1906, the Punjab government not only tightened the regulations and enhanced the discretionary power of government officers in the canal colonies but also increased the water rates in the central Punjab area fed by the Bari Doab canal. These actions led to mass protest meetings and discontent among recruits in the Indian army who came from the affected districts. This agitation, in which rural Punjabis of all religions united, drew support from an urban press grown increasingly critical of the highly paternalistic Punjab government. The government, after responding initially with strong action against those it considered guilty of 'sedition', backed down and the agitation subsided. However, for the remainder of this period, and especially during World War I, the Punjab government remained ever watchful of any challenges to its paternal wisdom and authority.[13]

Despite growing anti-British and anti-Western sentiment, the people of north-west India were not in a position to challenge British rule effectively. They had begun the process of political mobilization on a communal rather than nationalist basis, in pursuit of communal rather than broadly national objectives in the urban areas and in a more ad hoc fashion around economic issues in the villages. At this stage they seemed more interested in competing with each other for power and influence within the framework of the Raj than in overthrowing the Raj itself. Nonetheless, the fact of change, the prospects of change, and the fear of change during this period enabled Christianity to engage north-west Indian society at deeper levels than previously. It had acquired too much cultural prestige to be ignored

[12] Imran Ali, 'Canal Colonization and Socio-Economic Change', in Indu Banga (ed.), *Five Punjabi Centuries*, pp. 341–57.

[13] N. Gerald Barrier, 'The Punjab Disturbances of 1907: the Response of the British Government in India to Agrarian Unrest', *The Panjab Past and Present*, VIII (October 1974), pp. 444–76; Satya M. Rai, 'Agrarian Movement in the Punjab 1906–09: The Role of Lala Lajpat Rai and Sardar Ajit Singh', *Punjab History Conference Eighth Session Proceedings December 15–16, 1973*, Patiala: Punjabi University, 1975, pp. 132–47.

and was better equipped to address some of the social questions facing north-west Indian society in general than it had been earlier. Those sections of society with which its engagement was most intense were the urban elites, (predominantly urban) women, and rural Dalits. Each of these will be examined in turn before analysing the evolving and expanding Christian community of this period.

The Urban Elites

North-west India was overwhelmingly rural throughout this period. In 1881, the population of its three largest cities—Delhi, Lahore, and Amritsar—was very small by present-day standards (173,393, 157,287, and 150,665 respectively) and only 12.65 per cent of the population of the region was urban.[14] In the ensuing years both the urban and the rural population grew in size, but the urban percentage of the total population remained below 12 per cent.[15] Moreover, urban growth was uneven: high in Delhi, Lahore, and Sialkot, but negligible in Amritsar and Ludhiana.[16] Thus the north-west was not highly urbanized nor did it experience significant urbanization during this period.

However, at the outset of this period, the Christian missions and Christian community of the north-west were based in the urban areas. There was at least one Christian mission station in each major city as well as in almost every district headquarters of the north-west.[17] This predominantly urban institutional base continued to expand and develop, even as institutions and organizations created by the new religious associations sprang up all around them. The resulting level of persistent religious competition and conflict was greater than what Christians had experienced before. Of all their rivals, the Arya Samaj posed the most serious challenge.

[14] *Punjab Census 1881*, I, p. 17.

[15] *Punjab Census 1891*, II, Table I; *Punjab Census 1901*, II, Table I; *Punjab Census 1911*, II, Table I.

[16] *Punjab Census 1881*, I, pp. 514–5; *Punjab Census 1911*, I, p. 15; II, Table IV.

[17] A list of nineteenth-century Christian mission stations and their institutions is given in John C. B. Webster, 'Mission Sources of Nineteenth-Century Punjab History', pp. 215–8.

The Arya Samaj challenged Christianity on the very terms which Christians themselves had laid down during the preceding decades. At the institutional level, the Arya Samaj established their own schools as alternatives to the mission and government schools already in existence. It also took the lead in organizing the Hindu Orphan Relief Movement during the famines of 1897–1902.[18] The Arya Samaj also challenged Christians at the theological level, adopting in its newspapers, tracts, pamphlets, and books a style of argumentation that Christians themselves had popularized. Just as Christians had used 'Christian Evidences' to support their claims to the truth, so now the Arya Samajis used a list of 'Arya Evidences' to support theirs. These 'evidences' assumed that the Vedas were given at creation; that natural revelation is inherently superior to historical revelation; and that miracles (a standard Christian 'evidence') were not merely unacceptable as evidence of truth but a sign of weakness as well, because they stood in opposition to the teachings of modern science.[19]

Perhaps the most significant Christian response to the Arya Samaj challenge was simply to persevere. Arya Samaj agitators disrupted evangelistic meetings.[20] Its press attacked Christian motivations, moral superiority, and the rightness of their cause.[21] Christian schools lost students when the Arya Samaj opened up rival institutions. At the theological level, one can discern two types of Christian response to the Arya Samaj. One was simply to carry on the debate both by responding to Arya Samaj arguments and by attacking the authority of the Vedas. The most prolific debater of this type was the Rev. T. Williams, an SPG missionary in Rewari who read the Vedas in Sanskrit and used that to argue that the Arya Samaj had built 'their house

---

[18] On famine relief, see John C.B. Webster, *The Christian Community and Change*, pp. 179–84.

[19] For a much fuller account, see John C.B. Webster, '"Arya Evidences"—A Study of Christian Influence', pp. 1–19.

[20] See, for example, *CMS Proceedings 1889*, p. 117.

[21] See, for example, 'Christian Missionaries in India', *The Arya Patrika, Lahore* (16 March 1883), p. 4; *Arya Gazette*, 1 February 1893 cited in *Punjab Press Reports 1893*, p. 73.

upon a foundation of sand'.[22] Williams's style was highly combative, being aimed at seeking out and exploiting weak spots in order to vanquish opponents.[23] The other type of Christian response was best represented by Dr H.D. Griswold, an American Presbyterian professor at Forman Christian College in Lahore from 1894 to 1914, who had studied Sanskrit at Oxford and Vedic Religion under Max Weber in Berlin. Unlike earlier missionaries, Griswold was well schooled not only in the new historical critical methods of studying ancient sacred texts but also in the new field of comparative religion. His differences with Swami Dayanand and the Arya Samaj were, therefore, as much methodological as religious, which complicated the issues at stake. While quite critical on technical grounds of the Arya Samajis' interpretation of the Vedas, he was also judiciously fair in his treatment of them and genuinely appreciative of what they were attempting to do.[24]

As Griswold's work suggests, all was not rivalry and combat between Christians and the Arya Samaj during this period. Before it was over, Christians were being invited to address Arya Samaj meetings and reporting favourably upon the experience.[25] They were also writing excitedly about the 'new India' the Arya Samaj had helped create as well as about the fresh challenges it offered to Christian missions.[26] The Arya Samaj had demonstrated that Hindu religion was, contrary to earlier missionary assessments, capable of revitalization and change. This new 'ground reality' as well as the new theological liberalism in which he was trained in the West, led

---

[22] 'Rewari', *MF* (October 1887), p. 312.

[23] See his 'Exposure of the Character of the Yajur Veda', *MF* (August 1891), pp. 295–301 and his *Exposure of Dayanand Saraswati and his Followers*.

[24] See H.D. Griswold, *The Dayanandi Interpretation of the Word 'Deva' in the Rig Veda*, Lodiana, 1897 and 'The Arya Samaj', *Report of the Fourth Decennial Indian Missionary Conference Held in Madras December 11th–18th, 1902*, London: Christian Literature Society, 1903, pp. 312–35.

[25] Ibid., p. 73; J. J. Johnson, 'Conferences with Hindu and Aryan Pandits', *CMI* (July 1907), p. 418; S.S. Allnutt, 'A Brush with the Aryas', *DMN* (July 1909), pp. 140–1; *CMS Proceedings 1910*, p. 140.

[26] Griswold himself wrote a lot about new religious movements current in north India and J.N. Farquhar used much of Griswold's work in his well-known *Modern Religious Movements in India*.

Griswold and others like him to change their apologetic for Christianity. Instead of juxtaposing Christianity as true and Hindu religion as false, they offered a much more positive assessment of Hinduism's moral and spiritual power, but at the same time argued that only in Christ would religious aspirations nurtured in Hindu religion find their own proper fulfilment.[27]

Christian religious interaction with Muslims during this period resembled in many respects their interaction with the Arya Samaj. Muslim students were withdrawn from Christian schools when Muslim educational institutions were established[28] and Christians faced attacks in the Muslim press as well as periods of severe Muslim opposition in many cities. However, public controversy played an unusual prominent role in Christian–Muslim relations. This took the form of formal public debate and of running arguments through pamphlets, tracts, and books in which writers sought to advance their own new evidence or new lines of reasoning and respond to those produced by the other side. In 1893, in a paper written for the World Parliament of Religions, the Rev. Imad-ud-Din, a leading figure in these controversies, wrote of the stimulus and increased knowledge they had provided. 'So the hidden things of various faiths have been thoroughly brought to light. It is not necessary for Christians or Mohammedans now to engage in further controversy. All about Mohammedanism that it was necessary to say has been said, and whatever Mohammedans could do against Christianity they have done to the utmost.'[29] This judgement was obviously premature but it is indicative of how thorough and conscientious each side was.

---

[27] For example, H.D. Griswold, *The Religion of the Rigveda*, pp. 357–64, 373–5. For more on Griswold, see John C.B. Webster, *The Christian Community and Change*, pp. 98–102.

[28] In an unusual case of this kind, the missionaries in Peshawar felt obligated to protest against undue Government favouritism towards the newly established Islamia College there; redress was given and enrolment at Edwardes College picked up afterwards. *CMS Proceedings 1914–1915*, pp. 116–7.

[29] 'Dr. Imad-ud-Din's Paper for Chicago', *CMI* (August 1893), p. 583. A decade later the Rev. S. Ghose in Delhi wrote that the old 'Mahommedan Controversy' had run its course and people were tired of hearing the same old arguments being put forth on both sides. 'Mahommedan Controversy', *DMN* (April 1902), pp. 73–4.

The tone of these controversies varied considerably. The SPG built Bickersteth Hall in Delhi for public religious debates, discussions, and lectures. George Lefroy reported in 1891 that he had participated in a series of debates at the Fatehpuri Mosque, one of the largest in Delhi, in which each side spoke on the day's topic in half-hour turns over a three-hour period. These weekly debates drew large attentive crowds and no one was declared victor or vanquished.[30] Subsequent reports from Delhi indicate that this pattern continued for another decade or two.[31] In 1893, a twelve-day debate of considerable notoriety took place in Amritsar. Abdullah Athim, an active pamphleteer and Muslim convert to Christianity, and Mirza Ghulam Ahmad of Qadian covered such topics as the relative superiority of the Bible and Quran, the divinity of Christ, the prophethood of Muhammad, and generated widespread interest. At the close of the debate, Mirza Ghulam Ahmad indicated that God would give a sign vindicating the true prophethood of Muhammad: Abdullah Athim, who was already elderly and infirm, would die within fifteen months unless he 'turned to the truth'. When Athim survived the fifteen months, the Christian community celebrated its victory while Mirza Ghulam Ahmad stated that Athim had 'turned to the truth' because he had not spoken or written publicly against Islam during that entire period.[32]

It is difficult to discern any major shifts or innovations in the ways Christians came to approach their religious encounter with Muslims by the end of this period. The writings of E. Morris Wherry, an American Presbyterian missionary specializing in 'The Muslim Controversy', reveal only refinements in the positions Christians had been taking.[33] Wherry's basic method was to argue on the basis of

[30] 'Delhi', *MF* (September 1891), pp. 325–9.

[31] See G.A. Purton, 'Mahommedan Views of the Death of Christ', *DMN* (July 1906), pp. 139–40; Maulvie Ahmad Masih, 'Religious Discussions with Educated Mahommedans in Delhi and Agra', ibid. (July 1907), pp. 36–7.

[32] See H. Martyn Clark, 'A Controversy with Mohammedans', *CMI* (February 1894), pp. 96–105; Spencer Lavan, *The Ahmadiyah Movement*, pp. 67–70.

[33] Compare E.M. Wherry, 'The Sinless Prophet of Islam', *The Indian Evangelical Review*, VI (April 1879), pp. 283–90 with E.M. Wherry, 'Some Unfounded Muslim Claims', *North Indian Conference of Christian Workers 1911*, pp. 36–49.

the Quran itself for the claims of Christ over against those of Muhammad. He used a literal, rather than historical critical, approach to both scriptures and found irreconcilable differences between them. Even in his later writings, he saw Muslim reform movements as ultimately undermining rather than transforming Islam, for Islam was, in his view, set in a fixed, unchangeable mould.[34] What had changed over the decades was neither Christianity nor Islam but the strategy and spirit of Christian evangelists in presenting their gospel to Muslims.[35]

Christians did not give the same serious attention to Sikhism that they gave to Hinduism and Islam, perhaps because the number of urban Sikhs was relatively low or because they were uncertain about Sikhism's future as a distinctive religion.[36] For their part, Sikh reformers seemed less concerned about the Christians than about threats from other quarters. Nevertheless, there were some Sikh tracts that were essentially defensive in nature, aimed at warning Sikhs against the missionaries and their message,[37] although missionaries were also held up as models of religious commitment in the Sikh press.[38] One tract made an empathetic comparison of Jesus Christ and Guru Nanak. It found Guru Nanak to be superior because his teachings were less ascetic and thus better suited to the general run of humanity, and because he was less confrontational in

[34] E.M. Wherry, 'Islam in North India', *The Mohammedan World of Today*, New York: Fleming H. Revell Company, 1906, p. 157; E.M. Wherry, *Islam and Christianity in India and the Far East*, pp. 190–1.

[35] Ibid., p. 145. For more on Wherry, see John C.B. Webster, *The Christian Community and Change*, pp. 102–3.

[36] On the latter point see C.W. Forman, 'Who are the Sikhs?', *FM* (November 1882), p. 256; J.F.W. Youngson, *Forty Years of the Panjab Mission of the Church of Scotland*, p. 50.

[37] One of these was *Iswi Prabodh*. Another, *Padrian de Wade*, is referred to and summarized by Guildford in *CMS Proceedings for 1896–97*, p. 227. A report of a more polemical exchange is given in the *Khalsa Sewak* of 30 April 1913 in *Native Press Reports Punjab, 1913*, pp. 445–6.

[38] See Chander Mani Khanna and John C.B. Webster, 'Views of Christianity and Christians in the Sikh Press, 1897–1930', *BCISS* 5 (January 1976), pp. 5–12.

trying to get his message across.[39] That appears to be about as deep as the religious encounter became during this period.

As the preceding paragraphs indicate, Christians in the north-west were now facing a new and much more challenging religious situation. The missionaries could no longer describe the religions of the region as so moribund, so dependent upon superstition and dead habit for their continued survival, that they must inevitably give way to Christianity. All these religions had withstood the challenges of Christian evangelism and Western learning; they were now showing signs of great vitality, entering into the controversies of the day with fresh insight, skill, and confidence. This was apparent not only in theological debates but also in the educational and social service work the new religious associations were undertaking. By the 1890s, revitalized religion was providing an ideological and organizational basis not only for cultural renewal and modernization in the urban north-west, but also for the new politics of representative participation made possible by constitutional changes the government had instituted. As a result, Christians now had to address a religio-cultural nationalism that portrayed Christianity as a foreign religion, accepting which was considered 'unIndian'.

It seems that Christians in Lahore and Delhi were the first to recognize that they were living in a 'new India', that the religious situation had changed, and that they had now to find new ways of responding to it.[40] What these Christian spokespersons did was to develop a new apologetic for Christianity not only to counter the stereotype of Christianity as a 'foreign religion' but also to take seriously the new religious and political nationalism of north-west India that they themselves either shared or identified with. They sought to develop a 'Christian nationalism' by asking what the moral and spiritual foundations of the 'new India' ought to be and by

[39] S. Thakar Singh, *Comparison of Guru Nanak with Jesus Christ.*

[40] See C.F. Andrews, 'The Religious Unrest of Northern India', *CMI* (October 1905), pp. 739–41; Surendra Kumar Datta, *The Desire of India*; S.K. Datta, 'Christ the Fulfilment of India's Need', *Madras Christian College Magazine* (December 1910), p. 7; H.D. Griswold, 'Review of the Last Decade in the History of the Punjab Mission (1901–1910)'; S.K. Rudra, 'Religious Changes in India During the British Period', *EW*, XI (July 1913), pp. 290–307.

assuming that religion would have to provide those foundations. They then evaluated the religious options available in the north-west, less in terms of their relative truth or falsity (as in the past), than in terms of their adequacy in meeting the moral and spiritual requirements of the 'new India'. They found that the existing religions, while having much good in them, were fundamentally flawed in this respect; they believed that only Jesus Christ Himself, the fulfilment of India's religious aspirations, could provide those foundations. At the same time, they also recognized that the Christian Church in India would have to undergo some major changes in order to bear faithful witness to that fact. The result was some serious rethinking and experimentation in the years leading up to World War I.

Traditional methods of evangelism came under scrutiny for being culturally too Western; the Church would now have to make a more authentically Indian witness in the confidence that 'the ultimate victory of Christianity [is] certain if only the Person of Christ Himself is raised high before the eyes of India without any intervening Western medium'.[41] Two Indian innovations in Christian witness near the end of this period sought to do this. One was the National Missionary Society, founded in 1905, which had a Punjab Committee made up of members of the educated Indian Christian elite. It appointed John Williams, a graduate of Forman Christian College, as its first missionary in the Punjab to work in Montgomery district in conjunction with the CMS. Sadhu Sundar Singh, who grew up in Rampur village near Ludhiana, provided the other innovation. A year after a life-changing vision of Christ when he was fifteen years old, Sundar Singh was baptized in September 1905 and immediately became a sadhu. While there had been Christian faqirs and sadhus before him, Sundar Singh was the first in the north-west to appeal to educated urban people. He spent much of his time during this period wandering in the Himalayas, but his travel diary was extracted regularly in the Christian newspaper, *Nur Afshan*, and this created considerable interest in educated circles.[42]

[41] S.K. Rudra, 'Religious Changes in India During the British Period', p. 307.

[42] A.J. Appasamy, *Sundar Singh: A Biography*, pp. 19–91.

Rethinking Christian involvement in education showed signs of a similar sensitivity to the requirements of a 'new India'. Christians were prominent and invested heavily in the field of education. Christian schools both increased in number and were upgraded during this period. In 1881, the SPG added a college department to their St. Stephen's school in Delhi. The Presbyterians started a college in Lahore on a permanent basis in 1886 which they named after Charles W. Forman after his death in 1894. In like manner, in 1893, the United Presbyterians added a college department to their school in Rawalpindi and named it after the founder of their mission, Andrew Gordon. The Church of Scotland started Murray College in Sialkot in 1909 and the CMS started Edwardes College in Peshawar in 1910 by adding to and upgrading their schools in those places. In addition to this impressive institutional presence, individual Christians continued to occupy prominent positions within the educational system as a whole. Charles Forman was a Fellow of Punjab University and a regular participant in the educational conferences convened by the Punjab government. His successor, J.C.R. Ewing, continued in his footsteps and in 1910 became vice chancellor of Punjab University. H.D. Griswold served for some time as dean of the university's Oriental faculty.

Nevertheless, Christian schools and colleges faced increasing competition during this period. Their critics and rivals used the press to criticize their evangelistic aims as well as their failure to honour prevailing caste practices and important holidays of other religions.[43] They also had to face periodic 'religious panics' and public demonstrations when students either accepted baptism or showed a serious interest in Christianity. These panics, and the rumours which

---

[43] For example, see the abstracts of the *Rahbar-i-Hind* of 25 June 1890 in *Punjab Native Press Reports 1890*, p. 244; *Rahbar-i-Hind* of 18 June 1894 in ibid. of 1894, p. 285; *Sat Dharm Parcharak* of 24 July 1896 in ibid. of 1896, p. 464. In 1896, abetted by a local Hindu newspaper, 200 Hindu boys in the Mission Boarding School at Jullundur left in protest when a Christian used the well in the mission compound. The Muslims offered to share their well, but the missionary stood firm and the Hindu students, asking only that the Christians not use their side of the well, returned to the school. *Lodiana Mission Annual Report 1896*, pp. 23–4.

fed them, caused temporary drops in enrolment and contributed to unstable enrolments.[44]

There were also missionary critics of this heavy investment in 'educational evangelism'. Andrew Gordon considered mission schools to be both ineffective in converting people and instrumental in creating a more effective opposition to Christianity. Using a military analogy, he argued that Christian schools should focus on those inside rather than outside the Church.

> If a British officer should enter Russian territory, there to drill an army of Russians, in the hope that some of them would enlist and fight loyally for the Queen of England, we would all pronounce his course unwise, and say that he had better enlist them first and drill them afterwards. So men should first be enlisted under Christ's banner, and *then* trained up to power and efficiency in our institutions of learning.[45]

Gordon's priority on upbuilding the Church gained wider acceptance as the Christian community grew in size.[46] Christian educational leaders, however, were not as pessimistic as Gordon about the consequences of their work among other students. Few Christian educational institutions confined themselves to teaching only Christians and Christian educators took pride in the fact that their schools, like those of the government, drew students from all religious communities and not just their own.[47] They did, however,

[44] See, for example, Report of the Principal on the Forman Christian College, Lahore for the Year 1897–98 in *DPI Report 1897–98*, p. viii; K.C. Chatterjee, 'The Report of the Forman Christian College for the Year 1897', *IS* (1 March 1898), p. 4. Robert Morrison had remarked earlier on how Forman Christian College had to face the cry of 'India for the Indians' used by the D.A.V. College to recruit students. R. Morrison, 'The Crisis of Missions in India', *CHA* (April 1895), p. 319.

[45] Andrew Gordon, *Our India Mission*, p. 470.

[46] J.C.R. Ewing, 'Christian Education in India', p. 439; *Minutes of the Conference with Dr. Stanley White, held in Allahabad, 18–20 February 1913*, pp. 17–8.

[47] For example, in 1897–8 at Lahore, the Islamia College had only fifty-two Muslim students, the D.A.V. College had two Muslims and thirty-six Sikhs but 377 Hindus; Forman Christian College had 114 Hindus, sixty-nine Muslims, thirteen Sikhs, twenty-seven Christians and two others. While proportions varied slightly in subsequent years, the college retained its inter-communal character. *DPI Report 1897–98*, pp. ii, ix, xiii, xix.

begin to justify educating other students in two different ways. One was to emphasize character-building, with Jesus Christ as the premier model of what constitutes 'good character'.[48] The Christian school with perhaps the most dramatic emphasis upon character-building was the CMS school in Srinagar run by C.E. Tyndale Biscoe, a staunch advocate of 'muscular Christianity'. While converts were few (only four between 1890 and 1909), he concentrated heavily upon 'manliness' by creating a strong counter-culture in the school through a rigorous and highly disciplined programme of athletics, social service, and hostel life, undergirded by a strict moral code and the nurturing of school pride.[49] The other justification was that Christian schools influenced both the thought and attitudes of the new urban elite in the province (the 'new India') in ways that were favourable rather than hostile towards Christianity.[50]

Christian rethinking was also evident in how they addressed the changing political situation. With the gradual introduction of local self-government schemes at the municipal level and then of broader involvement in decision-making at the provincial level, Christians, including missionaries, became actively involved in politics. The Rev. Kali Charan Chatterjee was a member of the Hoshiarpur Municipal Committee from 1874 to 1890 and served as its president when local

---

[48] For example *Lodiana Mission Annual Report 1891*, p. 65; ibid. 1900, p. 9; D.J. Fleming, *Problems in School and College Work* (Cawnpore, 1907), p. 5; H.D. Griswold, 'Commemoration Address,' Commemoration Exercises of the Founding of Forman Christian College at the Quarter-Centenary Celebration held in the City of Lahore, India May 2, 1911, pp. 9–10; F.J. Western, 'Religious Training in Indian Missionary Schools', *EW*, IX (April 1911), pp. 121–38. By 1910, Griswold had come to believe that 'It may be that other forms of evangelism will gradually take the place of educational evangelism for non-Christians'. 'Review of the Last Decade in the History of the Punjab Mission (1900–1910)'.

[49] C.E. Tyndale Biscoe, 'School Life in Kashmir', *EW*, VII (April 1909), p. 191; *CMS Proceedings 1901–2*, p. 258; ibid. *1905–6*, p. 201; 'A Mission High School in Kashmir', *CMI* (February 1906) pp. 113–7; C.E. Tyndale Biscoe, 'A Mission School and Social Service', ibid. (April 1910), pp. 223–30.

[50] *Lodiana Mission Annual Reports*, 1886, p. 36; 1900, p. 3; 1901, p. 8; and 1907, pp. 159–60. J.C. Chatterjee, 'Missionary Education', *DMN* (January 1911), pp. 58–9.

self-government was introduced in 1882.[51] The Rev. H.U. Weitbrecht became president of the Batala Municipal Committee in 1884.[52] Sardar Didar Singh became vice-president of the Gujarat Municipal Committee and District Board.[53] In addition, Rajah Harnam Singh became a member of the Punjab Legislative Council and there opposed the Land Alienation Act of 1900.[54] He also became president of the Punjab branch of the Indian Christian Association.

Then the rise of anti-government agitation, particularly between 1905 and 1907, forced Christians in the north-west, for the first time since 1857, to re-examine their political assumptions and loyalties. At the outset of this period, a Lodiana Mission report had stated that they found both secular history and British rule providing 'a frame-work for the unfolding panorama of God's purpose of grace towards man, and India is no exception to the rule'.[55] It welcomed Lord Ripon's introduction of local self-government as enlightened, progressive, and courageous, and delighted in pointing out that 'our native Church has, for years, been learning the lesson [of self-government], and putting the principle into successful practice in the Church Session, Presbytery and Synod'.[56] In 1905, the Japanese victory over Russia, the *swadeshi* and boycott movements in response to the partition of Bengal, as well as agitations closer to home in 1907 when the mission premises in Rawalpindi were attacked,[57]

[51] J.C.R. Ewing, *A Prince of the Church in India*, p. 56.

[52] *CMS Proceedings 1884–85*, pp. 114–5. In a letter dated 31 January 1886, H.E. Perkins noted that 'In at least three of the new municipalities the heathen have elected a missionary as the president of a municipality. In two others a missionary is a member, though not the president. In your own at Sialkot, you have two native Christian members, and there are doubtless many others that I do not know of.' Cited by Robert Stewart in 'Are Indian Missions a Failure?', *UP* (3 June 1886), p. 340.

[53] Punjab District Gazetteers, Vol. XXV-A Gujarat District (1921), p. 56.

[54] *Indian Christians*, p. 229.

[55] *Lodiana Mission Annual Report 1882*, p. 3.

[56] Ibid., p. 38. It added that Lord Ripon would be encouraged if he had a population trained in the Presbyterian system of self-government! Ibid., p. 39.

[57] During the 1907 agitations a crowd, which had gathered outside the court in Rawalpindi to witness the hearing of two Hindu lawyers, turned violent when the deputy commissioner postponed the hearing. They attacked several buildings before ransacking the house occupied by two United Presbyterian missionary families

caused a sufficient upheaval to provoke serious rethinking. J.C.R. Ewing, Principal of Forman Christian College, considered British rule to be still good for India but took the liberal line in stating that its purpose was to train Indians for self-government, for which Indians were not as yet ready.[58] S.S. Allnutt at St. Stephen's College saw India's recent unrest and desire for 'a fuller, freer, completer national life' to be a natural consequence of Western education.[59] S.K. Datta and Satish Chatterjee wrote as patriots who identified, not uncritically, with the aspirations of the educated elites.[60] H.C. Velte, citing the attack upon the mission school in Rawalpindi, expressed concern about the anti-Christian aspects of the Arya Samaj-led nationalist movement in the Punjab and advocated an attitude of aloofness. 'We must keep in sympathy with the people, in sympathy with all their just aspirations. On the other hand we must not be blind to the tremendous problems that lie before the Government, before India can be brought into a line with the British colonies.'[61] G.L. Thakur Das, who had been active in the religious controversies of the day, believed that from the early years of the Indian National Congress the real agenda behind political agitation against the Raj had been basically religious in nature.[62]

However, it was C.F. Andrews who, after arriving at St. Stephen's College and the Cambridge Brotherhood only in 1904, came to

---

and pelting the fleeing missionaries and their children with stones. After attacking a second missionary home, they entered the church, smashed the windows, broke the organ and pulpit, set the benches on fire, and then ransacked the YMCA reading room before being dispersed by cavalry. M.E. Barnes, 'The Outbreak in Rawal Pindi', *UP* (6 June 1907), pp. 24–5; Robert Stewart, 'Unrest in India', ibid. (13 June 1907), p. 18; Josephine L. White, 'Letter from a Witness of the Rawal Pindi Outbreak', ibid., p. 20; Robert Maxwell, 'India News Letter', ibid., p. 30.

[58] J.C.R. Ewing, 'England and India', *UP* (16 January 1908), pp. 8–9.

[59] S.S. Allnutt, 'New Year's Letters', *DMN* (January 1908), pp. 1–3.

[60] S.K. Datta, *The Desire of India*, passim; Satish C. Chatterjee, 'Indian Christians and National Ideals', *EW* (April 1914), pp. 209–15.

[61] H.C. Velte, Letter to Mr. Speer, 6 June 1907.

[62] *Nur Afshan*, 27 September 1888 (*Selections from the Vernacular Newspapers— Punjab, 1888*, pp. 235–6); G.L. Thakur Das, Things Commendable and not Commendable in the Thought and Practice of Arya Samaj (handwritten, n.d.). The context indicates that this was probably written in 1908 or soon afterwards.

articulate not only for Christians but also for many others in north India a Christian nationalism for India. What Andrews discovered soon after arriving was racial antagonism, social distance, and distrust between British officialdom (especially in the Punjab) and the educated Indian elites, which was to be aggravated by the events of the next few years. Andrews spoke out early and often about this, using letters to newspaper editors, articles in magazines, public lectures, and sermons not only to express sympathy with the national aspirations articulated by the educated elite but also to criticize Western racism in India as both unchristian and out of keeping with the British imperial mission in India. In the latter effort he was joined by G.A. Lefroy, who had become the Anglican Bishop of Lahore in November 1899.[63] Andrews was a critical idealist who held to a moderate position akin to that of G.K. Gokhale on political issues. During the pre-war years he became not only increasingly disenchanted with Western arrogance and moral complacency but also more persistent in highlighting all that he considered positive in Indian life. He also found himself called upon to mediate between the British and educated Indians in specific cases of conflict.

As a missionary who had quickly become convinced that God's Spirit was incarnate in the 'national awakening' and 'Indian Renaissance', Andrews found the Church ill-equipped to carry out its own mission properly. The missionaries were too infected with the disease of 'Sahibism',[64] and their work too caught up in the project of Westernization.[65] The Christian community was too dominated by foreign missionaries[66] and divorced from the Indian religious ideal of renunciation[67] to be an effective witness. Only the Christian colleges were in touch with the 'new India'[68] where the Spirit of God was at work. Andrews was a strong supporter of the National Missionary Society, of Sadhu Sundar Singh, of the short-lived

[63] Daniel O'Connor, *Gospel, Raj and Swaraj*, pp. 64–101.

[64] C.F. Andrews, *North India*, pp. 160–3.

[65] Ibid., p. 157.

[66] C.F. Andrews, *The Renaissance in India*, pp. 201–3.

[67] C.F. Andrews, *North India*, pp. 170, 175.

[68] Ibid., p. 217.

Brotherhood of the Imitation of Jesus,[69] as well as of the transfer of power and responsibility within the Church from foreign missionary to Indian Christian hands. In 1910 he wrote that

> If Christianity is to succeed, it must not come forward as an antagonist and a rival to the great religious strivings and yearnings of the past. . . . It must come as a helper and a fulfiller, a peacemaker and a friend. It must be able to gather up all that is great and noble in a higher synthesis. There must no longer be the desire to capture converts from Hinduism, by any and every means, and take advantage of her hour of weakness and desolation; but rather the desire to come to her help in the needful time of trouble, and to aid her in the fulfillment of duties which she has long neglected.[70]

Andrews issued an important 'wake-up call', which was heard and seriously noted within Church and mission circles, even if his views did not win full or widespread acceptance. At the Lahore Diocesan Conference held in November 1909, his fellow Anglicans spent time hearing and discussing papers on 'The National Movement'. Comments at and around the conference indicated that assessments of the movement varied greatly. There were those who, like Andrews, saw it as basically progressive in nature and thus open to, if not aspiring towards, Christian social ideals. Others, however, saw it as basically conservative in nature, seeking to hold on to as much of the past as possible, and hence inherently antagonistic towards Christianity and Christian influence.[71] These crucial differences were by no means resolved at the time, but carried over into the ensuing period. Meanwhile, the Punjab government took steps to silence critical political opinion as well as to stifle political action. In 1907, it issued a circular prohibiting teachers in government and aided

---

[69] This small brotherhood, based on the Franciscan ideal of poverty, lasted from 1910 to 1912.

[70] C.F. Andrews, *India in Transition*, p. 12.

[71] See the following articles in the *Delhi Mission News*: 'Lahore Diocesan Conference Report' (October 1910), pp. 47–9; S. Ghose, 'What Has Happened in India?' (October 1910), pp. 49–50; S.S. Allnutt, 'A Note on "What Has Happened in India"' (January 1911), pp. 57–8; 'Lahore Diocesan Conference Report II' (January 1911), pp. 61–2.

colleges from discussing political questions in front of their students.[72] Then, during World War I, the British government issued an order prohibiting members of non-British missionary societies from engaging in any form of anti-government activity whatsoever under penalty of expulsion from India.[73] None were actually expelled, but the threat was taken seriously.

Urban Women

The Christian encounter with urban women in the north-west began quite differently from that with urban men. Christian women met other women individually or in small groups in their homes rather than in public, whether in bazars or institutional settings or through the printed word. It was thus not only based much more on person-to-person relationships than on mass appeals but also confined largely to the domestic realm, where many of the early schools were located, until men chose to make a public issue out of it.

By 1880, the Christian missions had already established themselves as pioneers in and major contributors to the education of women in the north-west. Both Indian Christian and missionary women had already begun visiting other women in the zenanas of the towns and cities where their mission stations were located. Their visits were both educational and evangelistic in nature. In Delhi, the SPG had introduced medical work exclusively for women as yet another form of Christian outreach to women. This work of education, evangelism, and medical treatment, primarily among urban Indian women, developed and expanded greatly as increasing numbers of single women and even women's missionary societies entered the region. In order to appreciate the dynamics of this encounter and the issues at stake, it is best to begin with a brief description of the

[72] Ibid., pp. 52–3.

[73] 'His Majesty's Government must hold every missionary body responsible for every member of its staff in India, and that should any such member be considered to have acted in a manner hostile to the government of India as by law established, the Government of India must be considered as justified in ordering the expulsion from India of the entire Mission involved.' Cited by Robert E. Speer in his letter to the North India and Punjab Missions, 21 February 1917.

women of urban north-west India as the Christian missionaries found them during this period.

The 'middle class' urban women whom the zenana missionaries visited were secluded, deliberately cut off from much of the outside world.[74] The visitors found them to be friendly, hospitable, curious, often lacking the Victorian virtue of 'seriousness'. Three features of these women's lives particularly disturbed the missionaries. The first they perceived to be a combination of superstition, fear, and ignorance (not lack of intelligence), which they considered to be a consequence of seclusion.[75] While missionary women generally accepted this as a routine challenge, the medical missionaries found it especially frustrating because they had to overcome these obstacles quickly and gain their patients' trust if the simple remedies they prescribed were to be followed.[76] The second feature was that these women's lives were so deeply embedded in such tight family networks and traditionally prescribed roles that they had virtually no lives of their own. The women existed to serve their families, not to become persons in their own right. While some women bitterly resented this,[77] the men and mothers-in-law enforced the traditional system rigorously and with force. Thirdly, the missionaries were particularly shocked at the treatment of widows as mere domestic chattel.[78] In short, the women they met appeared to be in psychological and social

---

[74] Mrs K.C. Chatterjee, 'Our Zenana Work in the Punjab', *Woman's Work for Woman and Our Mission Field* (April 1888), pp. 96–8.

[75] 'Umritzur', *IW* (October 1880), p. 41; 'Report of the Amritsar Medical Mission', ibid. (July–August 1883), p. 193.

[76] See, for example, 'Three Years...', *DMN* (January 1896), p. 8.

[77] In Batala some women told the missionaries that 'we have been living like monkeys'. 'Foreign Items', *IW* (September–October 1885), p. 271. That same year a missionary in Lahore wrote, 'It is strange how contented some of the inmates of Zenanas are with their shut up isolated condition, merely saying it is the custom of their country. But more than one Bibi has bitterly said to me the Zenana was like a prison...' 'Miss M'Phun's Report', *IFE* (January 1886), p. 221.

[78] 'Punjab and Scinde Mission', *IW* (May–June 1884), p. 120; Miss Wauton, 'Plead for the Widow', ibid. (May–June 1889), pp. 124–31.

bondage to particularly oppressive, religiously sanctioned customs and traditions.[79]

Missionaries had been aware for more than a decade that specialized evangelistic and educational work among these women was a necessary step forward. Not only did God's love include these women, who needed to be told about it, but their influence within their own homes was also such as to affect the eternal destinies of other family members as well. The obstacles that missionaries had to overcome reveal as much about the status and condition of urban women as about missionary frustrations. A Ladies Missionary Conference at Lahore in December 1882 summed up the difficulties they faced in their schools for Hindu and Muslim girls as:

1. Caste prejudices; 2. Religious beliefs; 3. Combination of priests, moulvies, and parents to keep children from imbibing too much of our teaching and influence; 4. Low estimate of female worth and education; 5. Early engagement and marriage of the pupils; 6. Want of properly educated and efficient teachers for the secular work; 7. Daily attendance of the pupils often of short duration, and very irregular.[80]

Partly because of what they found in the zenanas and partly because of the missionaries' assumptions about womanhood drawn from their own (largely middle-class) Victorian backgrounds and missionary vocations, 'women's work for women' became (and was certainly perceived as) quite radical in its implications. The aim of women's work, like all other mission work at the time, was evangelistic, but it wasn't simply that; as Dana Robert has pointed out, it was also more broadly emancipatory, including 'enlightenment' and 'social uplift' along with conversion.[81] Women missionaries were not, however, of one mind concerning the competing claims of home

[79] See, for example, S.S. Hewlett, *Daughters of the King*, pp. 10–13; 'Umritsar', *IW* (July–August 1883), p. 184; 'Plead for the Widow', ibid., (May–June 1889), p. 124.

[80] Miss C.E. Wilson, 'Woman's Work in India', *UP* (1 April 1886), p. 198.

[81] Dana L. Robert, *American Women in Mission*, pp. 130, 160, 188. One report from Delhi referred to it as emancipation from 'slavery'. 'Zenana Workers at Delhi', *DMN* (January 1896), p. 7.

and family on the one hand and liberation and/or conversion on the other. Young girls could go to school, become enlightened, return to their homes and social networks better equipped to transform them from within. Adult women, especially those who were married, faced the more radical choice between staying and leaving. The evidence indicates that the choice was theirs to make; only if a woman left her home of her own accord would she be given shelter and protection by the missionaries.[82]

What is remarkable is that there were some women who did leave their homes to convert to Christianity. One was Fatima, a Muslim woman from a good family in Amritsar, who had resolved to become a Christian. On the night before she had arranged to be baptized, she informed her husband of her intentions. 'A host of relations and friends beat her and threatened her and tore off her jewels.' In the morning, after her husband had gone to his shop, she slipped away, was baptized as Nur-ul-Nissa, and took up residence in the mission compound.[83] Nur-ul-Nissa became a Bible woman (a single woman evangelist employed by the mission) in Amritsar. From there she was transferred to Batala where she was instrumental in the conversion of a young Muslim widow, Fazl Nissa, who, when she left her home to be baptized, had to leave her eleven-year-old daughter behind with her relatives and was unable to see her again. She too became a Bible woman but subsequently married a Christian.[84] Another Bible woman in Amritsar was Susan, who had converted long before Nur-ul-Nissa. Born a Brahmin, she had been married at an early age and had become so concerned about her sins that she went on pilgrimages to expiate them, but without success. On hearing a Christian preacher she found the divine forgiveness she had been seeking and refused to return to her husband. For this she was put in

[82] For some of the discussion on cases of this type, see 'Here and There', *IW* (March–April 1884), p. 96; 'Amritsar', ibid. (July–August 1881), p. 174; 'Punjab and Sindh Missions', ibid. (May–June 1887), p. 151.

[83] 'Umritzur', *IW* (October 1880), p. 37.

[84] 'The Punjab Mission', *IWCD* (July 1896), p. 162; 'Punjab and Sindh Mission', ibid. (September 1896), pp. 205–7; 'Batala', ibid. (July 1897), pp. 107–8; 'The Baqar 'Id at Batala', ibid. (October 1900), p. 222.

jail for several months (the law favoured a husband's rights over a wife's freedom) and then, upon release, sought out missionaries in Amritsar for further Christian instruction.[85]

As these examples indicate, conversion was fraught with difficulties. Nur-ul-Nissa was beaten and lost her jewels, probably the only personal wealth she possessed. Susan had to spend time in prison. Fazl Nissa lost her daughter. In another case, however, a Muslim widow who converted had one of her three children taken by her late husband's brother. She took the matter to court and won custody of the boy on the grounds that this was in his best interests.[86] An especially tragic case was that of a Brahmin woman who decided to leave her home to live openly as a baptized Christian. Her husband let her go, but took their two children from her. She missed her children greatly and decided to go back to him, but he would neither take her back nor allow her to see their children. She ended up looking after her father-in-law whom his son had also deserted.[87]

However, most of the women who left their families to become Christians during this period were already socially if not culturally alienated prior to their conversion. A few were employees of the mission or of the missionaries, but most came to them with special social burdens. Several were widows. A larger number were patients who were blind,[88] crippled, paralysed, or suffering from such serious ailments that they too had been rejected or abandoned by their families.[89] There were also abused women who found their home

[85] 'Susan, the Late Amritsar Bible-Woman', *IW* (January–February 1890), pp. 15–6. Another example is found in 'Medical Work on the Frontier', *IWCD* (November 1910), p. 172.

[86] *Lodiana Mission Annual Report 1883*, pp. 11–2.

[87] S.S. Allnutt, 'Zenana Converts', *DMN* (July 1904), pp. 33–5; 'Head of the Mission's Page', ibid. (October 1904), p. 43.

[88] In 1887, a special Institute for the Blind was established at St. Catherine's hospital in Amritsar. By 1903, of the ninety blind people who had been at the Institute since its founding thirteen were Muslims and the other seventy-seven were Christians. 'North India Missionary Institute for the Blind', *IWCD* (February 1903), p. 41.

[89] See, for example, 'Amritsar', *IW* (July–August 1884), p. 192; 'Our Medical Mission Page', *IWCD* (February 1903), p. 30.

life intolerable and went to the mission as a refuge.[90] Some came in desperation after being widowed during a famine so that they and their children might simply survive.[91] Conversion among school girls, however, was very rare. The radical option was neither popular nor common nor easy, but it did exist and just enough women took it to create public anxiety.

It is apparent from their reports and correspondence that women missionaries faced considerable opposition to their work throughout the region during this period. Much of it was simply individual resistance (zenana visitors were not welcomed into homes or girls were not sent to schools) and most was unorganized. The more organized opposition was sporadic. Some incidents were provoked by a particular case of baptism,[92] but even these fed upon a pervasive perception that Christian women's work was a constant threat. As one Muslim tract circulated in Amritsar in 1885 put it,

The missionaries, who pour like a flood into this country, are striking deadly blows at the *root* of our faith. They know how much depends upon the women, so, on various pretences of teaching reading and needlework, they enter your houses, and sometimes even plant schools there! By this means a loophole is made for the Bible. Soon the women learn to despise their own religion, and the evil seed is sown in their hearts.[93]

The writer used this Christian threat to urge Muslims to educate their women and specifically to start 'an Islamic Madrassa for our girls'.[94]

This tract was part of what was the most serious concerted effort to close down 'women's work for women' in the north-west during

---

[90] See, for example, 'Foreign Items', *IW* (March–April 1887), p. 103; 'Medical Work on the Frontier', *IWCD* (November 1910), p. 172; 'Baptism of a Brahman Woman', *DMN* (October 1895), pp. 3–5.

[91] 'The Punjab Mission', *IWCD* (May 1898), p. 110; 'Our Medical Page', ibid. (October 1905), p. 220.

[92] See, for example, *Lodiana Mission Annual Report 1895*, p. 7; 'Foreign Notes', *IWCD* (February 1896), p. 44.

[93] 'A Mohammedan Tract', *IW* (September–October 1885), p. 232.

[94] Ibid., p. 233. See also 'Foreign Items', *IW* (September–October 1890), pp. 272–3.

this period. In 1885, the Amritsar Arya Samaj moved aggressively to provide alternative Vedic schools to the CEZMS girls schools there. They placed their schools close to the CEZMS schools and did all they could to get the girls and their parents to switch schools. This campaign was very successful; whole classes left, one mission school was closed down, and only in the following year did the girls start coming back. Meanwhile, some influential Muslims launched a parallel campaign to boycott mission schools and close their zenanas to mission visitors. 'They even threatened to place guards at the doors of the houses we visited to prevent our entrance. They succeeded in closing two.'[95] The Muslim opposition prevailed for some time, but the missionaries reported that it had also increased interest in education among Muslim women![96]

The same thing happened at Lahore in 1885, only there the agitation was confined to Muslims. One missionary of the Zenana Bible and Medical Mission reported that maulvies 'have been preaching near our schools, and through fear of the threats of excommunication, that is, that no one will smoke the huqqah, or drink water with them, many have removed their children from our teaching'.[97] Attendance dropped and more than a few schools had to be closed down. A tract of the Society for the Promotion of Islam on 'Education of Females' warned not only of the religious threat but also that 'Christian women teach Mohammedan women that they should have the liberty which they possess'.[98] Reports of Muslim opposition and of consequent school closings appeared in the CEZMS magazine in 1886 and 1887; in 1889, it reproduced another Muslim tract in which several maulvies stated that it was unlawful for Muslims to allow Christian women from the missions into their homes. 'The unbelieving woman of another faith is as a strange man; that is, that just as it is unlawful for a woman to appear before a strange man, so it is not lawful to show herself to such a woman.'[99]

[95] 'Punjab and Sindh Missions', *IW* (May–June 1886), p. 116.
[96] An account of this agitation and its aftermath is provided in ibid., pp. 114–9.
[97] 'Miss Healey's Report', *IFE* (January 1886), p. 223.
[98] 'A Mohammedan Appeal', ibid. (July 1885), p. 145.
[99] 'The Latest Mohammedan Manifesto', ibid. (July 1889), p. 117.

These were not isolated efforts. Earlier, in 1884, the Hindus in Jhelum held public meetings to prevent their women from receiving zenana visitors and their girls from attending mission schools. This boycott could be sustained for only a few months.[100] The Lodiana Mission reported in 1886 that Muslims had temporarily disrupted zenana work in Ludhiana.[101] In 1890, missionaries in Peshawar reported that in the mosques, mullahs were publicly warning their people not to allow missionaries in their homes. Women whose husbands were away were told that if they allowed Christians to visit them, this would be reported to their husbands who would divorce them.[102] In 1893, the *Wazir-ul-Mulk* in Sialkot published a fatwa against permitting missionary ladies from entering Muslim homes.[103] In 1894, Muslim opposition in Narowal was so strong that almost all the girls were removed from the mission school there.[104] In 1895, the Arya Samaj nearly succeeded in closing down the zenana meetings and the SPG girls' school in Karnal.[105] In 1897, in an effort to disparage mission work, the *Akhbar-i-Am* stated that missionaries had converted 'children and *purdah nashin* ladies and married the latter to *chamars* and sweepers'.[106] In 1900, the Amritsar Arya Samaj again made a systematic effort to persuade parents to withdraw their daughters from mission schools.[107] In Srinagar, the missionaries were challenged by the maharaja's many schools (and the rich gifts given to the girls who attended them), as well as by Annie Besant and the Theosophical Society that opened a school and offered the students

---

[100] 'Sialkot Presbytery, India', *UP* (17 July 1884), p. 455. 'Sialkot Presbytery—India', ibid. (28 August 1884), p. 551.

[101] *Lodiana Mission Annual Report 1886*, p. 6.

[102] *The Tenth Annual Report of the Church of England Zenana Missionary Society for the Year ending 31st March 1890*, 45 [hereafter referred to as the *CEZMS Annual Report* with the date]. 'A Year of Labour etc.' *IW* (July–August 1890), pp. 201–2.

[103] Wazir-ul-Mulk of 7th April 1893 cited *in Punjab Native Press Reports 1893*, p. 195.

[104] 'The Past Year at Narowal', *IW* (June 1895), p. 305.

[105] *SPG Annual Report 1895*, p. 61.

[106] *Akhbar-i-Am* of 23 March 1897 in *Punjab Native Press Reports, 1897*, p. 256.

[107] *CEZMS Annual Report 1901*, p. 54.

free books.[108] In 1906, a young Muslim woman, a former student at
the Baptist school in Delhi who was being forced into a marriage she
did not want, left home and went to the mission compound. This
was taken to court where she testified that she would not go back
home and that she was willing to become a Christian. The deputy
commissioner said that she was old enough to decide for herself and
that he could not force her to return home. This adverse decision
upset the Muslims who had brought the case to court and they
virtually accused the missionaries 'of being wholesale kidnappers'
and the mission girls' school had to be closed.[109]

All, however, was not opposition. There were large numbers of
zenanas that remained open to Christian visitors, some of them
during organized boycotts, and significant numbers of girls continued
to attend Christian schools.[110] One medical missionary in Dera Ismael
Khan commented in 1895 that ten years earlier 'people were beaten
for coming to me; others had to go down to the river to wash off the
defilement of my having felt their pulse. Now instead of fear, people
want me to stay longer and come more often.'[111] This was attributed
to a gradual dying out of old prejudices and taboos through personal
contact or to a growing appreciation of the health and educational
benefits the missionaries had to offer. However, something deeper
may also have been at work. One missionary told the story of a man
asking his wife why she was inclined towards Christianity and she
replied, 'Well, one thing you will allow: whatever Christianity may
be for *men*, it's a good religion for *women*.'[112] Other missionaries noted
that where they were working men led the opposition whereas
women were more welcoming.[113] When the Amritsar Arya Samaj

[108] S. Kutter, 'Sowing the Seed in Kashmir', *IWCD* (March 1906), p. 38; Eva
F. Goodall, 'Pupils in Srinagar, Kashmir', ibid. (December 1908), p. 182.

[109] Miss Fiennes, 'Opposition Versus Indifference', *DMN* (October 1906), p. 47.

[110] For example, in 1887, soon after the agitation described above, the CEZMS
reported that 150 homes in Amritsar and Tarn Taran were open to their zenana
visitors; in 1890, they reported that they were visiting 1382 zenanas throughout
the region. *CEZMS Annual Report 1887*, p. 34; ibid. *1890*, p. 12.

[111] *CEZMS Annual Report 1895*, p. 51.

[112] 'Amritsar', *IW* (July–August 1881), p. 175.

[113] Ibid., p. 186; 'Work in the Punjab', *IFE* (July 1884), p. 321.

launched their 1900 boycott campaign by appealing to parents to withdraw their daughters from the mission schools, the fathers and brothers were inclined to go along, whereas the mothers, 'many of whom had themselves been in these schools, were in favour of allowing the children to continue their attendance, in spite of threats and entreaties. The young people themselves have no idea of being kept away, and often cleverly evaded their pursuers, who were watching for them in the street.'[114] A similar contrast in the attitudes of men and women was noted earlier when the Arya Samaj succeeded in closing down the mission girls' school at Ludhiana back in 1894.[115] Organized opposition to women's work in Jagraon that same year had served to increase the women's interest in it![116] This evidence, while fragmentary, does suggest that while urban men saw Christianity primarily as a threat, growing numbers of women appreciated it for the affirmation and opportunities it offered them.[117]

One of the lasting legacies of women's work from this period were some important educational and medical institutions for women. The Alexandra School was started in 1878 as a Christian girls' boarding school in Lahore and then in 1880 was moved to Amritsar. Most of the girls were 'children of better-class native Christians—pastors, head-masters, doctors and professors'.[118] Among its early students were the first two girls to pass the Punjab Middle School examination as well as the first two girls from the Punjab to pass the Calcutta University entrance examination.[119] A good number of former students were employed in the medical, educational, and

---

[114] *CEZMS Annual Report 1901*, p. 54.

[115] *Lodiana Mission Annual Report 1894*, p. 5.

[116] Ibid., p. 12.

[117] In 1899, Robert Stewart reported that United Presbyterians were experiencing more open access than opposition to zenana visitors. 'The prospect of learning to read and getting acquainted with a more advanced condition of society is usually sufficient inducement to overcome every objection.' Robert Stewart, *Life and Work in India*, p. 176. Other missions shared a similar experience.

[118] 'Alexandra School', *IW* (July–August 1883), p. 187.

[119] *CEZMS Annual Report 1886*, p. 34; 'Foreign Items', *IW* (September–October 1886), pp. 265–6.

evangelistic work of the mission.[120] Some moved into positions of considerable importance as educators and doctors during this period.[121] Near the end of this period, in 1913, the Zenana Bible and Medical Mission started college classes in the Kinnaird Christian Girls High School in Lahore so as to enable Punjabi Christian women to improve their qualifications as teachers.[122] This was the beginning of Kinnaird College which quickly became interdenominational and the only Christian arts and science college for women in the north-west prior to 1947.

In addition to schools, the missions also created a large network of women's hospitals from Kashmir to Quetta to Delhi during this period. In order to staff these hospitals with properly trained Christian women, the North India School of Medicine for Christian Women was started in 1894 at Ludhiana. The original plan was to begin by training compounders, then develop a four-year course for medical assistants, and, if all went well, to introduce a five-year course for university-recognized assistant surgeons.[123] A committee in India, on which seven mission societies were represented, governed the school.[124] By 1902, it had received government recognition as a medical school and Punjab University had indicated a willingness to make it an affiliated college as soon as it met the university's standards.[125] In 1909, the Punjab government asked that it admit non-

[120] Some lists of what recent former students were doing can be found in 'Alexandra School', *IW* (July–August 1883), p. 188; *CEZMS Annual Report 1900*, p. 56.

[121] In 1888, Robert Clark reported that Miss Lajwanti Rallia Ram was in charge of all government girls' schools in Amritsar and Miss Mona Bose held the same position in Lahore. Both were products of CMS schools, as was Mona Bose's sister Kerith, who later became doctor in charge of the mission hospital (and the entire mission) at Asrapur, near Amritsar. 'Foreign Items', *IW* (July–August 1888), p. 222.

[122] Michelle Maskiell, 'Social Change and Social Control: College-Educated Punjabi Women 1913 to 1960', p. 56. Earlier women had been admitted to Forman Christian College in Lahore and Gordon College in Rawalpindi.

[123] 'The North India School of Medicine for Christian Women', *IW* (April 1895), pp. 149–54.

[124] 'North India School of Medicine for Christian Women, Ludhiana', *IWCD* (September 1897), p. 200.

[125] 'The North India School of Medicine for Christian Women', *IWCD* (March 1902), p. 59.

Christian students and in 1915 closed the Women's Department of its Lahore Medical College and transferred all the women students there to Ludhiana.[126] By 1918, it had produced sixty-eight graduates in medicine and fifty-two certified compounders.[127] Indeed, by the end of this period, Christian women held a commanding position in the field of Western medicine, as in the field of education, throughout north-west India.

Perhaps no aspect of mission work received more bitter criticism in the north-west during this period than did women's work among women.[128] This is not surprising. Christian evangelism, especially when wedded to a gospel that included 'enlightenment', 'uplift', and 'emancipation', was very threatening to the domestic order but, judging from missionary accounts, was very much appreciated by the women and girls it was intended for. It helped to open up new worlds, new options and alternatives, new opportunities, and even new images of themselves as women.[129] Anshu Malhotra has shown how upper-caste male Hindu and Sikh reformers soon absorbed the 'enlightenment' and 'uplift' components into their own agendas for controlling women's sexuality in ways that could promote their own social aspirations. This they did by retaining patriarchy while rejecting both certain prevalent social customs and the more emancipatory aspects of what the Christians were advocating.[130] There is also evidence in the Muslim tracts cited above that Muslim men were also fearful of the emancipatory consequences of their women's

[126] 'Women's Christian Medical College, Ludhiana', *The Indian Witness* (11 August 1920), pp. 608–9.

[127] *The Report for the 36th Year of the Women's Christian Medical College, Ludhiana, Punjab, 1929–1930*, pp. 35–9.

[128] In addition to the references cited above, see the *Akhbar-i-Am* of 8 September and 8 November 1888 in *Punjab Press Reports, 1888*, pp. 217, 284; *Kaistha Conference Gazette* of 15 September 1890 in ibid. *1890*; *Sanatan Dharm Gazette* of 15 March 1897 in ibid. *1897*, p. 229; *Arya Gazette* of 20 January 1898 in ibid. *1898*, p. 68; *Singh Sahai* of 15 February 1900 in ibid. *1900*, p. 92 as well as Kenneth W. Jones, *Arya Dharm*, p. 192.

[129] See also John C.B. Webster, 'The Women of Amritsar through Missionary Eyes'.

[130] See Anshu Malhotra, *Gender, Caste, and Religious Identities*.

exposure to Christianity.[131] Christian 'women's work' certainly provoked urban Hindu, Muslim, and Sikh men into taking steps for at least the enlightenment and uplift of the women in their families, if for no other reason than to diminish the attractiveness of the Christian alternative, especially as Christian women began to move into public life and influence what the 'new woman' in the 'new India' might look like. The result was not only to push women's issues to the forefront of regional reform agendas but also to promote female education. In playing this provocative role and forcing the pace of change, Christian women helped to lay foundations for the women's movement in north-west India.

This, however, lay in the future. Despite the significant catalytic and modelling roles which Christian women had played during this period, not a great deal of overall progress had been made, even among urban women. Women missionaries certainly reported greater receptivity to their work as well as a greater desire among women generally for education and emancipation, but the actual accomplishments made during this period remained very modest indeed. For example, the literacy rate among women had increased from a mere 0.17 per cent in 1881 to 0.60 per cent in 1911.[132] A missionary reported in 1910 that purdah was still commonly practised in Delhi and that women's education there was making only very modest advances.[133] Nevertheless, the ground had been broken in the face of much opposition. A start had been made, and there could be no turning back.

The Rural Dalits

Up to this period, Christianity had been an almost exclusively urban phenomenon in north-west India. Both missionaries and converts were based in the towns and cities. Their winter tours through the

[131] This is most obvious in the 'Education of Females' tract of The Society for the Promotion of Islam. 'A Mohammedan Appeal', *IFE* (July 1885), pp. 144–5.

[132] *Punjab Census 1881*, I, p. 403; *Punjab Census 1911*, I, p. 340. The former figure is only for the 'Total British Territory'.

[133] M.A.H. Taylor, 'The Education of Women in India', *LDR*, VI (1910), pp. 191–8.

many villages surrounding their urban mission stations, camping
for only a day or two in one place before moving on to the next one,
meant that their contact with the rural population was brief,
intermittent, and thus basically superficial. All this started to change
in 1873 when a mass conversion movement among rural Chuhras
began within the central Punjab. This conversion movement took
place solely at Chuhra initiative. The missionaries and mission
workers neither planned nor created it, but were caught by surprise
and had to adjust to it. By the end of this period, over 100,000 villagers
had been baptized and a rural church had been established.
Christianity thus ceased to be simply a passing show and now became
a settled fact of rural life in many parts of the region. The attention
of a good number of missionaries became focused upon the problems
of those at the very bottom of rural society. The Christian
community in the region was changed from a tiny, literate, and
progressive urban community into a much larger, predominantly
illiterate, poor rural community. The 'Dalit issue' also forced itself
upon public attention not merely as a 'social problem' but as a political
fact to be reckoned with as well. Thus, the Chuhra conversion
movement remains probably the most permanent legacy of this
momentous period for the Christian community in north-west India.

The Chuhras, one of the largest castes in the north-west, were
concentrated in the central Punjab. They were rural menials whose
traditional occupation was listed as sweeper although most actually
worked as agricultural labourers. Almost all worked for village
landowners on a daily wage basis, but some were tenant farmers,
generally on an annual renewable lease. Very few owned land. They
were thus totally dependent upon village landowners for their
livelihood. Since wages or shares of the harvest were kept as low as
possible, the Chuhras lived in poverty, eating whatever they could to
keep alive. They were, moreover, considered to be untouchables due
in part to the ritual impurity of the traditional occupation assigned
to them and in part to the lifestyle which severe poverty forced upon
them.

Chuhra religion did not fit into the neat exclusive categories used
to classify religions. Chuhra life-cycle rituals resembled those of other

castes in many respects and Chuhras shared many aspects of village religion: belief in spirits, omens, the evil eye, auspicious and inauspicious times. They worshipped at Hindu, Muslim, and Sikh shrines as well as at shrines of their own. They also tended to adopt some of the beliefs and practices of the dominant castes in their villages. If they accepted Islam, they were called Musallis and were often enjoined to give up carrying night soil. The same prohibition existed for those who became Sikhs; they were called Mazhabis and were expected to wear long hair and give up smoking.

Chuhras also had their own distinctive religion, but used different names to identify the deity they worshipped. In the western Punjab the predominant name was Bala Shah; in the eastern Punjab it was Lal Beg. Scattered throughout the Punjab, the name Balmik was also used. It was by no means clear whether these were simply three names for the same deity, three distinct deities, or three incarnations of one deity. Two important features of Chuhra religion were of special significance. One was that in their 'myth of origins' they claimed equality with members of other castes; their present ascribed status as untouchables was due to a gross injustice inflicted upon them in the past. The other was the affirmation that on the day of judgement they would be vindicated and their 'social superiors' punished. Until that day, however, the deity offered neither ethical guidance nor assistance in dealing with caste hierarchy and oppression.[134] Thus, while their religion affirmed their inherent equality with others in Punjabi society, it also reflected a passive acceptance of their fate in this world.

The origins of the Chuhra mass conversion movement have always been traced to Ditt, an illiterate dealer in animal hides who lived in the village of Shahabdike in Sialkot district. Ditt first became acquainted with Christianity through a recent convert who lived in a neighbouring village. Missionary sources do not say why he was attracted to Christianity or what his motives for conversion were.

---

[134] Much fuller treatments of the Chuhras and their religion can be found in John C.B. Webster, *Religion and Dalit Liberation*, pp. 15–23 and Vijay Prasad, *Untouchable Freedom*, pp. 25–45.

His friend taught Ditt all he knew and then accompanied him to Sialkot to receive baptism from the United Presbyterian missionary resident there, the Rev. Samuel Martin. Following a short period of further instruction and his baptism in Sialkot, Ditt returned to his village. Three months later he brought his wife, daughter, and two neighbours for baptism; six months after that, in February 1874, he returned yet again with four more neighbours desiring baptism. Not long afterwards and completely independently of Ditt, Karm Bakhsh and Chaughatta were baptized and stirred up interest in Christianity among fellow Chuhras near Gujranwala and Dinanagar (Gurdaspur district) respectively.[135] By the end of 1875, the United Presbyterian missionaries were aware of a conversion movement among the Chuhras, even though few had as yet converted. Because of its novelty they treated it with caution, responding to it by instructing those who had already made professions of faith and letting them 'operate upon their friends and neighbors'.[136]

Thus, at this early stage, the conversion movement really belonged to converts like Ditt, Karm Bakhsh, and Chaughatta rather than to the mission and its preachers.[137] News of the new religion spread by word of mouth at weddings, funerals, melas, and wherever Chuhras met for business or social reasons. It is unclear how Christianity was described or explained by one Chuhra to another, but Gordon did report that the news of Jesus, 'Saviour of sinners, Friend of the poor', was spreading through the surrounding villages.[138] Serious inquirers came as individuals, like Ditt's neighbours, or in small clusters of

---

[135] This account follows that of Andrew Gordon in *Our India Mission*, pp. 421–6, 428, 440–3. See also John C.B. Webster, 'A Quest for the Historical Ditt', pp. 53–68.

[136] *The Seventeenth Annual Report of the Board of Foreign Missions of the United Presbyterian Church of North America Presented to the General Assembly in May 1876*, p. 19; ibid. *1877*, p. 15. [Hereafter referred to as *UPCNA Annual Report* with the year added.]

[137] In Gordon's account, Ditt was so active as a volunteer evangelist that his business suffered and so the mission gave him a modest stipend. Andrew Gordon, *Our India Mission*, pp. 426–7.

[138] Ibid., p. 425.

families, as in Chaughatta's village of Awankha.[139] Touring
missionaries found Chuhras either interested primarily in religious
questions of sin and salvation or, more frequently, requesting help
in dealing with the oppression of their landlords.[140] Those whom
the missionaries considered to be sincere in their new faith had to
meet certain requirements before they could be baptized.

They must know Jesus Christ the Son of God, the sinless One, and only Saviour
of sinners; they must know that he came from God, became man, laid down
his life for sinners, and welcomes all, even the poorest and vilest, to come to
him; they must turn their backs upon idols, and every religion but that of Jesus,
heartily receiving and resting upon him alone, and promising obedience to
him. If we are satisfied with them on such simple points as these, we think it
our duty to receive them.[141]

In addition, the missionaries insisted upon three life-style changes.
They prohibited work on the sabbath as well as eating carrion and
they insisted upon faithfulness in the marriage relationship.[142] Those
who decided to convert remained in their villages and occupations,
and faced almost inevitable persecution from their landlords. Not all
those baptized remained Christians; persecution led some to give
up Christianity and others simply preferred to live according to their
old customs.[143]

During this initial stage of the conversion movement, the number
of converts baptized annually remained small. The first year in which
the total number of Chuhra baptisms exceeded one hundred was
1882, almost ten years after Ditt had been baptized. These numbers
increased, however, as the mission became more and more involved
with the movement. This happened quite naturally and gradually.

[139] Ibid., pp. 443–5.

[140] Contrast a letter by J. H. McKee in 'Foreign Missions', *UP* (20 July 1874),
p. 2 with *UPCNA Annual Report 1880*, p. 21.

[141] Andrew Gordon, *Our India Mission*, p. 462.

[142] These three demands are given in S. Martin, 'Work among the Depressed
Classes', *Report of the Third Decennial Missionary Conference Held at Bombay, 1892–93*,
Bombay, 1893, I, p. 23. Among Chuhras divorce was common and quite easy.

[143] *UPCNA Annual Report 1879*, p. 19; ibid. *1880*, pp. 22, 30.

When requests for Christian instruction came to the mission from a village or cluster of villages where a group of Chuhras was seeking baptism, the mission sent a trained catechist or teacher to live in that village in order to teach the inquirers the basics of the Christian faith, Christian worship, and Christian life. By 1882, the demand for such catechists/teachers from both inquirers and convert groups had exceeded the mission's capacity to supply them.[144] From then on it became a constant struggle to provide adequate attention to the requests of groups of inquirers and adequate pastoral care for the newly emerging village congregations.

Mission involvement brought the Chuhra conversion movement to a new stage in its development. While volunteer evangelists like Ditt continued to roam the countryside spreading the Christian message to fellow Chuhras, Christianity had now become a visible presence in the villages of the Sialkot, Gujranwala, and Gurdaspur districts. Chuhras could see what the mission was doing and what differences conversion to Christianity was making in the lives of rural Chuhras. The 'demonstration effect' of a literate catechist, and possibly a school, for the Chuhras in the village now supplemented whatever verbal messages the volunteer evangelists and the mission preachers shared to commend Christianity as a religion to the Chuhra people. This, of course, influenced the motives with which groups of Chuhra inquirers now approached the mission's representatives for baptism; many seemed more interested in the 'worldly advantages' conversion brought than in undergoing the inner transformations which made those advantages possible.

It was when the movement had already reached this stage that it spread beyond the borders of the Sialkot Mission into the 'mission fields' of neighbouring missions. In March 1885, the CMS missionaries at Batala received a request from the Chuhras in the nearby village of Fatehgarh for Christian instruction and a school. Equally important, these Chuhras promised to provide the land and build the brick walls for the school if the mission provided wood for the roof, doors, and windows. The mission sent people to instruct

---

[144] *UPCNA Annual Report 1883*, p. 30; ibid. *1884*, p. 84.

them and within a year sixty-five were baptized.[145] That same year, Dr Youngson of the Church of Scotland mission visited the village of Amoutrah in Sialkot district at the urging of his assistant, Nathu Mal. There he found Chuhras who had heard the Christian message and had relatives who had already become Christians. Initially, five walked the fourteen miles into Sialkot to be baptized. Three weeks later nine more came, of whom four were baptized. The following month twenty-four more were baptized in the village itself. Not only were the landlords who opposed the baptisms present but so also were Chuhras from neighbouring villages who came to see for themselves what the rite actually involved.[146] Nathu Mal subsequently became the resident pastor in Amoutrah which became yet another centre of the mass conversion movement. Charles Forman of the Lodiana Mission reported that the conversion movement had reached two villages in the Lahore district in 1884;[147] it would later spread from that district into Ferozepur district as well. The Rev. K.C. Chatterjee also reported considerable conversions among the Chuhras in Hoshiarpur district. While never very large, this development seems to have followed upon the conversion of a number of local Chamars rather than to have been an eastward expansion of the original Chuhra conversion movements.[148]

The Chuhra conversion movement also drew new missions into the central Punjab: the American Methodists, the Salvation Army, and the Roman Catholics, the latter two more as competitors than as collaborators. The Salvation Army's initial 'invasion' of the north-west had been in the person of a British faqir and former member of the Indian Civil Service, Frederick de Lautour Tucker.[149] What distinguished their subsequent work among rural Dalits was a difference in style, marked not just by their distinctive red uniforms

---

[145] *CMS Proceedings 1885–86*, pp. 111–2.

[146] 'Baptisms at Sialkot', HFMR (February 1886), p. 343; 'Sialkot', ibid. (March 1886), p. 374; *Church of Scotland Report 1886*, pp. 97–8.

[147] C.W. Forman, 'The Chuhras', *The Presbyterian Monthly Record* (July 1885), p. 263.

[148] *Lodiana Mission Annual Report 1891*, p. 55; ibid. *1892*, p. 65; ibid. *1893*, p. 70.

[149] 'A Tour of the Punjab', *All The World* (August 1885), pp. 191–3.

but also by a radical simplicity of life as well as racial and gender equality.[150] From 1888 onwards the Roman Catholics were represented in the villages of the north-west by the Belgian Capuchins. While initially based in the cities like the Protestants, they were quickly pulled into the villages in June 1889 when some disgruntled Protestant catechists told the Catholic chaplain in Sialkot that they and their followers wanted to convert. They were placed under instruction and in September Bishop Mouard baptized seventy-five of them. However, there was nothing to this change of affiliation. 'Being displeased with their former masters, they now preached adherence to the Catholic Church by promising the people food, money and fields while they themselves ran away with fat salaries as catechists and interpreters of the missionaries.'[151] When the deception was discovered, the catechists and their followers disappeared. Nonetheless, the bishop believed that a door had been opened and so in two villages he placed priests who began long-term work among the Chuhras.[152]

The expansion of the Chuhra movement also pushed all the missions beyond their existing boundaries. When in 1892 work began on the Chenab canal in the west Punjab, many Chuhras from the central Punjab, including a significant number of Christian converts, migrated there searching for land and higher wages. The converts' migration certainly had a disruptive effect upon the congregations they left behind; the United Presbyterians alone lost an estimated five thousand members to migration and some village congregations completely disappeared as a result.[153] The missions responded to this new challenge in two ways. One was to follow the migrants, to locate as many as possible, and to establish new congregations among them. The other was to acquire land of their own in the canal

[150] Jeffrey Cox, *Imperial Fault Lines*, pp. 233–9. See also Jai Singh, 'Facts and Figures of the War in North India', *All the World* (August 1899), pp. 429–33.

[151] 'Pauperes Evangelizantur', *Collectanea Lahorensia* (October–December 1938), p. 163.

[152] Ibid., pp. 162–4.

[153] William B. Anderson and Charles R. Watson, *Far North in India*, pp. 238–9.

colonies where they could create Christian villages. The Roman Catholics took the lead in this, creating first Mariabad in 1892 and then Khushpur in 1900.[154] They were followed by the CMS, which got the tract they called Montgomerywala in 1898 and a second one they called Batemanabad about five years later. In 1899, the United Presbyterians and Church of Scotland missions each got a tract that they named Martinpur and Youngsonabad respectively. While these settlements, with their churches and schools, became centres of Christian life and outreach, they also, quite unintentionally, linked conversion to Christianity with satisfaction of land hunger in the minds of many Chuhras, especially after the Punjab Land Alienation Act of 1900 denied them land ownership.

One other significant form of expansion deserves special mention. The Chuhra movement began, and remained throughout this period, largely a movement of men. In villages where conversions took place in small batches (which was the general pattern), the first batch generally consisted almost exclusively of men. Some women and children might follow in the second or third batch some time later, or they might not follow at all.[155] Men, like Ditt himself, often took the decision without really consulting the women in their families. Women were also considered to be more deeply immersed in and thus more firmly attached to their traditional religions than were the men. One of the earliest single women missionaries to work among the Chuhras, Rose McCullough, noted another dynamic at work which made Chuhra women reluctant to convert at first. The women were concerned about their children's marriages and would even 'give their souls to Satan' to get that done. 'Therefore, when one family of a house or clan having sons and daughters embraces Christianity, they must have faith strong enough to believe that God will furnish husbands and wives for their children, as the Church forbids marriage with the heathen.'[156]

---

[154] 'Pauperes Evangelizantur', *Collectanea Lahorensia* (October–December 1938), pp. 163–4; Daniel D'Souza, *Capuchin Missions in India*, pp. 116–7.

[155] See, for example, 'Mission Work in India', *UP* (7 August, 1884), p. 502.

[156] 'Foreign Missions', *UP* (4 September 1884), p. 573. See also 'Sialkot Presbytery—India', ibid. (21 October 1886), p. 659.

To address a situation in which relatively few Chuhra women were coming forward for baptism, the missions transferred some of their single women missionaries from urban zenana work to rural work. The evangelistic challenges rural Chuhra women posed differed from those of elite urban women because, in the words of one missionary, of 'the poverty which crushes them, the squalor of their normal surroundings, the darkness and ignorance which paralyze their mental effort, the sordid ignoble toil which forms their daily round, and the utter dependence on the good will and good faith of their masters for the merest morsel of bread'.[157] In addition, assuming that the men of the village did not disrupt their women's meetings, the missionaries still had to cope with such distractions as crying babies and squabbling children when trying to teach the women. For these reasons they had to resort to endless repetition of basic teachings week after week in preparing women for baptism or communicant membership.[158] It is not clear whether a significant number of girls attended the village schools set up by the missions, but the CMS did start a Christian Girls Boarding School at Narowal for village girls.[159]

All of this numerical and geographic expansion came in the face of considerable opposition from local landlords, especially when groups of Chuhras, rather than just individuals or single families, were contemplating baptism. Initially, such opposition took the form of warnings and threats. For example, Chuhra inquirers were told that the missionaries would force them to eat frogs, pigs, and lizards or drink the blood of rabbits.[160] They were also threatened with trouble with the police, with loss of work, or even eviction from the village. If the Chuhras persisted and actually accepted baptism, they

---

[157] 'Survey in Tears in 1902', *IWCD* (February 1903), pp. 38–9.

[158] T. Marcella Sherwood, 'After Two Years in Batala', ibid. (July 1907), p. 102; 'Extracts from the Narowal Report', ibid. (July 1912), p. 132.

[159] 'Narowal Christian Girls Boarding School', *IWCD* (November 1909), p. 173.

[160] 'Sialkot Presbytery—India', *UP* (30 April 1885), p. 278; *Lodiana Mission Annual Report 1895*, p. 64. The rabbit was a totem and thus eating it a taboo among certain Chuhra clans.

then faced almost inevitable persecution. Two examples serve to illustrate the usual methods. In two villages near Narowal the converts were denied not only work at harvest time but also the payments due them at harvest time for the whole year's work. In one of them the leading Christian was charged and imprisoned for poisoning a cow, which as it turned out had been poisoned by the accuser himself while the Christian was away from the village.[161] In the same area the *zaildar* brought false charges against the Christians in his village and while they were away defending themselves, he turned his cattle loose in their fields.[162] Among other forms of persecution used to harass converts into submission were denying them water rights and making them the first sent for *begar* (forced labour) when government officials demanded it. The landlords' motives for persecution were seen as being more socio-economic than religious in nature; what seemed to concern them was the potential loss of a cheap and submissive labour force rather than of some co-religionists.[163]

What then was the attraction? Why did so many Chuhras seek Christian instruction and become baptized converts? This question constantly plagued the missionaries who tried to sort out who among their many inquirers were properly motivated and who were not. Given the wide range of requests made to them, it is impossible to generalize but one theme seems to be dominant in their reflections on what was happening around them. They saw the conversion movement as a basically social movement aimed at achieving a rise in social status, and with it greater dignity and respect. Christian teachings concerning God's love for all regardless of status; the life-style changes Christians mandated; the acquisition of a new label, 'Christian', to replace the despised label, 'Chuhra'; and the presence

[161] *CMS Proceedings 1891–92*, pp. 113–4.

[162] *CMS Proceedings 1892–93*, p. 121.

[163] *UPCNA Annual Report 1894–95*, p. 33. One mission reported that landlords opposed the conversion of Chuhra women who worked in their homes because they feared that they might influence their wives. *Lodiana Mission Annual Report 1900*, p. 66.

of help in the form of a literate catechist–teacher in the village all contributed towards this end and were valued accordingly. Pandit Harikishan Kaul, Superintendent of the 1911 Punjab Census, put it this way.

The depressed classes are in a condition of peculiar social and religious disadvantage and gain most by the equality of treatment preached and secured by the Missions. Their status is raised. An untouchable becomes touchable by adopting Christianity, and has the satisfaction and advantage of receiving spiritual instructions from highly educated and sympathetic clergymen exactly in the same familiar way as his fellow-beings of the highest position. He can receive education and follow better pursuits than his degraded hereditary calling.[164]

Kaul's comment also points to another, less conscious but no less real, motivation underlying the Chuhra conversion movement at its most advanced stage. Chuhras were bound and profoundly conditioned by the patron–client relationships which lay at the basis of the rural socio-economic order. Linked to their desire for freedom from bondage to these oppressive and degrading relationships was a perception that the missionary and the whole mission network might serve as an alternative, more benevolent patron, or even counter-patron, who would help them in their struggle with the local landlords and moneylenders. The missionaries were slower to see this dimension of the movement than its more obvious thrust towards higher social status, but when they did, they took differing attitudes towards it. Gordon and his fellow United Presbyterians described it as '*ma-bap*ism' and sought to stamp it out like a heresy.[165] They did this, on the one hand, by avoiding interfering in rural conflicts affecting their inquirers as much as possible and, on the other, by making their rural congregations as self-supporting as possible. In short, they considered a growth in independence and

---

[164] *Punjab Census Report 1911*, I, p. 192.

[165] Andrew Gordon, *Our India Mission*, pp. 438, 445. *Ma–bap* literally means mother–father and expresses a dependent relationship which Gordon neither welcomed nor considered healthy.

self-respect in the face of difficulties to be part of the 'growth in grace' they desired for their converts.[166] The CMS missionaries seemed more willing to interfere when their converts were being persecuted, using their contacts with district officials to give the converts a fair hearing or to otherwise help them out in times of difficulty. To return to one of the examples cited above, in one of the villages where Christians had been denied wages and employment, the mission helped out with the cattle poisoning case; in the other the mission hired the Christians to build a church. When the Muslim landlords claimed that the site for the church was a graveyard and took the matter to the police, the missionaries helped fight and win the case.[167] However, in general the missionaries preferred the role of guardian–advisor to getting involved in all of the local disputes of countless rural Chuhras. This meant, in the end, that Christianity was not actually the threat to the rural social order which the landlords feared it might become.[168]

However, even though the Chuhra conversion movement did not change the imbalance of power or hierarchical social relationships within the villages where Chuhra converts lived, there is evidence that it did change the converts themselves. This seems to have been what Christian evangelists were aiming at. K.C. Chatterjee in Hoshiarpur indicated that 'Our aim is to raise them socially intellectually morally and spiritually and put them side by side with the best Christians from the upper classes.'[169] This was a gospel of social mobility through inner transformation rather than of structural change through united political action. It meshed quite

[166] They also believed that 'persecution has an important function to perform in excluding hypocrites from the pale of the Church and purifying saints'. 'Sialkot Presbytery—India', *UP* (20 November 1884), p. 751.

[167] The bones dug up turned out to be those of goats and dogs. *CMS Proceedings 1891–92*, pp. 113–4.

[168] For a fuller examination of the images and expectations rural Chuhras and missionaries brought to their encounter, see John C.B. Webster, 'Dalits and Christianity in Colonial Punjab: Cultural Interactions'.

[169] *Lodiana Mission Annual Report 1893*, p. 70.

well with Chuhra aspirations and did achieve some success.[170] While circumstances varied from individual to individual and from village to village, conversion did seem to bring some rise in social status, especially after Chuhra converts made some of the required life-style changes. Some converts, or their children, acquired an education and thus could move into occupations other than those assigned to them within the rural economy. A good number became mission workers. Of equal importance was the greater sense of personal dignity, self-respect, and independence converts gained as they discovered inner capacities that they did not know they had. Unprecedented opportunities were opening up before them; they were no longer as bound by fate and rigid social custom as before.[171]

The urban elite reform bodies, which had challenged Christian evangelists so effectively in the towns and cities, were very slow to respond to the challenge of the Chuhra conversion movement. One newspaper sneered at the missionaries for going after Chuhras and Chamars because they could not get enough respectable converts to make their annual statistical reports look good.[172] The Arya Samaj in Sialkot began performing *shuddhi* on Meghs only in 1903.[173] Moreover, Jones has pointed out that with the exception of some Kabirpanthis in Hoshiarpur, the Arya Samaj 'refrained from *shuddhi* among the lowest of the untouchables' during this period.[174] Mission sources reveal little or no competition from the Arya Samaj and other urban reform bodies for Chuhra and other Dalit converts.

[170] Harding also found that 'those individuals upon whose networks or experiences the initial spread of information about Christianity relied acted out of a desire to improve the lives of people or groups with whom they were familiar, and were not actuated by any notions of a wider pan-Chuhra or pan-Chamar consciousness or agenda'. Christopher Harding, 'The Dynamics of Low-Caste Conversion Movements', p. 262.

[171] This issue is dealt with more fully in John C.B. Webster, 'Christian Conversion in the Punjab: What Has Changed?'.

[172] Excerpt from the *Sat Dharm Parcharik* of 24 March 1902 in *Selections from the Vernacular Newspapers—Punjab 1902*, p. 216.

[173] Kenneth W. Jones, *Arya Dharm*, p. 212.

[174] Ibid., p. 311.

However, following the Aga Khan deputation to the viceroy in 1906, which not only requested separate electorates for Muslims but also argued that the depressed classes not be included in the Hindu totals when determining proportional representation, conversion assumed a political significance it had not had before. As some missionaries had noted,[175] following the grant of communal electorates to Muslims in the 1909 constitution, there were in the press expressions of concern for the welfare of the depressed classes emanating from various reform bodies and public figures. When the 1911 Census returns came in, educated Punjabi Hindus became increasingly alarmed about the numerical decline of their community and helped form the All India Shuddhi Sabha in 1911 in order to stem the tide. While this was not the intention of the Chuhra conversion movement, before the end of this period it had succeeded in helping to make 'the Dalit issue' a public issue which could no longer be ignored as if it did not exist. In this respect the Chuhra conversion movement succeeded well beyond its own expectations.

The movement's influence upon Christianity in north-west India was also profound. For one thing, it gave Christianity in the north-west its rural base, which remains to this day, as well as a distinctively rural Dalit form of Christianity. Cox has rightly described this as neither indigenous, nor foreign, nor hybrid so much as *sui generis*, cultivating a piety 'based on the singing of hymns and Psalms, memorization of Scripture verses, festival visits by dignitaries foreign and Indian, and Christmas observance'.[176] To this the Roman Catholics added elaborate ritual and devotion to the saints, especially the Virgin Mary.[177] The movement also totally changed the demographics of the Christian community. It had begun this period with a small number of converts from miscellaneous backgrounds concentrated in the towns and cities. By World War I it had become

---

[175] *Punjab Mission Annual Report 1909*, p. 24.

[176] Jeffrey Cox, *Imperial Fault Lines*, pp. 149, 152.

[177] Christopher Harding, 'The Dynamics of Low-Caste Conversion Movements', pp. 133, 218, 279.

a much larger and overwhelmingly rural Dalit community. With this change came a corresponding shift in the image of the Christian community. One missionary reported colleagues being stigmatized as 'gurus of the Chuhras'.[178] Christianity's Dalit image did not have as negative an impact upon the conversion of people from other backgrounds as the missionaries had feared it might.[179] Others continued to enter the churches as individuals and nuclear families at the same slow, steady rate as before. Finally, the Chuhra movement was to have a polarizing effect within the missions and churches of the north-west. As missionaries concentrated more fully upon the villages, they identified themselves increasingly with the interests and aspirations of those at the bottom of rural society, just as their urban colleagues were identifying increasingly with the interests and aspirations of the educated elites. This polarization of missionary opinion would become more obvious after World War I when the north-west became much more highly politicized.

The Christian Community

It was during this period that the Christian community emerged as a distinct social entity within north-west Indian society. To some extent this was a consequence of increased size and a high growth rate; there were many more Christians in the north-west at the end of this period than there had been when it began. More importantly, two other processes were also at work as the community grew in numbers. One was that Christians in urban as well as rural settings continued to develop their own shared pattern of life which set them apart in certain respects both from other communities and from the missionaries. The other was that Christians in the north-west were becoming more highly integrated as a community across lines of denomination, class, caste, and religious background. Each

---

[178] H.C. Velte, 'Mission Work Among the Low Caste Tribes of the Punjab', p. 11.

[179] See, for example, *UPCNA Annual Report 1876*, p. 19; *1877*, p. 15; *1884*, pp. 85–6; *1885*, pp. 25–7.

of these developments needs to be examined in turn for a clearer picture to emerge.

At the outset of this period the 1881 Census recorded a total of 3912 Indian Christians in the Punjab and its dependencies.[180] By 1891, this total had increased to 19,750 and in 1901 to 38,513.[181] However, in 1911, the number jumped to an astounding 163,994 with another 877 in the newly created North-West Frontier Province.[182] This number perplexed missionaries, as it far exceeded those in their own statistical reports; their only explanation was that Chuhras who had not yet been baptized were reporting themselves as Christians.[183] During World War I, they discovered 'free lance missions' going around the countryside promising Chuhras land if they became Christians and then charging them from one to five rupees for each baptism. Several of these entrepreneurs were caught and convicted of fraud.[184]

The rapid growth of the Christian community was largely due to the Chuhra conversion movement. The 1911 Census listed 92,769 Presbyterians of one sort or another (56.6 per cent of the total) up from 1284 in 1881; 29,051 Anglicans, up from 2030 in 1881; 18,007 Salvation Army and 8,497 Roman Catholics (up from 300 in 1881), both of whom had enjoyed evangelistic success almost exclusively among rural Chuhras.[185] However, perhaps the most striking feature of the 1911 Census for the Indian Christian population was its literacy figures. The male literacy rate among Indian Christians was 4.4 per cent as compared with the Punjab average of 6.8 per cent. This literacy rate was lower than the comparable Hindu (9.5 per cent)

---

[180] *Punjab Census 1881*, I, p. 151.

[181] *Punjab Census 1891*, I, p. 97; *Punjab Census 1901*, I, p. 172.

[182] *Punjab Census 1911*, I, p. 178; *Northwest Frontier Province Census 1911*, p. cxvi.

[183] *CMS Proceedings 1911–12*, pp. 94–5; H.U. Weitbrecht, 'The Christian Population of the Panjab as Shown in the Last Census', *IWCD* (March 1912), p. 44; C.F. Hall, 'A Suggested Policy for Mass Movements', *CMR* (May 1914), p. 280.

[184] These 'missions' are described in W.P. Hares, 'Mass Movement Work in the Central Punjab', *CMR* (September 1918), p. 318.

[185] *Punjab Census 1881*, I, p. 152; *Punjab Census 1911*, I, p. 196.

and Sikh (9.4 per cent) rates, but higher than the Muslim rate (2.7 per cent), and significantly higher than the overall Chuhra (0.20 per cent), Chamar (0.70 per cent), or even Jat (1.7 per cent) rates.[186] The Indian Christian female literacy rate was 3.5 per cent which placed them higher not only than all Hindu (0.7 per cent), Sikh (1.2 per cent), and Muslim (0.20 per cent) women but also higher than women of every caste except the Khatris (6 per cent).[187] This was a truly remarkable achievement given the fact that the overwhelming majority of Christians were from rural Chuhra backgrounds.

THE URBAN CHURCHES

The foundations of the urban churches in the north-west were laid during the previous period. This period witnessed more continuity with the past than significant change. As far as can be determined, the social composition of the urban churches remained proportionately about the same, even though the urban churches grew in size. Neither the statistical information nor the summary statements concerning the backgrounds and/or occupations of the members of urban congregations are as readily available for this as for the earlier periods. However, a few statements can be made with confidence. One is that both the Baptist and the Anglican churches in Delhi remained predominantly Chamar and most Chamar converts remained in their traditional or related occupations. A second is that the churches established on the fringes of the region tended to draw their membership from migrant workers rather than from the local population. In 1886, the Baptists described their congregation in Simla as made up mostly of Mazhabi Sikh workers coming up to Simla from the villages below Kalka,[188] while in 1905 the Anglicans described theirs as comprised of English-speaking Bengalis working in government offices, government press employees most of whom spoke Urdu, and servants.[189] Similarly,

---

[186] *Punjab Census 1911*, I, pp. 319, 322, 340.

[187] Ibid., I, p. 322.

[188] *Baptist Missionary Society Annual Report 1886*, p. 16.

[189] *CMS Proceedings 1904–1905*, p. 243.

the congregations in Dalhousie and Quetta were comprised almost exclusively of migrants from elsewhere.[190] Major exceptions would be Chamba and Ladakh which continued to draw their membership from the local population.[191] The church in Kashmir included both Kashmiris and outsiders, including servants of European summer visitors.[192] The urban churches in the central Punjab, where the Chuhra mass conversion was going on in the villages, continued to receive a small number of converts each year from other backgrounds just as they had in the past.

Perhaps the most striking feature of this period is that the urban-educated elite really came into their own as leaders within the churches and, to a lesser extent, in the public life of the region. Of these, Raja Harnam Singh was by far the most prominent, both as a member of the Punjab and Imperial Legislative Councils and as kind of 'patron-in-chief' of the Punjabi Christian community.[193] Sushil Kumar Rudra, friend and mentor of C.F. Andrews, became the first Indian principal of any Christian college in India when he became principal of St. Stephen's College in 1907. In fact, education, including higher education, became the main professional field for the Christian elite, with medicine being perhaps the second most popular field. Others, sharing the aspirations of the Western-educated elite in general, entered government service.[194] Charles

[190] *Church of Scotland Annual Report 1915*, p. 142; *CMS Proceedings 1888–89*, p. 125.

[191] By 1893, the Moravians reported forty-eight converts in the region. John Brown Myers, ed., *The Centenary Celebration of the Baptist Missionary Society 1892–93*, London: The Baptist Missionary Society, 1893, p. 330.

[192] *CMS Proceedings 1891–92*, p. 120.

[193] For example, he set up a Rs. 50,000 scholarship fund for Christian students; he gave a community entertainment in Amritsar at the time of Queen Victoria's Diamond Jubilee; and was active in the Punjab Branch of the Indian Christian Association to represent the political interests of the community. *CMS Proceedings 1902–03*, p. 230; 'Royal Gifts and Loyal Festivities in the Punjab', *IWCD* (January 1898), p. 4.

[194] Twenty Christian 'old boys' of the elite Baring School in Batala are listed by occupation in a history of the CMS in Punjab published in 1904. Of these, half

Golaknath, a barrister, was a member of the Indian Association of Lahore and in 1906 its vice-president. He attended the 1886 and 1888 sessions of the Indian National Congress, serving on its Steering Committee in 1888, 1893, and 1900.[195] Alfred Nundy was editor of *The Tribune* but few other Christians entered into these important professions. Finally, there were elite, English-speaking clergy attached to virtually every mission. Among the more prominent were G. L. Thakur Das, John Williams, P.C. Uppal, Henry Golaknath and K.C. Chatterjee.

Two issues seem to have been central in the life of the urban churches throughout this period. The first of these was basically a boundary issue. To a great extent others drew boundaries between the Christian community and other communities. When high-caste Hindus, Muslims, or Sikhs were baptized, they were still ejected from their former caste and religious communities. The government also defined boundaries by passing separate laws concerning marriage, divorce, and inheritance that applied only to Christians.[196] However, Christians also were active in defining boundaries as well. This was most dramatically illustrated in the case of the Chamar Christians in Delhi who continued to live and work alongside their fellow Chamars after baptism. For Baptists, who were concerned about developing a Christianity rooted in Chamar culture, the boundaries were deliberately left blurred and porous. The SPG, on the other hand, sought to socialize Chamar converts within an Anglican framework and thus believed a sharper break with the past was necessary. They denied communicant membership to those converts who contracted betrothals or marriages with non-Christians

---

were in government service, three were missionaries, and five were educators. Robert Clark, *The Missions of the Church Missionary Society*, p. 84.

[195] Barrier and Wallace, Punjab Bibliographic Project. The sources of material on their data cards are the *Tribune* and Annual Reports of the Indian National Congress.

[196] For example, Act XXI of 1866 (The Native Converts Marriage Dissolution Act), Act XV of 1872 (The Indian Christian Marriage Act), and Act VII of 1901 (Administration of Estates of Native Christians). For more details, see John C.B. Webster, *The Christian Community and Change*, p. 250.

or who participated in life-cycle rituals and community meals for which food had been previously offered to idols. In 1883, they acquired four bastis for Christians to settle in and made these prohibitions, plus another one against work on Sundays, mandatory for all residents.[197] Converts were thus forced to choose between membership in the Chamar *biradari* and the Christian Church. A defining moment in this struggle occurred at a public meeting of Chamars in June 1884 when a group of converts announced that they wished to separate themselves formally from the biradari.[198] A few years later another sifting of members took place when a faqir arrived in the Chamar basti of Delhi promising the residents equality with other castes. In time he turned against the Christians, forcing them to choose between their Chamar and Christian associations. Both the Baptists and the SPG lost heavily, as many converts and even some catechists succumbed to social pressure and left. This effectively ended the Baptist strategy and from that time on the Delhi Christian community became more separate and distinct from their fellow Chamars.[199]

The flip side of the boundary issue during this period of increasing Westernization and rising nationalism concerned the cultural identity of the urban Christian community. Clear-cut evidence on this subject is difficult to find, as is a clear reference point for comparison. Compared to the missionaries, urban Christians were profoundly Indian in life-style, associations, and psychology.[200] Educated Christians appeared to be not only as Indian and as westernized as other members of the educated elite, but also more Westernized than less well-educated urban and rural Christians. In their corporate life Christians developed their own melas and holidays. Churches were being built using Indian architectural styles. However, perhaps

[197] 'Delhi', *MF* (October 1884), p. 318.

[198] This is described in great detail in G.A. Lefroy, *The Leather-Workers of Daryaganj*.

[199] See John C.B. Webster, 'Missionary Strategy and the Development of the Christian Community: Delhi 1859–1884'.

[200] These can be found in missionary comments and explanations to the churches and boards back home.

the greatest and most lasting change was made in the area of music when the Rev. Imam-ul-Din Shahbaz translated the psalms into metrical Punjabi and set them to Punjabi tunes. These *zaburs* (psalms) became very popular, adding to the depth and appeal of Christian faith. There was, however, little experimentation in theology beyond the use of the fulfilment theory already described and formal worship remained more Western (in translation) than Indian in inspiration.

The cultural identity of the Christian community had an important internal political dimension as well. At this stage this was primarily an elite issue. The educated elite had already begun to challenge the exclusive authority of the foreign missionaries within the churches and community; that challenge became more pronounced during this period. As indicated in the previous chapter, the elite clergy related to the Lodiana Mission wanted to become full members of the mission where real power lay. This solution, supported by the Lodiana Mission, was rejected by the Board of Foreign Missions in New York, which wanted local leaders to identify with their churches and presbyteries rather than with the foreign missions. To this end it denied local leaders membership in the mission and decided instead to transfer, incrementally, the missions' decision-making powers and responsibilities to the churches. The Board also linked those increments to the degree of financial self-support the churches attained, whereas the view in India was that Indian Christians would support financially only those churches that they themselves governed. [201] Moreover, as Kanwar Raghbir Singh pointed out to the Lahore Presbytery in 1914, if self-support were given priority, then the Church would get only the quality of clergy which it could afford, rather than the quality of clergy it needed to minister effectively both to its own members and to an awakened India.[202]

---

[201] For a fuller treatment of this case, see John C.B. Webster, *The Christian Community and Change*, pp. 215–23; Daniel Johnson Fleming, *Devolution in Mission Administration*.

[202] The title of his presentation was significant: 'The Causes Preventing the Young Educated Indian Christians from Taking up Mission Service'.

The Church Missionary Society began this period with a parallel mission and Church structure but then proceeded to unify them. The two parallel bodies, the Missionary Conference and the Native Church Council, were under the Corresponding Committee, which related to the CMS in London. The Native Church Council got off to a good start. It undertook responsibility for rural mission around Amritsar in 1881–2 and offered to take further responsibility for work elsewhere in the diocese, but failed to sustain its initial enthusiasm because it remained subject to foreign oversight and veto power.[203] In an attempt to overcome not only festering racial suspicions and divisions built into this structure, but also the functional divisions between evangelists (under the mission) and pastors (attached to the churches), the Corresponding Committee, Native Church Council, and Missionary Conference were combined into one body known as the Punjab Mission Council in 1905. This was divided into six district mission councils, each of which met annually, and a central mission council, which also met annually with the bishop of Lahore as its chair. Indian representatives were elected to the central mission council, but it was heavily dominated by Europeans because, as in the Presbyterian case, most of the money came from overseas.[204]

Whether transferring power from mission to church bodies[205] or unifying the two into a single body,[206] the missionaries throughout this period remained paternalists caught in the bind of both retaining and letting go of leadership. The result was a nationalist movement

---

[203] Both Cox and Harding make this point. Jeffrey Cox, *Imperial Fault Lines*, p. 103; Christopher Harding, 'The Dynamics of Low-Caste Conversion Movements', pp. 117–20. See also, John C.B. Webster, 'British Missions in India', p. 44.

[204] H.U. Weitbrecht, 'The Punjab Mission Council', *CMI* (September 1905), pp. 664–8; H.G. Grey, 'Native Church Organization in India', ibid. (August 1909), pp. 476–81.

[205] This approach was also followed by the United Presbyterians who described the mission as a committee of the General Assembly (in the USA) and handmaid of the presbytery (in India). 'Sialkot Presbytery—India', *UP* (2 October 1884), pp. 631–2.

[206] The SPG, like their fellow Anglicans in the CMS, also worked through a unified council which had Indian members.

within the churches which resembled the Indian nationalist movement in general, with the Indian elites and entrenched Europeans arguing over similar issues concerning the sharing and transfer of power. There were, however, three significant differences. One was that the missionaries were earlier and more deeply committed in principle to the independence of the Church than the Raj was to Indian independence, which may explain why the nationalist movement began earlier in the churches than within the wider society. Another difference was that whereas the Raj lived off income derived from Indian taxpayers, the missions (and to a lesser extent the churches) lived off money sent from abroad. The mission boards thus saw self-support and self-propagation to be essential to, if not a requirement for, ecclesiastical independence.[207] Finally, the nationalist movement within the churches of the north-west never developed an 'extremist' wing creating an alternative, culturally Indian Church completely independent of all ties with the Western missions, as was the case with the Christo Samaj in Bengal.[208]

THE RURAL CHURCHES

Demographics provide the key to understanding the rural churches during this period. They were overwhelmingly Dalit churches: some Megh in Sialkot district, some Chamar near Delhi, but most were Chuhra. Only in the new Christian canal colony settlements and in isolated villages here and there did Christians own land. For purposes of analysis it is, therefore, necessary to distinguish the Christian canal colonies where Christians were both numerous and prosperous from the rest of the region where Christians were scattered in relatively small clusters working as village menials totally dependent upon others for their livelihood. Social and geographic location played a major role in shaping rural Christian culture and its piety, as well as in defining the boundary issues Christians faced in the villages throughout this period.

---

[207] This was made explicit by Robert E. Speer, Secretary of the Board of Foreign Missions of the Presbyterian Church in the USA Letter to JJ Lucas, 3 August 1911.

[208] Kaj Baago, 'The First Independence Movement among Indian Christians', pp. 65–78.

The most important boundary issue was adopting and retaining a distinct Christian ritual and worship life. For Chuhra Christians this meant giving up the worship of Bala Shah, which does not seem to have been too difficult. In 1912, one mission reported that Bala Shah shrines were gradually disappearing, even though none were to be removed until all the Chuhras in its village had been converted.[209] However, the issues surrounding marriage, which was where Chuhra ritual was most elaborate, were far more complex and difficult. Chuhra Christians, unlike higher-caste Christians, had not been outcasted upon conversion and so retained relationships with their caste fellows. The mission requirement that converts marry Christians according to Christian rites posed two serious problems which strained those relationships. One was that betrothals and payments made with non-Christian families according to Chuhra rites prior to conversion could not be broken easily. The other was that at times relatives refused to attend marriages performed according to Christian rites because they deviated so markedly from Chuhra practice. Attempts to reconcile the differing rites were sometimes negotiated but were not always successful.[210] However, by the end of this period, this problem was less serious in those areas where conversions were most numerous and thus Christian marriages were easier to arrange.[211]

Rural Christians also drew boundaries between themselves and their fellow Chuhras by organizing their own panchayats. This was most obvious in the Christian villages where the panchayats governed the entire village. For example, Montgomerywala had two panchayats at the end of this period. The pastorate committee, chaired by the pastor, looked after church affairs, including marital disputes, discipline cases, and poor relief; the village committee,

---

[209] *Church of Scotland Annual Report 1899*, p. 133; ibid. *1912*, p. 113.

[210] See, for example, *Lodiana Mission Annual Report 1899*, pp. 3–4. For example, Rev. Puran Chand Uppal allowed the couple to walk around a fire but would not allow butter for Agni to be poured into it or verses from the Shastras recited. Ibid. *1900*, p. 26.

[211] *UPCNA Annual Report 1903*, p. 49; W.T. Anderson, 'Progress in the Village Christian Communities', ibid. *1909*, p. 173.

chaired by one of the two lambardars who dealt with police and government matters, maintained the village guest house and settled local water disputes.[212] In other villages where (Protestant) Christians were sufficiently numerous to have either a formally organized congregation with its own lay leadership or at least an unorganized fellowship with a catechist or teacher, they developed their own internal organization with functions similar to that of a caste panchayat.[213] The missions conducted a variety of training courses for these local lay leaders.[214]

However, perhaps the most telling boundary marker was the growing sense of Christian identity among rural Christians. The Punjab Census Commissioner commented on this in 1891 when he found that 97 per cent of the Indian Christians returned themselves as 'Native Christians' with no reference to their caste backgrounds.

The Christian pastors very properly object to their flock being called on compulsorily to return the name of their former caste. In the first place the Native Christians from one point of view renounces caste as inconsistent with Christianity; in the next place, and from another point of view, the Native Christians form a genuine caste of their own; and, thirdly, it would be impossible to describe the original caste of Native Christians in the second or third generation whose progenitors had sprung, as they often do, from several different castes; and, lastly, the Native Christian being in most cases originally of a low caste, wishes to rise socially as well as morally above the level of that caste and is anxious to avoid being classed by the name he formerly bore.[215]

This growing sense of Christian identity was enhanced by subsequent government actions during World War I when the rural Punjab became a major recruiting ground for the army. The

[212] Anne W. Gross, 'The Local Government of an Indian Christian Village', *IWCD* (June 1914), pp. 111–12.

[213] *CMS Proceedings 1914–15*, p. 112. The Roman Catholics kept all power and responsibility was in the hands of the missionary priest. Christopher Harding, 'The Dynamics of Low-Caste Conversion Movements', p. 312.

[214] For a description of the United Presbyterian case during this period, see Frederick and Margaret Stock, *People Movements in the Punjab*, pp. 123–6.

[215] *Punjab Census 1891*, I, p. 98.

government was persuaded to recruit Christians who were formed initially into two, then three double companies (one CMS and two Presbyterian), and finally into a regiment, the 71st Punjabis. The formation of this regiment was a matter of considerable community pride and among its volunteer chaplains were some American missionaries![216]

Rural Christian culture and piety were also very much a function of demographics because corporate Christian worship, systematic Christian nurture, and consistent pastoral care could be maintained only where Christians were concentrated in sufficiently large numbers to support, or at least warrant, the presence of a pastor, catechist or teacher. Even in the canal colonies, most Christians lived in scattered villages as much as 10–15 miles apart and could be visited only once or twice a year. As a result their 'Christianization' could only be very modest at best.[217] In the Christian settlements, however, much more could be done. The Catholic colony of Mariabad became a model of Christian socialization.[218] The Anglicans at Montgomerywala not only built the largest church in the area but also maintained a resident pastor and school at their own expense,[219] as did most of the Christian settlements.[220] Culturally these villages seem to have been similar to other Punjabi villages, except that they observed Christian holidays and had Christian melas.[221] In Clarkabad and Santokh Majra, where the missions functioned as landlords responsible for paying land revenue

[216] William Dalgetty, 'A Christian Panjabi Regiment', *LW* (November 1915), pp. 345–6; 'From the Outposts', ibid. (May 1916), pp. 142–3; R.B. Love, 'Men—Real Men', *IS* (August 1919), pp. 231–2.

[217] T. Holden, 'The Jhang Bar C. M. S. Mission', *CMI* (April 1904), pp. 265–8; *CMS Proceedings 1906–07*, p. 202.

[218] Christopher Harding, 'The Dynamics of Low-Caste Conversion Movements', pp. 318–9.

[219] 'The Mission Field', *CMI* (August 1903), p. 617.

[220] See, for example, *Church of Scotland Annual Report 1906*, p. 152; 'Bishop Whitehead in the Punjab: Extracts from his Journal', *CMI* (August 1913), pp. 485, 488; *Church of Scotland Annual Report 1906*, p. 152.

[221] For a description of Christmas and the Christmas mela at Clarkabad, see *CMS Proceedings for 1901–02*, p. 251.

to the government, there were open conflicts over the acquisition of land ownership rights, while in Montgomerywala and Batemanabad, where Christians leased from the government directly, there were fights over the selection of the lambardars through whom they paid.[222]

In the central Punjab, the picture is somewhat different, primarily because of the converts' poverty and dependence on the goodwill of their landlords. In his reports about the rural churches around Narowal between 1899 and 1906, C.M. Gough presented a picture of religious indifference and discouragement, of continued use of charms, and of pressure from landlords which made sabbath observance difficult. Although their status relative to other Chuhras was rising, they seemed to Gough to have wanted only to replace their despised label, 'Chuhra' with the more respectable one of 'Christian', but showed little interest in spiritual growth or inner transformation.[223] Seven years later, W.P. Hares presented a much more positive picture of the same rural churches. Christians were more clean and godly than their fellow Chuhras and so their status had risen. Attendance at worship was good and the level of giving to the church quite remarkable, even in hard times.[224] Elsewhere in the Punjab at that time, a United Presbyterian missionary was making similar comments about the growing spirit of self-respect, self-support, and 'independence' among converts whose 'ma-bapism'

---

[222] 'The Mission Field', *CMI* (July 1901), p. 549; *CMS Proceedings 1902–03*, p. 239; *Punjab Mission Annual Report 1905*, p. 126. In Mariabad, the Lahore diocese was the landlord, but in the later Roman Catholic villages 'the Government mortgaged land directly to Christian tenants' with the diocese acting as government agent and tax collector. Christopher Harding, 'The Dynamics of Low-Caste Conversion Movements', p. 322.

[223] *CMS Proceedings 1898–99*, pp. 224–5; ibid. *1900–01*, p. 286; ibid. *1901–02*, p. 249; ibid. *1902–03*, p. 236; ibid. *1905–06*, p. 191. The Lodiana Mission Report for 1893 made some similar observations, adding that as village menials they had little leisure time for learning, p. 10.

[224] W.P. Hares, 'Mass Movements and their Consequences', *CMI* (January 1913), pp. 31–5.

and dependency had, a generation earlier, been lifted up as a major spiritual problem.[225]

Worship in the rural churches showed little western influence. People sat on mats or rugs; liturgies and sermons were simplified to adapt to an oral culture. Music played a central role for devotional and teaching purposes, particularly since traditionally the Chuhras were good singers,[226] and new hymns with Punjabi tunes were being composed, often by Chuhra converts themselves. Two of these, translated by John Youngson of the Church of Scotland mission, give some hint of the Chuhra Christian piety of this period. One tells the story of Jesus raising Lazarus from death and ends by saying,

If any desire to go to heaven, let them believe in this Jesus.
God gave Him all power in heaven and in earth.
O seeker, my Saviour, Jesus, is Lord of all![227]

The other meditates upon the death of Jesus and closes with these words.

We are all beggars at Thy door
And Thou hast fed us all;
In Thy hand is all my life,
The shadow of Thy mercy is over me;
O beloved, show kindness to me,
Who am oppressed by many sorrows.[228]

Near the end of this period there was a revival in the Punjab, the focal point of which became the annual Sialkot convention. Begun in 1904 with an attendance of 200, it grew to 300 in 1905, and then the following year to about 1500, not all of whom stayed the entire ten days. Much time during the conventions was devoted to prayer;

---

[225] W.T. Anderson, 'Progress in the Village Christian Communities', in *UPCNA Annual Report, 1909*, p. 172.

[226] 'Panjab', *HFMR* (2 January 1895), p. 260.

[227] 'Sialkot', ibid. (February 1887), p. 26.

[228] 'Sialkot', ibid. (January 1887), p. 6.

prayer tents for men and women were kept open throughout the day and night. Repentance, intense devotion, singing of zaburs, and reconciliation of parties in conflict were some of the 'manifestations of the Spirit' mentioned in reports of the conventions which by 1907 were attracting Christians of all denominations, even from other parts of India, as well as curious Hindus and Muslims.[229]

INTEGRATION

Even as the Christian community grew in size and its boundaries became more clearly defined during this period, it was becoming more diverse and several of its internal cleavages becoming more apparent. Of these perhaps the most obvious one was that between foreign missionaries and Indian Christians. Both the nationalist movement within the churches and sympathetic missionaries like C.F. Andrews were committed to exposing and overcoming this racial/national barrier to Christian unity. On the other hand, the gender issue was hardly addressed at all. Instead, 'women's work' was treated as a largely autonomous and subordinate sphere of mission activity; women had little voice in the councils of the churches or community during this period.[230] Any cleavage between converts from different religious backgrounds was an exclusively urban and generally local problem which seems to have warranted far less attention than three others which came into prominence during this period. The first of these might best be described as a class and cultural cleavage between the urban educated elite and the rapidly increasing rural poor. The second was the related caste cleavage between the higher-caste and Dalit converts, whether urban or rural. The third was the denominational cleavage between the

---

[229] 'Some Impressions of the Sialkot Convention', *UP* (11 January 1906), pp. 10–11; 'India News Letter', ibid. (4 October 1906), p. 25; 'The Sialkot Convention, 1906', ibid. (11 October 1906), pp. 11–12; 'The Sialkot Convention', ibid. (25 October 1906), p. 10; 'India News Letter', ibid. (26 December 1907), p. 24.

[230] For example, it was only in 1906 and under much pressure from women's missionary societies in the USA that the Lodiana Mission allowed single missionary women to become voting members of the mission. Punjab Mission of the Presbyterian Church in the USA, *Minutes of the Annual Meeting 1906*, p. 22.

already established Protestant missions and the Roman Catholics. Each of these warrants a brief description.

Prior to this period there were few rural converts or congregations; those that did exist were located near urban areas and thus were, in a sense, rural extensions of basically urban congregations. The Chuhra conversion movement changed that by producing clusters or congregations of rural converts unconnected to pre-existing urban congregations. Mission reports during this period often refer to 'city work' and 'village work' separately as quite distinct spheres of activity. At this stage only two things brought the two together. The first was their absorption into shared ecclesiastical structures such as presbyteries or district councils where the new rural congregations were represented alongside the older urban congregations. There they did the planning and decision making for the Church together under the careful guidance of the attending missionaries. The second was through the 'home mission work' conducted either by these bodies or by local congregations. For example, the CMS Native Church Council took responsibility for rural evangelistic work in the villages near Amritsar and the Ludhiana Presbytery did the same for the villages near Jullundur, Ludhiana, and Ambala, while the Naulakha Presbyterian Church in Lahore supported a lot of home mission work. The urban elites sponsored and oversaw the work of the National Missionary Society in the canal colonies. While urban and rural Christians were thus in touch with each other in these ways, it is difficult to determine how meaningful their inter-action was.

Caste divisions were not as prominent a feature of church life in the north-west as they were in south India. They also seemed to have been more closely associated with class divisions than in the south, probably because ritual purity and pollution were less important status indicators to Punjabis than were such secular criteria as land ownership, wealth, education, and lifestyle. As has already been pointed out, Christians saw themselves as a 'community without caste' and took pride in that self-image. However, that does not mean that they were blind to caste within their own ranks. For example, when the Chuhras of Fatehgarh village approached the

CMS missionaries at Batala concerning instruction, baptism, and a school, the Christians in Amritsar became concerned that their status would suffer as a consequence. This concern was addressed at a meeting of the Central Church Committee after the delegates had visited Fatehgarh. The result was 'a general agreement that no considerations of caste ought to prevent admission to full Christian rights; but that converts should be carefully separated from degrading heathen habits and social distinctions [between converts and other Chuhras] be duly maintained'.[231] At about the same time, when a much smaller conversion movement was just beginning among the Chamars near Hoshiarpur, the Rev. K.C. Chatterjee, a Brahmin convert, wrote that caste was not an issue there except in matters of intermarriage.[232]

Relations between the seven missions working in the north-west at the outset of this period were, on the whole, quite cordial. Each had its own sphere of activity and did not encroach upon the territory of the others without permission, an arrangement called comity. Moreover, they collaborated with one another in a number of areas, most notably in the production of Christian literature, and in transferring converts in danger from one locale to another. During this period, the collaboration grew closer, for example in sponsoring the Kinnaird College in Lahore and the North India Medical College for Christian Women in Ludhiana as well as in their involvement in the Sialkot Convention. The biggest challenge to Christian unity of this type was posed by the Chuhra mass conversion movement which expanded in accordance with its own internal dynamic rather than at the convenience of the missions affected. In 1889, the United Presbyterian, Church of Scotland, and CMS missions redefined their territorial boundaries and thus, in effect, exchanged rural converts in order to reduce conflict between their respective mission workers

---

[231] H.U. Weitbrecht, 'Work among the Chuhras', *CMI* (October 1886), p. 766; 'Punjab Mission: Tokens of Blessing and Calls for Service', *CMI* (August 1887), p. 476. See also John C.B. Webster, 'Christian Conversion in the Punjab: What Has Changed?', pp. 364–5.

[232] *Lodiana Mission Annual Report 1885*, p. 69. See also ibid for 1893, p. 70.

and provide better ongoing pastoral care for the scattered congregations the movement had created. In this exchange the Scots gave the United Presbyterians 1111 converts in 110 villages and received 512 converts in 53 villages in return, while the CMS received 1283 converts in 75 villages from the United Presbyterians.[233] In addition, the Lodiana Mission welcomed the New Zealand Presbyterians into their 'mission field' and gave them the area around present-day Chandigarh, which they had received earlier from the Baptists. However, the most significant unity effort was the creation of the Presbyterian Church in India in 1904, which joined presbyteries of the Church of Scotland and Presbyterian Church in the USA into one independent Indian church, of which Rev. K.C. Chatterjee was the first moderator.[234]

There were Protestant groups who did not fit into the prevailing mainstream Evangelical ethos. The Plymouth Brethren and Salvation Army did not respect comity agreements already in place but simply entered uninvited into the 'mission fields' of others. They were, however, minor irritants to the existing missions[235] compared to the Catholics who posed a more serious threat to the established mission order. When in 1886, the Roman Catholic Church formally established a territorial hierarchy in India and posted a bishop at Lahore who, as has been seen, began work among Dalits by receiving opportunistic Protestants, the Anglican bishop of Lahore objected. 'In a province which alas! still offers abundant scope for the evangelist among Hindus, Sikhs and Mussulmans, without touching ground already broken by any Christian organization, I deem it my duty to protest against this marauding policy, this wanton aggravation of bitterness and of those divisions which we deplore.[236] This complaint was not without justification because, as Harding has shown, the

---

[233] *Church of Scotland Annual Report 1890*, p. 121; *UPCNA Report 1889*, p. 54.

[234] John C.B. Webster, *The Christian Community and Change*, p. 220. The United Presbyterians did not join.

[235] See, for example, *CMS Proceedings 1895–96*, p. 216; ibid. *1917–18*, p. 56.

[236] *CMS Proceedings 1889–90*, p. 115.

Roman Catholics did seek to displace the Protestants.[237] They were also deeply moved by the needs of the rural Dalits and by their requests for Catholic instruction, especially in villages Protestants had 'abandoned'.[238] The Catholic challenge united the Protestants who formed a joint committee to figure out 'the best way of resisting the aggression'.[239] Throughout the remainder of this period complaints about Roman Catholic intrusion kept appearing in Protestant mission reports.

Aside from the disruption caused, and often the 'sheep-stealing' which resulted, two less obvious complaints were made. One was that it caused considerable confusion among recent, uneducated converts who had more than enough difficulty internalizing the basics of the Christian faith without the added burden of understanding the differences between Protestantism and Catholicism. The other was that this competition undermined discipline among mission employees who now had the option of joining the other side (and taking some converts with them) whenever they were unhappy. On the other hand, one United Presbyterian missionary, in lamenting the loss of converts to the Catholics, commented, 'Village after village has gone over to them, and we grieve the more because we know that in most instances the people were not being instructed or cared for by us. Some say plainly they were not being visited and taught. Few if any villages which were receiving regular instruction from any worker have gone over.'[240] Clearly, intra-Christian competition was freeing Dalit converts from tight missionary control. If they were not satisfied with one mission patron, they could change to another nearby without ceasing to be Christians.

---

[237] Christopher Harding, 'The Dynamics of Low-Caste Conversion Movements', p. 168.

[238] Letter of Fr Lievin de Grimmingen in 'Missio Punjabensis', *Analecta* (1890), pp. 17–25; Letter of A.R.C. in 'Missio Punjabensis', ibid., pp. 48–51.

[239] *CMS Proceedings 1889–90*, p. 115. The traffic moved in both directions. See Fr Leo, *The Capuchin Mission in the Punjab*, p. 153.

[240] *UPCNA Annual Report 1913*, p. 85; see also ibid. *1914*, pp. 164–5.

With this one notable exception, the new Christian community had become remarkably well integrated by the time World War I broke out. Cleavages were there, some of which would grow wider and others narrower over time. Nonetheless, the community had established boundaries which set them apart from other communities, baptism being the central boundary marker. In addition, Christians had developed their own patterns and prohibitions concerning worship and life-cycle rituals, celebrated their own festivals, created minimal codes of conduct, and shared a sense of common identity as Christians. There is also ample evidence of a functional interdependence across denominational lines within the community. The missions, missionaries, and the educated elite were actively collaborating not only in the field of women's higher education but also through such associations as the Young Men's Christian Association and Young Women's Christian Association (both at Simla and Lahore), the Sunday School Union with headquarters at Jullundur, the Christian Literature Society with headquarters at Ludhiana, and the Punjab Religious Book Society at Lahore, all of which served the needs of all Protestant denominations. A branch of the Indian Christian Association had been established at Lahore around 1900 whose main activity up until the creation of communal electorates in 1909 had been to provide college scholarships for deserving Christian students. After that it became active in trying to provide a political voice for Christians in the north-west.[241]

Conclusions

The years between 1880 and the end of World War I proved to be a time of profound transition for Christianity in north-west India. The confident white male Evangelical missionary guardian who had occupied centre stage and had made such an impact in the 1860s and 1870s was now being challenged on all sides and facing intense competition for that measure of cultural dominance he had enjoyed

---

[241] The Indian Christian Association, Punjab, *Eleventh Annual Report.*

earlier. Instead of following his lead, the Hindu, Sikh, and Muslim elites, whom he had helped to educate, were now organizing their own religious associations with their own religious and socio-political agendas. By the end of this period the religio-cultural initiative had passed from his hands to theirs. In like manner, within the church structures his exclusive leadership was being challenged by the educated elite among the Indian clergy and laity, as well as by the increasing numerical preponderance of single women missionaries, while the Roman Catholic presence was now offering the north-west an alterative form of Christianity to his. In the villages, the initiative always lay with the Chuhras who were approaching him for instruction, baptism, and help in their struggles for greater dignity and justice. They accepted those aspects of his visions and methods that overlapped with their own; he never had real control over them. Women's work, the only area where the missions still retained the initiative at the end of this period, especially in the cities, was largely outside his domain.

What this chapter documents is Christian resourcefulness, not only in rethinking their purposes and methods, but also in making some institutional adjustments under new, challenging circumstances. The most obvious example was the Christian response to the rise of religious nationalism which forced a re-examination of their evangelistic message and methods, their educational work, the Indianization of Church and community leadership. No less important for the future, however, was their responsiveness to the Dalits who, by their very presence in it, transformed the Church into a Church of the poor and oppressed seeking a better life not only in heaven but also here on earth. Responsiveness included both subtle changes in the focus of the Christian message and training previously illiterate people to nurture scattered groups of believers in their new faith and assist them in their daily struggles. It also involved redirecting a good portion of the women's work away from the urban elites towards rural Dalits among whom men were converting at a much faster rate than women.

This flexibility and adaptability enabled Christianity to keep up its momentum as a religious movement with evangelism as its central aim. Its representatives both spoke and acted as part of an organized effort to bring about change. Their movement gained enough interest and support among the personally alienated within urban society and the socially alienated within rural society to shake, or at least disturb, the socio-cultural foundations of both. Ostensibly the foreign missionaries were the movement's leaders, but in actual fact it was the Indian converts who gave the movement its dynamism and made it appear so threatening to the status quo. Had Christianity won no Indian converts, it could not have become a movement from within Indian society or offered a credible challenge to existing belief systems and social relationships. As it happened, during this period it grew at a rate so high in the north-west as to be both unprecedented and publicly alarming.

It would certainly be wrong to attribute all of the ferment so characteristic of this period to the influence of Christianity. Nonetheless, Christianity did play a provocative role and make its own distinctive contribution to the ferment. As indicated earlier, its most direct impact was felt among the urban elites, both male and female, as well as among rural Dalits, from whose ranks they drew almost all of their converts. Specifically, the Christian movement provoked urban elite men to re-evaluate the very foundations and guiding convictions of their religious traditions, to promote change from within their own communities, and to redefine their relationships to women, Dalits, and the victims of famine and natural disaster. What Christianity offered elite urban women was education, medical care, alternative ways of seeing themselves and their own possibilities. For rural Dalits Christianity provided a potentially 'emancipatory identity', [242] opportunities for social mobility, and occasional assistance in local struggles against oppression. Perhaps most important of all, the Chuhra conversion movement was one of several in different parts of India which placed the plight of the Dalits on the public agenda and forced those concerned about 'the Christian threat' to address the Dalits' plight in meaningful ways.

---

[242] This very apt phrase is taken from G. Aloysius, *Religion as Emancipatory Identity*, pp. 1–23.

The elites would take their time in doing this, but were now clearly aware of the Dalit issue and its political consequences. In short, as with other social groups, so also with the Dalits, Christian evangelism with its built-in threat of conversion, proved to be a most effective means by which fundamental human rights and social justice issues were raised in the late nineteenth- and early twentieth-century north-west.

5 Towards Independence and Partition: 1919–47

In order to gain fuller Indian support during World War I, the British government committed itself in 1917 to 'the progressive realisation of responsible government in India as an integral part of the British empire'.[1] This decision represented such a major step forward in sharing legislative and administrative power with Indians that politics came to dominate all aspects of Indian public life once the war was over. The ensuing power struggle between politically active Indians and the British Raj for responsible and independent government went hand-in-hand with an internal power struggle over who would rule in the place of the British and who would have how much influence on those who did rule. In no other region of India did these power struggles prove to be as tumultuous as in the north-west. The tumult began almost immediately after the war with the Rowlatt satyagraha and Jallianwalla Bagh massacre in 1919 and ended with the partition riots of 1947. The history of Christianity in the north-west was severely affected by this momentous shift in regional priorities from the socio-cultural to the political. Whereas Christians had played a significant catalytic role in provoking and sustaining socio-cultural change in the region, they were now to be pushed to the sidelines as little more than spectators to power struggles in which others had become the prime movers.

'The progressive realisation of responsible government' began with the Government of India Act of 1919, which transferred some 'nation-building' and 'welfare' portfolios in the provincial governments to Indian ministers. The Government of India Act of 1935 did the same for the central government, while handing over the remaining portfolios at the provincial level. Both constitutions granted only a very limited franchise. In 1947, India became independent and was partitioned. Each of these 'steps' was taken

[1] The declaration of E.S. Montagu, Secretary of State for India, 20 August 1917.

against a background not only of large-scale demonstrations against the Raj, but also of serious political competition and conflict within north-west Indian society. At stake were both the political visions of differing nationalisms and the political interests of those segments of society being mobilized on the basis of either religion or class and caste. The 1917 Declaration had opened up in the north-west a veritable Pandora's box of political assertiveness long suppressed by the 'Guardians' of the Punjab civil service. Christians now had to find their way in the midst of considerable political turmoil.

Meanwhile, important theological and missiological developments in the Christian West were making their presence felt. Perhaps the most significant for north-west India, presaged in the writings of H.D. Griswold and C.F. Andrews described in the previous chapter, was the breakdown of a general Evangelical consensus with the rise of theological modernism and social Christianity. One of its leading proponents, William Adams Brown,[2] saw the religious life, and that which is distinctive in the Christian religious life, as the starting point for a modern Christian theology.[3] He distinguished the essential content of Christianity from its ever-changing forms in order to set forth its essence in terms which not only were true to the Christian scriptures and tradition but also reflected the 'new learning' in science, history, social psychology, and comparative religion. Social Christianity started with the Old Testament prophets' demand for social righteousness as well as Jesus' teachings on the Kingdom of God and then set forth progressive agendas for a transformation of the social order aimed towards the Kingdom of God. In working these out, it not only used an organic view of society and its evolutionary development but also relied upon the social sciences both for understanding current problems the Church had to address and for determining how best to proceed.

These 'new theologies' were to influence Protestant thinking about mission during the inter-war period. Up to this point two

---

[2] Brown's *Christian Theology in Outline* (1906) became a widely used theological textbook and came out in a new edition in 1919.

[3] Ibid., p. 23.

missiologies had shaped Protestant mission policy in India. One gave priority to evangelism and the other to planting churches that were to become self-supporting, self-governing, and self-propagating. These mission priorities remained intact throughout this period but now a 'Kingdom of God' missiology aimed at social transformation was added. In this missiology, Christian service projects involving the wider society—education, medical work, rural development, 'uplift' work—acquired a degree of theological autonomy. They could now be evaluated and justified not solely in terms of their evangelistic influence or contribution to the strengthening of the Church, but in terms of the quality of the service they provided as measured by 'Kingdom of God values' and commonly accepted professional standards. These new theologies and missiologies found their way into north-west India through a new generation of missionaries and visits by international commissions or denominational deputations from abroad.

This chapter begins by looking at how the Christian community itself was developing under these circumstances, assessing its assets and liabilities in the struggles and strife of this period. It then examines the community's involvement in nationalist and communal politics, an important dimension of which was a nationalist movement within the churches themselves which closely paralleled that in the region at large, so that when India became independent, ecclesiastical power had largely shifted from foreign missionary to Indian Christian hands.

The Christian Community

Whereas the preceding period had been one of remarkable growth in the size of the Christian community in the north-west, this was to be a period primarily of consolidating and strengthening the gains made earlier. To some extent this was a matter of policy; the missions responsible for large numbers of baptized rural believers were concerned that they grow in Christian faith and life rather than lapse back into their old loyalties and old ways. It was also due in part to the fact that the older, larger missions had so overextended their available human resources that they could not respond to the needs of both existing and prospective converts. Whereas earlier, when touring the villages during the cool season, missionaries had spent most of their time responding to requests for instruction and baptism from potential converts, they now made a point of visiting the villages where Christians already resided so as to converse, instruct, and worship with them. Other interested villagers could attend these open worship services and 'overhear' the Christian message as it related to the lives of those who already accepted it.[4] Only the newer missions, like the Methodists, were still baptizing new converts in large numbers during this period.[5] As a result of this emphasis upon consolidation, the Christian population grew by a modest 31 per cent from 318,701 in the 1921 Census to 418,926 in the 1931 Census, and only by 22 per cent up to 511,299 in the 1941 Census.[6] It also remained only a very small portion of the regional population as a whole; in the Punjab, where they were most numerous, Christians were only 1.4 per cent of the total population and in Delhi 1.1 per cent in 1941.

The Christian community was now predominantly rural, thanks to the Chuhra conversion movement. The best estimate available, drawn from the 1931 Punjab Census, is that there were about 43,000 urban Indian Christians (about 11 per cent of the Indian Christian population) at that time.[7] The 1941 Census shows how unevenly

[4] This was stated most explicitly in the *Survey of the Evangelistic Work of the Punjab Mission 1929*, p. 19, but see also Lillian Henderson, 'Disappointments and Hopes in Village Work', *DMN* (April 1930), p. 192; W.P. Hares, 'Building the Church in the Panjab', *MMQ* (June 1930), p. 21; Robert C.H. Kinloch, 'Our Punjab Church', *OL* (January 1945), p. 29.

[5] This is apparent from the reports of the Northwest India and Indus River Annual Conferences from this period.

[6] The 1921 Census figures for Indian Christians (not Europeans or Anglo-Indians) were 2353 in the North West Frontier Province, 315,031 in Punjab and Delhi, and 1317 in Kashmir. By the 1941 Census they increased to 5997 in the North West Frontier Province, 493,081 in the Punjab, 10,494 in Delhi, and 1727 in Jammu and Kashmir.

[7] The Census reported that there were 395,629 Indian Christians and 352,608 rural Christians in the Punjab that year. It is assumed that virtually all of the rural Christians, with the exception of a European missionary here and there, were Indians. Thus the urban total is arrived at by subtracting the rural total from the Indian Christian total. *Punjab Census 1931*, I, pp. 98, 313.

Indian Christians were spread out throughout the region. Two-thirds of them were in the six districts of the central Punjab (Lahore, Amritsar, Gurdaspur, Sialkot, Gujranwala, and Sheikhapura) where they constituted 4.7 per cent of the entire population. Another 15 per cent were in the canal colony districts of Lyallpur and Montgomery, where they constituted 3.7 per cent and 1.8 per cent of the total population respectively.[8] On the other hand, the entire Ambala division in southern Punjab and Delhi district had just over 10,000 Indian Christians each, while in Jammu and Kashmir the tiny urban Christian population actually outnumbered the rural Christians there (56.1 per cent vs. 43.9 per cent).[9] An astute SPG missionary working in the villages around Delhi, struck by this difference between his area and the central and western Punjab, did not attribute it to the fact that the latter was an area dominated by Muslims and Sikhs, while his was dominated by Hindus.

> The real point of comparison is that they are working amongst people who are historically accustomed to *change*, whereas we are working in an area where traditions, however much they may have developed from the simple to the complex, or *vice versa*, have never been broken. In short, we are up against a more formidable barrier of conservatism and loyalty to tradition than they are.[10]

Two other sets of census statistics are important for understanding the Christian community during this period. The literacy rate for Christians recorded in the 1921 Census for Punjab and Delhi was 4.6 per cent for men and 3.4 per cent for women. This represents a slight drop from the 1911 rate, due primarily to the large influx of illiterate Chuhras that had almost doubled the Christian population during the intervening decade. While below the 6.3 per cent general literacy rate for men, Christian men continued to have a higher literacy rate than either the Muslim men (2.7 per cent) or the Chamar (0.50 per

---

[8] *Punjab Census 1941*, pp. 42–3.

[9] Ibid., p. 43; *Delhi Census 1941*, p. 80; *Jammu and Kashmir Census 1941*, II, pp. 103, 105.

[10] Roy Randolph, 'Village Problems in the Punjab and Delhi', *DMN* (July 1938), pp. 131–2.

cent) and Chuhra (0.50 per cent) men from whose ranks the vast majority of the Christian men had come.[11] The literacy rate for Christian women, on the other hand, was more than four times higher than the 0.80 per cent literacy rate for women in general. Sex ratio data has become a prime indicator of the status of women in India.[12] The 1941 Census indicated that, although not evenly distributed throughout the region, the sex ratio among Christians (856 women per 1000 men) was still more favourable than that among the population as a whole (845 women per 1000 men).[13] When taken in conjunction with the female literacy rates of the various religious communities, this suggests that the Christian community was somewhat justified in seeing itself as a progressive community as far as gender issues, as well as caste issues, were concerned.

This demographic data provides important insights into the nature of the Christian community, but says nothing about the most historically significant cleavage within the community, namely that between the urban and the rural churches. While interrelated within common mission and church structures, the two were so different that their histories are best described separately. This section is, therefore, divided between a consideration first of the urban and then of the rural Church.

The Urban Church

The Church in the north-west began in the cities and, despite its extraordinary growth in the villages between 1880 and 1920, its centre of gravity and public influence remained urban. The apex of the ecclesiastical structures created by the many Christian missions was still urban, as was most obvious in the case of the hierarchical Roman Catholic and Anglican churches. The former had its diocesan headquarters in Lahore (1887), Simla (1910), Multan (1936), and Delhi (1937), while the latter had its in Lahore (1877) and Delhi (1947),

[11] *Punjab and Delhi Census 1921*, I, pp. 292–3.

[12] See *Towards Equality: Report of the Committee on the Status of Women in India*, pp. 9–17.

[13] *Census of India, 1941. Volumes VI, X, XVI, XXII.*

even though the Indian membership of both was overwhelmingly rural. The other more decentralized missions and churches had also established their own institutional complexes and posted most of their top leadership, whether missionary or Indian, in the cities where cultural influence was considered vital to the Church's mission.[14] Moreover, the urban churches were constantly fed by the rural churches as migrants moved from the villages to the towns and cities in search of education and better jobs; there was little or no flow in the opposite direction.

The urban Christian population was relatively small (11 per cent) and spread out among a large number of cities. While no occupational data on them is available in the census, it is apparent from the incomplete quantitative data, impressionistic information, and biographical materials drawn from mission sources that class differences now existed within the urban Christian community. On the one hand, there were educated Christians in white collar work as professionals or government servants (but very rarely in business) who provided the Indian leadership and defined the issues for the churches; on the other, were the Christian labourers, with varying degrees of education and specialized skill, who were either long-term urban residents, as in the Chamar bastis of Delhi, or more often recent Chuhra migrants from the overpopulated rural areas of the central Punjab.

Class differences did not necessarily mean class churches. While separate European churches could be found wherever large concentrations of British military and civilian personnel existed, Indian congregations tended to be not only multi-class and multi-caste but also upward mobile in nature. A good case in point is the Christ Methodist Church in Delhi. In 1925, its pastor, Rev. Amar Dass, reported,

The congregation here consists of two classes of people—one the well-to-do both in means and in intellect. This class works in offices, workshops, hospitals, schools, railroads, etc.…The other class is the domestic servant class. They are

[14] *Survey of the Evangelistic Work of the Punjab Mission 1929*, p. 59.

bearers, motor or taxi drivers, cooks, butlers, guides, etc. Of both classes about 33 per cent remain for seven months in the year in the hill stations and are here for only five months of the winter. The servant class people are very uncertain. They go wherever their officers are transferred or a change of officers automatically changes their residence. It is a job to keep track of them.[15]

A Presbyterian evangelistic survey pointed out that many Dalit Christian migrants to the cities had 'blended into' urban congregations so well that the other members were unaware of their 'mass movement' origins,[16] while an account of the Anglicans in Delhi described the remarkable movement away from traditional occupations, especially into educational and medical work, of its overwhelmingly Dalit membership.[17] The marriage register of Holy Trinity Church located in a Chamar basti of Delhi showed that the number of members engaged in shoe-making, which was the sole occupation of the original members, relative to the number in other occupations, declined sharply.[18] Exceptions during this period were the churches in the cantonments, especially on the north-west frontier, where Christians were employed as menials.[19]

[15] *Yearbook and Official Minutes of the North-West India Conference of the Methodist Episcopal Church Thirty-fourth Session held at Aligarh December 5–13, 1925*, p. 46. [Hereafter referred to as *Annual Conference Journal* with the name of the Annual Conference and the year added.] Ten years later, it was reported that of the 450 members of that church, one-third were domestic servants, ten were doctors, seventy were nurses or compounders, thirty-four were teachers, twenty-six were in clerical work, fourteen in the railways and the others were shopkeepers, drivers, mechanics, etc. Ibid. 1935, p. 120.

[16] *Survey of the Evangelistic Work of the Punjab Mission 1929*, p. 30.

[17] W.T.W., 'Christianity in Delhi', *DMN* (July 1925), pp. 64–5.

[18] See Monodeep Daniel, 'The People Who Believe that God is Faithful', pp. 127–9.

[19] *Survey of the Evangelistic Work of the Punjab Mission 1929*, pp. 92, 221; Olive Elwin, 'Echoes of the Punjab Mass Movement on the North-West Frontier of India', *CMR* (December 1927), p. 365; Lilian A. Underhill, 'The Afghan Frontier: Its Problems, Progress and Possibilities', ibid. (June 1927), pp. 114–24; O. Elwin, 'Punjabi Christians in Dera Ismail Khan', *MMQ* (September 1929), pp. 36–8; J.S. Dugdale, 'A Channel for God on the North-West Frontier', *CMO* (January 1933), pp. 5–7.

Two other features of urban church life in this period were also quite noteworthy. One was that by this time most of the older congregations had become self-supporting and self-governing, paying their own pastors' salaries and making their own decisions without relying on missionary paternalism. This speaks well of the level of both income and commitment their relatively small memberships had attained.[20] The other was that much of their membership consisted of employees of local Christian educational and medical institutions. For example, in Ambala the mission hospital for women employed an overwhelming majority of the congregation, while its pastor described the Naulakha Church in Lahore as an 'institutional church' because so many of its members worked in the Christian institutions of the city.[21] Thus, while independent of the missions, these congregations were at the same time heavily dependent upon the presence of local Christian institutions for their economic and political viability.

Most of those educated urban Christians who were not employed by the missions or by Christian institutions were in government service, and some rose to very high positions.[22] A brief survey of the genealogy of the Golaknath family, that includes information about the families into which they married, shows that government service was almost the exclusive career path of them all.[23] Those in high government positions or in the top mission positions, along with the leading independent professionals, constituted the Indian Christian elite. Then came the large number of pastors, teachers, medical personnel, and other educated clerical workers who made up the Christian middle class. Below them were the skilled and finally the unskilled labourers in the urban class structure of the Christian community.

[20] This was true of the churches in Ambala City, Ludhiana, Jullundur, Naulakha Church in Lahore, and Ferozepore City. *Survey of the Evangelistic Work of the Punjab Mission 1929*, pp. 91, 115, 151, 177, 221.

[21] Ibid., pp. 91, 177.

[22] In 1917, it was reported that there were twenty-one Indian Christians who held gazetted appointments in the Punjab government, almost half of them in the medical service. 'News of the Month', *CMR* (May 1917), p. 254.

[23] J.N. Mangat-Rai, compiler, *The History and Genealogy of the Golaknath Line*.

The Presbyterian evangelistic survey in 1929 noted a great change in urban evangelism since the previous century. Bazar and chapel preaching had declined. Occasional public lectures by such noted evangelists as E. Stanley Jones and the Rev. Abdul Haqq continued, as did zenana visitation, albeit on a reduced scale. However, urban evangelism relied primarily upon either evangelistic 'campaigns' of limited duration, the personal witness of committed individuals, the distribution of Christian literature, or the evangelistic efforts of Christian institutions.[24] Work among Muslims at Bickersteth Hall in Delhi continued[25] and there were well-attended public debates elsewhere.[26] There were also deliberate efforts made to create new congregations as large cities grew in size. In New Delhi, the Roman Catholic and Anglican cathedrals, St. Thomas Church, and the Free Church were planned and built during this period.[27] During World War II the Methodists sought to obtain property in New Delhi on which to erect a church for newly arrived war workers who lived too far away to attend the Christ Methodist Church, while St. Stephen's Church added a Tamil congregation to its Hindustani congregation in 1943.[28]

Certainly the most famous Punjabi evangelist of the time was Sadhu Sundar Singh. He had already acquired a national and international reputation when this period began. After the war he made three extensive trips of several months each to Burma, Malaya, Japan, and China in 1918–19; Great Britain, the United States, and

[24] *Survey of the Evangelistic Work of the Punjab Mission 1929*, pp. 61–6.

[25] H.J. Welles, 'Bickersteth Hall: Work Among Muslims', *DMN* (January 1929), pp. 33–7.

[26] There were 1000 present in 1924 at a Christian–Muslim debate in Sialkot. United Presbyterian Board of Foreign Missions, *Foreign Missions Handbook 1924*, p. 45.

[27] The SPG and Cambridge Mission in Delhi and the South Punjab, *Fifty-fourth Report of the Cambridge Committee with which is incorporated The General Report of the Other Branches of the Mission for the Year 1931*, p. 17. [Hereafter referred to as *SPG and Cambridge Mission Annual Report* with the year added.]; ibid. *1933*, p. 16; 'Consecration of Delhi Cathedral', *Collectanea Punjabensia* (January–February 1946), p. 73.

[28] *Delhi Annual Conference Journal 1945*, pp. 28–9; *LDM* (June 1944), p. 246.

Australia in 1920; and finally continental Europe in 1922. After that, his poor health kept him confined to Sabathu and its environs, except for his attempts to enter Tibet. In Sabathu, he devoted himself to writing short devotional books that contained the messages he often shared on his preaching tours. His style was simple, often anecdotal, with many analogies drawn primarily from nature, and, unlike the work of earlier evangelists, directed as much to religious intuitions and imagination as to the intellect. He appealed to the yearning heart, to religious experience, and to interest in the invisible world of angels, saints, and spirits he had entered through mystical visions. Yet his message remained basically an Evangelical message.[29] His books, written originally in Urdu, were translated into English with the help of good friends, as well into many other languages. In 1929, he made his final journey into Tibet and simply disappeared; no trace of him was ever found.

Education remained the Christians' chief urban 'industry' and their major point of engagement as a religious community with the rest of society. While some new schools were started and older ones expanded, the most significant changes in Christian education during this period tended to be qualitative rather than quantitative. The process of rethinking educational missions begun during the previous period was accelerated as Indian independence approached. Initial anxiety over the government introducing a 'conscience clause' allowing parents to exempt their children from participation in Christians religious instruction or observances did cause some rethinking of educational aims and investments at the outset of this period,[30] but some reordering of priorities occured and the earlier

---

[29] Sadhu Sundar Singh saw the invisible, spiritual world permeating the visible world of ordinary sense experience. These visions and the miracles he described evoked a lot of hostile criticism. A good example of his visions may be found in his *The Spiritual World*, originally published in 1926. His longest book, *With and Without Christ*, perhaps best conveys the flavour of his basic evangelistic message.

[30] The SPG in Delhi did not seem to have any objection to such a clause, but the American Presbyterians did. The Punjab Christian Council in 1935 asked that the conscience clause be limited to areas where there was only one school. 'Editorial Notes', *DMN* (July 1921), pp. 246–7; 'Indian Education and the Conscience Clause',

consensus about the purpose of education being evangelistic no longer held.

One can see a shift in priorities when comparing the aims of city schools and of Forman Christian College in Lahore as set forth in a Presbyterian educational survey in 1926 with the aims listed by a Presbyterian delegation in 1939. Whereas the former stated that evangelism remained the primary aim of educational work, the latter listed the aims of Christian schools in the following order: (1) to give Christian nurture to the children of the Christian community; (2) to make possible a literate Church; (3) to train leaders for all forms of Christian work in and through the Church; and (4) to witness to the Christian gospel [by carrying out its work in the 'Spirit of Christ'] in the non-Christian neighbourhood by admitting non-Christian children.[31] This shift in priorities from evangelism and 'Christian influence' to the upbuilding and equipping of the Christian community for its mission was also apparent in the decision of the SPG and Baptists in Delhi to close their schools and create the United Christian School which would concentrate on the education of Christians.[32] At the same time, many educators continued to give priority to evangelism, or more broadly to touching minds and hearts, to changing outlook and world-view, or to building character, all under the influence of Jesus Christ. It was recognized that very few converts would be won, but that Christian education would still make a lasting impact upon the Hindu, Muslim, and Sikh students who

---

CMR (December 1921), pp. 340–6; Arthur Judson Brown, *One Hundred Years*, pp. 623–6. *Punjab Christian Council Proceedings*, 1935, p. 6. As the Punjab correspondent for *The Guardian* pointed out, a conscience clause would affect Christian institutions, which generally served members of all religious communities, more than other private institutions, which did not. 'Punjab Letter', *The Guardian* (16 August 1934), p. 525.

[31] *Survey of the Educational Work of the Three India Missions of the Presbyterian Church in the United States of America 1926*, pp. 61, 90, 136, 137; *Reports and Recommendations of the Deputation of the Board of Foreign Missions, 22–25 March 1939*, pp. 25–6.

[32] 'Head of the Mission's Letter', *DMN* (October 1926), p. 161. The SPG handed over its St. Stephen's School to the management of the Anglo-Oriental College. 'Head of the Mission's Letter', ibid. (January 1929), p. 25.

would provide future leadership for the wider society;[33] some schools once intended for Christians alone were opened up to others as well, reversing the practice in Delhi.[34] Among Roman Catholics the dilemma of conflicting priorities—outreach vs. upbuilding those already converted—remained throughout the inter-war period.[35] The Methodists included the added objective of nation-building through imparting a 'balanced ideal of nationalism'.[36]

At the outset of this period, male educational missionaries were concentrated in the Christian colleges and generally provided leadership for them. An exception was St. Stephen's College where S.K. Rudra was principal and after a brief interlude was succeeded by another Indian, S.N. Mukarji. Forman Christian College invited Dr S.K. Datta to become its first Indian principal in 1932, but his successor was a foreigner. The vast majority of the Christian schools for boys were already under Indian headmasters. Christian educational institutions at all levels also retained their cosmopolitan faculties and student bodies, which led one school inspector to remark that they were the only truly national schools in the region, mixing students of all classes and communities together.[37]

The reports of educational institutions indicate that, apart from the political turmoil, the major preoccupations of the period were meeting the rising standards expected by the government, improving the physical plant to meet educational needs, and retaining the Christian character of these institutions in places where Christian

[33] This was certainly an important rationale for the Christian colleges. See, for example, the five-fold programme of Forman Christian College set forth in *Punjab Mission Annual Report 1926*, p. 65. See also O.C. Cocks, 'Some Problems of the Christian Schoolmaster in North India', *CMO* (July 1936), pp. 150–3; Robert C.H. Kinloch, 'Indian Missions and Education', *OL* (October 1940), p. 15.

[34] For example, Baring School in Batala and Kinnaird College in Lahore. The latter began by enrolling only Christian women, but in 1933 only thirty-five of its 130 students were Christians. Vinod K. Khiyalie, *Hundred Years of Baring's Mission to Batala*, p. 48; *UPCNA Annual Report 1933*, p. 64.

[35] Michael Anikuzhikattil, 'The Punjabi Century (1846–1947)', p. 64.

[36] 'The Delhi Area Educational Conference', *The Indian Witness* (August 8, 1929), pp. 504, 505.

[37] See *Punjab Mission Annual Report 1927*, p. 70.

students and teachers were relatively few in number.[38] There were, however, some attempts at educational innovation within a constricting and confining university and government grant-in-aid system.[39] In 1926, the politically active K.L. Rallia Ram, headmaster of Rang Mahal School in Lahore, introduced a civics course so that students could gain a better understanding of government and of the ideals of citizenship.[40] Forman Christian College had 'extra-curricular classes' to move students beyond the narrow confines of the prescribed curriculum.[41] The major concerns of the Lindsay Commission, which visited all the Christian colleges in the north-west, were the growing enrolments and low percentage of Christians in the colleges. It commended Forman Christian College for its postgraduate teaching and research work, as well as St. Stephen's College for its small size, Christian influence, and success in winning the confidence 'of a wide constituency of non-Christians who look upon it as their own college and contribute to its support'.[42]

Given the stated aims of Christian schools and colleges in the north-west during this period, it is very difficult to assess their achievements. In 1935, one missionary estimated that one out of every seven college students was studying in a Christian college.[43] Christian colleges continued to play an important role in the councils of Punjab University and St. Stephen's College was not only one of the three founding colleges of Delhi University in 1922 but also

---

[38] Josephine E. Martin, 'Christian Education in India', *WMM* (May 1922), pp. 404–10.

[39] See the comments of E.D. Lucas in *Punjab Mission Annual Report 1922.* p. 44.

[40] *Punjab Mission Annual Report 1926*, p. 62.

[41] *The Christian College in India*, p. 327.

[42] *The Christian College in India; SPG and Cambridge Mission in Delhi and South Punjab Annual Report 1924*, p. 46.

[43] E.L. Porter, 'Building the Church in India', *WMM* (February 1935), p. 286. In 1928, the Report of the Director of Public Instruction in the Punjab (p. 46) had shown that D.A.V. College in Lahore had the highest enrolment (1082), followed closely by Forman Christian College (1013), Government College, Lahore (818), Islamia College (664), and Khalsa College in Amritsar (604). Murray College in Sialkot had 353 students and Gordon College in Rawalpindi had 305.

provided many of its senior faculty.[44] While indicative of the fact that Christian institutions were still carrying a diminishing but nonetheless significant portion of the educational 'load' in the province, this estimate says nothing about the kind of impact a Christian education was having upon the minds of the students who received it. Michelle Maskiell, in her study of Kinnaird College, has argued that while it had little impact upon the world-view or religious beliefs of its students, its ethos greatly influenced the subsequent lives of its students,[45] particularly as a counter-culture to the purdah culture in which most of them had been raised. In the conviction that the education of women should be equal to that of men, it provided them with important professional and social skills which went beyond simply performing well on university examinations.

Non-academic social and civil skills, such as polished English conversation, and responsible 'civic spirit,' were crucial to the college experience. Absence of *pardah* arrangements; emphasis on extracurricular participation and community democracy; nurturing of individual initiative and assertiveness; anticipation of professional careers; the college experience was heavily laden with foreign values held by the missionary staff. These ideals attempted to turn students' attentions from their individual family concerns towards public issues. Students were not presented with gender-free models for behavior at Kinnaird College. Rather, they were presented with *expanded* models of what Hindu and Muslim gender roles could encompass. The staff did not suggest that women should choose to be wives *or* citizens but that they could be both.[46]

---

[44] It supplied seven department heads as well as the deans of the faculties both of Arts and of Science. 'Editorial Notes', *St. Stephen's College Magazine* (February 1923), p. 3.

[45] The college's aim was less directly evangelistic than extending the Kingdom of God in India. D.A.L. Lyon, 'Kinnaird College for Women, Lahore', *LDM* (April 1936), p. 200.

[46] Michelle Maskiell, 'Social Change and Social Control', p. 69. In 1943, Miss V. Sutherland said of the counter-culture of the New Zealand Presbyterian girls' schools in Jagadhri and Kharar: 'The children all grow up at school, at least, in an atmosphere where each girl is judged on her merit and character, not by her caste or religion, where her possibilities are recognized apart from her status, and her needs are attended to, whoever she may be.' *Proceedings of the General Assembly of*

While the Hindu women who attended Kinnaird College used these skills to improve their marriage prospects and to work in voluntary associations, the Christians went into teaching—about 30 per cent of them preferring a career to marriage—and the few Muslims tended to follow the same path as the Christians.[47] In 1929, Kinnaird College reported that of the 199 women who had left the college since 1913, eighty had become teachers and two had become physicians.[48]

A similar pattern, at least for Christian graduates, seemed to prevail at lower levels of education as well. Just after independence, the Avalon Girls' High School in Pathankot reported that 290 of its 338 graduates were Christians.

Of these 290 Christian graduates: 89 are now teachers, 40 of whom are teaching in our own schools or in other Mission schools. The rest are in Gov't or private schools. 4 are managers in our Mission Schools. 3 are head teachers in our own schools. 5 are head mistresses in Government schools. 6 are Gov't Inspectresses of Schools. 15 are doctors of whom 7 are serving in Mission Hospitals. 16 are nurses of whom 8 are serving in Mission Hospitals. 58 are married and in homes of their own and 16 of these are still teaching or nursing. 19 have died. 23 are still training in colleges or training schools. 26–our last year's graduating class were still not settled when these figures were culled out. 26 we have lost track of or are not sure where they are or what they are doing.[49]

These figures give quantitative support to the claim made in 1932 that most of the women appointed in the government's educational and medical departments were Christians.[50]

---

the Presbyterian Church of New Zealand Held in Dunedin, November, 1943, p. 161. [Hereafter referred to as *NZ Presbyterian GA Proceedings* with the year added.]

[47] Michelle Maskiell, 'Social Change and Social Control', pp. 72–82. Maskiell based this portion of her research upon interviews with former students of the college from this period.

[48] *Punjab Mission Annual Report 1929*, p. 46.

[49] Vida Graham, 'The Products of Pathankot School', *WMM* (February 1948), p. 337.

[50] *UPCNA Annual Report 1932*, p. 71. This was to change as the Punjab government issued a two-year moratorium on hiring Christian women in the education department and the Delhi government was considering something similar. 'Women's Work', *Delhi* (October 1934), p. 69.

The impact which Christian schools and colleges had upon their male students, whether measured in terms of general character development or of the upbuilding of the Christian community, is not as well documented or researched. The schools educated far more boys than girls; enrolments were larger and personal contact, especially with missionary teachers, was less intense; male institutions neither sought nor achieved a totally counter-cultural ethos in this nationalist era, but, while largely ignoring gender issues, did work at creating a cosmopolitan unity across the lines of caste and creed that were hardening during this period. It may thus be safe to conclude that the impact of Christianity was far greater upon the education of women than of men during this period.

The same was also true of medical care, the other great service in which Christians in the north-west invested heavily. While there were mission doctors, dispensaries, and hospitals for men in Kashmir and along the north-west frontier, medical missions were set up throughout the region primarily to serve the needs of women and children. The heavy majority of these mission hospitals were run and staffed by women. Many also served as formal and all were informal training centres for nurses and compounders, thus opening up employment and service opportunities for women. The North India School of Medicine for Christian Women, or Women's Christian Medical College in Ludhiana, as it later came to be called, also trained only women for medical work.

One can see the same pressure to raise standards operating in the medical as in the educational field.[51] A brief history of St. Stephen's hospital in Delhi illustrates this broader trend quite clearly. In its early years the hospital recruited its nurses from among those 'young women, educated in our schools, married at an early age, and, either widowed or deserted by their husbands, [who] sought the hospital as a refuge and means to help them support a young family'.[52] However, the medical tasks that they could perform were very

[51] For an overview of the early stages of the professionalization of medical missions for women, see Rosemary Fitzgerald, 'Rescue and Redemption: The Rise of Female Medical Missions in Colonial India during the late Nineteenth and early Twentieth Centuries'.

[52] 'S. Stephen's Hospital, Delhi', *DMN* (January 1930), p. 172.

limited. With the advent of trained missionary nursing sisters and the attempt to standardize nurses' training from about 1913 onwards, the nursing profession came to be seen in a new light. By 1930, St. Stephen's Hospital had two Indian nursing sisters and four Indian staff nurses who could assume responsibilities far beyond what the earlier nurses had been capable of doing. The hospital also trained *dais* to become properly certified midwives and provided a prenatal clinic for expectant mothers.[53]

The main Indian source of trained medical women was the Women's Christian Medical College in Ludhiana. A list of graduates in medicine prepared in 1930 indicated that between 1919 and 1929 there had been 129 graduates. Of these, forty-seven were working in mission hospitals, two in Hindu hospitals, twenty-two in other hospitals, and twenty-two for the government. Eleven were in private practice, two were engaged in further study, eight had died, and fifteen (most of whom had just graduated) were unaccounted for.[54] In 1933, they reported that eighty-six of their 133 licentiate students and all of their nursing students were Christians.[55] They struggled with academic standards, especially for entering students,[56] and during this period had Indians on the college faculty.[57]

In addition to these service institutions, Christians had also created many specialized organizations to serve the Christian mission: the British and Foreign Bible Society which was engaged in the translation and distribution of scriptures; the Punjab Religious Book Society; the Young Men's Christian Association (YMCA) and Young Women's Christian Association (YWCA);[58] and the Henry Martyn School of Islamics, the primary purpose of which was 'making a close study of present day movements among Muslims, and [preparing] Christian

[53] Ibid., pp. 173–4.

[54] *The Report for the 36th Year of the Women's Christian Medical College, Ludhiana, Punjab, 1929–1930*, pp. 36–8. [Hereafter referred to as *Women's Christian Medical College Annual Report* with the year added.]

[55] *Women's Christian Medical College Annual Report 1932–1933*, pp. 45–6.

[56] *Women's Christian Medical College Annual Report 1935–1936*, p. 11.

[57] *Women's Christian Medical College Annual Report 1929–1930*, p. 4; ibid. *1935–1936*, p. 3.

[58] *Directory of Christian Missions and Churches in India, Burma and Ceylon 1940–1941*, pp. 170, 256–7.

literature more adequate to the needs of the day'.[59] In addition, the missions created the Punjab Representative Council of Missions, which became the Punjab Christian Council and sought to function as a clearinghouse, coordinating body, service agency, and public spokesperson for the various missions working in the Punjab. All of these organizations were Protestant; there was only ad hoc cooperation between Protestants and Catholics.

The picture of the urban Christian community in north-west India that emerges from the preceding description is of a small, institutionally based, service-oriented community with clear boundaries separating it from other urban caste and religious communities. While strongly committed to its own Christian faith, it was at the same time cosmopolitan in its engagement with members of other religious communities. It was also very progressive, as was most obvious in the case of its women, large numbers of whom worked at respectable jobs outside the home, thus setting a trend which other women were later to follow. This was also true in the case of caste as well, for it also included many Dalits who had not only 'moved up' through education and subsequent occupational mobility, but also 'blended in' to the point where their caste origins were not always apparent or important. The community's chief assets were its institutions, which continued to attract others for the quality of service they offered, as well as some truly exceptional individuals. Its chief liabilities were its small size, its lack of independent wealth, and its denominational divisions, especially between Protestants and Catholics. As will become apparent, its nature, assets, and liabilities affected its relations with the rural church, with members of other communities, and with the foreign missionaries in their midst.

THE RURAL CHURCH

What rural church existed in north-west India at the time of the 1881 Census had been a mere appendage of the urban church. However, the Chuhra conversion movement had changed that.

---

[59] The Henry Martyn School (of Islamics) Lahore, India, *Annual Report 1933*, p. 8.

Although the rapid pace of conversion of the earlier period did not, and perhaps could not,[60] continue, the rural church nonetheless remained the place where numerical growth through conversion (as opposed to migration) still occurred. Converts still faced persecution from landlords[61] and the missions faced considerable competition, not only from each other[62] but also from such outside bodies as the Arya Samaj.[63] The rural church continued to be, with rare exceptions, a Dalit church and all its members, except a few in Christian villages and in the villages near Delhi, came from one caste background. Aside from those in mission service, the vast majority of members were dependent upon agriculture for their livelihoods.[64] Most were landless agricultural labourers, economically dependent upon village landlords. Unlike their urban upper- caste or Muslim counterparts, they maintained cordial and even matrimonial relationships with their caste fellows following conversion. These relationships helped not only to maintain the hold that Dalit cultures had upon converts, but also to keep the religious boundaries separating them from their caste fellows blurred and porous. Converts did not completely lose

[60] W.P. Hares reported in 1930 that 'in the older Mission Districts practically all the Chuhras have become Christians.' 'Building the Church in the Panjab', MMQ (June 1930), p. 21.

[61] See, for example, 'The Annual Day of Thanksgiving and Intercession', DMN (July 1919), p. 59; R.M. King, 'Experiences among India's Outcastes: I. In the Villages of the Punjab', CMO (July 1923), pp. 138–9; NZ Presbyterian GA Proceedings 1923, p. 166; Punjab Mission Annual Report 1927, p. 55; North-West India Conference Journal 1933, p. 28.

[62] See, for example, W.P. Hares, 'Great Encouragement and a Great Disappointment', MMQ (July 1922), p. 10; 'Missiones: Les Conversions en masse au Punjab', Analecta (1925), pp. 153–4; Punjab Mission Annual Report 1926, p. 29; ibid. 1930–31, p. 20; UPCNA Annual Report 1931, pp. 88–9. 105.

[63] See, for example, Indus River Annual Conference Journal 1924, p. 26; NZ Presbyterian GA Proceedings 1924, p. 98; Punjab Mission Annual Report 1930–31, p. 24; Punjab Mission Annual Report 1933, p. 19; 'Ambala District Women's Work', Punjab Mission Annual Report 1933–34, p. 1; UPCNA Annual Report 1931, p. 94; Indus River Conference Journal 1938, p. 155.

[64] The others either dealt in animal hides, worked in brick kilns, or lived close enough to a town or city to have an urban occupation.

the pragmatic 'religious flexibility' viewed as characteristic of the Chuhras generally.[65]

Whether in areas of Christian concentration or not, and regardless of denomination, village churches took one of three different forms throughout this period. One was the church of the Christian village where virtually the entire population, including the landowners, was Christian. All but one of these were in the canal colonies of the western Punjab.[66] These churches resembled the urban churches. They tended to be somewhat socially diverse, self-supporting with a school, perhaps a dispensary, a full range of activities including Sunday schools, women's groups, Christian melas, and even a resident missionary at times. Another was the fully organized church in a village where the landowners were not Christians, but where there was a large enough concentration of Christians to warrant a resident pastor or catechist/teacher and perhaps a building that served as a church as well as a school. This gave some regularity and reinforcement to Christian religious practice as well as opportunity and help in the struggle for a better life. The most common type, however, was the small cluster of unorganized believers, perhaps only a few families in one or neighbouring villages, who had no regular services of worship and infrequent pastoral care or instruction. They would be visited periodically by catechists resident elsewhere, and perhaps once or twice a year during the cool season or when emergencies arose, by district missionaries and pastors.

[65] Supra p. 169 and Joseph Thakur Das, 'A Great Door and Effectual', *MMQ* (December 1929), p. 52.

[66] By 1929, Mariabad, the original Roman Catholic village, had 408 Christians as well as a resident priest, schools and orphanages for boys and girls, a dispensary, and a convent for a new community of Indian Franciscan sisters. Khushpur and Francisabad were similarly well established. This concentration of limited resources made all three villages major centres of Christian life and influence. 'Missiones', *Analecta* (1929), pp. 42, 70. In 1937, the Salvation Army reported that Shantinagar, a tract of land given them for the rehabilitation of criminal tribes, had succeeded so well that the government had closed it and allowed the settlers to go where they wanted. Shantinagar thus became a totally Salvationist village. *Salvation Army Year Book 1924*, p. 64; ibid. *1937*, p. 87; David C. Lamb, 'Migration and Settlement', in ibid. *1938*, p. 19.

The history of these churches is not easily told. The rural Dalit Christian voice remains more silent in this part of the historical record than in the past, but can be heard when examining at least four clusters of interrelated concerns around which their struggles took place. The first and most important of these was economic, focusing on emancipation from poverty, indebtedness and economic dependence. The second consisted of socio-cultural and psychological identity issues. The third were educational issues and the final one concerned their negotiations with their well-intentioned but strong-minded missionary patrons over the steps to be taken towards creating self-governing, self-supporting, and self-propagating churches. Each of these aspects of rural church life will be examined in turn to gain some sense of its history during this period.

Miss R.M. King, a CMS missionary at Gojra, described the bitter complaints of Dalits she heard in the early 1920s as she toured the villages in the canal colonies. 'When are you going to deliver us from this dung and filth?' 'It isn't land and wealth we want; it is only to be able to have a bite to eat in peace. We toil and slave, but get no pay for it.' 'Can't you manage to get the farmers to give us water? We must drink, but they refuse to let us draw water from the village well, and when we wanted to make a special pond for ourselves they opposed us and refused to let us dig.' 'What shall I do? I hired myself for a year to a farmer and have done nine months' service without a penny of wages. The agreement was that I should be paid in grain every six months. To-day he has given me notice and says he will employ me no longer as I am a Christian, nor will he pay me anything that is due.' 'The farmers here have turned us all off. What are we to do? Our women sweep the compounds and carry off the manure, but they get a mere pittance for that work, and unless we can get field labour how can we put bread into our children's mouths?'[67] Another district missionary in the central Punjab observed that while the converts are 'humble and hard-working menials', they 'are treated more as slaves than as farm labourers'.[68]

[67] R.M. King, 'Experiences Among Indian Outcastes. I. In the Villages of the Punjab', *CMO* (2 July 1923), p. 138.

[68] *Punjab Mission Annual Report 1925*, p. 117.

Other comments were more analytical than evocative. In 1926, R.B. Nesbitt, a Presbyterian missionary at Hoshiarpur, surveying eleven people 'in contact with village conditions', found that landlords frequently mistreated village Christians, in many cases as a consequence of normal conflicts over such things as debt payments, the division of grain, and enforced labour rather than religion. However, his respondents also believed that Christians were mistreated more frequently than other village menials primarily because the landlord 'feels intuitively that the Christian is escaping from the control which has been exercised over him and his ancestors for generations'.[69] One reason for this, indicated in his survey but elaborated upon at greater length by the Rev. Barakat Ullah, was the growing willingness of rural Dalit Christians to openly challenge their landlords because they felt that the missionaries, who were well connected with local officials, would protect them from reprisals.[70] Barakat Ullah was disturbed by this trend and was quite critical of missionary paternalism not only because missionaries could be easily manipulated by such tales of oppression as those Miss King had heard, but also because, with the increasing nationalization of the Punjab administration, the intercessions of missionary patrons could no longer be as effective as in the past.

In 1937 and 1938, Frank Thakur Das and E.D. Lucas carried out the most thorough study of the economic situation of rural Punjabi Christians from this period. They concentrated upon twelve villages around Pasrur (a United Presbyterian station) and six around Narowal (a CMS station). They found that over two-thirds of their sample consisted of landless labourers and another 15 per cent were tenant cultivators on yearly contracts, both of which were very insecure arrangements. Most of the remainder were engaged in gut-making, trading in hides and skins, making bricks, and casual labour; only a few of the better educated had become cobblers, potters, or mission

[69] R.B. Nesbitt, 'Disabilities of Village Christians', *NCCR* (June 1926), pp. 329–30.

[70] Ibid., pp. 328–9; Barakat Ullah, 'An Aspect of the Mass Movement Problem in the Punjab', *NCCR* (May 1927), pp. 291–300.

employees.[71] They found 81.9 per cent of the Pasrur sample and 90.9 per cent of the Narowal sample were in debt, the average debt being equivalent to 19 months' average income and the amount borrowed each year exceeding the amount repaid.[72] General interest rates were high, averaging about 25 per cent per year.[73]

Poverty and indebtedness were major obstacles to the creation of a self-supporting rural church. Creating cooperative banks among rural Christians so as to reduce interest rates and increase independence from moneylenders did not solve the problem and some missionaries moved into direct rural reconstruction work, although this had to be limited to only that very small percentage of Christians who either owned or held land on long-term tenancies. When J.C. Heinrich moved into Martinpur, a United Presbyterian village in the canal colonies, he found the village to be full of conflict, which he attributed to severe overcrowding (an increase in population from 400 to 1600 in thirty years) and the presence of a new generation of educated but unemployed youth.[74] One of his early campaigns was to get all the manure piles removed from the village and he even instituted a Clean Village Challenge Cup to achieve his objective.[75] By 1939, he and some of the pastors working with him, in collaboration with the Punjab government's rural reconstruction programme, set up demonstration plots among Christian tenant farmers in and around Martinpur to convince other farmers both to use new rust-resistant seed for their wheat crops and to sow cotton in rows.[76]

However, the more common approach to the problems of poverty and debt that the missionaries adopted was to promote thrift by

[71] E.D. Lucas and F. Thakur Das, *The Rural Church in the Punjab*, pp. iii–iv.

[72] Ibid., p. 17.

[73] Ibid., p. 23.

[74] J.C. Heinrich, 'Blessed are the Peacemakers', *UCR* (September 1934), pp. 228–9.

[75] J.C. Heinrich, 'Rethinking Missions in Martinpur Village', *WMM* (March 1936), pp. 393–4.

[76] J.C. Heinrich, 'Rural Reconstruction and Village Self-Support', *UCR* (June 1939), pp. 166–9.

encouraging their rural parishioners to give up some of their 'needless expenditures'.[77] At this point economic and socio-cultural identity concerns clashed, with the former usually giving way to the latter. Nowhere was this more apparent than in the expressions of missionary anguish over marriage practices that frequently appeared in mission reports. The first task the missionaries had undertaken was to persuade their rural Dalit converts to marry their children only to other Christians and to use Christian rites for engagements and weddings. Persuasion became easier as the rural Christian population increased in size, but was by no means completely successful when this period began.[78]

During the 1920s and 1930s, two other issues tended to dominate discussions of marriage practices. One concerned the practice of bride price. The Chuhras considered a woman to be an economic asset who was being transferred from one family to another and for whom, therefore, compensation was expected.[79] To the missionaries this practice not only involved the buying and selling of women, which was wrong in principle, but also led to endless quarrels over price and payment. The other issue concerned the expense of the wedding festivities themselves. Gifts had to be given; people had to be entertained, fed, and even allowed to drink to excess, thus increasing the chances for quarrels and fights.[80] Thakur Das and Lucas found that the Christian labourers interviewed in Pasrur spent about 9.3 per cent of their average annual income of Rs 156 on marriages, while in Narowal it was 12.2 per cent of their average annual income

[77] 'The Editor to his Readers: Hoshiarpur Conference Summons Christians to Advance', *IS* (June 1925), p. 178.

[78] See R.B. Nesbitt, 'Engagement and Marriage among Village Christians', *NCCR* (July 1925), pp. 278–80.

[79] See H.J. Strickler, 'The Religion and Customs of the Chuhra in the Punjab Province', India, p. 10.

[80] Digby R.M.F. Creighton, 'Facing Facts, Dark and Bright', *MMQ* (October 1922), pp. 13–4; R.B. Nesbitt, 'Engagement and Marriage', *NCCR* (July 1925), pp. 282–3; C.L. Richards, 'A Mass Movement Church and its Ethical Needs', *MMQ* (December 1927), p. 59; C.L. Richards, 'The Average Village Christian', *CMO* (April 1931), pp. 72–3; Bishop Banerji, 'Evangelism', *LDM* (March 1936), p. 135; W.F. Hawkes, 'India's Future Generations', *MMQ* (December 1936), p. 35.

of Rs 153.[81] Bride price ranged from Rs 100 to Rs 200.[82] They also found that marriage was the main reason for heavy borrowing; 57.7 per cent of the loans taken by 105 families in the Pasrur area were for marriage expenses, the average loan being about Rs 162 or more than a full year's wages.[83] Yet, in the villagers' perception, hospitality at marriages was a necessity if one was to be a respected member of the community. Moreover, debt was not considered a totally bad thing; it was a sign of trust and a guarantee of protection.[84]

'Marriage reform' was but one point of attack in the missionary effort to both Christianize and emancipate rural Dalits from a bondage which was perceived to be as much cultural as socio-economic.[85] A much deeper identity issue was the sense of helplessness and dependency that was carried over from village patron–client relationships into Church relationships. While this was a major obstacle to the creation of self-supporting, self-governing, and self-propagating rural churches, district missionaries often saw the creation of such churches as the chief means of moving rural Dalits beyond helplessness and dependency towards greater initiative, competence, self-confidence, and respect.[86] At the same time, as J.C. Heinrich pointed out, when Dalit Christians began to experience the beginnings of emancipation from helplessness and dependency, they often took out their pent-up anger over long-term oppression and humiliation not only on each other, as in the past, but also

[81] E.D. Lucas and F. Thakur Das, *The Rural Church in the Punjab*, pp. 23–4. They had to contribute to the wedding expenses not only of their own family but also of caste-fellows within the village. Mrs. Kenneth McKenzie, 'A Christian Village Wedding', *WMM* (November 1923), p. 225.

[82] One Christian used the Rs 120 he received to feed the wedding guests (Rs 30), buy a buffalo (Rs 45), repay a debt (Rs 35), and keep some cash on hand (Rs 10). E.D. Lucas and F. Thakur Das, *The Rural Church in the Punjab*, p. 24.

[83] Ibid., p. 39–41.

[84] Ibid., p. 17.

[85] The only evidence of successful 'marriage reform' I have found was a reference to an agreement among Christians in Jullundur district on standards of giving and expenditure for marriages in 'The Editor to His Reader: Hoshiarpur Conference Summons Christians to Advance', *IS* (June 1925), p. 178.

[86] This is most apparent in missionary discussions of self-support.

occasionally upon their oppressors (which had greatly concerned the Rev. Barakat Ullah),[87] and more often on the mission workers who had helped liberate them. The pastoral care of newly and partially emancipated rural Dalit Christians was, therefore, a very challenging task, requiring considerable psychological stamina and sophistication.[88]

Rural Dalits and missionaries alike saw education as a vital key to social emancipation and to the development of the Church. Dalit requests came early for both Christian instruction and primary schools for their children. Those early village schools, providing basic literacy and Christian teaching, served also as important recruiting grounds for the missions' growing demands for rural workers. Dalit enthusiasm for education was by no means universal, as parents often needed the small extra income their children could provide.[89] Thakur Das and Lucas found that in the three villages around Pasrur with Christian schools, 51 per cent of the children ages 6–14 were enrolled, whereas in the nine villages without Christian schools 35 per cent were enrolled.[90] Moreover, 79 per cent of the girls enrolled in school in those villages were attending Christian schools.[91] The presence of a Christian school obviously made a difference to the education of Christian children.

The issue, however, was not just whether rural Christian children were going to school; it also concerned what they were learning and what kind of life that was preparing them for. In 1919, the Punjab government made education compulsory for boys between the ages of six and eleven. In 1923, under some pressure from Dalits, it

---

[87] Supra p. 227.

[88] J.C. Heinrich, *The Psychology of a Suppressed People*, pp. 90–144.

[89] E. Guilford, 'Some Hindrances to the Progress of the Mass Movement', *MMQ* (November 1918), pp. 10–11; J.D. Finlay, '"Building" at Batala', ibid. (November 1928), p. 64; 'Gojra Village Mission, 1943', ibid. (June 1944), p. 16; *Punjab Mission Annual Report 1925*, p. 44; Arsene de Berlare, 'Relatio Missionis Lahorensis', *Analecta* (1938), pp. 91–3.

[90] E.D. Lucas and F. Thakur Das, *The Rural Church in the Punjab*, p. 42.

[91] Ibid.

formally committed itself to equal opportunity for all in education.[92] Yet the prescribed curriculum retained its acknowledged urban bias. Meanwhile, in 1919, the International Missionary Council's commission on rural education placed the vocational middle school (which combined academic with industrial, agricultural, or household training) at the centre of their recommendations for improvement, but were ambivalent about whether the missions were to educate rural Christians for migration to the towns and cities or 'to help the various rural Christian communities to live a more abundant life where they are'.[93]

Education for the transformation of village life was no easy task. The village primary school teachers in the mission system were not trained or equipped to carry it out. The Christian Girls' Boarding School at Narowal did try to prepare their girls to become good Christian wives and mothers back in their villages. 'They have no idea of order and cleanliness when they come to us, so besides teaching them to read their Bibles, we try to inculcate habits of cleanliness, thrift, and economy so that they may be able to order aright the homes of their husbands.'[94] So, in addition to the prescribed government curriculum and a considerable amount of Christian teaching, they learned such practical tasks as making and mending clothes, grinding and cooking, as well as bead work and embroidery.[95]

However, the most radical experiment in rural education was the Training School for Village Teachers at Moga. Begun in 1908, it became a middle school in 1917 and added a two-year teacher's training course in 1923. William McKee introduced the 'project method' of education in 1919. Each boy was given a small plot of land to cultivate; he could sell its produce to help pay his school expenses and earn spending money. He thus had a strong incentive to learn not only improved methods of agriculture but also arithmetic

[92] William J. McKee, *New Schools for Young India*, pp. 44, 51–2.

[93] *Village Education in India*, p. 156.

[94] M.W. Morrison, 'A Girls' Boarding School in the Punjab', *MMQ* (January 1919), p. 12.

[95] M.W. Morrison, 'Education in a Mass Movement District', *IW* (November 1917), p. 126.

and basic accounting! In addition, each class had a special project (for example, the village home, the village farm, the village bazar, etc.) around which learning for the year would be organized and through participation in which the boys acquired some additional skills, came to understand their immediate environment, and learned to work together for the common good. This approach to education was applied to religious education as well. As Irene Harper, who taught at Moga for many years, pointed out,

Bible teaching and religious instruction must all be centred around the pupils' actual needs and around the practical everyday needs of the adult village Christians. Problems of conduct, problems of worship and individual experience, problems of service:– these must be made the centre of the courses of religious instruction.[96]

Moga's influence was considerable, as it was seen, both inside and beyond the Punjab, as a model for educating the rural poor. Between 1922 and 1926, eighty-eight of their ninety-six candidates in the teacher training course became teachers, seventy-five in village day or boarding schools. Moga not only continued to supervise them after they graduated but also published *The Village Teacher's Journal*, which was translated into five languages.[97]

It is extremely difficult to generalize about the impact of education upon the development of the rural church and Christian community during this period. It seems safe to conclude that literacy and hence education's potential impact was highest in Christian villages and lowest where small numbers of Christians lived in scattered villages. Thakur Das and Lucas provide the best available benchmark of any progress made. In the eighteen villages they studied the overall literacy rate was 10.7 per cent, well above the Census average for the Christian community or for the province as a whole. One village had a 29 per cent literacy rate for Christians and another had no

[96] Irene M. Harper, 'The Religious Education of Village Christians', *IS* (May 1925), p. 140.

[97] William J. McKee, *New Schools for Young India*, pp. 181–2. See also, ibid., pp. 133–84; Arthur Judson Brown, *One Hundred Years*, pp. 614–6; and *25 Years: Moga Training School for Village Teachers*.

literate Christians, so the range was considerable. However, only five adult women were literate.[98] What impact literacy and education had upon their individual, community, and church lives is even more difficult to determine. There were no correlations made between education and either occupational mobility, improved income, or patterns of expenditure and hence of life-style changes. Thakur Das and Lucas recommended both that 'the more capable boys and girls should be so trained that they can preferably return to the villages as skilled workers and raise the general economic level' and that 'those, however, who have both the keen desire and the ability to enter urban life, should be helped to do so'.[99]

Given their continued poverty and indebtedness, the dictates of their culture and dependency, the still unrealized potential of transformative education among them, as well as the steady departure of their most talented and ambitious for more economically and psychologically rewarding work in the towns and cities,[100] it is not surprising that rural Dalit Christians had the most difficulty developing self-supporting churches. Sunday offerings, harvest festivals, Christmas melas, gifts at the time of marriage, the distribution of earthenware pots in which a measure of grain or flour could be put each day, and other payments in kind were used to increase the gifts necessary to pay for the pastor's salary and the maintenance of church buildings. The United Presbyterians, considered the most successful in developing self-supporting churches, had each village pastor, together with the elders, raise his own support. This was considered to be an indigenous practice, which kept the pastor conscientious, even if it did put him 'too much at the mercy of his people'.[101]

---

[98] E.D. Lucas and F. Thakur Das, *The Rural Church in the Punjab*, p. 44. In 1946, S.N. Talibuddin found that literacy and school attendance was still low. 'A Study of Self-Supporting Churches in the Punjab', *UCR* (June 1947), pp. 301–2.

[99] E.D. Lucas and F. Thakur Das, *The Rural Church in the Punjab*, p. 52.

[100] See, for example, *Punjab Mission Annual Report 1925*, p. 93.

[101] C.H. Loehlin, 'Self-Support in Village Churches; A Report of a Survey', *IS* (April 1929), p. 91. J.C. Heinrich later pointed out in *The Psychology of a Suppressed People* (pp. 38–40) that in the process of collecting these offerings the pastors were often subject to considerable mockery and humiliation.

Two studies conducted during this period give some data on the progress towards self-support made by 1947. Thakur Das and Lucas found that the key factor in developing a self-supporting church was how highly concentrated or widely dispersed its membership was. It was generally agreed that it took 100 to 150 families to support a pastor and that pastors earned about double the income of the people they served. Contributions, made primarily in kind twice a year at harvest time, averaged out to about one per cent of each family's annual income. Generally people gave willingly; excuses for not giving usually centred around not receiving the services (legitimate or otherwise) expected or demanded of the pastor.[102] S.N. Talibuddin conducted the other study in 1946 within six districts of central Punjab where Christians were even more widely dispersed than in the Pasrur and Narowal areas. The consequences of dispersal for the quality of church life became very clear at a conference, included in the study, at which the following points emerged.

(a) The parish of each Pastor contains 20 to 60 villages, scattered over an area of 10 to 20 square miles. (b) The means of transportation at the disposal of Pastors is the bicycle, in addition to the occasional use of bus and train services. During certain parts of the year the bicycle is not very useful because of poor roads. (c) It is not possible for the Pastor to visit the different groups in his parish more than 1 to 4 times during the year. (d) Sunday Services can be held only in one fifth of the area of each parish. (e) Communion Services are held about 4 times a year in places where Pastors reside, in other places not more frequently than once a year.[103]

The rural church seemed to have expanded beyond its capacity to properly sustain itself. As indicated earlier, the resulting inadequate pastoral care explains why clusters of rural Christians moved from one denominational group to another.

While self-support was the major challenge, self-government and self-propagation were considered to be matters of proper training. In this connection it is important to distinguish the training of full-

[102] E.D. Lucas and F. Thakur Das, *The Rural Church in the Punjab*, pp. 46–51.

[103] S.N. Talibuddin, 'A Study of Self-Supporting Churches in the Punjab', *UCR* (July 1947), p. 325.

time rural workers—whether clergy, catechists, or Bible women—from the training of local lay leadership. With regard to the former, each mission had its own training school and continuing education programmes for village workers.[104] Each also had its own educational standards for each level of worker. As far as can be determined, the Roman Catholics did not ordain any Punjabis to the priesthood during this period; all of their priests were foreigners. The Anglicans had the highest educational standards for ordained clergy; as a result they had very few of them and in the rural areas their role, like that of the district missionary, was largely sacramental and supervisory rather than pastoral, as they were responsible for large areas. On the other hand, the United Presbyterians had much lower ordination standards and by far the largest number of ordained pastors; most were resident in villages and had full pastoral roles within a much more limited area. Lay education tended to be more informal, occasional, and on the spot. Beyond the level of instruction in the basic 'village catechisms' there were specially organized one-day classes, Bible schools, and week-long courses held at central locations during the summer for *lambardars, chaudhries,* and elders. This effort at training became more intense as independence approached and the future of missionaries in India became more uncertain.[105]

What then did the rural church in north-west India look like at the end of this period? S.N. Talibuddin, in his 1946 survey, listed his observations under the headings of 'Encouraging Features' and 'Limitations and Weaknesses'.[106] Several of these, reinforced by other contemporary observations, are of special importance in the light of what has already been said. Heading his list is the transformation

---

[104] See, for example, A. Dungworth, 'A Training School for Village Workers', *MMQ* (October 1921), pp. 5–7; L.H. Woolmer, 'Gojra Village Mission, 1943', ibid. (June 1944), pp. 16–7; Angus Nicolson, 'Theological Teaching in the Punjab', *OL* (January 1942), p. 52.

[105] Christopher Cox, 'Gojra Village Mission', *MMQ* (June 1945), p. 14.

[106] This study, 'A Study of Self-Supporting Churches in the Punjab', was spread over several issues of *The United Church Review*: May 1947, pp. 278–81; June 1947, pp. 300–06; July 1947, pp. 325–9; August 1947, pp. 351–4, 362; September 1947, pp. 375–80.

of individual lives brought about by Christianity, despite the poverty and disabilities from which they continued to suffer as rural Dalit menials. Talibuddin did not provide details at this point, but it seems clear that there was more literacy and thus probably more occupational mobility among Christians than among other rural Dalits. They also seem to have had higher standards of public sanitation than did their Dalit neighbours. Moreover, if Barakat Ullah and J.C. Heinrich are to be believed, there was among them more evidence of psychological rebellion against the oppression meted out to them by village landowners[107] and, despite continued dependency, more signs of growing self-confidence among them than among other village menials belonging to the same caste. Another 'encouraging feature' was the fact that the Church had 'taken root' in the rural Punjab and a 'church consciousness' (as opposed to dependency upon foreign missions) had grown among its members. There were some well-organized village congregations with trained, responsible, and committed leaders. He also noted a 'broadened outlook' and a growing desire for church buildings among rural Christians. Yet he also saw the rural church, despite these encouraging signs, as being highly vulnerable because of the poverty and low educational attainments of its members, as well as the inadequacies in pastoral care, provision for leadership development, and work among women he discovered. He considered the level of spiritual life in the village congregations to be, on the average, 'exceedingly low'. Animistic ideas, sorcery, the use of charms, idolatrous practices (undefined), and fear of evil spirits were all quite common. General sabbath observance was not good and regular Sunday worship was, in his estimation, lacking in dignity, beauty, and congregational participation.

The rural churches obviously did not measure up to urban and more middle-class standards. They were less structured, more informal and relaxed, more widely dispersed, with blurred and porous

---

[107] The high level of litigation among rural Christians, which Talibuddin bemoaned, could be taken as further evidence of a new-found freedom to rebel, if it was directed against landowners rather than against each other. Ibid. (June 1947), p. 304.

boundaries between them and their fellow villagers of other religions. Their economic base was weak and always precarious, except in the Christian villages. The second generation of rural Dalit converts had, in some places, moved beyond the attainments of the first generation, but their overall progress towards personal and communal transformation under the influence of Christianity remained slow and uneven.

Christians and Political Movements

The Christian community in the north-west was not well positioned to deal with the mass politics that Gandhi inaugurated in 1919. It did have some highly gifted individuals, but it was very small in size, institutionally based in the urban areas, and in the villages composed almost entirely of Dalit menials. It also had very few members drawn from those social groups which were most active in the politics of this period. In addition, it was, at this stage, missionary dominated, with only a few Indian members capable of providing political leadership for the community. Some Christians had found places within the very limited, paternalistic political structures of the pre-war Raj; a few had attended some of the early sessions of the Indian National Congress and of the Indian Association of Lahore. The Indian Christian Association, Punjab, became interested in political issues after 1909 and there were signs of growing politicization among Christian college students. The government itself was at best indifferent to Christian interests. During World War I it had not only been very reluctant to recruit Christians while virtually press-ganging other Punjabis into the army[108] but had also required all non-British mission societies to make certain that their missionaries and employees either refrain from all political activity and work in loyal cooperation with the government or face the expulsion of all their missionaries from India.[109] Opinion among Christians about the Congress-led nationalist movement was divided, ranging from deep

[108] See John C.B. Webster, 'Punjabi Christians and the Indian Nationalist Movement', pp. 69–70.

[109] The 1917 warning was renewed after the war and specifically included 'the work of missionary societies and of missionaries, employees, and agents of missionary societies'. Robert E. Speer, Letter to the North India and Punjab Missions

suspicion because of its perceived anti-Christian religious basis to approval out of love for India and a conviction that Christianity had a contribution to make to her regeneration.[110] Those Christians who were nationalists at this time were clearly more sympathetic to the moderate than to the extremist style and ideology.

In March 1919, Gandhi called for a nationwide hartal to protest the passage of the Rowlatt Bills, which allowed the government to take extraordinary measures and suspend due process of law in order to combat terrorism and sedition. In Delhi there were hartals on both 30 March and 6 April as well as an extended hartal between 9 and 18 April protesting Gandhi's arrest. Lahore had a hartal on 6 April and held major demonstrations on 9, 10, and 11 April that led to the imposition of martial law on 13 April. However, the worst affected was Amritsar where there were hartals on both 30 March and 6 April. The imposition of martial law, the arrest of Gandhi, and the deportation of two local leaders resulted in mass protest, a police firing, and a violent reaction on 10 April. The notorious Jallianwala Bagh massacre on 13 April when General Dyer and his troops shot hundreds of helpless people, further aggravated the prevailing unrest there and in other parts of Punjab. Gandhi called off the satyagraha on 18 April and the Punjab government ended martial law only in mid-June.

Mission reports from Delhi indicate that Christians did not participate in the hartals and that students at St. Stephen's College attended classes regularly.[111] S.K. Rudra pointed not only to a rapid rise in both national consciousness and Indian–British estrangement in the city following events in the Punjab, but also to C.F. Andrews's tireless efforts to mediate between British officialdom and the Indian

---

[of the Presbyterian Church in the U.S.A.], 21 February 1917; Board of Foreign Missions of the Presbyterian Church in the United States of America. Minutes No. 37 1919–1920 (meeting of 19 January 1920), pp. 265–6.

[110] See supra pp. 151–5, p. 278 and John C.B. Webster, *The Christian Community and Change*, pp. 200–4; John C.B. Webster, 'Punjabi Christians and the Indian Nationalist Movement, 1919–1947', pp. 68–9; Narayani Gupta, *Delhi Between Two Empires*, p. 200.

[111] 'Editorial', *St. Stephen's College Magazine* (June 1919), p. 1; F.J. Western in *Delhi Mission News* (July 1919), pp. 57–8.

leaders there.[112] In 1920, when the government was conducting an inquiry into the actions of the martial law regime in the Punjab, twenty-five British missionaries (eleven of whom were resident in Delhi and south-eastern Punjab) published a joint statement condemning, as fundamentally disloyal to the spirit of the recent Royal Proclamation and to the best traditions of the British Empire', some of the government's actions, its contemptuous attitude towards the Indian people, its arrogant assumption of racial superiority, and its self-justifying arguments, 'implying that India exists mainly for the white man's profit or pleasure'.[113] An editorial in the *St. Stephen's College Magazine* was equally blunt and more explicitly Christian.

Better, a thousand times better, in our view, if India were lost to the British Empire, than preserved only by such methods. The ideal of an India held for England only by naked and ruthless force is one no follower of Jesus Christ can consistently tolerate for an instant. We believe it to be also entirely out of relation to the facts; the links which bind India and England together are of nobler and more durable material than brute might. But it is with principles rather than facts that we are here concerned; and with principle we repudiate with detestation a policy based on a belief in the cementing efficacy of "blood and iron".[114]

The students of Forman Christian College in Lahore took a far more active role in the agitations of 6 and 10 April than had the St. Stephen's College students, despite the efforts of the American principal, E.D. Lucas, and his colleagues. On 11 April, only fifty of the 750 students attended classes; the others were fined and seven were punished more severely for their involvement in the agitation. Lucas and his predecessor, J.C.R. Ewing led a committee of Lahore educators which resolved to educate the students there on the actual provisions of the Rowlatt Act, an action which C.F. Andrews publicly condemned. Other missionaries helped the government coordinate the use of commandeered vehicles for about three weeks. The list of those

---

[112] 'St. Stephen's College, Letter from the Principal', *The Forty-Second Report of the Cambridge Committee with which is incorporated The General Report of the Other Branches of the Mission for the Year 1919*, pp. 7–8.

[113] 'Correspondence', *Young Men of India* (September 1920), pp. 568–9.

[114] 'Editorial', *St. Stephen's College Magazine* (July 1920), p. 2.

arrested in Lahore under martial law contained only one obviously Christian name, Joseph, a *tongawala* who was arrested twice and beaten both times.[115]

In Amritsar the mob violence following the police firing on 10 April had an anti-Christian dimension. Among the buildings burned were the Religious Book Society's depot in Hall Bazar and the Indian Church. The CMS Girls' Normal School was being attacked when the police arrived. A CEZMS missionary, Marcella Sherwood, was assaulted while cycling through the bazar, was left for dead, and was then rescued by the people of the locality. Missionaries and Indian Christians spent that night in the Alexandra School; they moved to the fort the next day for greater safety.[116]

Elsewhere in the Punjab there was damage to church and mission property in Gujrat, Wazirabad, and Gujranwala where a crowd moving towards the mission premises was stopped by bombing from the air. Under martial law, missionaries were advised to take special precautions and some of the women were even escorted to safer places. In Lyallpur district, village Christians were reportedly harassed by the Hindu and Muslim landlords. W.P. Hares also reported with pride that they remained staunchly loyal to their faith as well as to the Raj, and even offered to defend the Europeans in Lyallpur if necessary. Hares said that he knew of only two Christians who were implicated in the agitations.[117]

The Rowlatt satyagraha and its suppression proved to be quite a traumatic experience for Christians, especially in the Punjab.

[115] The Principal's Report to the Board of Directors, 27 September 1919; Personal Labour Report, J.M. Benade; Personal Labour Report, E.D. Lucas; Personal Labour Report 10 October 1918–11 October 1919, John B. Weir; *Evidence Taken Before the Disorders Inquiry Committee*, IV: pp. 120–24; C.B. Stuntz in *The Indian Witness* (30 April 1919), pp. 280–81; C.F. Andrews, 'The Rowlatt Act to be Taught in Schools', *Indian Social Reformer* (11 May 1919), p. 491. A fuller picture of Christian involvement with the Rowlatt satyagraha in Lahore is found in John C.B. Webster, 'Presbyterian Missionaries and Gandhian Politics, 1919–1922', pp. 251–2.

[116] 'North India: Punjab', *The C.M.S. Gleaner* (2 June 1919), pp. 93–4; V.N. Datta, ed., *New Light on the Punjab Disturbances in 1919: Volumes VI and VII of Disorders Inquiry Committee Evidence*, pp. 248–75.

[117] See John C.B. Webster, 'Punjabi Christians and the Indian Nationalist Movement', p. 74 and 'Presbyterian Missionaries and Gandhian Politics', pp. 251–2; see also Martha Payne Alter, *Letters from India to America 1916–1951*, pp. 110–1.

Missionary opinion ranged from the staunchly pro-British, represented by Hares and the American C. Herbert Rice, to the deeply conflicted E.D. Lucas, who had been supportive of the government but was at the same time forthrightly critical of some of the measures the martial law regime had taken.[118] Marcella Sherwood, while clearly pro-government, did not wish to become part of its self-justifying propaganda campaign. She turned down a gift of Rs 50,000 as compensation for the injuries she suffered during the Amritsar riots because she felt that her injuries had been 'more than compensated for by the action of those Indians to whom she owed her life and rescue'.[119] Members of the Punjabi Christian elite presented equally mixed views. Whereas Alfred Nundy told the All-India Conference of Indian Christians (AICIC) that the 'Indian Christians of Gujranwala fully sympathized with their fellow countrymen in the Punjab', Hakim Din cited instances in both 1907 and 1919 to show that 'the national movement had manifested an Anti-Christian character on several occasions and at several places'.[120] The AICIC Council, at a special June 1920 meeting, condemned the excesses not only of the martial law regime but also of the agitation's leaders (including Gandhi) and appealed for the end of 'all religious animosities and racial hatred'.[121] When the governor who had imposed martial law upon the Punjab departed, deputations of loyal and appreciative Muslims, Hindus, and Sikhs presented him with farewell addresses, but, interestingly enough, there is no indication that any Punjabi Christian deputation did so.[122]

[118] C. Herbert Rice, Letter to Mr. Putnam, 1 June 1919; *Evidence Taken Before the Disorders Inquiry Committee*, IV, pp. 120–4.

[119] 'An Explanation', *IW* (April 1920), p. 58; 'Notes', *The Indian Social Reformer* (15 February 1920), p. 378.

[120] *The Report of the Fifth All India Conference of Indian Christians Held in Cuttack on December 29th, 30th, and 31st, 1919*, p. 13; *The Report of the Sixth All India Conference of Indian Christians Held in Calcutta on December 28th, 29th, 30th and 31st, 1920*, p. 29. [Hereafter referred to as *AICIC Conference Report* with the year added.]

[121] 'Statement of the Council of the All-India Conference of Indian Christians on the Punjab Disturbances in 1919', *The Young Men of India* (September 1920), p. 570.

[122] See V.N. Datta, ed., *New Light on the Punjab Disturbances*, pp. 823–35.

The British failed to set things right when martial law was lifted. Their verdict on the excesses of martial law was highly ambivalent, their constitutional reforms were deemed most inadequate, and the Treaty of Sevres with its broken wartime promises alienated Muslims. Gandhi's faith in British justice was broken and he launched a non-cooperation campaign which included a boycott of government-aided educational institutions. Although he conceived the plan while staying in S.K. Rudra's home at St. Stephen's College, with Rudra and C.F. Andrews as his revisionists for a portion of it,[123] he was unable to convince either Rudra or the students of the Delhi colleges to join the boycott.[124] Rudra's own view of the movement, stated in his report for 1920 directed to a British readership, was very positive.

Mr. Gandhi's movement of non-co-operation means renunciation of association and fellowship with Government. It does not mean renunciation of association and fellowship with Englishmen or with Christians as such, for he has many of his esteemed and valued friends among these. The essential character of the movement is that it is a mighty spiritual call to righteousness, both in public, private, social and business life of the people, with an implicit childlike faith in God who wants righteousness to flourish upon the earth. If this is not clearly grasped, it may be easily misunderstood not only as a purely destructive movement confined to the immediate political issues in this country, but also an anti-foreign and anti-Christian movement.[125]

F.J. Western of the Cambridge mission was more ambivalent, appreciating Gandhi's moral idealism, and especially his commitment to non-violence, but more sceptical about the kinds of consequences for India and Indo-British relations his campaign was fostering.[126]

[123] Quoted from *Indian Christians*, pp. 318–9.

[124] He addressed a meeting of students from all three colleges on 24 November 1920, but the next day work resumed as usual in all of them. Donald W. Ferrell, 'Delhi, 1911-1922', pp. 487–8. Rudra's policy with regard to student participation was 'The principle of the liberty of conscience has been upheld strenuously, but precipitate mass action has been strongly deprecated at the same time.' 'Report of St. Stephen's College for 1920', *The Forty-third Report of the Cambridge Committee with which is incorporated The General Report of the Other Branches of the Mission for the Year 1920*, p. 12.

[125] Ibid.

[126] F.J. Western, 'The Problem of Mr. Gandhi', *DMN* (July 1922), pp. 57–60.

It was in the Punjab that the differences between the non-cooperation movement and the Rowlatt satyagraha were most apparent. While Christians opposed the boycott of their own and other aided institutions, Forman Christian College lost 156 of its students, Gordon College lost thirty of its 175, while many mission schools reported unstable enrolments during the campaign.[127] There were, however, no acts of violence against Christians or Christian property, as had been the case in 1919, even if in places Christians also had to bear the brunt of bitterness at the Raj and Westerners in general.[128] In some cities Christian evangelistic work ran into difficulties and was curtailed; in some others the very opposite was the case. Some 1800 loyal rural Methodists marched into Lahore to welcome the Prince of Wales whose visit was being boycotted by the Lahore Municipal Committee, the Christian Secretary of which, K.L. Rallia Ram, was the headmaster of the Presbyterian school in Lahore and a member of the Punjab Legislative Council.[129]

However, perhaps the best indicator of educated Punjabi Christian opinion on non-cooperation was the meeting of the AICIC held between 28 and 30 December 1921 at Forman Christian College, as all but two of the 75 members of the reception committee and fifty-four of the seventy-one delegates were from the Punjab. The conference followed the lead of K.L. Rallia Ram who, in his welcome address, defined the role of Christians in the conflict as peacemakers. While the AICIC welcomed the Prince of Wales, it also urged the government to adopt a policy of conciliation by ceasing to put into force several measures 'as have a repressive effect', to release those

[127] E.D. Lucas, 'The Report of the Principal, 1920–21', *The Forman Christian College Monthly* (March-April 1921), p. 10; *Triennial Report of Foreign Missions of the United Presbyterian Church of North America, 1919–1921*, pp. 128, 155; *Eighty-third Annual Report of the Church of Scotland Women's Association for Foreign Missions 26th May 1921*, pp. 11–2.

[128] *CMS Proceedings 1920–1*, p. 60; *Foreign Mission Handbook 1923*, United Presbyterian Board of Foreign Missions, pp. 70–71.

[129] *Reports and Minutes of the Women's Foreign Missionary Society of the Indus River Conference, Ajmer Nov. 1–6, 1922*, pp. 38–9. When the Prince visited Taxila, the mission hospital had a welcome banner, staff, and workmen out on the road to cheer him on. Martha Payne Alter, *Letters from India to America 1916–1951*, p. 163.

imprisoned under those Acts, to convene a Round Table Conference, and to grant a much larger measure of self-government than the 1919 Constitution had provided. While urging Christians to give full support to the swadeshi movement, it urged its leaders to suspend non-cooperation.[130] Like the National Liberal Party, the Conference was sympathetic to many of the objectives of non-cooperation but was too ideologically moderate to endorse non-cooperation as a method.

The events of the Rowlatt satyagraha and non-cooperation movement had placed the Christian community in a difficult political dilemma. Their government-aided urban educational institutions placed them in the midst of the turmoil and forced them to take a stand. Rudra and Lucas came down on the side of both freedom of conscience and the student's primary responsibility to study.[131] The educated urban Christian elite was definitely being drawn towards the nationalist cause, albeit in its moderate form and with some reservations, because some Christian institutions came under attack. Educational missionaries in the major cities were becoming more sympathetic to Indian nationalism and more conflicted about British rule. At the same time, rural Dalit Christians, insofar as they were politically active at all, tended to be supportive of their foreign patrons under whose aegis they had gained whatever liberation they had. Rural missionaries tended to sympathize with their loyalist views, just as the urban missionaries sympathized with the nationalism of those with whom they worked most closely. Christian nationalism at this time was far more pro-Indian than anti-British. In fact, Christian nationalists saw themselves as mediators between their British co-religionists and their Indian fellow countrymen.

With the end of non-cooperation in 1922, politics in the north-west moved largely within the framework of the gradual, incremental devolution of power set forth in the Montague declaration of 1917. In the Punjab, the influential minister of education and local self-

---

[130] *AICIC Conference Report 1921.*

[131] S.K. Rudra, 'Report of S. Stephen's College for 1920', *The Forty-third Report of the Cambridge Committee . . . for the Year 1920*, p. 12; E.D. Lucas, 'The Report of the Principal 1920-21,' *The Forman Christian College Monthly* (March–April 1921), p. 10.

government, Fazl-i-Husain, formed the 'Rural Block' which in 1923 became the Unionist Party, a party of big landlords committed to rural development, communal harmony, and the attainment of dominion status by constitutional methods,[132] that ruled the province until 1946. Christian political initiatives in the north-west during the latter half of the 1920s seemed to be confined to attempts at lowering communal tensions and addressing women's issues, mainly through their educational institutions. In addition, Gandhi invited Dr S.K. Datta to attend the Delhi Unity Conference in 1924 and publicly praised his work there to bring about communal harmony.[133] Punjabi Christians, led by B.L. Rallia Ram, took a public stand against communal electorates for themselves and for others, but insisted that if they were granted to some minority communities they should be granted to all.[134] From 1929 onwards, Rajkumari Amrit Kaur became involved in the All-India Women's Conference, which served as an effective elite, non-communal lobby on a range of women's issues,[135] and by 1930 several missionary women were members of its Punjab branch.[136]

In December 1929, frustrated by British unwillingness to make dominion status the basis of negotiations for a new constitution of

[132] Raghuvendra Tanwar, *Politics of Sharing Power*, pp. 50–1.

[133] 'Late Dr. S. K. Datta', *The Guardian* (25 June 1942), p. 298; 'Gandhiji's Tribute to Dr. S. K. Datta', ibid., (2 July 1942), p. 306.

[134] B.L. Rallia Ram came out strongly against communal electorates in 1923 and did not change his position. *AICIC Conference Report 1923*, p. 53. Opposition to separate electorates was reaffirmed at the Lahore meeting of the AICIC in 1929 at which Punjabis were in a majority. Ibid. 1929, p. 25. The Punjab Christian Conference came out strongly against the Communal Award in 1932, and especially against the communal divisions imposed upon Indian women. It also refused to enter into any communal pacts or agreements, preferring to 'play the role of a neutral community' in the communal politics of the 1930s and thereafter. 'Punjab Christians and the Communal Award', *The Guardian* (22 September 1932), pp. 394–5; 'Brief Notes', ibid. (30 June 1932), p. 255; R.M. Chetsingh, 'The Communal Problem in the Punjab', ibid. (18 August 1932), pp. 333–4.

[135] Aparna Basu and Bharati Ray, *Women's Struggle*, p. 178. The Conference was begun in Pune in 1927.

[136] Nettie D. Clark, Station Letter from Lahore and Shahdara, Punjab Mission, Fall–1930 (The Board of Foreign Missions, Presbyterian Church in the USA).

India, the Congress decided to demand total independence and launch a campaign of civil disobedience. Gandhi inaugurated the campaign in March 1930. It lasted until May 1934 with a truce from March 1931 to January 1932, during which Gandhi attended the Second Round Table Conference in London on behalf of the Congress. Civil disobedience did not evoke the same level of response in the north-west as had the Rowlatt satyagraha and non-cooperation movement. Muslim participation dropped significantly and even urban Hindu participation declined after the end of the truce in January 1932. As in earlier campaigns, the work of urban educational institutions in the Punjab and Delhi was disrupted, but this seems to have been more an inconvenience than a serious threat. Rural evangelism was also affected, but in the villages the 1931 Census appeared to be a more significant political event than the civil disobedience campaign, as the census would determine the proportional representation of the various communities under the forthcoming constitution. In several districts, rural Christians, like other Dalit menials, faced intense local pressure to return themselves as adherents of the same religion as their landlords.[137]

Missionary opinion concerning civil disobedience is difficult to assess, as each missionary spoke as an individual rather than as a leader or spokesperson of some larger body. While some like E.D. Lucas and Miriam Benade in Lahore were quite pro-nationalist,[138] most were more cautious. One can note a far greater degree of detachment from British rule in their writings during civil

[137] A.J. Mortimore, *Forward: The Story of the Year 1930–31* (London: CEZMS, n.d.), p. 28; Baptist Missionary Society, *Indian Report: Bengal, Orissa, Northern India and Ceylon for 1930* (Calcutta, 1931), p. 94; 'News from Overseas', *CMO* (November 1930), p. 235; *Punjab Mission Annual Report 1930–31*, pp. 10, 27–8. The same thing happened again at the time of the 1941 Census. *North-West India Annual Conference Journal 1942*, pp. 29, 30; *Indus River Conference 1941*, p. 33.

[138] Frank Thakur Das later recalled that Lucas gave shelter to revolutionary students during civil disobedience, while Benade spoke most enthusiastically about the transforming influence that participation in the nationalist movement was having upon Indian women. See Frank Thakur Das's review of *The Christian Community and Change in Nineteenth Century North India* in *Religion and Society* XXIII (December 1976), p. 81 and Miriam M. Benade, Letter to Mr. Strickhouse, 8 May 1930.

disobedience than during non-cooperation or the Rowlatt satyagraha. What seems to have concerned them most about Indian nationalism at this stage was its inability to resolve the communal problem and its methods of mass civil disobedience rather than its ultimate goals.[139] At its annual meeting in 1931, the Punjab Mission of the Presbyterian Church in the USA passed a resolution opposing the principle that its Indian employees were bound by the same regulations with regard to political activities as were its missionaries, on the grounds that 'Indians associated with the Mission on a paid basis are nevertheless citizens of India, and are, in consequence, entitled to exercise all the rights and privileges of Indian citizenship',[140] and won their point.[141] This was especially important to them as some were planning to invite Dr S.K. Datta, an active nationalist who was a personal friend of Gandhi and Nehru, to become the next principal of Forman Christian College.

For educated urban Christians in the north-west, however, civil disobedience marked an important turning point. At Lahore, in 1929, the Punjabi-dominated meeting of the AICIC had supported the Nehru Report and dominion status as the basis for the Round Table Conference negotiations[142] and the Delhi correspondent of *The Guardian*, a Christian weekly published in Madras, who had been present commented, 'The traditionally loyal and conservative Indian

---

[139] A fuller discussion of this is provided in John C.B. Webster, 'American Presbyterian Missionaries and Nationalist Politics in the Punjab, 1919–1935', pp. 63–9. For a sampling of views from other missions, see W.M. Ryburn, 'The Present Situation in India and the Duty of Christians', UCR (August 1930), pp. 235–9; R.H. Ewing, 'Things New and Old', UCR (July 1931), p. 228; 'Editorial', DMN (January 1931), pp. 2–3; 'Editorial', DMN (April 1931), pp. 22–3.

[140] *Minutes of the Annual Meeting of the Punjab Mission of the Presbyterian Church in the USA, 1931*, pp. 45–6.

[141] They later learned that the regulations applied to Indians in mission employ only when engaged in activities under mission control and not otherwise. H.C. Velte, Letter to Mr Paton, 7 January 1932 and Mr. Paton, Letter to Dr Velte, 27 January 1932.

[142] Unlike the Congress whose leaders had received clarification of the viceroy's assurances, the AICIC assumed that dominion status would be the basis of the negotiations, *AICIC Conference Report 1929*, pp. 23–5.

Christian community is becoming restive and the younger generation is anxious to keep up fully with the most radical element in the nationalist movement.'[143] In the summer of 1930, several Presbyterian missionaries in the Punjab wrote that nationalism was as rampant among educated Christians as among other educated Indians.[144] S.K. Datta, who had represented the Christian community at the Second Round Table Conference, told the AICIC that the British were simply taking Christian loyalty for granted. Whereas two Christians had been invited to represent the community at both the First and Second Round Table Conferences, none had been invited to the Third. He urged the delegates to stop depending upon the government for small favours, but to rely instead upon their own resources and to get organized for effective political action.[145]

Datta's advice was very sound. The government was far more interested in satisfying those whom it deemed powerful and influential in north-west Indian society than in showing any partiality towards Christians. Christians in the north-west were no better positioned for the communal politics of separate electorates than they were for Gandhian politics. They had no Christian party equivalent to the Muslim League, the Hindu Mahasabha or the Central Sikh League to champion Christian interests. Up to 1935 they had only nominated members in the Punjab and Delhi governments to do that. The AICIC, while in many ways modelled on the Congress, did not see itself as a political party. It was opposed to communalism and communal electorates and, therefore, did not believe that it could act as a communal political party but only as a

---

[143] 'Our Delhi Letter', *The Guardian* (16 January 1930), p. 29.

[144] A.E. Harper, Letter to Robert E. Speer, 21 June 1930; Mary C. Helm, Letter to Friends, 21 July 1930; Jane S. Ewing, Letter to Dr. Speer, 29 June 1930. W.W. Duff, a rural missionary, wrote to friends in 1930 that 'The Indian Church is divided in its sympathies. The leaders are probably mostly Nationalist in sympathy, while the village pastors and teachers, and the mass of the village population is strongly in favor of the British government and fearful of what might happen under Hindu rule.' W.W. Duff, Letter to Friends in Birmingham, 11 September 1930.

[145] *AICIC Conference Report 1933*, pp. 7–22.

fellowship of concerned Christian citizens.[146] As a result, Christians in the north-west were, in the 1930s, politically disorganized and ineffective with little clear sense of common direction. In 1933, the Punjab Christian League was formed as an alternative to the Punjab Indian Christian Association. The League, claiming to represent the interests of the Christian masses, opposed the anti-communal stand of the more elitist Association.[147] Other Christian political associations were to follow but none could claim to speak for the community as a whole.

Neither the nominated Christians in the government, nor the Christian political associations, nor the missionaries were successful in their attempts during the 1930s to overcome three forms of discrimination that kept current power relations, especially within rural society, intact. The British had closed off opportunities for occupational mobility to rural Christians by denying them not only the right to own land on the grounds that they were not an 'agricultural caste' and did not have sufficient numbers to qualify as an 'agricultural community', but also recruitment into the Indian army because they were not a 'martial race'.[148] In addition, Christians were unable to prevent Fazl-i-Husain's attempt to open up the educational services to Muslim women by placing a two-year moratorium on the recruitment of the numerically predominant Christian women as teachers in government schools.[149] In response

---

[146] 'Our Delhi Letter', *The Guardian* (16 January 1930), p. 29.

[147] Venturo Eternon, 'Punjab Letter', *The Guardian* (9 February 1933), pp. 66–7; 'Punjab Letter', ibid. (18 January 1934), p. 38; 'Punjab Letter', ibid. (16 August 1934), p. 524; Interview with Mr Eric Banerji, 9 September 1980.

[148] 'The Batala Mission and a Disconcerting Discovery', *LDM* (May 1933), p. 5; 'Editorial', ibid. (July 1933), pp. 5–6; 'Editorial', ibid. (September 1933), p. 4; 'Punjab Letter', *The Guardian* (17 May 1934), p. 314; *Punjab Christian Council Proceedings 1935*, pp. 3, 31–2. The 71st Punjabis were disbanded soon after the end of World War I. Punjabi Christians were recruited into the Territorial Battalions, but not the regular army until November 1941, two years after the British had entered World War II. See 'A Governor's Appreciation of Punjabi Christians,' *The Indian Standard* (August 1923), p. 255; 'The Bishop's Tours', *LDM* (December 1941), pp. 567–8; 'Indian Christian Battalion', *The Indian Witness* (25 December 1941), pp. 827–8.

[149] 'Women's Work', *Delhi* (October 1934), p. 69.

to Christian petitions on these matters the government was unwilling to change either their categories or their policies to help out the Christians. Another affront to the community came in 1934 when Kunwar Dalip Singh, the Senior Justice of the Punjab High Court, was passed over as Chief Justice in favour of a European from outside the Punjab.[150]

Under the provisions of the 1935 constitution, Christians in the Punjab were granted two seats in the Punjab Legislative Assembly. In the elections that followed in 1937, S.P. Singha, the Registrar of Punjab University and the Indian Christian Election Board candidate, won the East Central Punjab (Indian Christian) seat and Chaudhri Jalal Din Amber, a retired tehsildar and independent candidate, won the West Central Punjab (Indian Christian) seat.[151] Both then joined the Unionist Party which had won the election. It seems, however, to have made little difference. The Punjab Correspondent of *The Guardian* reported that

Indian Christians have been rigidly excluded from all Committees appointed by the Government in spite of both the Christian members having joined the Party in power as its full-fledged members. The Premier invited leaders of all communities to a Conference to consider communal situation in the Punjab, but no Indian Christian was asked.[152]

Christians also entered into another, very different political alliance during this period. Dalits in the north-west were slower in developing their own independent political organizations than in other parts of India. Mangoo Ram had launched the Ad Dharm movement in 1925 and won a major victory in getting Ad Dharm listed as a separate religion in the 1931 Census. Despite intense pressure from Arya Samajis and Sikhs, 418,789 Dalits recorded themselves as Ad Dharmis

[150] Kunwar Dalip Singh, was the son of Rajah Harnam Singh. 'Notes', *The Guardian* (22 February 1934), p. 14; 'Punjab Letter', ibid., p. 125.

[151] *The Tribune* (10 February 1937), p. 1. A noteworthy feature of this election was that 95 per cent of the Christian women registered to vote in Lahore actually voted, a far higher percentage than the men achieved. *The Tribune* (23 January 1937), p. 2.

[152] 'Punjab Letter', *The Guardian* (5 August 1937), p. 492.

at that time. Their second victory came during the 1937 elections when they won seven of the eight seats in the Punjab Legislative Assembly reserved for the Scheduled Castes.[153] In June 1936, a major Dalit conference had taken place in Jullundur in the wake of Dr Ambedkar's decision to leave Hinduism.[154] Among the speakers was Arthur Ghose, a missionary in Jullundur who helped organize another conference, attended by about 500 Dalits, in the American Presbyterian Mission compound in Jullundur in July 1937. Among the resolutions submitted by Mangoo Ram as president of the Punjab Ad Dharm Federation, and accepted unanimously by the conference members, was an appeal to the government to consider and appreciate the rights and claims of the *achhuts* and Christians as well as a decision that 'for the welfare of both the communities, i.e., *Achhuts* and Christians, in respect of political views, they will in and out of the Legislative Assembly work together'.[155] Like the decision of Singha and Amber to join the Unionist Party, this alliance proved to be more of symbolic than practical value. It could not be binding upon the Christian legislators, as they were not a party to it;[156] the alliance was also hindered both by considerable external opposition and by a lack of funds for continued joint conferences.[157]

Christians do not appear to have been politically active from the 1937 elections until the end of World War II. The AICIC leadership, in which Punjabi Christians were well represented, was critical of both the Cripps Mission proposals for post-war India and Gandhi's Quit India Movement in 1942.[158] In the 1946 elections, when demands

[153] Mark Juergensmeyer, *Religion as Social Vision*, p. 145.

[154] 'At the Jullundur District Adi-Dravida Conference', *The Indian Witness* (2 July 1936), pp. 421–4.

[155] 'News of Church and Kingdom', UCR (October 1937), pp. 301–2.

[156] Cooperation at that level cannot be ruled out because Mangoo Ram and the Ad Dharmis did work in close cooperation with the Unionist Party, of which the two Christian legislators were members. Mark Juergensmeyer, *Religion as Social Vision*, pp. 142–55.

[157] 'News of Church and Kingdom', UCR (October 1937), pp. 301–2 and (February 1938), pp. 56–7.

[158] 'Indian Christians and Cripps Proposals', *The Guardian* (7 May 1942), p. 215; 'Christian Leaders Meet Gandhiji', ibid. (6 August 1942), p. 370.

for a separate state of Pakistan were being articulated and the Unionists were soundly defeated, S.P. Singha managed to retain his seat in the Punjab Legislative Assembly, but then resigned from the Unionist Party because it had 'lost all significance as a non-communal organisation and now appears to exist only in the interests of a few Muslims'.[159] He believed only a government comprised of the two parties with popular support behind them (the Congress and Muslim League) could save the province. When a Congress–Unionist–Akali coalition government was formed instead, he formed a 'Christian bloc' with the other Christian, the Anglo-Indian, and the European members.[160] On 1 March 1946, the governor asked Singha to serve as temporary Speaker of the Legislative Assembly. When the Assembly met on 21 March 1946, Khizar Hyat Khan, the leader of the coalition government, proposed that Singha be the elected Speaker on the grounds that 'The Speakership could go only to a person who is above party politics and command confidence of the House'. Singha defeated the Muslim League candidate by ninety-one votes to seventy-nine, but offered to step down if the Assembly agreed on a Muslim instead.[161] Since they could not do this, Singha became the last elected Speaker of the Punjab Legislative Assembly and presided over the vote to partition the Punjab.

As events in late 1946 and 1947 led inexorably towards both independence and partition, Christians were excluded from the negotiations and their interests were ignored. They were not even invited to the Punjab Minorities convention held on 1 May 1947 in Delhi.[162] Earlier S.P. Singha had expressed the view that

Our position has always been to support any Government in office in the maintenance of law and order but our votes are not available to the League Party for the purpose of the formation of their ministry in the Punjab.... If the

---

[159] *The Tribune* (7 March 1946), p. 12.

[160] Ibid.

[161] Ibid. (2 March 1946), p. 3 and (22 March 1946), pp. 1, 8.

[162] V.P. Menon, *The Transfer of Power in India*, p. 301; 'The Punjab Joint Christian Board's Demand for Separate Electorate', *The Indian Witness* (22 May 1947), p. 173; 'An Explanation of the Basic Policy of the All India Christian League', ibid. (12 June 1947), p. 181.

Muslim League wants the whole Punjab in Pakistan I can never be with the League for I stand for united India. But if the League would agree to the partition of the Punjab—partition to be decided upon either by the communities themselves or failing that by any third party—then I think agreeing to Pakistan will be the shortest cut to Indian unity and peace.[163]

On 3 June 1947, the procedure for voting on the partition of the Punjab was announced. On 23 June, the Punjab Legislative Assembly would be divided into two parts, members from the Muslim-majority districts and those from the other districts voting separately. Both Christian seats were counted as belonging to the Muslim-majority districts as that was where most Christians lived. Singha presided first over the brief joint session of the Assembly on 23 June and then over the West Punjab meeting. He and the other Christian MLA voted for a united Punjab under a new constituent assembly.[164] As his widow later pointed out, as soon as the voting procedure was announced, partition was a foregone conclusion and Singha realized that Christians would need the goodwill of their new rulers.[165] Ten days before the vote, Eric Banerji, the general secretary of the Punjab Indian Christian Association, had indicated that it was unclear where Christians would go following partition. 'To my mind neither any Christian leader nor the Christians collectively can give any declaration in a representative capacity in favour of Pakistan or Hindustan. It would be purely a personal matter....'[166]

Christians were only minor players in the politics of this period and were in no position to influence the outcome. This was due in large measure not just to the community's small size but also to its peculiar social composition. The missionaries were a cautious lot, either because government policy forced them to be or because they chose to be for a combination of ideological and pragmatic reasons. There is evidence that they not only viewed the events of the period both through their own lenses and of those with whom they worked

---

[163] 'Punjab Christians and Pakistan', *The Indian Witness* (24 April 1947), p. 123.

[164] *The Tribune* (24 June 1947), pp. 1, 5.

[165] Interview with Mrs S.P. Singha, 9 September 1980.

[166] *The Tribune* (14 June 1947), p. 3.

most closely, but also that they shared in the same sense of uncertainty and helplessness over their inability to shape the course of events which prevailed within the community at large. So, instead of politics they concentrated upon building up the Church to prepare it for whatever future lay ahead.

Among Indian Christians there was the small urban-educated elite and the rural Dalit menials with hardly anyone in between. The Dalits had no vote and were largely outside the political process of the period; those who did get involved seemed to identify more with broader Dalit than with distinctively Christian interests. The elites shared the political outlook of the elites of other communities, joining or forming similar organizations. What perhaps distinguished the Christian from the other elites were a fairly consistent, politically moderate, anti-communal stand and a concentration upon nation-building activities, including Hindu–Muslim unity, rather than upon mass politics.[167] As the reality of independence became inevitable, Christians expressed some anxiety about the possible loss of their religious liberty under the new regimes.[168] Because they were such a small minority, they had nothing to gain and much to lose if the communal politics and communal ideologies of this period were to continue on and shape their post-independence world. Not only would their interests be ignored, as the British had ignored them, but their minority rights might be taken from them as well. First, however, they had to go through the horrors and dislocations of partition. There, as it turned out, their neutrality in the communal conflicts of the immediate past proved to be a national asset, because Christians had established their bona fides well enough to be trusted, as few others could be trusted, as impartial and effective public workers for the relief of suffering and the promotion of the common good.

[167] This was most obvious in Christian educational institutions.

[168] See, for example, Barakat Ullah, 'A Sermon', *LDM* (February 1944), p. 57; Reba Hunsberger in *WMM* (July–August 1947), p. 764.

Nationalism and 'Missionary Raj'

The Montagu declaration of 1917 and the ensuing nationalist agitations accelerated a long-standing but fitful nationalist movement within the churches themselves. The missionaries who dominated ecclesiastical decision-making bodies had long been committed to developing fully independent (that is, self-governing, self-supporting, and self-propagating) churches in the north-west, but were not convinced that self-government should precede self-support. Moreover, as good paternalists (and maternalists!), they were reluctant to share or transfer significant power and responsibility. However, the wider nationalist fervour of this period made both missionaries and Indian Christians aware of the necessity and urgency of making fundamental changes within their churches which would be in keeping with, if not ahead of, those taking place in the wider political arena. Although the goals, challenges, and debates within the various denominational missions and churches were often very similar, the pace of change was not the same for all. Each denomination paid attention to what was happening in the others, but the struggle for structural change was divided into separate denominational compartments. A brief survey of the major ecclesiastical structures existing in 1919 indicates that the political struggle within the churches would involve either increasing the power of Indians and decreasing that of foreign missionaries within a single ecclesiastical body or transferring power and responsibility from a missionary to an Indian ecclesiastical body.

The Roman Catholic Church was organized around the diocese and religious orders. Work among the Indian population within the Diocese of Lahore was assigned to the Belgian province of the Capuchin Order in 1887. Throughout this period all the Catholic bishops and priests of the diocese were Europeans. There were two congregations of Indian nuns in the diocese but no local Christian man rose above the level of a catechist until after independence. There was thus no nationalist struggle within the Catholic Church in this part of India; what structural changes took place within the region involved the rearrangement of ecclesiastical boundaries and the development of some lay organizations,[169] not the Indianization of the Church hierarchy. The Salvation Army also had a top–down hierarchical structure with Europeans at the top of the chain of command, and no nationalist movement from below.

The Anglican Church structure was similar to that of the Catholic Church, but the dynamics within that structure were different. The Lahore diocese, created in 1877, had a functional division between the chaplains who, as part of the ecclesiastical establishment, served the resident European population, while the two Anglican mission societies worked among the Indian population. Both the CMS and the SPG were answerable to their home mission societies as well as to the bishop of the diocese. The Indian congregations they had established were part of but had little voice in the diocese. By 1919, the CMS and the SPG were working through separate Mission Councils, both of which had Indian as well as missionary members. The difference between the two was that the CMS congregations elected delegates to their district councils which in turn elected delegates to the Central Mission Council, whereas the SPG Mission Council did not have elected delegates from the congregations, even after its constitution was revised in 1918. Nonetheless, missionaries dominated both councils.[170] The (American) Methodist Episcopal Church was quite similar but had no ecclesiastical establishment to deal with. Its North-West India (1893), Indus River (1926), and later Delhi (1939) Annual Conferences had elected members from the congregations, but missionaries held all the top positions, including that of bishop. For Anglicans and Methodists alike, the struggle would involve increasing the Indian and reducing the missionary share of power within the diocese / annual conference.

---

[169] In 1911, the Catholic Association was formed to promote Catholic interests in the diocese and the Indian Catholic Union was later established in Sialkot (1930), Amritsar (1936), and Lahore (1937). 'Collandate Dominum Mecum', *Collecteana Lahorensia* (October–December 1938), p. 157; Fr. Nathanael, 'Catholic Social Action in Lahore Diocese', *Collecteana Punjabensia* (September–October 1945), p. 50.

[170] John C.B. Webster, 'British Missions in India', p. 44; F.J. Western, 'The Early Years of the Cambridge Mission to Delhi', pp. 110–11.

The Presbyterian structure was somewhat different. The missionaries organized themselves into missions, while the congregations that they had created were organized into presbyteries. All three Presbyterian missions had chosen to grant power to Indians by transferring the mission's powers and responsibilities piecemeal out of the mission and into the presbyteries where Indians had a majority of the votes. In 1904, the presbyteries associated with the Presbyterian Church in the USA and the Church of Scotland (but not the United Presbyterian Church of North America) had joined with others to form the Presbyterian Church in India.[171] However, even by 1919 very little real power had been transferred to that body from the related missions and missionaries remained in control.[172] In 1924, the Presbyterian Church in India joined with Congregationalists in western India to form the United Church of Northern India. The only real change this brought about in the north-west, where there were no Congregationalists, was that the presbyteries were renamed Church Councils.[173] The Baptist polity was similar to the Presbyterian and involved a similar transfer of power from the foreign mission to the Indian churches.

By the end of World War I both missionaries and Indian Christian leaders were clearly aware that the time had come for some significant steps towards granting the churches in the north-west more control over their own destinies. Three statements made in 1918 pointed in this direction. The Rev. Henry Golaknath argued that at this time, when India and the world were changing, the Indian Church must develop from within, starting at the local level. For this to happen, two things were essential: foreign models of the Church should not be imposed upon it and Indian Christians must identify fully with it, rather than with the missions, and make it the centre of all Christian

[171] The New Zealand Presbyterians were not in the Punjab when the Presbyterian Church in India was formed, but joined up with it when they came.

[172] See John C.B. Webster, *The Christian Community and Change*, pp. 208–23 and 'American Presbyterian Missionaries and Nationalist Politics in the Punjab, 1919–1935', pp. 59–60.

[173] Kenneth Lawrence Parker, 'The Development of the United Church of Northern India'.

activity.[174] H.D. Griswold was more cryptic. 'It is perfectly obvious that just as there is to be "the progressive realization of responsible government" in the State, so there must be in the Church'.[175] The Rev. A.B. Chandu Lall argued for a 'Swadeshi Church', and gave priority to self-support over self-government in the realization of this goal.[176] However, by October 1919, when his article was published, he had reversed those priorities.[177] As part of a 1921 mission report, the Rev. Andrew Thakur Das of Lahore wrote that a Church which was united, indigenous, and self-sustained was what was needed. 'The grand task before the Church in this land is the re-expression of Christianity in our own terms.'[178] He saw foreign support and control as 'narcotics' checking 'the spontaneous development of Indian Christianity'.[179]

All four were clergymen writing in Church publications. All four considered a 'Swadeshi Church' to be necessary for the more effective evangelization of India in the new, post-war situation. In December 1921, the Punjabi-dominated meeting of the All India Conference of Indian Christians in Lahore was more cautious in their proposals but less cautious in the rationale they offered. They passed resolutions, first indicating that the Protestant missions 'should be completely merged in the Indian Church and that in future all Foreign Missionaries should be related to it', and then urging the missions in the meantime to 'appoint Indians of ability and character on an increasing scale'.[180] Among their supporting arguments were that 'Indian Christians are not going to put up with colour and racial distinctions', that foreign missionaries could not solve the community's problems 'because of lack of sympathy', that the

[174] H. Golaknath, 'The Foreign Missions and Churches in India in Relation One to the Other', *IS* (December 1918), pp. 364–5.

[175] H.D. Griswold, 'Missions and the Great War', *IS* (March 1919), p. 77.

[176] A.B. Chandu Lall, 'Self-Support and Self Government in the Indian Church', *LDM* (October 1919), p. 15.

[177] Ibid., p. 18.

[178] A. Thakur Das, 'The New Day in the Indian Church', *Punjab Mission Annual Report 1921*, p. 9.

[179] Ibid., p. 10.

[180] *AICIC Conference Report 1921*, p. 41.

missions were too divided by denominational differences to bring about a united Indian Church, and that 'In these days Indians look up to Indians and do not pay much attention to foreigners.'[181]

The first significant attempt made during this period to move towards greater responsible government within the churches was the 'Saharanpur Plan' negotiated by the missions of the Presbyterian Church in the USA and their counterparts in the Presbyterian Church in India. When the Government of India interned German missionaries early in World War I, H.C. Velte had asked, 'Would our work stand, if we had to leave?'.[182] Velte was sceptical and by 1918 was convinced that the way forward towards a self-sustaining Church lay in the closest cooperation between the missionaries and the Indian Church.[183] Early in 1920, P. Carter Speers of Forman Christian College put it this way.

There has been a pile of talk about the lack of cooperation between Church and Mission in India, and there certainly has been mighty little cooperation really—and the reason is just this that we have been working from outside and above and not from within. We are the ones who have not been cooperating—not the Indian Church.[184]

It was, as another missionary pointed out later that year, the 'most pressing' issue of the day among the educated Christian elite.[185]

However, it was not Velte's prodding or Speers's confession, but an open letter written by four Indian Presbyterians in Allahabad in June 1920 that set the process in motion. They argued that the strict separation of mission and Church, while well intentioned, had the unfortunate consequences of producing pervasive misunderstanding between missionaries and Indian Christians, of increasing resentment among Indian Christians and an unwillingness among capable young men to enter into full-time Christian work, and of presenting to the Indian public a glaring failure of 'practical Christianity' at a time

[181] Ibid., p. 12.
[182] H.C. Velte, Letter to Dr Speer, 1 October 1914.
[183] H.C. Velte, Letter to Dr Speer, 20 July 1918.
[184] P. Carter Speers, Letter to Dr Speer, 6 February 1920.
[185] H.A. Whitlock, Letter to Robt. E. Speer, 29 December 1920.

when the growing gulf between East and West needed to be bridged.[186] These views were reinforced by a large deputation of Punjabi Christians [187] and in essence, as already noted, by the AICIC in December 1921.

From 30 March to 2 April 1921 eleven missionaries representing the three missions in India of the Presbyterian Church in the USA met with fourteen official representatives of their related presbyteries within the Presbyterian Church in India at Saharanpur, to develop a new, more equitable way of working together. This Saharanpur Plan combined elements of both sharing and transferring power. The missions and the presbyteries were to retain their separate identities. A set of joint committees to cover evangelism, education, medical work, and finance were created with both church and mission representatives to plan and oversee these aspects of their combined efforts. An Intermediate Board consisting of four Indians and four missionaries was placed above them to coordinate the work of the joint committees. The plan was finally approved by all parties in June 1923.

The Saharanpur Plan did not get off to a good start. It did represent an advance in that what were now joint committees had previously been only advisory committees of the mission. Moreover, the Indian members now represented their presbyteries instead of being the mission's selected appointees. What hurt the initial working of the Plan was the Board of Foreign Missions' unilateral decision to cut its appropriations to the Punjab Mission in such a way as to reduce the salaries of the already underpaid Indian mission workers, but not of the missionaries.[188] Subsequent missionary correspondence through the remainder of the decade indicates that for them the heart of the Saharanpur Plan lay in sharing the burden of making decisions on how best to both allocate and withhold appropriation money, as the

---

[186] *The Indian Standard* (September 1920), pp. 259–64.

[187] Robert E. Speer and Russel Carter, *Report on India and Persia*, pp. 635–7.

[188] H.C. Velte, Letter to Dr Speer, 6 March 1924; H.C. Velte, Letter to Dr Speer, 26 June 1924.

Indian share of the total costs remained low.[189] Increased self-government had not as yet led to a significant increase in self-support during what was seen as a transitional phase from mission to Church control.[190]

Unlike these Presbyterians, the Anglicans did not change their ecclesiastical structures until just before independence. However, while Indian Christians accepted the Mission Council structure, they did not accept the existing power relations within it. Back in 1917, the Rev. J.C. Chatterjee had noted that some of the better-off Christians in Delhi were withdrawing from Church life, in part to show 'their resentment against and independence of Missions and foreign missionaries'.[191] Later, during non-cooperation the editor of the *Delhi Mission News* noted the presence of both moderates and extremists within the Church, the former wanting a shift in power, while the latter were non-cooperators.[192] The moderate Anglican Rev. Barakat Ullah in the Punjab argued,

The best thing is to allow us to develop the Indian Church according to our own ways of thinking. We should be neither ruled by the Missionaries nor be crushed by the Diocesan Council. We should be allowed to form a Diocesan Indian Church Board with the Bishop at its head which should begin working according to Indian methods. All those places like Amritsar, Lahore, Clarkabad etc. which have got endowments should be immediately given over to this Board.[193]

The CMS had already expressed a willingness to hand over some of their mission stations, but it is not clear that that included the

[189] H.A. Whitlock, Letter to R.E. Speer, 16 July 1925; Agnes S. Weir and John B. Weir, Letter to Friends, 18 November 1926; H.A. Whitlock, Letter to Dr Rourke and Friends, 27 December 1928.

[190] H.J. Strickler, Letter to Col. Hoisington and Members of the Men's Bible Class, 22 May 1929.

[191] 'Letter from the Rev. J.C. Chatterjee', *The Fortieth Report of the Cambridge Committee with which is incorporated The General Report of the Other Branches of the Mission for the Year 1917*, p. 11.

[192] 'Editorial Notes', DMN (October 1921), p. 266.

[193] 'Indian Opinion', LDM (October 1922), p. 24.

endowments as well.[194] Control over finances was to be the major sticking point between Indians and representatives of the CMS for some time to come.[195]

The year 1929 provided two powerful stimuli for the Church in north-west India to take further steps towards full independence. One was the collapse of the stock market and ensuing Depression, which led to major reductions in the funds allocated to the missions in India. The other was the independence resolution of the Lahore session of the Indian National Congress. The cut in mission funding did not come immediately, but it did hit hard. In the case of the Presbyterian Church in the USA, the allocations to their Punjab Mission had risen steadily from 1919 onwards and reached a peak in 1930. Thereafter, they dropped off by 22.3 per cent in 1931, by another 10.5 per cent in 1932, and 15.9 per cent more in 1933.[196] By 1935, faced with a deficit of over a half million dollars, the Board of Foreign Missions had cut missionary salaries by twenty per cent, its allocations for 'native work' by thirty per cent, and recalled some missionaries from overseas.[197] The Punjab Mission not only had the salaries of missionary and Indian personnel cut, but also had to close some of its institutions.[198] The impact of the Depression upon the United Presbyterians appears to have been more swift and drastic, involving

---

[194] 'Church and Mission', ibid. (September 1922), pp. 11–4. The United Presbyterians also tried to turn over segments of their work to the presbyteries during this period but that did not produce any more independence than the other missions had. Harris J. Stewart, 'The Problem Contained in the Relation of the Mission to the Indian Church', *WMM* (November 1922), pp. 227–32; Martha Payne Alter, *Letters from India to America 1916–1951*, pp. 159, 162.

[195] Gordon Hewitt, *The Problem of Success*, p. 82.

[196] These percentages are based on figures taken from the Annual Reports of the Board of Foreign Missions of the Presbyterian Church in the USA of the years 1930 (p. 229), 1931 (p. 243), 1932 (p. 239), 1933 (p. 203).

[197] *BFM PC in USA Annual Report 1935*, p. 143.

[198] For example, Caroline S. Clark, Letter to Friends, 6 April 1934. Since missionaries shared some of the pain involved, this cut was taken in a better spirit by mission employees than was the earlier one. H.E. Wylie, Letter to Arch Street Church, 28 June 1933. For some of the principles involved, see *Minutes of the Annual Meeting of the Punjab Mission of the Presbyterian Church in the USA, 1933*, pp. 69–70.

the closing of more schools and larger reductions of missionary personnel.[199] As indicated earlier, the missions and churches placed a major emphasis upon encouraging self-support, especially among the rural churches where the level of economic dependency was so high, in part to compensate for these losses in overseas support.

On the political front, in 1927 the British Parliament had passed the Indian Church Measure by which the Church of England in India became ecclesiastically independent as the Church of India, Burma, and Ceylon but in communion with the rest of the Anglican Church. This measure, which did not alter the balance of power within the various dioceses, went into effect in 1930.[200] In November 1931, Canon John Bannerji from Allahabad was consecrated assistant bishop of its Lahore Diocese, which covered all of north-west India and was considered too much for one bishop to oversee properly.[201] In 1930, the Methodist Church had elected Jashwant Rao Chitamber to be its first Indian bishop.[202] Even earlier, probably in 1929, Narayana Muthiah, a high-caste Hindu convert from the Madras Presidency, became for about ten years the Territorial Commander of the Salvation Army's Northern Territory, covering the Punjab and United Provinces.[203] These changes, while important, were mostly symbolic; real power still remained in foreign missionary hands in the Anglican and Methodist Churches as well as in the Salvation Army. The impact of the civil disobedience movement is more clearly seen within the United Church of Northern India.

---

[199] *Triennial Report of the Board of Foreign Missions of the United Presbyterian Church of North America, 1929, 1930, 1931*, p. 93; 'A Message to the Church from the Board of Foreign Missions', *UP* (12 February 1931), p. 12; *A Century for Christ in India and Pakistan 1855–1955*, pp. 37–9.

[200] M.E. Gibbs, 'The Anglican Church in India and Independence', p. 54.

[201] 'A Second Indian Bishop', *CMO* (March 1931), p. 50; 'The Bishop's Charge to the Clergy, 1933', *LDM* (December 1933), p. 21.

[202] James K. Mathews, *South of the Himalayas*, p. 108.

[203] *The Salvation Army Year Book 1930*, p. 80. Muthiah, on his retirement, wrote in appreciation of the Salvation Army's efforts to break down racial prejudice through the adoption of Indian dress, to overcome caste prejudice, and to emancipate women. 'From High-Caste Hindu to Salvation Army Leader', ibid. *1939*, pp. 13–15.

In April 1930, when Gandhi was launching the civil disobedience movement, five Indian members of the Ludhiana Evangelistic Committee, one of the joint committees set up under the Saharanpur Plan, resigned in protest against two unilateral decisions taken by the Punjab Mission's Executive Committee on which consultation with their committee was required.[204] This was as close to civil disobedience within the Church in the north-west as its Indian members got. It is not clear whether this was a cause or a manifestation of a more widespread suspicion and unrest among the Indian leadership, which was reported in the missionary correspondence of that year. H.C. Velte attributed the suspicion and sensitivity of 'the Indian brethren' to the separation of Mission and Church along racial lines.[205] Two others attributed it to the pervasive political unrest and 'spirit of independence' in the air. As one put it, 'The political unrest of the country has struck the Church, and we find the leaders demanding a larger share in the control of the funds which come from America and of the work done by the American missionaries.'[206] While both were sympathetic to the demand, both also raised the question of whether the leaders 'are ready to assume the responsibility, financial and otherwise, which ought to go with authority'.[207]

The tension continued and at its 1931 annual meeting the Punjab Mission voted to tell the Lahore and Ludhiana Church Councils that it did not wish to continue the Saharanpur Plan beyond 31 March 1933.[208] Fresh negotiations in 1932 produced the 'Dehra Dun Plan', which had the Mission and Church Councils functioning separately but cooperatively, while the work of the joint committees and Intermediate Board reverted to the Mission.[209] This plan was initially accepted by all, but quickly faced strong Indian opposition, largely

---

[204] H.C. Velte, Letter to Dr Speer, 19 May 1930.

[205] Ibid.

[206] Mary C. Helm, Letter to Friends, 21 July 1930.

[207] W. Wendell Duff, Letter to Rev. Herman L. Turner, 17 May 1930.

[208] *Minutes of the Annual Meeting of the Punjab Mission of the Presbyterian Church in the USA 1931*, p. 49.

[209] Ibid. *October 21st to 31st, 1932*, pp. 51–3.

on the grounds that it enabled the missionaries to function quite independently, free from the constraints of cooperation, while many Indian leaders remained on the mission payroll and thus in a position of dependency.[210] Moreover, since financial cuts were in the offing at that time, the Indian leaders wanted a share in determining how those would be applied.[211] In November 1933, the Lahore and Ludhiana Church Councils invited the Punjab Mission to a Round Table Conference, which then drafted a new plan in January 1934. This 'Joint Church Councils Plan' transferred significant power from the Mission to the Church Councils by vesting all the responsibilities of the former joint committees and Intermediate Board, as well as the assignment of missionary personnel and allocation of money from the USA, to a forty-member Central Board elected by the Ludhiana and Lahore Church Councils. No proportion of Indians and missionaries was fixed but there were to be at least thirteen women members. This Central Board was answerable not to the Mission but to the Church Councils and was to report annually to a joint meeting of the two Church Councils. The Mission was left with responsibility for all work not transferred, for the care of its own personnel, and for property owned by the Board of Foreign Missions.[212] This plan went into effect in 1935, the same year that the British gave India a new constitution with less autonomy.

The New Zealand Presbyterians, whose main centre was Jagadhri and who in 1924 took over from the American Presbyterians work begun by the Baptists in Kharar, had a much quieter time. They had joined the Presbyterian Church in India as well as its Ludhiana Presbytery in 1924 and watched the developments in Mission–Church relations described above with great interest. However, perhaps because they were relatively recent arrivals and had not yet had the

---

[210] See [H. Hem Raj,] 'Church and Mission in the Punjab (A Layman's Sentiments)', *UCR* (August 1935), pp. 216–8; Harry E. Wylie, Letter to Robert E. Speer, 8 June 1933.

[211] H.J. Strickler, Letter to R.E. Speer, 14 June 1933; H.E. Wylie, Letter to Friends, 28 June 1933.

[212] *Minutes of the Annual Meeting of the Punjab Mission of the Presbyterian Church in the USA 1934*, pp. 101–8.

time to develop the kind of Indian leadership which could challenge missionary dominance, or perhaps because their provision for Indians to be either voting or associate members of the mission served as a safety value,[213] they did not face the nationalist challenges their neighbouring mission did. The United Presbyterians also had a relatively quiet time of it. They had not joined the United Church of Northern India but had their own Synod with six constituent presbyteries. While they had achieved a higher level of self-support among their congregations than had the other missions,[214] their clergy were neither well educated enough nor well paid enough to be in a position to challenge the missionaries' authority. Early in 1930, it was reported that the Mission had offered to hand over responsibility for all the evangelistic work, as well as the administration of all funds set aside for it, to the Synod. However, after a year's deliberation, the Synod decided to turn down the offer.[215] It was repeated and turned down again in 1935.[216]

One other major ecclesiastical change just prior to independence was the creation of the Archdeaconry and then the Diocese of Delhi in 1944 and 1946 respectively within the Anglican Church. This included the 'diocesization' of the responsibilities and resources of the SPG and Cambridge Mission to Delhi. The archdeaconry, and then the diocese, had its own council to which 'all management and control at present exercised by Mission persons ... or Mission bodies ... and missionary societies in England' were transferred.[217] The Rev. Arabindo Nath Mukherjee, the current head of the Cambridge Mission to Delhi, became archdeacon and was consecrated assistant bishop of the Lahore Diocese in October 1944. When the Delhi

---

[213] *Manual and Constitution of the Punjab Mission of the Presbyterian Church of New Zealand*, p. 10.

[214] Of their 111 congregations, seventy-two were supporting their own pastors. *Foreign Missions of the United Presbyterian Church of North America, 1931*, p. 114.

[215] W.B. Anderson, 'Foreign Affairs', *UP* (29 May 1930) p. 31; J.G. Campbell, 'Leadership in the Punjab Church', ibid. (1 January, 1931), p. 9; Mrs. W.H. Merriam, 'India News Letter', ibid. (11 June 1931), p. 25.

[216] *A Century for Christ in India and Pakistan 1855–1955*, p. 40.

[217] 'The Delhi Archdeaconry Scheme', *Delhi* (October 1943), p. 37. See also, 'Devolution from the Mission to the Church in Delhi', ibid. (July 1943), pp. 28–31.

Diocese was created two years later, he was enthroned as its first bishop on 21 April 1947.[218] The other change was the integration of the Baptist mission and churches in and around Delhi as well as the creation of the Baptist Union of North India at the time of independence.[219] This was the culmination of a process begun with the creation of the Delhi–Agra Church Council in 1917 and included first giving participation in mission station committees to some pastors in 1923 and then the formation of a joint advisory committee of representatives from both the Council and the Baptist Mission in 1936.[220]

Thus on the eve of independence and partition, the churches of north-west India had become self-governing. The Roman Catholic Church and the Salvation Army had only to replace foreign with Indian personnel at the top of their respective hierarchies. The Anglicans, whose chaplains were leaving, had vested full authority in Indian-controlled dioceses and had an Indian bishop in the new nation's capital. Both the Indus River and Delhi Annual Conferences of the Methodist Church had significant Indian majorities, while the Baptist and all the Presbyterian missions except the United Presbyterians had transferred power to Indian Church bodies. Although foreign missionaries continued for a time to have considerable personal influence as members of these churches, and problems of financial dependency continued, constitutional authority for virtually all decisions affecting the Church's future now lay in Indian hands, rather than in those of outside bodies. The Church's influence would increase, while that of the missions would decrease and finally vanish. This was thus an extremely important and timely transition.

As important as the transition itself was the process by which it had been achieved. Power and responsibility had been transferred

[218] F.J. Western, 'The Early Years of the Cambridge Mission to Delhi', p. 119.

[219] There is a difference of opinion about dates. Alter and Jai Singh put the formation of the Union in 1947 and Stanley puts it in January 1948. James P. Alter and Herbert Jai Singh, *The Church in Delhi*, p. 51; Brian Stanley, *The History of the Baptist Missionary Society 1792–1992*, p. 293.

[220] James P. Alter and Herbert Jai Singh, *The Church in Delhi*, pp. 50–1.

through a series of negotiations, which varied in frequency and timing from denomination to denomination, between foreign missionaries on the one side and clergy as well as lay members of the educated urban elite on the other. Unlike in the broader nationalist movement, these negotiations went on without recourse to mass agitation for change within the Christian community. Not only were both the missionaries and Indian Christian leaders involved averse to mass agitation, but it also proved to be quite unnecessary anyway. The result was basically an elite to elite transfer in which the ninety per cent rural Dalit majority of Christians was largely both uninvolved and bypassed throughout the negotiation process. This assured the small elite minority of at least initial dominance in the new Indian Church structures as the missionary presence and influence receded.

Conclusions

From 1858 through World War I both the present fact of British rule and a confidence in its continuation provided an overarching framework for the Christian community's ongoing life, mission, and encounters with others outside its fold. The Declaration of 1917 changed that. The British did not leave for another thirty years, but the permanence of the Raj could no longer be taken for granted. The Christian community and churches faced the prospect of, and had to prepare themselves for, an uncertain and potentially precarious future under a regime, or regimes, not merely indifferent (as the British were) but downright hostile to their aims as well as to their very existence. This realization did not come at one time or with equal force to all, but when it did come, one can see Christians facing that future with varying mixtures of confidence and anxiety. It is within this context of changing frameworks that three features of the Christian community's life from 1919 to 1947 stand out in unusually sharp relief.

The first of these is the adjustment process itself. Mission annual reports provide every indication that in most evangelistic and institutional activities the daily routines continued on much as before, albeit perhaps with an eye to a fresh relevance for their work and witness. There were, nonetheless, important adjustments and innovations made in response to the new requirements of the times. The missions had to 'let go' and transfer decision-making power to Indian church bodies. Educational institutions had to redefine their basic purposes and rearrange their priorities. Rural evangelism became linked with rural reconstruction and rural education in new ways. Overseas church delegations and expert international commissions visited the region, posing new questions and offering recommendations for consideration. Perhaps most important of all, Indian Christian leaders, at some risk, staked their community's future on a modern, secular, rather than communal, political ideology which set their negotiating positions throughout this period.[221] Taken together and in conjunction with the infusion of 'modernist theology', which placed a higher valuation on other religious traditions than did nineteenth-century Evangelicalism, one can discern an effort on the part of the Christian leadership to 'mainstream' the Church and community within a communally divided Indian nation without sacrificing a distinctive Christian identity.

A second feature of the north-west Indian Christian community's life, which emerges quite clearly during this period, is the profound social cleavage within it. In the towns and cities were the educated, progressive Christian elite drawn from diverse backgrounds as well as upward mobile Dalit migrants from the villages. In the villages were some Christian landowners of diverse backgrounds, who were confined almost exclusively to Christian villages, and a vast majority of Dalit labourers, most of whom were landless and uneducated, while only some had tenancy rights and a basic formal education. The former group was gaining independence and individuality, whereas the latter was dependent for their very survival upon caste-based, patron–client relationships. Although the two shared a common Christian identity, their social worlds as well as their political interests and natural alliances were very different. The gulf between

---

[221] One can sense both the pride and the uneasiness of a Punjabi Christian with regard to this political decision in S.J. Imad-ud-Din, *Gandhi and Christianity*, pp. 133–4. The contents indicate this was published either late in 1946 or early in 1947.

them was bridged to an extent through schemes by which elite-dominated urban congregations took charge of providing for the surrounding rural congregations. Thus, for rural Christians, urban or urbanized Indian patrons were replacing missionary patrons as a counter-balance to landlord patrons. In the wider Church and national context, this small minority of educated urban patrons represented and spoke for the Indian Christians as a whole in the north-west, while the rural Dalit majority was treated simply as 'silent masses' who could not speak for themselves.

The other feature of the history of Christianity in north-west India during this period is its transition from a movement to a community. Movement rhetoric continued, was even predominant, throughout this period, but the cumulative signs of a transition are unmistakable. The community's growth rate had slowed down. Rural missionaries, pastors, and evangelists were giving greater priority to consolidating gains already made than to reaching out to new inquirers, primarily because their human resources had been stretched beyond their capacity to provide adequate pastoral care to their widely scattered congregants. Educational priorities were shifting towards the upbuilding of the community. Much time and energy was being devoted to internal structural change and the empowerment of Indian leadership.

There is perhaps another dimension to this transition from movement to community as well. Back in 1918, the Rev. Henry Golaknath had written: 'We must create an Indian Church movement.' Hitherto the Christian movement had been led by and associated with the missions; now Indian Christians needed to identify with and invest themselves in the churches instead of the missions if such a shift from a mission-centred to a church-centred movement was to occur.[222] Two assessments made at the end of this period indicate that this shift in consciousness was not yet complete. In 1943, when introducing the Delhi Archdeaconry Scheme, the Anglicans

[222] H. Golaknath, 'The Foreign Missions and Churches in India in Relation One to Another', *IS* (December 1918), p. 365.

did not find much 'church consciousness' there.[223] In 1946, S.N. Talibuddin was heartened by the level of church consciousness he found among the rural congregations of the United Church of Northern India he visited, but the criteria he used for measuring church consciousness were not movement criteria.[224] A transfer of power had occurred without the desired transfer or awakening of consciousness. The Church was, in its consciousness, more a community than part of a movement in 1947.

[223] 'Devolution from the Mission to the Church in Delhi', *Delhi* (July 1943), p. 29.

[224] S.N. Talibuddin, 'A Study of Self-Supporting Churches in the Punjab', *UCR* (May 1947), pp. 279–80.

6 Christianity in North-west India Since Independence

The fifteenth of August 1947 marked a transition that was far more disruptive and traumatic in the north-west than in any other part of India. Not only did the governments of India and Pakistan replace the British Raj, but the line of demarcation between the two newly independent countries also ran through the middle of the region. Millions of people crossed the border in the weeks immediately preceding and following partition, while as many as a half million lost their lives. At the same time, the infrastructure of provincial administration in the East Punjab, now cut off from the former capital in Lahore, had to be created anew. Yet, despite these breaks with the past, certain important continuities remained: the predominantly agrarian economy, the hierarchical social structure, most of the religious and cultural milieu, as well as the legacies of both nationalist and communal politics.

The churches in the north-west also became independent of foreign control and had to be partitioned to conform to national boundaries. The power transfers begun earlier were soon completed and the foreign missionary gradually disappeared from the scene. The churches, now fully in Indian hands (initially those of the educated urban elites), sought to adjust to their new circumstances by redefining their relationships within both north-west Indian society and the wider Christian Church. While all this was going on, Christianity in the region was also becoming far more diverse than it had ever been before. The result was that the Christian churches and community in the north-west experienced as much change in this as in any previous period of their history.

This chapter begins by attempting to set the wider context for the story that follows. It then concentrates on ecclesiastical and institutional developments before turning to the changing nature of the Christian community, and hence of Christianity, in the region during this period. Unlike the previous chapters, this one examines

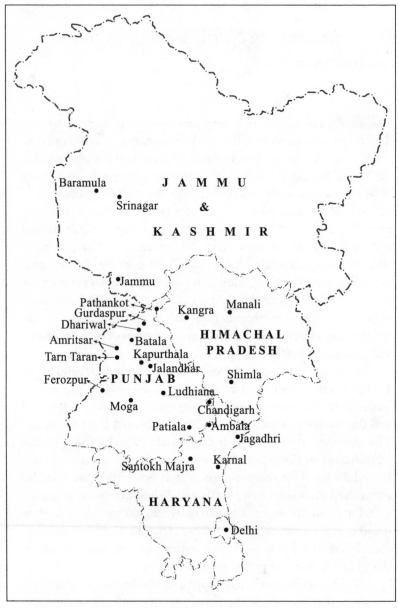

Map 3: North-west India in 2000

Source: Author.

what happened only on the Indian side of the border and offers no account of what happened in Pakistan during the post-independence years.

Partition and Its Aftermath

The transfer of power from the British to the government of independent India was an orderly process, but the partition of the north-west was not. The boundary line was announced only on 17 August, but the movement of refugees began before that. The Boundary Force proved ineffective in protecting minorities on both sides of the border. Refugee camps for both emigrants who no longer felt safe in their homes and immigrants coming across the border had to be set up and supplied. Property left behind by departing refugees was assigned to incoming refugees.[1] A deeply contested consequence of partition was the future of Jammu and Kashmir, a Muslim-majority princely state ruled by a Hindu maharaja who, on 15 August 1947, had still not decided whether to accede to India or to Pakistan. On 22 October, Pakistani tribesmen entered Kashmir and headed towards Srinagar, killing, looting, burning, and abducting as they went. On 26 October, the maharaja acceded to India and appointed Sheikh Abdullah as his prime minister. Indian troops arrived the next day and pushed the tribesmen back. Negotiations between India and Pakistan failed to produce a lasting settlement with the result that Kashmir has been a major point of contention between the two countries ever since.

Although communally neutral in the carnage of partition days, Christians could not escape its effects. It is difficult to estimate how many Christians migrated.[2] Most reports indicate that the vast majority stayed where they were. Many put crosses on their homes

---

[1] See Satya M. Rai, *Punjab Since Partition*, pp. 83–206.

[2] E.C. Bhatty of the National Christian Council estimated first that over 500 Christian families and then that 50,000 Christians had come from Pakistan to the East Punjab as refugees. 'Condition of the Rural Christian Community in West Pakistan', *NCCR* (April 1948), p. 168; 'Rural Christians in the Punjab', ibid. (September 1948). p. 354. See also 'Badomali City and District', *WMM* (July–August 1948), p. 802 and 'News from the Churches', *UCR* (September 1948), p. 200.

and clothes, or reverted to their distinctively Christian names, in order to identify themselves as Christians, but they still faced threats, property damage, and in a few instances, death.[3] The Methodists in Patiala state reported that many Christians there had to wear Sikh symbols, and a good number of pastors fled, in order to escape being killed, while on the other side of the border in Bahawalpur, Christians, who had been tenants of Hindu and Sikh landlords, faced forced conversion, beatings, and being driven from their homes.[4] In Amritsar, Sikhs threatened to burn down the CMS school for sheltering Muslims. St. Catherine's hospital was overrun by Muslims seeking refuge from the slaughter outside; about 1500 of them remained for three to four days before being taken away in government lorries.[5] The Presbyterian hospital in Sialkot was broken into three times by 'Muslim rascals' intent on killing its Hindu patients.[6] The worst case of deliberate anti-Christian violence occurred in Baramulla, Kashmir, where the tribesmen en route to Srinagar invaded St. Joseph's Franciscan convent, church, and hospital. They shot the Mother Superior, the Assistant Mother, a Christian nurse and her Muslim patient, an Anglo-Indian, and a European couple. They lined up all the nuns before a firing squad and would have shot them too had not one of their officers, who had studied at a convent school, arrived on the scene and stopped them.[7]

[3] Bhatty's estimate for the East Punjab was that 'Nearly 200 Christians had been killed during the disturbances, either because they joined the raiders, or were deliberately killed by their enemies, or were the victims of indiscriminate slaughter, or because they fraternised with Muslims'. E.C. Bhatty, 'Condition of the Rural Christian Community in West Pakistan', *NCCR* (April 1948), p. 168. See also 'The Bishop's Letter', *Delhi* (January 1948), p. 4; 'Christians in the Punjab', *NCCR* (December 1947), pp. 597–8; J. Leroy Dodds, 'Crisis for Christians in India', *Presbyterian Life* (19 April 1948), pp. 14–15; Martha Payne Alter, *Letters from India to America 1916–1951*, p. 552.

[4] *Indus River Annual Conference Journal 1948*, pp. 20–21.

[5] A.F. Atkins, 'Hatred Let Loose', *CMO* (November 1947), p. 3.

[6] Evelyn M. McKelvey, 'Sialkot Training School', *WMM* (July–August 1948), p. 820.

[7] This is the report of Fr Shanks in a white paper quoted by Josef Korbel, *Danger in Kashmir*, pp. 76–7. See also Dominic Thirunilath (ed.), *Christianity in Jammu & Kashmir*, pp. 45–8, 58, 61, 94–5.

Communal neutrality saved many Christian lives; it also put Christians in a trusted position to save other lives. Christian schools became refugee camps on both sides of the border. Christian hospitals and medical personnel worked tirelessly to treat wounds, malnutrition, dysentery, and assist in childbirth. Christian medical teams in Pakistan were invited to care for Muslim refugees in India, while those in India were asked to do the same for Hindu and Sikh refugees in Pakistan.[8] Christian mobile medical units even accompanied some of the columns of refugees to care for their medical needs, while others concentrated on public health work in order to prevent the spread of cholera, malaria, and smallpox.[9] Orphans and lost children were placed in the care of Christian hospitals as 'state children' until their parents found them or other arrangements for them were made.[10] Christian churches and organizations like the National Christian Council, the YMCA, and the YWCA mobilized volunteers, food and medical supplies from within India and abroad.[11] Christian schools situated in hill stations made arrangements with the government to evacuate their Muslim students and employees safely to Pakistan.[12] Perhaps the most striking instance where being a Christian made a crucial difference in relief work occurred in Delhi in September 1947, when Muslim refugees started collecting at Humayun's tomb. K.B. Lall, the ICS officer in charge of relief work in Delhi, asked Raja Ram, the principal of St. Stephen's College, to organize relief work in the camp because no

---

[8] D.F. Collier, 'Refugees in Amritsar', *The Growing Church* (March 1948), pp. 2–3; *Indus River Annual Conference Journal 1948*, p. 21; Marian T. Peterson, 'The United Bible Training Center, Gujranwala', *WMM* (July–August 1948), p. 803; Helen C. Sharp, 'Relief Medical Units', ibid., pp. 821–2.

[9] 'The Sign of the Cross', *The Growing Church* (June 1948), pp. 30–31; R.W.F. Wootton, 'Refugee Relief', *CMO* (February 1948), p. 5; Helen C. Sharp, 'Relief Medical Units', *WMM* (July–August 1948), pp. 821–2.

[10] Miss Parks, 'Relief Work', *MMQ* (December 1947), p. 62.

[11] 'Worse Than War', *MMQ* (December 1947), pp. 60–61; John R. Cole, 'The Relief of Refugees', *UCR* (March 1948), pp. 57–9.

[12] 'A Brief History of the School', *Convent of Jesus and Mary Chelsea Shimla, 2001 Calendar*, p. 12; Alicia Mitra, *A History of the Congregation of the Religious of Jesus and Mary in India, 1842–1993*, p. 81; 'Hundred Years of St. Bede's College, Simla', *St. Bede's College Shimla: 100 Years of Education*.

Hindu or Sikh could go there. 'The Christians alone can do it.' After the city's Christian leadership took up the challenge, they found that Lall was right. Initially, the refugees 'would only trust at the head of affairs a Padre in his white cassock'. It took ten days of hard work before they were relieved by the Government of India's food department.[13]

It was the resettlement process, compounded by severe September floods, which affected Christians most negatively, as the vast majority were landless agricultural labourers and tenants. In the East Punjab those who had worked for Muslim landowners as wage labour lost their share of the ripening harvest and those who cultivated land on a six-month lease did not expect their leases to be renewed by their new refugee landlords. In addition, many wells formerly used by Muslims and Christians together were now closed to the Christians and forced labour was introduced where it had not existed before. Throughout the region, Christians were not included in the redistribution of land, although the Kapurthala authorities considered it.[14] In West Punjab their situation was no better. They too lost their share of the crop to be harvested. In addition, because the incoming Muslim refugee population greatly outnumbered the rural Hindus and Sikhs who had departed, they received smaller plots of land and consequently had less demand for agricultural labour. Thus, an estimated 250,000 Christians lost the main source of their livelihood.[15]

[13] Kenneth Sharp, 'The Camp at Humayun's Tomb', *Delhi* (January 1948), pp. 9–12.

[14] E.C. Bhatty, 'Condition of the Rural Christian Community in West Pakistan', *NCCR* (April 1948), pp. 168–9; 'News from the Churches', *UCR* (June 1948), pp. 136–7. The government later allotted land near Ajnala for a model village of 100 Christian families, after some land on the border, deserted at partition time, had been given to Christians and, only after they had cultivated it, was forcibly taken from them by others. 'Annual Report—Rt. Rev. C.R.H. Wilkinson for the Year 1955' (Mimeographed); Heber Wilkinson, *Thirst of India*, p. 24; *The Church Militant* (1952?), p. 2.

[15] The estimate, which is probably on the high side, is that of the Anglican Bishop of Lahore in 'Village Christians in the Punjab', *The Guardian* (19 February 1948), p. 83. See also E.C. Bhatty, 'Condition of the Rural Christian Community in

While the human tragedies of partition were being played out throughout the north-west, the Constituent Assembly in New Delhi was drafting a constitution that envisioned creating a society based on liberty, equality, fraternity, and justice. Perhaps its most radical provision was the universal adult franchise, as under the British no more than ten per cent of the adult population had ever been eligible to vote. Not only did this enfranchise the entire Christian community, very few of whom had been entitled to vote before, but it also shifted power away from the more cosmopolitan elites to those numerous and assertive groups, like the Jats, whose interests, as it happened, often clashed with those of the Christians.

In addition, three issues came before the Constituent Assembly that had special significance for the Christian minority. The first concerned minority representation. Debate on this point focused not on communal electorates, but on reserved seats. Initially, the Advisory Committee on Minorities and Fundamental Rights recommended reserved seats for all religious minorities and the Scheduled Castes.[16] Then, on a motion from a Christian member, the Advisory Committee dropped the proposal for reserved seats, except for the Scheduled Castes. The Christian members of the Constituent Assembly supported this because they felt it depoliticized religious conversion and best served the long-term interests of the Christian community.[17] The second issue concerned religious liberty. The constitution granted freedom from religious discrimination by the state, the community's right to run its own educational institutions, and most importantly the right to 'freely profess, practice, and propagate religion'. The right to propagate, which the Advisory Committee had recommended, stirred up debate around the issue of conversion, but was ultimately affirmed, thanks to the

---

West Pakistan', *NCCR* (April 1948), pp. 166–7; 'Rural Christians in the Punjab', *NCCR* (September 1948), pp. 352–3; 'Christians in West Pakistan', *The Indian Witness* (4 December 1947), p. 289.

[16] The report is reprinted in Jose Kananaikil, *Scheduled Castes in the Constituent Assembly*, pp. 25–8.

[17] Jerome D'Souza, 'Constituent Assembly Discussions on Fundamental Rights', *The Guardian* (2 June 1949), p. 343.

efforts of Sardar Vallabhbhai Patel and much to the relief of the Christians.[18]

The other issue of special importance concerned eligibility for Scheduled Caste benefits which, according to the Presidential Order of 1950, was open only to Hindu Dalits. How this anomaly, which goes against the non-discrimination clauses of the constitution, got through the Assembly without a major fight is somewhat baffling. Jose Kananaikil has argued that in the early stages of the Assembly's work, when reservations for all minority communities still provided the framework for discussion, K.M. Munshi proposed an amendment to an Advisory Committee recommendation to say that 'The section of the Hindu community referred to as Scheduled Castes . . . shall have the same rights and benefits' as are provided for the other minorities, thus making the Dalits part of the Hindu and of no other religious community. Neither Dr Ambedkar, nor any other Dalit, nor any of the minority members of the Assembly raised any objections and so this passed without difficulty. Only when reservations for other minorities were dropped and those for Dalits retained did this understanding become problematic.[19] The National Christian Council made a protest in June 1949 and the Christian members of the Assembly voiced similar concerns.[20] Following the issuance of the Presidential Order which defined the Scheduled Castes as being Hindu, Prime Minister Nehru gave a written assurance that Christian Dalits were eligible for all Scheduled Caste benefits except reserved seats in elected bodies.[21] In December 1950, a deputation of Christians led by Dr H.C. Mookerjee, the vice-president of the Constituent Assembly, met with the president and gave him a memorandum from the Christian Members of Parliament protesting the discriminatory definition of the Scheduled Castes in the Presidential Order and pointing out that the assurance given by

[18] Ibid., p. 342; Donald Eugene Smith, *India as a Secular State*, pp. 181–4.

[19] Jose Kananaikil, *Scheduled Castes in the Constituent Assembly*, pp. 13–30.

[20] 'Correspondence', *The Guardian* (30 June 1949), p. 7; Jerome D'Souza, 'Constituent Assembly Discussions on Fundamental Rights', *The Guardian* (2 June 1949), p. 5.

[21] This may be found in 'Editorial Notes', *NCCR* (March 1951), pp. 104–5.

the prime minister was not being implemented. Despite further assurances, the distinction Nehru had drawn between political representation and other benefits, which President Rajendra Prasad had confirmed, was never made in practice.[22] In 1956, all Dalit Sikhs were included in the list of Scheduled Castes and in 1990 the Buddhists were added.

Missionary visas did not become an issue until 1952 when the Government of India rejected an unusually large number of applications, thus provoking discussion of its policy in both Church and government circles. In 1955, the Government of India laid down as policy that missionaries 'coming for the first time in augmentation of the existing strength of a mission or in replacement will be admitted to India, if they possess outstanding qualifications or specialized experience in their lines'.[23] As Smith has pointed out, the Government of India wanted to reduce the number of foreign missionaries as well as to 'transfer both routine jobs and positions of leadership from missionary to Indian Christian hands' so as 'to develop self-sufficiency of personnel in all aspects of the work of the church'.[24]

These early decisions aside, the social history of Christianity in the north-west was affected more by regional developments than by the central government. Following partition, the Punjab government had to establish itself, integrate the princely states within the region, and face a growing agitation for a Sikh-majority state. The Punjab was not included in the states' reorganization along linguistic lines in 1956, but after the 1965 war with Pakistan the demand for a Punjabi state drawn on linguistic rather than communal lines was granted. The result of this partition of the Punjab in 1966 was the creation of the present states of Punjab, Haryana, Himachal Pradesh, and the Union Territory of Chandigarh, which remained the capital city of both Punjab and Haryana. As Table 6.1 indicates, the Christian

[22] Ibid. Other benefits included eligibility for reserved government job quotas, financial aid for education, and development assistance.

[23] Cited by Korula Jacob, 'The Government of India and the Entry of Missionaries', *International Review of Missions*, 47 (1958), p. 413.

[24] Donald Eugene Smith, *India as a Secular State*, p. 200 and also p. 206.

population was spread very unevenly throughout the states of the region; only in the Punjab and Delhi, where ninety per cent of the Christians lived, did they have a chance at making any impact upon the wider society.

Table 6.1: Population Distribution in the North-west, 1971

State	Population	Per cent of Regional Population	Number of Christians	Per cent of State Population	Per cent of Regional Christian Population
Haryana	10,036,808	27.89	9,802	0.1	4.28
Himachal Pradesh	3,460,434	9.62	3,556	0.12	1.55
Jammu and Kashmir	4,616,632	12.83	7,182	0.16	3.14
Punjab	13,551,060	37.65	162,202	1.20	70.83
Chandigarh	257,251	0.71	2,540	0.97	1.11
Delhi	4,065,698	11.30	43,720	1.08	19.09
Total	35,987,883	99.99	229,002	0.64	100.00

Source: Religion Tables of the 1971 Census.

Following this second partition, Sikhism came to enjoy a quasi-establishment status within the Punjab[25] and the Chuhras gravitated towards Sikhism.[26] In politics, the Akali Dal, the Congress's main competitor, presented itself as the party of both regional and Sikh interests, often equating the two and drawing its support primarily from rural Jat Sikhs. Their 1973 Anandpur Sahib Resolutions, seeking greater provincial autonomy for the Punjab and a commanding position of power for the Sikhs within it, called upon Sikhs to make

[25] The state did much to promote Sikhism. In 1967 and in 1969, the Guru Gobind Singh and Guru Nanak Foundations were established with substantial government financial support. Guru Nanak University in Amritsar was created to encourage the study of Sikh religion and history as were new university departments or chairs.

[26] Whereas the 1931 Census had recorded only 169,247 Mazhabi Sikhs in a much larger Punjab, the 1981 Census recorded 1,221,131 of them. *Punjab Census 1931*, 1. p. 308; *Punjab Census 1981. Paper 1 of 1984: Household Population by Religion of Head of Household*, p. 738.

sacrifices in the struggle against the central government. By 1982, when the more extremist and confrontational Akalis had gained ascendancy and the secessionist Khalistan issue had been raised, this escalated into a violent *dharm yudh* (religious war). On 6 June 1984, the Indian army entered the Golden Temple premises in order to capture the extremist leaders and destroyed the Akal Takht, which they had chosen to make their headquarters. After two Sikh bodyguards assassinated Prime Minister Indira Gandhi in retaliation, there was uncontrolled anti-Sikh mob violence in Delhi. Bishop and Mrs Caleb hid overnight twenty-three Sikhs who had jumped over the Gurdwara Rakabganj wall into the diocesan compound to escape a violent mob, while elsewhere in Delhi, Christians, in close cooperation with human rights activists, especially at Delhi University, were active in providing relief to Sikhs.[27] In the Punjab, escalating violent confrontations between Sikh extremists, the police, and Home Guards took an estimated 25,000 lives. This ended late in 1992, but the issues that initially had given rise to it remained unresolved.[28]

In this political context, and within a profoundly hierarchical political culture based on caste and patron–client relationships, Christians and Christian interests were largely ignored. In 1949, Bashir-ud Din, the headmaster of the Christian school in Dhariwal, the section of Gurdaspur district with the largest concentration of Christians, revived the Indian Christian Council with Congress backing and renamed it the Masihi Sangat. He became a member and even deputy speaker of the Punjab Legislative Council, before

[27] Maqbul Caleb, *Count Your Blessings*, pp. 174–8; Interview with Fr T.K. John SJ, 23 August 2005; 'Indian Social Institute through the Fifty Years', *Indian Social Institute Golden Jubilee 6th January 1951–5th January 2001*, p. 42.

[28] This paragraph is based upon J.S. Grewal, *The Sikhs of the Punjab*, pp. 181–236 and the essays in Paul Wallace and Surendra Chopra (eds), *Political Dynamics and Crisis in Punjab,*. One study of thirty-one villages around Amritsar between 1984 and 1992 suggests that at the grassroots level the terror and violence were related to local rather than to larger Sikh religious or political issues. Harish K. Puri, Paramjit Singh Judge, and Jagrup Singh Sekhon, *Terrorism in Punjab: Understanding Grassroots Reality*, pp. 185–6.

his death in 1958. Since the 1966 partition of the Punjab, when the Punjab Legislative Council was eliminated in favour of a single house legislature, no Christian has been elected to any state legislature in the region. Several ran as independent candidates. In 1980, Isaac Das ran for the Punjab Legislative Assembly and then in 1985 for the Lok Sabha on the Akali ticket, the first Christian to get backing from a major party, while Abraham Irshad ran for the Punjab Legislative Assembly on the Congress ticket from Dhariwal, also in 1985, all without success. Christians have fared somewhat better in local panchayat and municipal elections. A number have also been nominated to government boards and two have served as directors of the Punjab Backward Classes Financial Corporation.[29]

Punjabi Christians, like Dalits in general, have largely supported the Congress, but in the 1970s some made contacts with the Akali Dal. Since then they have become more divided politically and Christian support for the Congress has diminished.[30] Rural Christians have been under enormous pressure to vote for the party backed by their village landlords, whereas urban Christians and those living near towns have been more independent. There were village Christians entrapped and even killed in the anarchy surrounding the confrontations between the government and the Sikh extremists during 1984–92.[31] The Home Guards occupied the Boys' Hostel at Baring Union Christian College, an alleged terrorist refuge, and left it in shambles with no compensation. Since then Christian political activism has been confined to localized Christian organizations which at times have linked up with either the Congress or Akali Dal, but there has been little ideological consensus, organizational unity,

[29] This information was gathered at a meeting of about twenty Christian political activists at village Shahpur near Dhariwal on 27 October 2003.

[30] A recent survey of 240 urban and rural Dalit Christians in the Punjab found only 42.5 per cent supporting the Congress, a further decline (judging from earlier studies) from a high of about 85 per cent in the 1960s. Emanual Nahar, 'Dalit Christians of the Punjab', *Dalit International Newsletter* (October 2006), p. 8.

[31] Harish K. Puri, Paramjit Singh Judge, and Jagrup Singh Sekhon, *Terrorism in Punjab*, p. 95. They reported eleven Christians killed by terrorists in the villages they surveyed.

recognized statewide leadership, or even a single mobilizing political issue in the Christian community. Some individuals have occupied positions in the Punjab Pradesh Congress Committee, the Youth Congress, and the Janata Dal, but the community as such remains politically unorganized and unaligned.[32]

Outside the Punjab, Christians have been too few in number or too widely dispersed to have any political impact at all, as they faced either the increasing appeal of Hindu nationalism as a political ideology and the aggressive activities of the Vishwa Hindu Parishad in promoting Hindu religion or, in Kashmir, destructive acts of Muslim outrage over events which took place outside of India.[33] In Delhi, a Christian was elected twice on the Congress ticket to the Metropolitan Council after it was formed in 1966.[34] Elsewhere in the region they have been politically marginalized and considered irrelevant. In touring the region after being appointed to the National Commission on Minorities in 1996, James Massey found Christians in all the states facing great difficulties in getting government officials to address their grievances, especially about government interference and property, including cemeteries.[35]

Most Christians in the region have had to function not only within this political culture, but also under rapidly changed socio-economic circumstances. The post-partition land settlement has already been referred to. This was followed in the 1960s by the Green Revolution in the Punjab and Haryana, which the state did much to sponsor by creating the necessary infrastructure. While greatly increasing production and wealth, this technological advance in agriculture

---

[32] Meeting of Christian Political Activists at Village Shahpur, 27 October 2003.

[33] All Saints Church in Srinagar was twice destroyed by Muslim mobs while the police stood by and did nothing. In June 1967, it and two other churches were attacked and looted by a mob shouting anti-Israeli slogans following the Arab–Israeli war. In 1979, it was attacked again following the execution of Z.A. Bhutto in Pakistan. (Pakistani Muslims decided on Bhutto's execution but the executioner they appointed was a Christian.) 'News from Many Quarters', *NCCR* (August 1967), p. 311; 'News Items', *NIC* (July 1979), pp. 14–5; 'A Letter of Protest from the Christians of Srinagar', ibid. (August 1979), p. 9.

[34] Vijay Laxmi Pandit, *Elites and Urban Politics*, p. 81.

[35] James Massey, *Minorities in a Democracy: The Indian Experience*, pp. 51–4.

required considerable inputs of capital that small landowners and tenant farmers could not afford. The net effect in the countryside was to increase disparities of wealth and to reduce many tenants and small farmers to the status of agricultural labourers. Mechanization both decreased the demand and increased the annual wages of agricultural workers.

The other important socio-economic change in which Christians became involved was the increasing urbanization of the region. Back in 1931 only about 11 per cent of the Christians were urban, whereas in 1971 that percentage had risen to 36.3 per cent (as compared with 27.7 per cent for the general population) and by 2001 it had reached 50.9 per cent (as compared with 40.8 per cent for the general population.) As Table 6.2 indicates, the urban population of the region tripled in the three decades between the 1971 and 2001 Census. Christians were already a predominantly urban community in all the states except the Punjab, where they were less urbanized than the total population. With increased urbanization between 1971 and 2001 Christians were becoming urbanized at a slightly higher rate and remained about ten per cent more urbanized than was the regional population as a whole.

The other significant social change that needs to be mentioned here has been the growing assertiveness of the Dalits of all religions in exercising their basic human and civil rights. This has been particularly noticeable in the Punjab where the Dalit portion of the population is now approaching thirty per cent, the highest in India.[36] The Dalit literacy rate has risen significantly (but still remains below the general literacy rate) and a much larger portion of them are getting an education than were able to do so prior to independence. Dalits increasingly have been moving out of occupations that made them dependent upon village landlords and into a wide range of new occupations.[37] In politics, the Chamars in particular have sought

[36] It was 28.3 per cent in the 1991 Census.

[37] See Paramjit S. Judge, 'Emerging Trends in the Caste Structure of Punjab', pp. 56–60.

Table 6.2: Urbanization in North-west India, 1971–2001

State	Urban Population in 1971	Percentage of State Population in 1971	Urban Christian Population in 1971	Percentage of State Christian Population in 1971	Urban Population in 2001	Percentage increase 1971–2001	Urban percentage of State Population in 2001	Urban Christian Population in 2001	Percentage increase 1971–2001	Urban percentage of State Christian Population in 2001
Haryana	1,772,859	17.66	5,119	52.22	6,115,304	244.9	28.9	17,510	242.1	64.4
Himachal Pradesh	241,890	6.99	1,907	53.63	595,581	146.2	9.8	3,317	73.9	43.2
Jammu & Kashmir	858,221	1.84	4,140	57.64	2,516,638	193.2	24.8	13,425	224.3	66.1
Punjab	3,216,179	23.73	26,907	16.59	8,262,511	156.9	33.9	81,640	203.4	27.9
Chandigarh	232,940	90.54	2,404	96.01	808,515	247.1	89.8	7,255	201.8	95.1
Delhi	3,647,023	89.70	42,547	97.32	12,905,780	253.9	93.2	123,953	191.3	95.1
Total	9,969,112	27.7	83,024	36.3	31,204,329	213	40.8	247,100	197.6	50.9

Source: Religion Tables of the 1971 and 2001 Census of India.

to move out from under the customary patron–client politics,[38] to supporting Dalit-led political parties like the Ambedkarite Republican Party of India, which enjoyed some early success,[39] and more recently the Bahujan Samaj Party. Dalits have also become increasingly involved in village politics and some (including a few Christians) have even won the post of village *sarpanch*. In religion, assertiveness has taken the form of a revival of Ad Dharm, of building Ravidas gurdwaras, and of building separate Sikh gurdwaras so as 'to assert their autonomy and avoid the humiliation they felt in the gurdwaras run by the local upper castes'.[40] One of the consequences of this assertiveness has been increasing caste conflict throughout the region.

What perhaps distinguishes this period from the preceding one was that with independence, the adult franchise, and the penetration of the institutions of self-government to the village level, Indians at all levels of the social hierarchy in the north-west gained more control over their own destinies than had previously been possible. Equally importantly, the pace of social and economic change within the region quickened significantly through a combination of private enterprise and state initiatives in planned economic development. The caste-based political culture of the region, reflecting rural social hierarchies and power relationships, however, remained the same. The Christian community, now under Indian leadership and as marginalized under Congress or Akali regimes as under the former colonial regime, had to respond to this increasingly complex and faster moving environment.

The Reorganization and Proliferation of Churches

In August 1947, the Christian churches in the north-west were better prepared organizationally for independence than for partition.

[38] See Satish Saberwal, *Mobile Men*.

[39] Lelah Dushkin, 'Scheduled Caste Politics', in J. Michael Mahar (ed.), *The Untouchables in Contemporary India*, Tucson: University of Arizona Press, 1972, p. 203.

[40] Surinder S. Jodhka, 'Caste and Untouchability in Rural Punjab', p. 1818. See also, Harish K. Puri, 'Scheduled Castes in Sikh Community: A Historical Perspective', pp. 2693–701.

Virtually all had ecclesiastical structures in place with adequate decision-making power to function effectively in the new political context. However, they now faced the task of adjusting their ecclesiastical borders to the new international boundary drawn between India and Pakistan, while completing the process of gaining full ecclesiastical independence from, and redefining relationships with, the overseas churches which had been so instrumental in creating them. Once viable, fully independent, and free from foreign missionary dominance, the churches could face the challenges of this new era in accordance with their own visions and priorities. Meanwhile, as the older churches were making these changes, new churches were either entering into or emerging from within the north-west. This combination of internal changes and new additions made the picture of the 'church scene' in north-west India at the end of the twentieth century appear far more complex than in 1947.

The churches were slower in adjusting their governing and administrative structures to the new international boundary than was the government. In 1952, the Roman Catholics created the Apostolic Prefectures of Jullundur as well as of Jammu and Kashmir, to cover those districts of the Lahore and Rawalpindi dioceses which were on the Indian side of the border.[41] The former was raised to the status of a diocese in 1971 and the latter in 1986. In 1959, the Archdiocese of Delhi–Simla was bifurcated to create the Diocese of Simla–Chandigarh and the Archdiocese of Delhi. The former included districts of Himachal Pradesh, Haryana, the Punjab, and the Union Territory of Chandigarh. The latter consisted of the Union Territory of Delhi and seven districts of Haryana.[42]

The major Protestant denominations in the region took similar steps. The [Anglican] Church of India, Burma, and Ceylon was

[41] The Apostolic Prefecture of Jammu and Kashmir was originally named Kashmir and Jammu but was changed in 1968 to conform to state usage. The diocese was named Jammu–Srinagar in 1986. *Diocese of Jammu-Srinagar India Directory 1996,* p. 131.

[42] *Diocese of Jalandhar Punjab, India: Directory 1999,* pp. 1–2; Fr Paul A. Cardoza, compiler, *Delhi Catholic Directory 2000,* pp. 23–5; *Catholic Diocese of Simla-Chandigarh Directory–2001,* pp. 1–2; *Capuchins in India 1972–1997,* pp. 208–9.

renamed The Church of India, Pakistan, Burma, and Ceylon following partition. In February 1949, its Lahore Diocese created the Archdeaconry of East Punjab that became the Amritsar Diocese in 1953, but the Lahore and Amritsar dioceses still remained within the same Church.[43] In the Punjab the United Church of North India (UCNI) also resisted complete bifurcation. Some territorial adjustments were made in defining the boundaries of its Church Councils. By 1952, the two West Punjab Church Councils had formed the Synod of Pakistan, while the three in East Punjab became the Punjab Synod.[44] Since the Gurdaspur Presbytery was the only United Presbyterian presbytery to fall on the Indian side of the border, it joined the UCNI in 1954.[45] Then the Moravian Brethren in Ladakh joined in 1956.[46] In the Methodist case, the portion of their Indus Valley Annual Conference which lay inside India was simply incorporated into the Delhi Annual Conference. The Salvation Army shifted the territorial headquarters for the districts in East Punjab from Lahore to Delhi by 1949.

At the same time the missions also completed the transfer of power to the churches begun earlier. Of the Presbyterian missions associated with the UCNI, the New Zealanders seem to have made this transition most easily. In 1952, they reported the transfer of control over all their mission's work to the Ambala Church Council of the UCNI and the following year transferred all of their property to the UCNI Trust Association.[47] The United Presbyterians entered this period with the most control still vested in the mission. In March 1957, they created a new mission on the Indian side of the border, separate from the Sialkot Mission in Pakistan, with the responsibility

[43] C.R.H. Wilkinson, 'For the Church in the East Punjab', *Into All The World* (March 1950), p. 2; M.E. Gibbs, *The Anglican Church in India 1600–1970*, p. 385.

[44] 'Directory of the United Church of Northern India'. *UCR* (January 1949), p. 18; Alexander McLeish, 'Far and Near', ibid. (March 1949), p. 51; E.Y. Campbell, 'Doaba Church Council', ibid. (November 1950), p. 209; 'Directory of the U.C.N.I.', ibid. (January 1953), pp. 19–20.

[45] Leonard A. McCulloch, 'What Befell Gurdaspur Presbytery?' *Missionary Horizons* (April 1958), p. 471.

[46] *The United Church of Northern India Survey 1968*, p. 11.

[47] *NZ Presbyterian GA Proceedings 1953*, p. 22a.

of integrating its work as quickly as possible into that of the Gurdaspur Church Council. This was done in just two weeks' time.[48]

By 1935, the Punjab Mission of the Presbyterian Church in the U.S.A. had transferred most of its responsibilities to a Central Board of the UCNI Church Councils to which it was historically related. In October 1956, it transferred its remaining responsibilities to the Punjab Synod of the UCNI and ceased to exist.[49] In 1960, the Presbyterians in the USA appointed a fifteen-member international committee to prepare *An Advisory Study* that might guide its policies in the coming years. Central to its recommendations was the conviction that a necessary prerequisite to mature relationships between churches was that each had 'achieved authentic selfhood', a key indicator of which was that a church be able to 'care for its worship, its teaching and pastoral ministries, the basic training and support of its clergy, some form of outreach in evangelism and service, and a minimum of church administration'.[50] Using this 'tough love' approach, the Presbyterians in the USA then decided to make no further financial contributions towards pastoral support or church administration in the UCNI. The Punjab Synod made some structural readjustments, rural workers dependent upon American Presbyterian support received a severance package, and Punjabi congregations increased their giving, at least initially, so that ninety per cent of the pastors continued to serve their congregations there.[51] The long-term effects, however, were not so salutary. The old securities were gone and everyone now had to fend for themselves. Pastors, institutional workers, and even their descendants claimed church housing as their own. Encroachments on and illegal occupation of church property increased. Soon the UCNI became bogged down in the legal complexities of gaining control of the

[48] *UPCNA GA Minutes 1948*, p. 178; ibid. 1950, p. 952; ibid. *1957*, p. 600; J. Morgan McKelvey, 'Integration of Mission and Church', *Missionary Horizons* (April 1958), pp. 473–4.

[49] *BFM PC in USA Annual Report 1957*, p. 46.

[50] *An Advisory Study*, pp. 70, 71.

[51] *Seventh Annual Report of the Commission on Ecumenical Mission and Relations* (1965), p. 66; ibid. (1966), p. 22; ibid. (1967), p. 23.

property previously owned by the Punjab Mission. In the ensuing disputes and court cases the UCNI lost members to other, seemingly more stable, denominations.

In the Anglican case the transfer of power and responsibility went hand in hand with the creation of the Delhi and Amritsar dioceses out of the old Lahore Diocese. While the Delhi Diocese had only the closely connected SPG and Cambridge Mission to deal with, the Amritsar Diocese had to concentrate within diocesan committees all decision-making previously done separately by members of the CMS, the CEZMS, and the Missionary Society of the Church of England in Canada.[52] Once this was done and ownership of property transferred to Diocesan Trust Associations, the related missions gradually withered away.

As the missions lost their collective power and slowly died, foreign missionaries now served at the pleasure of Indian church bodies and their leaders. The government's new visa policy, the growing number of Indian Christians qualified for positions of leadership, and the mounting costs of missionary support the sending churches had to bear, combined to move foreign missionaries first out of church work and then out of institutions. The older and the educated Dalit elites took over from the missionaries and became the new patrons within the churches, while the rural poor and the urban lower middle class remained the clients. As these ruling elites consolidated their power, the churches' political culture came to resemble north-west Indian political culture in general.

While these churches were redefining working relationships with overseas church bodies, they were also negotiating with each other about unifying into one Church of North India. These negotiations, begun back in 1929, were intensified following both independence and the formation of the Church of South India in September 1947. Church union led to the final ecclesiastical separation of the Anglican, UCNI, and Methodist congregations in West Pakistan from those in India and on 29 November 1970 six of the seven negotiating churches in India inaugurated the Church of North India (CNI).

[52] The latter entered the region in 1912. Heber Wilkinson, *Thirst of India*, p. 17.

(The Methodist Church of Southern Asia withdrew shortly before inauguration.) Two of the CNI dioceses were located in the north-west: the Diocese of Delhi and Rajasthan, which included Delhi and Haryana within its bounds and was headed by Bishop Eric Nasar, a former Anglican bishop, and the Diocese of Amritsar, which included the Punjab, Himachal Pradesh, Jammu and Kashmir, and was headed by Bishop S. Ghulam Qadir, a former UCNI pastor.[53]

Church union got off to a good start in the Delhi Diocese where the Baptists and Anglicans had been working together for a long time and where UCNI members in Haryana were very few in number. In 1981, a separate Diocese of Rajasthan was created, thus confining the Delhi Diocese entirely to Delhi and Haryana. Church union in the Amritsar Diocese was another matter. In this diocese, a majority of Anglicans, fearing Presbyterian domination, had opposed church union.[54] A group led by the archdeacon and diocesan treasurer used their position in the Amritsar Diocesan Trust Association, which held the property and financial reserves of the former Anglican diocese, to thwart progress towards unification within the new diocese and create a separate Anglican church of their own. In September 1973, the CNI divided the diocese in two, basically along denominational lines. The jurisdiction of the Amritsar Diocese included Himachal Pradesh, Jammu and Kashmir, and the Amritsar district of Punjab, while the new Chandigarh Diocese had the rest of the Punjab. This did not solve the Amritsar Diocese's problems with dissident Anglicans, who had made overtures to the Roman Catholic Diocese of Jullundur. Working with those dissidents, Catholic priests became involved in seizing what had been Anglican property and, for a time, the Catholic bishop of Jullundur Diocese claimed to be chairman of

[53] James Kellock, *Breakthrough for Church Union in North India and Pakistan*; D.M. Kennedy, 'The CNI History', and 'Work in Progress: The CNI History'; Dhirendra Kumar Sahu, *United and Uniting*.

[54] Amritsar was the only Anglican diocese to vote against church union, but by law had to accept it. Had two other dioceses joined them, they could have remained a separate Anglican province. Eric S. Nasir, Letter to Donald Clark, 29 November 1977. Nasir was the Anglican bishop of Amritsar at the time of the vote.

the Amritsar Diocesan Trust Association.[55] The dissidents had little popular support among former Anglicans who either remained loyal to the CNI or became Catholics, but the court cases over property and finance proved to be a long-term running sore in the life of the Amritsar Diocese.[56] The CNI won a significant victory when the court recognized it as the legal successor to the Church of India, Pakistan, Burma, and Ceylon in August 1988;[57] an appeal was made to the High Court, which has yet to hear the case. Meanwhile, in the overwhelmingly rural Chandigarh Diocese the major challenge was not division so much as providing financial support for its clergy.[58]

The transfer of power and responsibility from foreign missionary to Indian hands that had the most dramatic consequences in northwest India occurred within the Roman Catholic Church. Prior to independence its episcopacy and priesthood were almost totally foreign. With the creation of the Apostolic Prefecture of Jullundur in 1952, English Capuchins from the neighbouring Delhi–Simla Archdiocese were sent to help out. However, they were quickly supplemented and then replaced by Capuchins from Kerala, one of whom, the Rt. Rev. Dr Symphorian Keeprath OFM, became the first bishop of the Jullundur Diocese in March 1972. In the 1970s, two other male religious orders from Kerala, the Little Flower Congregation and the Order of the Discalced Carmelites, joined the Capuchins in the diocese.[59] Both the Simla–Chandigarh Diocese and the Delhi Archdiocese drew Indian priests, not just from Kerala but from other parts of India as well, to replace the Europeans. The

[55] Ibid; E. John, Letter to Donald Clark, 15 August 1976; Michael O'Connell, Letter to Donald Clark, 8 August 1977; Aziz William, Letter to Lawrence Cardinal Pichachy, 12 October 1979; Interview with Fr Emmanuel Y. Diwan, 17 September 2005.

[56] R.W. Bryan, 'Another Milestone: Synod Passes the Constitution and Debates Priorities', *NIC* (August 1974), pp. 3–4; 'Bishop John Reports on Amritsar Diocese', ibid., (September 1976), pp. 4–5; 'News from the Amritsar Diocese,', ibid. (March 1978), pp. 11–13.

[57] *Diocese of Amritsar 1989*, p. 9.

[58] 'Pastoral Letter to the People of Chandigarh Diocese', *NIC* (April 1974), p. 10; 'Diocese of Chandigarh, Bishop's Report 1973–74', ibid. (June 1974), pp. 3–4.

[59] *Diocese of Jalandhar Punjab, India: Directory 1999*, pp. 73–8.

former currently has members of twenty-two religious orders as well as diocesan clergy, while the latter has members of seventy-eight religious orders living in 162 religious communities within the diocese.[60] In Jammu and Kashmir, the Mill Hill Fathers decided to turn over their work to an Indian religious society following the 1971 India–Pakistan war. The Capuchins of St. Joseph's Province in Kerala responded and the transfer was completed in 1978. The Very Rev. Hippolytus Kunnunkal Ofm Cap became the first Indian Prefect Apostolic there in 1978 and the first bishop of the diocese in 1986. At the time of the transfer there were only three women's religious orders in the area; in 2004, there were nineteen, totalling 180 sisters, as well as six orders for men.[61]

The expansion resulting from this large influx of Indian priests was most noticeable in the Jullundur Diocese. Of the ninety-two parishes in the diocese in 1999 only four had existed prior to 1947: Dalhousie, Jullundur, Amritsar, and Ferozpur. Of the eleven female religious orders in the diocese in 1999, only the Sisters of Charity of Jesus and Mary had been there before 1947.[62] Post-independence expansion in the Jullundur Diocese began by reaching out to Protestants who were not receiving adequate pastoral care.[63] The Capuchins from Kerala arrived in the aftermath of the Presbyterian decision to withdraw financial support and the Anglican conflicts over church union. They set up new missions either near their original churches or in places where there were already a significant number of Christians, almost all of whom were rural Dalit Protestants and many of whom were won over.[64] In one case, a former Anglican priest became a Roman Catholic priest and brought nine village parishes with him.[65] The Delhi Archdiocese expanded from seven

[60] *Catholic Diocese of Simla–Chandigarh Directory 2001*, pp. 25–61; Fr Paul A. Cardoza, compiler, *Delhi Catholic Directory 2000*, p. 27.

[61] *Diocese of Jammu-Srinagar India Directory 1996*, pp. 4, 53–80; *Directory 2004 Diocese of Jammu-Srinagar* (Jammu Cantt: Bishop's House, 2004), pp. 25–37, 59.

[62] Ibid., pp. 78–107.

[63] Dr James Mundackal CST in, Fr George Cheruvil (ed.), *Christward*, pp. 43–4; Interview with Fr Mathew Kokandam, 22 October 2003.

[64] Fr George Cheruvil (ed.), *Christward*, p. 45.

[65] *Capuchins in India 1972–1997*, p. 205.

parishes or missions in 1947 to forty-six in 2000,[66] not by winning over Protestants but by finding migrant Catholics from other parts of India who had settled in and around Delhi.[67] The Archdiocese expanded very much by plan, first locating through existing parishes or schools where these migrants were living, and then creating missions and churches in those locations where there were enough Catholics to create a congregation.[68] The Jammu Srinagar Diocese increased from two parishes in 1952, when the Prefecture Apostolic was created, to seven parishes in 1978, when the Mill Hill Fathers handed over to the Capuchins, to twenty-nine in 2004.[69] Almost all of this increase has been Dalit.[70] As a result of all this expansion, the Catholics, who comprised less than ten per cent of the Christian population of the region at the time of the 1931 Census, made up about half of the region's Christian population by the year 2000![71] Unlike the historic Protestant churches in the region, which had long drawn their clergy almost entirely from the local population, virtually all the Roman Catholic clergy at the end of the century still came from outside the north-west. The Catholics also relied heavily upon funding from outside the region to support at least the early stages of their work there.[72]

Like the Catholics in Delhi, Protestants also responded to rapid urbanization by building new churches and creating new parish congregations. Christ Church in Chandigarh represents an unusual

[66] Fr Paul A. Cardoza, compiler, *Delhi Catholic Directory 2000*, pp. 49–134.

[67] Sebasti L. Raj, *Renewal–2000*, p. 47; Interview with Fr Leonard Fernando SJ, 21 October 2003.

[68] *Delhi Archdiocese Yesterday, Today and Tomorrow* (1971); *Renewal in the Archdiocese of Delhi 1959–1972*; Archbishop Angelo Fernandes, 'Delhi in the Sixties and Seventies: Church in Action' (mimeographed, 1975); Interview with Fr Benedict Santos, Secretary, Archdiocese of Delhi, 23 April 1980.

[69] *Diocese of Jammu-Srinagar India 1996*, pp. 20–50; *Directory 2004 Diocese of Jammu-Srinagar*, pp. 10–24.

[70] Interview with Deacon Joseph Jacob Gill, 27 August 2005.

[71] This is an estimate based on the figures for Roman Catholics given in the diocesan directories at around 2000 and projections for the total Christian population of that year made from the 1991 Census.

[72] Interview with Archbishop Vincent M. Concessao, 18 August 2005; Interview with Fr Emmanuel Y. Diwan, 17 September 2005.

example of inter-church collaboration in this regard. Christian families started moving to Chandigarh when it was just being built. In 1952, members of about thirty Christian families began meeting together in the home of Mr Dethe, the city's senior architect, for worship and a fellowship meal. In 1954, they got a deed for a site and in 1959 the new church building was dedicated with Anglican, Methodist, Baptist, and UCNI support. In 1971, it joined the Amritsar Diocese of the CNI.[73] Christ Church was the first church in Chandigarh, but since then a number of others have come into existence as the city has grown. By 2000, there were at least ten established congregations with their own church buildings in the city as well as a large number of independent congregations, prayer fellowships, and informal Christian groups.[74]

Delhi and New Delhi provide the region's best example of church expansion in response to large-scale urbanization and population growth. The Methodists who in 1947 had only four Hindi and two English-language congregations now have an additional ten Hindi and three English-language congregations spread throughout the city. Pastors in established congregations first organized prayer and Bible study groups in new residential areas and then sent lay preachers to those groups to conduct regular Sunday worship and organize Sunday Schools.[75] The Free Church on Sansad Marg in New Delhi was responsible for starting the Green Park Free Church, which in turn helped start the United Free Church in Dakhshinpuri (1982) and more recently the United Free Church in Vasant Kunj.[76] St. Francis Church in Anandgram grew from a simple request to the pastor of St. James Church in Kashmiri Gate for Christian funeral services in 1951 to a

[73] Douglas Milne Riddle, *Life and Light*, pp. 93–101; Interview with Mr E.D.M. Khan, 31 October 2003; two typewritten papers prepared for a court case in the 1980s given to me by Mr Khan.

[74] Interview with Mr Arvind Noel, 29 October 2003. The souvenir of a gospel music concert, '*Tu Mera Bal*', in Chandigarh on 17 October 2003 sponsored by the India Campus Crusade for Christ listed a total of ninety 'Pastors & Christian Workers in Chandigarh, Mohali, Panchkula'.

[75] Interview with Bishop Nimrod Christian, 17 August 2005.

[76] The Diocese of Delhi (The Church of North India), *Reports: Diocesan Council 9th–10th September 2005* (Delhi: 2005), pp. xvii, 92, 95.

large thriving church today within a community defined neither by caste nor even by religion, but by the presence of leprosy in its families.[77] This church has grown as new members have joined from both within and outside this distinctive community.[78] Some congregations have offered worship services not only in English and Hindi, but also in one or more regional languages in order to serve the needs of migrant populations. Almost all of this growth has come from Christian families rather than through converts from other faiths.

While these 'historic' churches were reorganizing and responding to the demographic challenges before them, new churches were either coming into or emerging from within the region itself. Several Evangelical organizations based in south India adopted north-west India as a 'mission field'. Unlike the south Indian Catholic priests who came to strengthen and expand an existing Church, these groups started their own fellowships and churches outside the existing Protestant churches. One such group, the Indian Evangelical Team founded by P.G. Vargis, began evangelistic work in Jammu and Kashmir in 1972. By 1997, it had seventy-eight congregations in Jammu and Kashmir, one hundred forty-six in Punjab, fifteen in Himachal Pradesh, thirteen in Haryana, and eight in Delhi (almost all of which are 'house churches' meeting in the homes of members), as well as the Beersheba Theological College, in Pathankot, Punjab.[79]

The Pentecostals also came to the north-west from south India. While ecstatic speech has generally been their defining characteristic, in north-west India they are better known for their emphasis upon divine healing in response to fervent prayer. In addition to regular Sunday worship and personal visitation, they have used large public meetings or conventions, which have included prayer for and laying

---

[77] A most unusual feature of this church is that both Christian and Hindu graves lie side by side in its cemetery. Today, very few people in this community have leprosy.

[78] *An Invitation to Share: To Build St. Francis Church with the people of Trans-Yumuna Pastorate*, Delhi: Diocese of Delhi, 1998(?); Visit to St. Francis Church, 14 August 2005.

[79] *Indian Evangelical Team Silver Jubilee Souvenir*, pp. 24, 88–94.

hands upon those requesting healing. These have attracted large crowds which, in a few instances, have been disturbed or broken up by Hindu militants. However, the Pentecostals' mission in the region began modestly, first in Delhi and then in the Punjab. Pastor Sam Paul of the Ceylon Pentecostal Mission (now The Pentecostal Mission) came alone to the Punjab and Jammu and Kashmir in the 1950s. Others followed. Their greatest response has come in the Gurdaspur district of the Punjab where in 1978 they acquired a large campus in Dhariwal. Twenty years later that campus included residences for the celibate brothers and sisters in full-time service as well as a large hall where up to 1000 people worship every Sunday morning and eat at the *langar* afterwards. There are twenty-six other centres in their Punjab Ministry alone, but the one in Dhariwal is the largest and serves as headquarters for the Punjab.[80] Meetings in Jullundur and Ludhiana with other Pentecostal pastors, the vast majority of whom are recent Punjabi converts, provide further evidence that these churches are proliferating rapidly because of their strong emphasis upon prayer and faith healing in addressing the many, varied problems of personal life brought to them by people seeking help. During Sunday worship they give such individuals opportunities to testify to the wonderful changes God was been working in their lives.[81]

There are also churches that have emerged from within the north-west itself rather than through the efforts of outsiders. Three examples must suffice. The Evangelical Church of God traces its history back to 31 January 1965 when Sadhu P.D. Benjamin baptized six members of the Howell family in Ferozpur and two other people. This church grew slowly among local Christian labourers until 1969 when they met Sister Alice from Canada, who had the gift of healing. Howell arranged week-long meetings for her in eight different places. The converts won through these and subsequent public meetings were placed under the care of locally acceptable pastors, with the

---

[80] Interviews with Pastor Mohan and Mother E.V. Thangamma, Dhariwal, 26 October 2003.

[81] Meetings with Pastors, Carmel Church, Jullundur, 26 October 2002 and Bethsaida Prayer Tower, Ludhiana, 28 October 2002.

result that the movement grew as much through local initiative as through large public meetings. Its major centres are in Ferozpur and Ludhiana, but there are now 150 pastors working primarily among Dalits in 800 villages of Punjab, Haryana, and Rajasthan.[82] Pastor Munir Masih started the Azad Masihi Kalisia in 1971. Like the Pentecostals, he places much emphasis upon prayer and faith healing. There are fifty Azad Masihi Kalisia congregations in the Punjab and more outside, the two largest being in Gurdaspur and Dhariwal where the annual convention is held.[83] The Open Door Church at Khojewala village in the Kapurthala district of the Punjab was founded by a Jat Sikh landowner named Harbhajan Singh who converted to Christianity in 1986 while working in Australia. After returning home in 1987, he attended nearby churches but found them spiritually lacking. In 1989, he started praying at home for sick people and in 1991 built a prayer hall on his own land. He also emphasizes prayer, healing, and personal testimony. His daily worship services include preaching and opportunities for personal healing. His style resembles that of a Hindu or Sikh Baba in his *dera*, except that he is Christian. He baptizes all who desire it when he considers them ready; by 2002 he had baptized about 2700 people.[84]

In Delhi, the newer charismatic and Evangelical churches, whether originating inside or outside the region, have proliferated almost beyond counting. Among the larger charismatic churches are the Assemblies of God with many well-established congregations in the city and the Pentecostal Church of India. The more Evangelical Delhi Bible Fellowship, founded in 1973 by some upper middle-class Christians, who felt that the existing churches suffered from a dearth of Bible teaching, is much smaller but well established and growing.[85]

[82] Baptism Register, Church of God [Renamed Evangelical Church of God in 1969]; Interview with Reginald Howell, 31 August 2005.

[83] Interview with Pastor Munir Masih, Hosanna Church, Dhariwal, 26 October 2003.

[84] This description is based upon a Sunday morning visit to Open Door Church on 27 October 2002 when fifty-five baptisms were performed; on interviews with Sant Harbhajan Singh and ten of those baptized that morning; and on his autobiographical tract, *True Story*.

[85] Interview with Rev. Devinder Verma, 27 September 2005.

The number of small, perhaps independent, house churches in the city changes from month to month. New Delhi also has a shrine of Our Lady of Health, Vailankanni,[86] close to Khan Market, started soon after independence by some working-class Tamil Catholics. One of them, Michael Anthony, brought a replica of Our Lady's statue from the south and installed it in a small hut of its own in the colony. (The colony was later demolished but the shrine was not.) From that small beginning it has become a much larger marble shrine in the Tamil temple architectural style. Most of the people who visit the shrine are south Indians and not all are Roman Catholics. Devotees of other faiths have also experienced healing through her and are among the many visitors to the shrine.[87]

Organizationally, the Christian Church in north-west India was not the same in 2000 as on 15 August 1947, when the missionary presence was highly conspicuous, ties with churches in West Pakistan were intact, and the major Protestant denominations together dominated the 'church scene'. Fifty years later, the foreign missionaries were almost completely gone, the churches were firmly in Indian hands, and all organizational ties with churches in Pakistan had long since been severed. An undetermined but large number of new, more independent and less connectional, Protestant churches had appeared on the scene. While no estimates are available concerning the relative numerical strength of the older and newer Protestant churches in the north-west, it is clear that the latter have grown rapidly, while the former may actually have declined. Add to that the growing Catholic presence in the region and the result has been a far wider diversity of 'Christianities' in the region than seemed imaginable back in 1947. Christianity thus exhibits a religious diversity similar to that long characteristic of the north-west Indian religious scene as a whole.

[86] Vailankanni is located on the Tamil Nadu coast near Nagapattnam. The miracles that led to the shrine being built there occurred in the late sixteenth and early seventeenth centuries. *Pilgrims Prayer Book Vailankanni*, 1981, pp. 4–10.

[87] Visits to the Shrine of Our Lady of Vailankanni, New Delhi, 18 and 20 August 2005; Interview with Rosemary Brown, daughter of Michael Anthony, 20 August 2005.

The Institutional Complex

Apart from the churches, the other major legacy from the missionary era was the large complex of Christian educational, medical, and other service institutions. The missionaries of the colonial era, in Cox's words, believed in 'the gospel of institutional presence'.[88] Many of their institutions had been the first and best of their kind in the towns and cities where they were located. However, since independence there has been a tremendous proliferation of public and private educational, medical, and service facilities in the region that has forced Christian institutions into playing much more modest roles than previously. The dreams of cultural influence through institutional presence entertained by earlier generations of missionaries simply had to be scaled down or redefined to be realistic in this changing environment.

Christian schools, colleges, and hospitals have held a special place in the minds and hearts of the Christian community. On the one hand, they have been the most visible symbols of the community's public presence and prestige. On the other, they have also been major employers of urban Christians and a major vehicle for their upward mobility. Yet, in this period they had to face the problem of 'authentic selfhood' just as the churches did. At one level, this required mustering the financial resources necessary to remain viable, when the churches were so poor and supporting funds from abroad were increasingly limited. At another it involved maintaining standards and 'the Christian character' of their institutions when there were so few qualified Christians in the region to provide adequate professional staff. At still another level it meant innovation to maintain or recover a 'pioneering' role in their respective fields of service. This section examines these struggles and transitions, first in the educational, then in the medical, and finally in some other service institutions run under Christian auspices.

---

[88] Jeffrey Cox, *Imperial Fault Lines*, p. 52.

EDUCATIONAL INSTITUTIONS

In 1947, each major Christian denominations had a network of village primary schools. Education beyond that level was confined, with rare exceptions, to urban schools, often with boarding facilities for rural students who wished to continue their education. At the apex of this pyramid were the Christian colleges with hostels for students coming from beyond commuting distance. These educational institutions were underwritten by a combination of government grants-in-aid, student fees, and subsidies or endowments from overseas mission societies. Virtually all were under Indian leadership. With few exceptions, Christian education above the primary level was oriented towards preparing students for urban rather than for rural life.

Partition threw these Christian educational institutions into temporary disarray. All schools and colleges were closed from as early as July 1947 until the end of February 1948;[89] in the interim many served as refugee camps. Muslim teachers and students left for Pakistan, creating staffing and enrolment problems. The medium of instruction had to change from Urdu to Hindi. Educational links to Punjab University in Lahore were transferred to a new Panjab University in India. The Avalon Girls' School in Pathankot lost not only its Muslim teachers and students but also most of its Christian students who had come as boarders from towns and villages now in West Punjab.

During the years following partition, Protestant leaders decided to close down their village schools and consolidate their educational efforts in a small number of urban schools, both for financial reasons and to avoid competition with the village primary schools that the government was setting up and Christians could attend anyway. Highly symbolic of this trend towards consolidation was the creation of United Christian Schools in Suranussi, near Jullundur. Presbyterians and Methodists began negotiation in the 1930s and officially registered the school in 1941. It began classes in 1943, and in 1948 moved to its enlarged Suranussi campus. Its boys' school,

---

[89] Satya M. Rai, *Punjab Since Partition*, p. 111.

girls' school, industrial training centre (1952), and residence halls brought together students from several struggling urban schools and numerous village schools.[90]

In 1962, a survey team undertook an evaluation of the educational institutions related to the UCNI. Of these, seven were located in north-west India: United Christian Schools in Suranussi, Milne Memorial Mission High School in Dhariwal, Avalon Girls' Higher Secondary School and Training Centre in Pathankot, the Church of Scotland Mission High School in Jammu, the Training School for Village Teachers at Moga, the Henderson Girls' Higher Secondary School as well as the Christian Higher Secondary and Basic Training School in Kharar. The team's descriptions of these schools as well as their recommendations offer considerable insight into the nature of Christian education in north-west India fifteen years after independence. In fact, there are four striking features shared by all seven schools.

The first is that their main purpose was to provide the children of the Christian community with access to a good Christian education. This meant, on the one hand, seeking the highest academic standards which the school and its students were capable of attaining and, on the other, providing Christian instruction, worship, and community life to Christian students. All the schools had a good percentage of Christians both as students and as teachers. This ranged from 62 per cent at the United Christian Schools down to 8 per cent of the student body at the Kharar Boys' School, and from 47 per cent at the Jammu School to 87.5 per cent of the teachers at Avalon. The schools were closely related to local churches, often providing almost the entire worshipping community.[91]

Secondly, none were elite schools. Their medium of instruction was Hindi or Punjabi and a good proportion of their students were rural Christians and other Dalits. Christian schools for the elite, with

---

[90] 'A Brief History of the UCI', *Golden Jubilee–1994 Anniversary Letter, United Christian Institute*, p. 5; *Report of Survey Evaluation of Twenty-Eight Schools and Colleges*, p. 167.

[91] *Report of the Survey Evaluation of Twenty-eight Schools and Colleges*, pp. 167–79, 189–239.

the exception of the Alexandra Girls' Higher Secondary School in Amritsar and the Tyndale-Biscoe School in Srinagar, were located either in hill stations or in Delhi. A third common feature was that all these schools were facing tight budgetary problems as they struggled to meet government requirements, maintain their physical plant, basic equipment, and scholarship assistance for (mostly rural) Christian students. Finally, while relationships with officials of the education department were considered good in all cases, the fact is that the government had forced the closing of Moga's Teacher Training Department, of Avalon's Junior Secondary Training Centre, and the training class at the Boys' School at Kharar, [92] thus effectively terminating the important role Christian schools had played in teacher training.

The major development in Protestant school education since the 1962 Survey has been the creation of a number of self-supporting and even income-generating English-medium schools for which the Green Revolution and its accompanying prosperity created a market. Among the first to open were the St. Thomas School in Jagadhri founded by the Rev. Doreen Riddel in 1966; the Ewing Christian English Medium School (renamed St. Thomas School when it moved to its own campus) at Ludhiana in 1971; the St. Thomas School which was added to the existing schools at what was renamed the United Christian Institute at Suranussi in 1972; and the Baring Public School in Batala in 1973. The elite Anglican and Roman Catholic schools originally founded in Simla for European children made a relatively smooth transition from European and Anglo-Indian to Indian, and even international, student bodies at the time of independence and partition.[93] All have greatly expanded their student bodies since that time.

[92] Ibid., pp. 197, 213, 230.

[93] This transition had begun, in most cases, well before 1947. Bishop Cotton School admitted its first Indian student in 1881 and, judging from a photograph of the 'Batch of 1912–13', St. Bede's College had Indian students from its earliest years. Auckland House School definitely had Indian students well before 1932, most probably admitted them in 1909, and may have admitted them earlier. 'A

The Roman Catholic Church did the most to increase the number of Christian schools throughout the region during this period. Like the early Protestant missionaries, they created schools in many of the places where they chose to organize parish churches. A good number of these were located in rural centres where Protestants had closed their schools. Catholic expansion in education is most evident in the Jullundur Diocese where prior to 1947 only four of their schools existed: Sacred Heart High School in Dalhousie, Sacred Heart Convent High School and St. Mary's High School in Amritsar, and St. Joseph's High School in Ferozpur Cantonment. Between 1947 and the creation of the Jullundur Diocese, six secondary and two primary schools were added. Afterwards, there was a veritable explosion in new school development: twenty-three in the 1970s, twenty-two in the 1980s, and thirty-seven schools as well as four vocational training centres in the 1990s. Of the fifty-one secondary schools in the diocese in 1999, thirty-eight were English medium (including some village schools); of the forty-four primary schools, twenty-eight used English as the medium of instruction while two others combined English with either Hindi or Punjabi.[94] At the close of the century, the Simla–Chandigarh Diocese had four senior secondary schools, twenty-six high schools, fourteen primary schools, and two technical training schools, while the Delhi Archdiocese had thirty-nine secondary schools, twelve primary schools, and seventeen nursery schools.[95] In the Jammu-Srinagar Diocese the number of schools increased from three in 1952, to four in 1978, to twenty in 1996.[96]

Brief History of Bishop Cotton School, Simla (1859)' in *Bishop Cotton School Shimla: An Introduction* (the School brochure); *St. Bede's College, Shimla: 100 Years of Education* (1992); Minutes of the Governors, Auckland House 30th March 1889–15th May 1958: Minutes of the 209th Meeting (2 November 1909) and Minutes of the 257th Meeting (18 June 1932). The Convent of Jesus and Mary also had Indian students in 1947, but the situation of St. Edwards School and the Loreto Convent School, Tara Hall, at that time is unclear from the sources available.

[94] *Diocese of Jalandhar Directory 1999*, pp. 107–30, 139–40.

[95] *Catholic Diocese of Simla-Chandigarh, Directory 2001*, pp. 63–70; *Delhi Catholic Directory, 2000*, pp. 173–81.

[96] *Diocese of Jammu-Srinagar India Directory 1996*, pp. 88–102.

The aim of all these new schools has been very similar to that attributed by Cox to the earlier Protestant schools: cultural influence through institutional presence, despite the paucity of Catholic teachers and students. All of them have emphasized value education, explicitly through the curriculum and implicitly through the school ethos. Two secondary purposes also seem to have undergirded this large investment in education. One is the uplift of the poor, and especially the Christian poor, through subsidized education. The other is helping to finance, within the limits set by law, both the subsidized education of the poor and the other social welfare work of the Church. Catholic schools, headed in almost every case by priests or nuns from outside the region, are very popular and meet a growing demand for quality English-language education.[97]

There have been four[98] Christian colleges on the Indian side of the border in the north-west. The oldest is St. Stephen's College in Delhi. From its inception in 1881 it has modelled itself on Cambridge University, seeking not only to provide a sound academic education but also to develop character worthy of a ruling elite through clubs, sports, tutorials, a close community life, and moral and religious instruction. After New Delhi became the capital of India, St. Stephen's drew its student body increasingly from the sons of government officials and products of elite boarding schools situated in hill stations.[99] In the years following partition this changed. Admissions became more competitive as Delhi's population increased and diversified. Enrolments increased and the proportion of hostel students decreased. Co-education was introduced in 1975. Academic standards rose but the college became more impersonal.[100] In 1967, the principal, 29 per cent of the faculty, as well as 13 per cent of the students were Christians; the college had a chaplain and there were

[97] Interview with Thomas Kunnunkul, 18 August 2005.

[98] There have been others that have opened and closed but these four, have continued. Only recently the Catholics opened Trinity College in Jullundur and the Salvation Army started Catherine Booth College for Girls in Batala.

[99] 'Mr. K.C. Nag at Seventy: St. Stephen's Through Four Decades', *The Stephanian* (Annual 1962–63), pp. 10–11.

[100] David Baker, 'St. Stephen's College, Delhi, 1881–1997', pp. 100–9.

classes on Christianity for Christian students.[101] By 1995, the student body had grown from 703 to 1158 and the faculty from forty-two to eighty; however, more students (26 per cent) and fewer faculty (11 per cent) were Christians; the chaplaincy and classes in Christianity have continued.[102]

In June 1980, Delhi University challenged St. Stephens' long-established admissions criteria and procedures. The case went to the Supreme Court, which in December 1991 found in favour of the college. It decided that the college was in fact a minority-run institution and, as such, was not bound by the university circulars concerning admissions. It also decided that 'the minority aided educational institutions are entitled to prefer their community candidates to maintain the minority character of their institutions', subject to conformity to university standards and to making available to others at least fifty per cent of the annual admissions.[103]

Because of its location and constituency, Baring Union Christian College in Batala stands in sharp contrast to St. Stephen's. Begun in 1881 as an Anglican boarding school for the sons of the north Indian Christian elite, it merged with two local day schools in 1934, became an intermediate college in 1944, and a degree college in 1948. In 1949, the Presbyterians, Methodists, and Quakers joined with the Anglicans to make it a union college. It has been co-educational and has drawn almost all its student body from the local population; in 1965–6, 58 per cent of them were urban but by 1975–6 58 per cent were rural. In only two of the intervening years did the number of students receiving fee concessions drop below 40 per cent and in two years it exceeded 50 per cent.[104] The number of Christian students reached 100 in 1971–2 and remained fairly constant after that, being 6.4 per

---

[101] Richard Dickinson and Nancy Dickinson, *Directory of Information for Christian Colleges in India*, pp. 49–50.

[102] Mani Jacob (compiler and editor), *Directory of Church-Related Colleges in India*, pp. 42–3.

[103] John Vallamattan and Mani Jacob (compilers and editors), the entire verdict is reproduced in *Judgments on Minority Rights. Volume I Supreme Court of India 1951–95*, pp. 794–867. The quotation is on p. 835.

[104] Vinod K. Khiyalie, *Hundred Years of Baring's Mission to Batala*, p. 79.

cent of the student body in 1995 and 6 per cent in 2001, while the proportion of Christian teachers dropped gradually from 37.1 per cent in 1963 to 15.4 per cent in 2001.[105] The college had a regular chaplain and Bible classes for Christian students through the 1970s.

Following a Christian–Sikh religious dialogue at the college in October 1963, the principal, Dr Ram Singh, created the Christian Institute of Sikh Studies in 1966 to continue such dialogues, to foster research on Sikhism, and to educate the Christian Church on the religion of the now dominant Sikhs. Dialogues at the institute set a tone in engaged religious discussion,[106] stimulated some serious reflection about the role of modern critical scholarship in religious studies,[107] and encouraged Christians to re-examine their own faith in the changed context of a Sikh-dominated Punjab. Following Operation Bluestar, when terrorism was rampant in the area around Batala, interfaith dialogue was curtailed and the management renamed the institute, the Christian Institute of Religious Studies.

The Congregation of the Religious of Jesus and Mary established two Roman Catholic colleges for women in the north-west. The first was St. Bede's in Simla, which opened up a teacher-training college in 1904 with fifteen students to meet the growing demand for school teachers. Originally intended for Christian students, it opened its doors to other students and began undergraduate classes only after independence. Enrolments increased from 125 undergraduates and twenty teacher trainees in 1967 to a total of 1300 students in 2001. Half of the teacher trainees are Christians, but few of the under-graduates or faculty are Christians.[108] Jesus and Mary College in New

---

[105] Ibid., pp. 79, 84; Reny Jacob and Carolyne John (compilers and editors), *Directory of Church-Related Colleges in India*, p. 250.

[106] Reports of these dialogues are given in the *Bulletin of the Christian Institute of Sikh Studies*, which began publication in January 1972.

[107] This was provoked in good part by the publication of W.H. McLeod's *Guru Nanak and the Sikh Religion*. McLeod taught at Baring Union Christian College from 1965 to 1969 and was director of the institute his final year there.

[108] Richard Dickinson and Nancy Dickinson, *Directory of Information for Christian Colleges in India*, pp. 57–8; Reny Jacob and Carolyne John (compliers and editors), *Directory of Church-Related Colleges in India*, pp. 50–51; 'Hundred Years of St. Bede's

Delhi was begun only in 1968 with less than 150 students; it had 450 in 1979 and 2510 in 2001 studying arts and commerce. As a matter of policy it admits an increasingly high proportion of Christians (20.4 per cent in 1995, 24.1 per cent in 2001, and 29 per cent in 2004–5) for whom it has worship, special classes, assemblies, and retreats.[109] While located in quite different settings, the two colleges have shared the common purpose of empowering women students, through both academics and a wide range of extracurricular activities, to move out of a relatively sheltered girlhood into the modern job market with social skills and self-confidence. In addition, both have shared a commitment to empowering the poor through their admissions and financial-aid policies as well as in their social service projects. One sister was particularly pleased at their success in creating an atmosphere within the colleges in which differences between the rich and the poor are obliterated as much as possible.[110]

MEDICAL INSTITUTIONS

There were eighteen Christian hospitals of varying sizes in north–west India in 1947. Of these, four were in Kashmir, four in what became Himachal Pradesh, two in Haryana, one in Delhi, and the remaining seven in the Punjab. They ranged in size from the large hospital connected with the Women's Christian Medical College in Ludhiana to the small rural hospitals at Asrapur in Amritsar district and Manali in the Kulu Valley. About two-thirds of them were started as zenana hospitals for women and children, but during this period all of them either closed down or became general hospitals. In 1947, virtually all of their medical superintendents, as well as their head nurses or nursing superintendents, were foreign missionaries. One

---

College, Simla,' in *St. Bede's College, Shimla: 100 Years of Education*; Interview with Sister Melba Rodrigues, 10 September 2005.

[109] *Jesus and Mary College Handbook 2005*; Reny Jacob and Carolyne John (compilers and editors), *Directory of Church-Related Colleges in India*, pp. 39–40; Interview with Mrs Sylvia Lal, 24 August 2005; Interview with Sister Jovita, 24 August 2005.

[110] Sister Jovita emphasized this in her interview on 24 August 2005.

of them, the CMS general hospital in Srinagar, was taken back by the Kashmir government in 1948.[111]

Once the partition riots had subsided and medical assistance to refugees was no longer at crisis levels, Christian hospitals faced some long-term challenges. One was the replacement of foreign missionary with Indian Christian professional staff. However, the most apparent and the most enduring need was financial. The older hospitals had buildings requiring either major repairs or replacement. All had equipment to be replaced and expensive, new medical technology to purchase, usually from overseas, if acceptable standards of medical care were to be maintained. The costs of medicines, X-rays, common surgical procedures, and salaries constantly rose, even if the patients' capacity to pay did not. The financial crisis provoked much soul-searching about the fundamental purposes and priorities of these expensive institutions. In January 1966, a young medical missionary sent from Canada to the Maple Leaf Hospital in Kangra wrote a letter to his bishop in which he described the long-term financial drain of maintaining 'the general Christian witness of subsidized medicine' in an area considered 'backward'. His problem concerned the very purpose of such a hospital, given the fact that it had had no noticeable impact upon the religious thinking of the people in the area over the half century it had been there. Was he there simply to hand over the hospital to the Indian Church and to Christian doctors, or to serve a philanthropic institution helping people until such time as other indigenous hospitals inevitably arose to meet local medical needs, or was he to offer the 'bait' of medical care for an evangelistic mission aimed at individual conversions?[112]

Those were not the only possibilities under consideration as medical personnel and church leaders faced harsh financial realities. In 1950, after Dr E.R.B. Snow had left to become principal of Women's Christian Medical College in Ludhiana, the diocese decided to close down the aging St. Catherine's hospital in Amritsar. The underlying rationale was that the limited medical resources at their

---

[111] C.R.H. Wilkinson, Letter to L.A. Dixon, 23 July 1952.
[112] R. Bradley, Letter to the Rt. Rev. K.D.W. Anand, January 1966.

disposal should be integrated more closely with the other work the Church was doing. They, therefore, chose to focus on rural as well as preventative medicine in an area where there was already a sizable and growing Christian population. They selected Tarn Taran, upgraded the small hospital there to forty beds, and engaged in public health work in the surrounding villages.[113] On the other hand, in 1958, the same diocese rebuilt the rundown Maple Leaf Hospital in Kangra, where there was only a small Christian population.[114] The difference would seem to be that the medical needs of women in Amritsar were being met by other hospitals there, whereas in Kangra only the Maple Leaf hospital was meeting the area's medical needs.[115]

Perhaps the best way to gain insight into the changing Christian medical picture is to examine in somewhat greater detail the recent history of two major medical institutions. The Women's Christian Medical College in Ludhiana was founded in 1894 to train Christian women for service in mission hospitals. The hospital attached to it first admitted men during the partition riots of 1947.[116] Four major interrelated themes run through the minutes of its governing body since then: upgrading, Indianization of senior medical staff, maintaining the Christian character of the institution in the face of government requirements, and, underlying all of them, finance. By 1951, it had become clear that the college had to upgrade from the licentiate to the MBBS standard or close down. The estimated cost of this was Rs 5,000,000, half of which would come from government sources and half from the cooperating missions. The college had to meet certain government requirements to get government funds. It would become co-educational and change its name to Christian Medical College. At least half of its students would be from the Punjab and at least a quarter from the rest of India. It would have

---

[113] Findings and Recommendations of Amritsar Sub-Committee, St. Catherine's—December 1950; C.R.H. Wilkinson, Letter to L.A. Dixon, 30 March 1951; Heber Wilkinson, *Thirst of India*, p. 59.

[114] 'In India—Diocese of Amritsar', *M.S.C.C. Popular Report—1958*, p. 18.

[115] Reports from the hospital at that time mention serving patients from as far away as Palampur and Dharamsala.

[116] Forrest C. Eggleston, *Where is God Not? An American Surgeon in India*, p. 66.

two representatives of the Punjab government, two from the Government of India, and the chief nursing superintendent, Government of India, on its governing body.[117] The Punjab government also insisted that it be run on non-communal, non-sectarian lines and both parties agreed that 'no compulsory instruction or preaching in any religion will be given in the Institution.'[118] Rajkumari Amrit Kaur who, as Union health minister, had played a key role in the upgrading, laid the foundation stone for a new hospital building in 1954. In 1973, the School of Nursing was upgraded to a College of Nursing offering a B.Sc. nursing degree; in 1985, M.Sc. classes in nursing were started. In 1991, a dental college was opened.

Along with upgrading went the Indianization, and north Indianization,[119] of the senior medical staff, almost all of whom were foreigners during the 1940s and 1950s. In 1962, the governing body still saw Christian Medical College as a place where missionaries could fulfil their professional and Christian vocations,[120] but in 1969, a study committee recommended that the college move towards Indianization gradually and at all levels; foreigners should now remain only as long as the institution required them.[121] The first Indian director of the college and hospital was Dr K.N. Nambudripad, who was confirmed in 1975 and served until 1982.[122] His successor, Dr Forrest C. Eggleston, who served from 1982 to 1986, was the last missionary director.

Throughout this period the college sought to be true to its founding purpose of training Christian medical personnel for work in Christian hospitals, especially in north India. To that end the

[117] Women's Christian Medical College, Ludhiana, Governing Body Minutes Vol. I, Special Meeting of 12 January 1951; Christian Medical College, Ludhiana, Governing Body Minutes Vol. I, Special Meeting of 15 November 1951.

[118] Ibid., 33rd Annual Meeting 3 June 1953; 34th Annual Meeting 27 April 1954.

[119] The transfer of responsibility to Indians in general and to north Indians in particular is discussed in some detail by Ernest B. Chander, *Trishul to Trinity*. See also Kenneth M. Scott, *Around the World in Eighty Years*, p. 212.

[120] Christian Medical College, Ludhiana, Governing Body Minutes Vol. III, Meeting of 27 October 1962.

[121] Ibid., Meeting of 19 and 20 November 1969.

[122] Ibid., Vol. IV, Meeting of 22 August 1975 and 17 and 18 August 1982.

governing body sought to retain control over admissions and appointments in the face of government pressures and university regulations, to which it was especially vulnerable in times of financial strain.[123] These pressures led first, in 1962, to its setting a minimum of 25 per cent Christian MBBS admissions[124] and then to creating quotas within the original quotas. Candidates sponsored by member organizations of the CMC Society were required to spend the first two years after receiving their MBBS degree in a hospital either run or designated by their sponsoring organization.[125] By the end of the 1980s the college was forced to pursue several court cases, alone or in conjunction with other prestigious minority institutions, in order to protect their right to select their own staff and students, as they had when first upgraded to the MBBS standard.[126] Internally, the governing body sought to maintain the Christian character of the institution by providing for Christian worship and pastoral care within both the college and the hospital through its chaplaincy office.

Holy Family Hospital in New Delhi was begun through an arrangement between the Delhi Archdiocese and the Medical Mission Sisters who began arriving from the USA in 1950 while the hospital was being built. It was opened to outpatients in 1954 and to in-patients in 1955, with a major emphasis upon not only the care of women

---

[123] Ibid., Vol. III, Meeting of 18 and 19 November 1970.

[124] Ibid., Meeting of 17 October 1962.

[125] Ibid., Meeting of 7 and 8 March 1984. In 1988, non-sponsored candidates had to sign service agreements to serve two years in rural, peripheral/institutionally needy areas or in mission hospitals. Meeting of 11 March 1988. These service obligations were increased to three years in 1994. Ibid., Meeting of 9 and 10 March 1994.

[126] Ibid., Meeting of 22 and 23 September 1989. Soon afterwards, the governing body decided to decline a Rs 800,000 government grant in order to retain its independence. Ibid. Meeting of 20 January 1990. It was also a party to the Supreme Court of India Civil Appellate Jurisdiction (Civil Appeal No. 5031 of 2005) case in which the Court decided on 12 August 2005 not only that the government could not impose reservations or quotas upon private unaided institutions, but also that minority institutions are free to admit students of their own choice and could set their own fee structures. [Christian Medical College supplied the author with a copy of this decision.]

and children but also community health. In 1956, it added nurses training and later training for laboratory and X-ray technicians. By 1971, the hospital had 130 beds and today it has 300. It also offers its patients a choice of modern allopathic, traditional ayurvedic, and homeopathic treatments. The hospital has been run on American lines with a trained hospital administrator rather than a doctor as its head. The Medical Mission Sisters handed over first the administrative leadership (1972) and then (1979–84) the management of the hospital to Indians. The last overseas staff member left in 1995. In 1991, the Archdiocese took over management from what had been for seven years an essentially independent board. Like the Protestant hospitals, Holy Family has had to struggle continuously with the competing claims of providing the very best possible medical care using the latest technology, of service to the poor, and of financial viability.[127]

Holy Family Hospital is symbolic of a major and relatively recent Roman Catholic commitment to medical care. Prior to 1947 the only Catholic hospital in the region was the hospital in Baramullah that had been attacked by Pakistani tribesmen in 1947. In the Jullundur Diocese the first hospital was established only in 1973, but by the end of the century there were five, ranging in size from twelve to 150 beds, all of which were run by nuns. In addition to these hospitals they set up twenty-three dispensaries, all but two of which had women in charge.[128] Each hospital had rural health teams serving the surrounding villages and the diocesan mobile catechetical team included a nurse.[129] The Simla-Chandigarh Diocese has one hospital and ten dispensaries,[130] the Jammu-Srinagar Diocese has two hospitals as well as a health centre and nine dispensaries,[131] while the Delhi Archdiocese has five hospitals as well as two hospices and twelve maternity homes and dispensaries.[132]

[127] *Delhi Catholic Directory 2000*, p. 200; Interview with Mr Edward David, associate director, 18 August 2005.

[128] *Diocese of Jalandhar Directory 1999*, pp. 133–8.

[129] Fr. George Cheruvil (ed.), *Christward*, pp. 29–30, 86–97.

[130] *Catholic Diocese of Simla-Chandigarh Directory – 2001*, pp. 72–3.

[131] *Diocese of Jammu-Srinagar India Directory 1996*, pp. 106–8.

[132] *Delhi Catholic Directory 2000*, pp. 183–6.

The foregoing analysis suggests that in medicine, as in education, a general consolidation of older Protestant institutions combined with the creation of new Catholic institutions in the region. For the former it was a matter of weighing viability over against a continuing witness not so much of subsidized as of compassionate and competent medical care. For the latter, as with the Protestants before them, medical mission complemented an expanded educational and evangelistic mission to the whole person rather than just to the mind or soul.

OTHER SERVICE INSTITUTIONS

When, however, one turns from education and medicine to other forms of institutionally based social service, one finds proliferation and diversification, as both Protestants and Catholics responded to the changing circumstances and needs of the times. This was most obvious in Delhi which, as India's capital city, became the headquarters for many Christian organizations. In addition, there were church-sponsored projects that produced a large number of small institutions of their own. For example, by the end of the century, the Archdiocese of Delhi had not only schools and hospitals under its management but also community centres, social service centres, a media centre, a book centre, a library, a variety of vocational training centres, employment bureaus, homes and orphanages for children, crèches and day care centres, hostels for working women, several regular publications, and a printing press.[133] According to a 1975 development plan, the first three guiding principles for this expansion were: 'The emphasis in all our projects is to help people help themselves. 2. The poor have a special priority among the people we serve. 3. The discovery of the real and felt needs of the people is the beginning and basis of the projects.'[134]

The New Delhi YMCA, started in 1927, has moved into a wide range of service and educational activities, beginning with refugee

---

[133] *Delhi Catholic Directory 2000*, pp. 169–203.

[134] Archbishop Angelo Fernandes, 'Delhi in the Sixties and Seventies: Church in Action', Mimeographed, 1975, p. 2.

relief and social service training during partition. It began development work in Jhugistan, a coolie camp in New Delhi, in the 1950s, and established major development centres in Nizamuddin East and at Hondal in Haryana during the 1970s. It also created an Institute of Management Studies, Institute of Secretarial Services, and Institute of Civil Services in the heart of New Delhi.[135] In like manner, the YMCA in Chandigarh, begun in 1954 with a hostel and recreational programme, has expanded into training programmes as well as social service and development projects.[136]

The Indian Social Institute, which the Jesuits moved to New Delhi from Pune in the 1960s, began its work within a social work/social welfare framework of national development similar to that of the YMCA, but with a strong study component. However, when it saw development strengthening the unjust structures of society during the 1970s, it began to focus attention upon the underprivileged and redefine priorities in terms of contributing through research, training, and extension programmes 'to the process of social change through the creation and strengthening of people's organizations', especially those of the economically and socially exploited.[137] Starting in the early 1980s they concentrated upon Dalits, Tribals, women, most backward castes, and minorities in their action research, training programmes, documentation, publication, networking, and advocacy efforts. More recently they have added such categories of people as bonded labourers and domestic workers as well.[138]

Christians have also created important institutions within the region to meet the specific needs of the Christian churches and community nationwide. For example, the Indian Society for Pro-

---

[135] Mark S. Clive (compiler), *Towards the Mission: A Monograph of New Delhi YMCA's Vision, Commitment & Achievements 1927–1997.*

[136] YMCA National Survey Commission, *Survey of the YMCAs of India 1966–1968,* New Delhi: The National Council of YMCAs of India, 1968, p. 40; Interview with Arvind Noel, 29 October 2003.

[137] 'Indian Social Institute through the Fifty Years', *Indian Social Institute Golden Jubilee,* p. 39.

[138] Ibid., pp. 35–67; *Indian Social Institute Annual Report 2004–2005; Indian Social Institute Brochure 2004–2005.*

moting Christian Knowledge (ISPCK), set up in 1935, concentrated upon bookstores and publishing Anglican books for worship in Indian languages.[139] However, with the appointment of James Massey as general secretary in 1985 it soon grew to become India's leading Christian publishing house. Sales quadrupled between 1985 and 1991,[140] and publications diversified greatly in response to new demands in theological education and within the churches. This trend has continued and made the ISPCK both financially independent and capable of providing book grants for theological students and pastors.[141]

Two important institutions for the training of clergy and Christian workers are also located in Delhi. St. Mary's College, founded by the Jesuits in 1889, moved to Delhi in 1972 and changed its name to Vidyajyoti. It also opened its student body to non-Jesuits in 1974 and to women in 1976. It has become a major centre of theological research, publishing its own theological journal and building relationships with the universities and research institutes of the city.[142] The Delhi Bible Institute was founded in 1954 and built Bible Bhavan in 1964 to provide short-term training opportunities for evangelists and church workers through conventions, radio, correspondence courses, literature, and residential courses ranging from one week to one year in length. By training a large number of young men and women (an estimated 3300 between 1984 and 2004 alone), they have both helped to lead and to resource much of the recent expansion of Evangelical and charismatic churches throughout north India.[143]

The missionary commitment to a strong institutional presence did not vanish from the north-west when the missionaries left. The

[139] Victor Koilpillai, *The SPCK in India 1710–1985*, pp. 45–60.

[140] Indian Society for Promoting Christian Knowledge, *Triennial Report 1989–1990–1991*, p. 14.

[141] Indian SPCK General Secretary's Report (1998–1999–2000), pp. 7, 13.

[142] *Vidyajyoti College of Theology Handbook and Calendar 2005–2006*, pp. 2–3; G. Gispert-Sauch SJ, 'A Century of Theology Part II: The Delhi Period', *Centenary Souvenir 1889–1989*, Delhi: Vidyajyoti Institute of Religious Studies, 1989, pp. 13–7.

[143] The Delhi Bible Institute published two booklets on the occasion of their golden anniversary in 2004, both entitled *Standing Steadfast for the Word*; Interview with the Rev. Isaac Shaw, executive director, 26 September 2005.

preceding pages suggest that Christians in the region have carried that commitment forward by making significant changes in the institutions they have inherited and by creating new ones to address the changed circumstances and perceived needs of the post-independence Christian Church, Christian community, and Indian society. In addition to the older Evangelicalism, which has continued to exercise a strong influence throughout this period, two more recently developed Christian theologies seem to have undergirded and guided these institutional adjustments and innovations. The first was a 'Christian Participation in Nation-Building' theology which sought to develop 'a Christian understanding of certain crucial issues in the political, economic, and social development of modern India', to make a Christian contribution to the cultural foundations of this new India, and to rethink the Church's life, mission, and service in the light of this.[144] The other was liberation theology and its Indian variant, Dalit theology, which employs a conflict rather than developmental model of society, views salvation in terms of liberation from systemic oppression, and gives priority to the claims of the oppressed upon the Church.

The Christian Community

Finally, there are the Christian people of north-west India themselves to consider. What has happened to them since independence and the disruptions of partition? Part of their story has already been told and the context for the rest of it has been provided in the opening section of this chapter. This section attempts to round out their story by offering first a social profile of the Christian community during this period, then a description of some of its struggles, particularly in relation to the wider society, and finally a look at its inner religious life, as seen in congregational as well as broader Indian and global Church settings.

---

[144] P.D. Devanandan and M.M. Thomas (eds), *Christian Participation in Nation-Building*, pp. vi–vii. Its most direct impact on Christian institutions can be seen in *The Christian College and National Development*.

SOCIAL PROFILE

In the volumes on the Punjab, Haryana, Himachal Pradesh, and Delhi in its *People of India* series the Anthropological Survey of India depicted Christians as a caste-like community, in many respects functioning like a caste in a caste-based society, even though the Survey recognized its defining characteristic to be religion rather than caste.[145] In these brief anthropological profiles Christians are described as denominationally and occupationally diverse, speaking local languages and eating locally available food. They marry within the community, although exceptions do exist, and marriage alliances are based, with relatively few exceptions, on such class criteria as education, income, and occupation rather than on caste. Dowry is not practised but gifts are given, and widow remarriage is permitted with a full marriage ceremony. The dead are generally buried. The Punjab and Haryana volumes describe the Christian family as patriarchal with women clearly subordinate to men, while the Delhi and Himachal Pradesh volumes describe women as enjoying virtual parity with men.[146]

This description is important because it highlights not only the fact that anthropologists, as well as others,[147] view the Christian community through a caste lens but also through the caste-like ways in which the community behaves. What the description omits are some of the important changes the Christian community has undergone over the past half century, a few key indicators of which are found in the religion tables of the decennial Census of India. The most obvious of these changes has been the Christian

[145] There is no separate entry on Christians in the volume on Jammu and Kashmir.

[146] Virinder Singh, 'Christians', in K.S. Singh (ed.), *People of India, Volume XXXVII: Punjab*, pp. 147–52; B.K. Nagla and J. Prasad, 'Christians', in ibid. *Volume XXIII: Haryana*, pp. 126–31; T.K. Ghosh, 'Christians', in ibid. *Volume XX: Delhi*, pp. 143–8; Vatsala Sarkar, 'Christians', in ibid. *Volume XXIV: Himachal Pradesh*, pp. 158–62.

[147] Philip Dayal takes note of this in his study of social interaction between Christians and members of other communities in 'Level of Social Integration of Ethnic Minorities: A Case Study of the Christians of Gurdaspur District in the Punjab', pp. 106, 292.

Table 6.3: Growth of the Christian Population of North-west India, 1971–2001

State	Christian Population 2001	Percentage Growth Since 1971	Percentage Growth of State Population Since 1971
Haryana	27,185	177.3	110.7
Himachal Pradesh	7,687	116.2	75.6
Punjab	292,800	80.5	79.8
Jammu & Kashmir	20,299	182.6	119.7
Chandigarh	7,627	204.6	250.1
Delhi	130,319	198.1	240.7
Region as a Whole	485,917	112.2	112.4

Source: Religion Tables of the 1971 and 2001 Census of India.

community's growth in size, paralleling the growth of the population as a whole. Table 6.3 shows that, while there are variations within the region, both the Christian and the general population more than doubled in size, and grew at almost exactly the same rate, in the years between 1971 and 2001.

Another change recorded in the 2001 Census is enormous growth in literacy in all sectors of society, with both general literacy and female literacy among Christians being well above the state average everywhere except in the Punjab (Table 6.4). Nazir Masih argued in 1991 that the closing of village schools and consolidation of educational work in urban institutions during the 1950s and 1960s had led to increased illiteracy within the Punjabi Christian community. He cited as evidence a Chandigarh Diocese survey, which put the Christian literacy rate at 15 per cent, and another survey in Dhariwal, which found that within a two-kilometre radius of their school 96 per cent of the Hindu children, 87 per cent of the Sikh children, but only 65 per cent of the Christian children were attending school.[148] The most recent study, Dogar's 1993 survey of 750 rural Christian families in Punjab (550), Haryana (100), Himachal Pradesh

[148] Nazir Masih, 'Education and Development of Punjabi Christians', pp. 47–50.

Table 6.4: General and Female Literacy Rates for the Total Population and for
Christians in North-west India, 2001

State	General Literacy (%)		Female Literacy (%)	
	Total Population	Christians	Total Population	Christians
Himachal Pradesh	47.4	66.2	36.5	52.3
Jammu & Kashmir	66.5	72.2	59.0	68.8
Punjab	60.6	45.8	55.5	39.5
Haryana	57.2	74.8	47.2	71.7
Chandigarh	71.4	77.8	66.2	74.7
Delhi	69.8	83.2	63.5	81.8
Region as a Whole	60.2	59.2	52.5	55.0

Source: Religion Tables of the 2001 Census.

(50), and Jammu & Kashmir (50), put the literacy rate of rural
Christians throughout north-west India at 46 per cent.[149] According
to the 2001 Census, the literacy rate for rural Christians in the Punjab
was 40.4 per cent, as opposed to 83.3 per cent for urban Christians,
thus illustrating the enormous disparity between them.[150]

There was a less dramatic change in the sex ratio. Back in 1941 it
had been a very low 845 women per 1000 men for the region and 856
women per 1000 men for the Christians within the region. The sex
ratio has continued to be low in the entire north-west, but has
improved in the years following independence (867 in 1971 and 869
in 2001 for the population as a whole, and 895 in 1971 and 924 in
2001 for the Christians). The improvement in the Christian sex ratio
was not uniform throughout the region; in 2001, their lowest sex
ratio was in Jammu and Kashmir (594) and the highest was in Delhi
(1076).[151]

[149] Vidya Sagar J. Dogar, *Rural Christian Community in Northwest India*, pp. 49,
102.

[150] The literacy rates for rural Christians in the other three states were markedly
better: 61.8 per cent in Jammu and Kashmir, 64.3 per cent in Himachal Pradesh,
and 63.8 per cent in Haryana. *Census of India 2001. India: The First Report on Religion
Data*, pp. 13–15, 25–7.

[151] *Census of India 1971. Series I: India, Paper 2 of 1972: Religion*, pp. 42–5, 60–3,
78–9; *Census of India 2001. India: The First Report on Religion Data*, pp. 1–3.

This sex ratio data should be read in conjunction with the female literacy data given in Table 6.4 as well as the data on the percentage of women in the urban workforce provided in Table 6.5, as all three have been used as important indicators of the status of women. Table 6.5 shows that the proportion of Christian women in the urban workforce at least doubles the state averages everywhere except in the Punjab where it exceeds the state average by more than 40 per cent. Taken together these three indicators suggest that Christian women within the region continue to have a somewhat higher status than do women in the north-west generally. These census figures and their implications are reinforced by Jane Caleb's survey of 307 members of the various women's fellowships throughout the Delhi Diocese of the CNI. Both their literacy rate (90.4 per cent with 35.8 per cent college educated) and their participation in the workforce (36.8 per cent and 41.5 per cent in full-time jobs in Delhi and Haryana respectively) were much higher than the census figures.[152] More to the point, the survey showed that Christian parents were offering equal opportunities and responsibilities to their sons and daughters. 'People, particularly girls, are valued in economic terms. Christians see with their own eyes that Christian girls can earn for themselves and even support their parents just as well as their boys and this makes them interested in their development.'[153] In fact, the survey indicated that the respondents saw giving girls equal status to boys as a distinguishing mark of the Christian community. 'As one respondent wrote in answer to the question, "In what way does your Christian faith influence your life?"—"I feel good within to be a Christian specially when I see other women, Hindu, Muslim, etc."'[154]

The other social indicator highlighted by the census, mentioned earlier in Table 6.2, concerns the relative urbanization of the Christian community which rose from an estimated 11 per cent in 1931 to 36.3 per cent in 1971 and 50.9 per cent in 2001. With urbanization has come increased diversification of occupation and decreased economic dependence upon the Church and its institutions, as several micro studies of Christians within the region have shown. As early as 1960,

[152] Jane R. Caleb, *Women in the CNI Diocese of Delhi*, pp. 22–3, 39–41.
[153] Ibid., p. 36.
[154] Ibid., p. 74.

Table 6.5: Percentage of Urban Women Workers and of
Urban Christian Women Workers, 2001

State	Urban Women Workers	Urban Christian Women Workers
Jammu & Kashmir	10.4	22.5
Himachal Pradesh	15.2	54.4
Punjab	10.4	14.9
Haryana	10.6	22.5
Chandigarh	14.5	30.8
Delhi	9.3	36.5
Region as a Whole	10.2	27.8

Source: Religion Tables of the 2001 Census.

Campbell found in one village close to Jullundur only three Christians working for the village landlords while twenty-one worked in the city, five had other skilled jobs, thirteen had semi-skilled jobs, three were in business, one owned land and another was a school teacher.[155] Of the thirty-seven members of the Jullundur city church, six were part-time or apprentice labour, eight were industrial labourers, three were sanitary workers, four were clerks, three were carpenters or masons, four were teachers, two were professors, four were businessmen and three were administrators.[156] As this list of occupations indicates, the proportion of urban Christians who had become economically independent of the Church was very high. Twenty years later, Dayal found a similar economic diversity among the Christians of Batala, virtually all of whom are Dalits.[157] The Anthropological Survey for Delhi also saw considerable occupational diversity, obviously independent of Church employment.[158] In Jagadhri, where one would expect virtually all of the Christians to be employed in the local Christian hospital and school, many of the

---

[155] Ibid., p. 37.

[156] Ibid., p. 77–8.

[157] Philip Dayal, 'Level of Social Integration of Ethnic Minorities', pp. 94–5.

[158] T.K. Ghosh, 'Christians,' in K.S. Singh (ed.), *People of India, Volume XX*, pp. 145–6.

men work in the steel, sugar, plywood, and paper mills, while the women work as domestic servants.[159]

A third social profile of the Christian community is provided by Dogar's survey of rural Christians across the region. He found that a full 85 per cent of the interviewees were fourth- of fifth- generation Christians and three-quarters of them lived in nuclear families.[160] While virtually all owned their own houses, most of them lived in poverty; 56.43 per cent ate only simple *dal* with either rice or *roti* and only about 17 per cent could afford to eat meat once or twice a month.[161] Nearly three-quarters were employed as labourers, about half of them being casual labour, and only 6.15 per cent as skilled labour. The others worked in institutions, had small jobs or were self-employed in occupations ranging from shopkeeper or mechanic to self-supporting clergy.[162] Just over half of the children in these families went to school, while the rest were a source of child labour either inside or outside the home.[163] Only about a third of the families reported experiencing upward occupational mobility since their first ancestor converted to Christianity around a century ago; 5.57 per cent had experienced downward mobility and the rest had experienced no mobility at all.[164] Clearly those rural families, which were already part of the urban workforce, have had the most opportunities for occupational mobility.

A series of snapshots of various parts of the Christian community at different moments during the past half century help to fill out the picture provided by this statistical data and highlight sub-regional differences. In 1975, Bishop Ernest John reported meeting with two Christian families in Kargil, four in Kalaze, twenty in Leh, and six in

[159] Interview with Rev. George Lazar, 21 September 2005.

[160] Vidya Sagar J. Dogar, *Rural Christian Community in Northwest India*, pp. 54, 58–9. There appears to be a serious misprint in the numbers of families in the table he provides, but the percentage makes sense.

[161] Ibid., pp. 60, 62. He put the percentage of those in poverty at 80.28 per cent. Ibid., pp. 90–1.

[162] Ibid., pp. 69, 71.

[163] Ibid., pp. 78–9. He puts the percentage of actual child labour at 20.19 per cent.

[164] Ibid., p. 83.

Shey on his visit to Ladakh. All he described as prosperous and some held good positions, especially in Leh, even though the Christian community was very small.[165] Fifteen years later, Bishop Anand Chandu Lal described the Christian community in Srinagar as comprised of 'Kashmiris, Maharashtrians, Punjabis and individuals from different parts of the country'.[166] Very few of the Christians there or elsewhere in Kashmir are actually Kashmiris.[167] By way of contrast, Christians in Jammu have been overwhelmingly local Dalits, among whom are individuals who have experienced considerable upward mobility.[168] In Himachal Pradesh the picture is mixed. In places like Kangra, Manali, and Dalhousie the Christian community consists almost entirely of employees of local Christian institutions and retirees. In Simla, Christians historically have been seasonal employees from outside, along with some resident staff of Christian institutions and government offices. In Chamba, Ani, and Kotgarh the Christians are local people.

In Haryana two sites are particularly worth mentioning. One is Jagadhri, the former headquarters of the New Zealand Presbyterian mission, which has one of the largest Christian populations in the state. There is a Christian middle class, many of them from out of state and concentrated in the Christian hospital and English-medium school, as well as a Christian working class, many of whom are resident in the Christian colony of Isapur and work in local factories. Christ Church (CNI) has helped to bridge the gap between the two not only through shared worship and community events but also through a growing scholarship programme which now helps subsidize the education of about twenty-five students per year.[169] The other is the Christian village of Santokh Majra. Since the land was handed over to the tenants in 1946, the village has witnessed not

---

[165] Ernest John, 'Episcopal Commissary for the Diocese of Amritsar Visits Ladakh', *NIC* (November 1975), pp. 11–12.

[166] Anand Chandu Lal, 'The Kashmir Diary', ibid. (April 1990), p. 5.

[167] Interview with Deacon Jacob Joseph Gill, 27 August 2005.

[168] Esther William, 'Jammu–Its Christian Community–A Background', *NIC* (October 1987), p. 16.

[169] Interview with Rev. George Lazar, 21 September 2005.

only significant urban migration and resultant land sales to outsiders, but also increased class differentiation among the Christians who continue to live there. Of the 150 Christian families who still remain, about twenty own around five acres of land each, down from about fifty in 1967, while the rest work as labourers.[170]

In carrying out field research on the Protestant churches in Delhi in 1959 and 1960, Alter and Jai Singh found both descendants of the converts described in earlier chapters of this history and migrants from elsewhere in India. Some lived in government housing, some in a few small Christian bastis, but most were scattered throughout the city. Their data indicated that about one-third of the Christians were poor, facing constant problems of unemployment and underemployment. About 15 per cent were well-off and the remaining half were in the middle, working as skilled or white collar labour. Alter and Jai Singh noted that 'the strongest single force in the lives of most Delhi Christians appears to be the desire to get ahead, economically and socially'.[171] They also found a strong community consciousness, which was expressed in terms of considerable social mixing among Christians and of helping one another out in times of need.[172]

In one of the oldest Christian bastis near Turkman Gate, there were sixteen families and six widows or ninety people in all, most of whom were in the lowest income category, living in eighteen small residential quarters. Some of the old biradari practices like marrying outside the basti (since all living there were considered to be related) continued, but the authority of the biradari and parish priest were on the decline.[173] Forty years later, two major changes had taken

---

[170] This paragraph is based on an unpublished history of Santokh Majra by the Rev. Suresh Kumar, who served as pastor there from 1988 to 1992. A survey of the village published in 1986 reported that of the young people between the ages of sixteen and thirty, only 29 per cent were employed, 37 per cent were unemployed, and 34 per cent were students or housewives. 'Diocesan News', *NIC* (May 1986), p. 9.

[171] James P. Alter and Herbert Jai Singh, *The Church in Delhi*, p. 94.

[172] Ibid., p. 95.

[173] Ibid., p. 87.

place. The basti was more built up with more amenities and more people. The other was that the basti residents had experienced considerable upward social mobility by moving into a variety of skilled and professional occupations in the modern sector of the economy. However, with varying degrees of mobility have come class divisions within what had once been a socially homogeneous basti.[174]

Like the Protestant churches, the oldest Roman Catholic parishes in Delhi were primarily local and Dalit in social composition.[175] However, while among Protestants these still predominate, among Catholics they are completely outnumbered by large numbers of migrants from other parts of India.[176] The most conspicuous among these are the many members of religious orders, virtually all of whom have come from either south or western India. The same is true of the rest of the Catholic population, except that it also includes a good number of tribals from the Chota Nagpur area.[177] These migrants are divided not only by social class and language but also, in the case of those from Kerala, by religious rites as well.[178] Some of them have now been settled in Delhi for so long that they have produced a new generation that considers Delhi to be their home, even though their family roots lie elsewhere in India.

The Christian community in the Punjab which, as the census figures cited earlier indicate, is the largest in size, the most rural and most educationally backward in the region, has remained the best studied to date. Campbell's study, carried out in and around Jullundur between 1959–61, provides a helpful baseline for the others. In one village he described there were first-, second- and third-generation Christians. Relations with the local landlords were changing from traditional *jajmani* relations with a built-in right-to-serve, to short-

---

[174] Monodeep Daniel, 'The People Who Believe that God is Faithful', pp. 122–4.

[175] Joseman Ponnan and Savari Muthu Y., 'A Brief History of the Archdiocese of Delhi', Appendices, pp. 1, 2, 13, 18.

[176] Interview with Fr. Leonard Fernando SJ, 21 October 2003.

[177] Joseman Ponnan and Savari Muthu Y., 'A Brief History of the Archdiocese of Delhi', p. 12.

[178] Sebasti L. Raj, *Renewal—2000*, pp. 92–3.

term but potentially renewable contractual relations, so that tenants could not establish rights to the land under recently enacted land ceiling legislation. Seasonal contracts were being replaced by short-term contracts and manual labour by tractors, with the result that many of the young Christian men were either unemployed or underemployed. Some had left the village to seek employment elsewhere.[179] A follow-up conference of leading Christians confirmed the existence of these patterns throughout the Punjab.[180]

Subsequent studies of rural Punjabi Christians reinforce this picture of persistent rural poverty. A 1973 study of Christian–Sikh relations in six villages in Gurdaspur district[181] pointed to a very low level of full-time employment among them. The percentage of adult Christian males engaged in full-time employment ranged from 50 per cent in one village to only 10.4 per cent in another, with an average of only 25.8 per cent working as full-time labour. Almost all the rest were seasonal labourers. Philip Dayal's rural data (1982) is less about unemployment and poverty then about status, attitudes, and relationships. He found the vast majority of his Christian informants in two colonies of Fatehgarh Churian to be illiterate, in the lowest occupational prestige category, and in one of the two lowest of his nine income categories. In Sunaiya, close to Batala, almost all his Christian respondents were clustered in the second, third, and fourth lowest income categories but in the middle occupational prestige category, while 60 per cent were literate. Socially, the Fatehgarh Churian Christians were ranked two-thirds of the way down the local hierarchy, whereas in Sunaiya, where they were numerically and politically dominant, they were ranked in the middle. In both villages, Christians saw themselves as a caste and confined their social relationships largely to their own community.[182]

[179] Ernest Y. Campbell, *The Church in the Punjab*, p. 27.

[180] *The Social, Economic and Political Problems of the Christian Community in the Punjab*, 1961.

[181] John C.B. Webster, 'Christians and Sikhs in the Punjab: The Village Encounter', pp. 17–24.

[182] Philip Dayal, 'Level of Social Integration of Ethnic Minorities', pp. 91, 97, 100, 108, 250, 293, 295.

The other village study is Vidya Sagar's description of growing up in the village of Tibber. His memories were of the distinction within the village between the upper-caste locality and the low-caste locality in which the Christians lived. The landlords used insulting terms not only for the Dalit residential area but also for the Dalit menials who were at their beck and call. Christians were called *saa-i*, a distorted form of *Issai*, a follower of Jesus, with derogatory caste connotations. Education levels among Christians were low and apathy about educating their children high. The one bright spot was a band of Christian youth who looked after the church building and organized touring singing parties at Christmas time. Since then these men have become labour contractors for work on roads or at brick kilns, getting four months of full-time work a year for fellow Christians. The other Christians in the village continued to work for the village landlords and the women did cleaning work in the homes and courtyards. The church building was in a dilapidated state and the overall picture was one of stagnation within a deprived community that had very limited options.[183]

The most recent survey data on rural Punjabi Christians, drawn from sixty-six villages in the Amritsar and Gurdaspur districts in the early 1990s, reinforces this picture of stagnation. It found 31 per cent of the Christians literate and only 11.5 per cent of the children going to school, which means that literacy among them was declining. Occupationally, 92.73 per cent of the Christians were casual or seasonal labourers in the fields and brick kilns, and only 17.65 per cent had work for more than nine months a year. A mere 5.36 per cent owned some agricultural land. The majority of the women did cleaning work for higher-caste people in their villages and in 83.64 per cent of the cases the children went to work along with their parents instead of going to school. This lack of occupational and social mobility was attributed to the landlords' desire to keep the Christians (and other Dalits) down as a ready source of cheap and dependent labour, to the Christians' preoccupation with short-term

---

[183] Vidya Sagar, 'The Christian Community in Punjab: An Analogy', *Religion and Society*, pp. 3–17.

survival issues rather than with inter-generational mobility, and to the Church's failure to work at changing the circumstances in which its members lived.[184]

Two studies of urban Punjabi Christians provide glimpses of what happens to rural migrants. Campbell noted that most of the members of the city church in Jullundur were rural Dalits who had migrated to the city. Those in skilled trades or offices were second- or third-generation Christians. While the labourers were concerned primarily with employment and survival issues, the white-collar workers were more concerned with educating their children and other status-enhancement matters.[185] Dayal found the Christians in three different wards of Batala some twenty years later to be occupationally very diverse, economically more spread out but concentrated in the lower income and occupational prestige categories, although around 25 per cent were quite well placed in both respects. As a community, however, they were ranked third from the bottom with only weavers and Dalits below them, even though they saw themselves a few ranks higher. Their levels of modernity correlated more with their levels of education than with their occupations. They were better integrated with the rest of society than were their rural counterparts, although their social interactions (unless they were very well educated) were generally limited to those members of other communities with whom they worked or resided.[186]

When taken together, all of this data would seem to indicate that there has been considerable dynamism and change as well as considerable stagnation within the Christian community of the north-west since independence. On the one hand, they are far more urbanized, far more literate, and more occupationally diverse now than before 1947. There are also signs that along with these changes the status of Christian women has improved over the decades. On the other hand, Christians are perceived and often perceive

---

[184] Clarence O. McMullen, 'A Survey of the Christian Community in North West India', pp. 25–8.

[185] Ernest Y. Campbell, *The Church in the Punjab*, pp. 77–8.

[186] Philip Dayal, 'Level of Social Integration of Ethnic Minorities', pp. 94, 97, 100, 108, 112, 176, 264, 273, 298, 306.

themselves as a caste; almost all are Dalits and carry a Dalit image. The Christians who have remained in the villages continue to be poor, powerless, and stigmatized. This rather contradictory social profile of the Christian community is both its legacy from the past and its response to the changes of the post-independence era. The community's social base inherited from the past has been overwhelmingly rural and Dalit. Only exceptional individuals from that background, or those living near towns and cities, have been able to move out of the traditional occupations of their people as well as out of the poverty and degradation that have gone with those occupations. However, whereas either migration or socio-economic stagnation has characterized most of the rural Christian community, which has few middle-class landowners, the urban Christian community has become larger with the growing middle classes and skilled working classes seeking a better life both for themselves and for their children. It is within this section of the community that most of the social change since independence has occurred.

STRUGGLES

Given the social profile described above, it is not surprising that one of the most important struggles of the Christian community over the past half century has been the economic struggle either for survival or for maintaining and improving one's circumstances as the region's economy has undergone profound changes. The community has also been engaged in a socio-political struggle for respect as a religious minority within a region where communal ideologies and politics have been unusually strong. In addition, since the overwhelming majority of Christians are Dalits, they have been involved in the Dalit struggle for dignity, equality, and justice. These struggles have overlapped and not all Christians have been equally or similarly engaged in all three. However, all Christians have been affected by each of them, albeit in differing ways. Each will be examined in turn.

Much of the data on the economic struggle has already been provided and needs only to be summarized here. For rural Dalit Christians, partition accelerated the process by which they moved out of jajmani into contract labour relationships with village landlords and others seeking their labour on a seasonal basis. Whether they were able to move out of menial and semi-skilled work in the fields, on road crews, or at brick kilns, into work that was full-time and more rewarding, depended largely on the distance of their village from a town or city. Education has played a role in mobility, but the accidents of location determined whether opportunities for mobility would even exist for them.

In their struggle to survive, rural Christians received little help from the government. As Christians they could not benefit from the income enhancing programmes reserved for the Scheduled Castes. Few villages continued to have mission schools, and the government schools, which were to have been the alternative when retrenchment took place, have proven to be so poor in quality as to be hardly worth attending.[187] The Green Revolution has been, at best, a mixed blessing. Few if any Christians had the land or resources to use the new agricultural technology. While agricultural wages did rise significantly, many Christian labourers lost work as agriculture became more mechanized. The churches have not had the resources to be of much help to the vast majority of rural Christians and most of what they have had has been concentrated upon providing training opportunities for the most capable and enterprising or in giving ad hoc relief in times of emergency. These continued to be the major emphases when the Delhi, Chandigarh, and Amritsar dioceses of the Church of North India launched rural community development projects in the mid-1980s to address the problem of rural unemployment. Additional components in these projects involved raising awareness of government programmes from which rural Christians might benefit and developing some cottage industries that could provide supplementary or alternative sources of income.[188] These, however, impacted only a small number of families.

Urban Christians have had more job options than rural Christians. Although their religion has also made them ineligible for the

[187] Surinder S. Jodhka, 'Caste and Untouchability in Rural Punjab', pp. 1820–1.

[188] 'News from the Dioceses', *NIC* (February 1986), p. 14; ibid. (April 1986), p. 12; 'Diocesan News', ibid. (May 1986), p. 9; *Diocese of Amritsar 1989*, pp. 6–7.

Scheduled Caste job quotas for which they would otherwise be qualified, they have been better positioned than their rural counterparts to take advantage of the churches' institutions for education, job training, and employment. At the same time, housing, overcrowding, a higher cost of living, and the competition for decent jobs have posed major challenges. Two Punjabi Christians writing in the early 1990s on the problems of Christian youth saw the lack of meaningful employment as both the major issue they confront and often the root cause of many of their other problems. As one put it, 'Unfortunately, the Punjabi Christian youth have no resources, nothing to bank on as far as material or mental inheritance is concerned. There is no family trade or tradition of sound education or material inheritance of an important size. Everything has to be built anew.'[189] This he attributed in part to social background and in part to a failure of leadership within the Christian community.

The hard fact is that we could never evolve an effective, educated, intelligent leadership. So much so that now there is a crisis even in running our own schools, colleges and hospitals because we had never planned to prepare Christian leadership at an appropriate time. A few who were in control of community resources looked after their own families and fulfilled their own interests.[190]

This analysis has much to commend it. Historically, the churches have placed much emphasis upon social mobility and have taken pride in their successes. Yet, except for a small minority, their members have at most only a generation or two of literacy and formal education within their families. There is little inherited or individual wealth within the community. Its major assets to date have been communal, in the form of institutions and properties that overseas mission societies have handed over to their successor churches. A great deal of 'church politics' thus revolves around who gets to allocate these communal resources as well as who gets to benefit

---

[189] Anil Sagar, 'Problems of Christian Youth in Punjab', *Religion and Society*, p. 66.

[190] Ibid. See also Alwan Masih, 'Christian Youth Issues in Punjab: A Challenge', ibid., pp. 51–3.

from them. In this way the denominations have become arenas in which members of the community struggle for the means of survival, of upward mobility, and of protection against loss of security or status. Since virtually all of the older churches are hierarchically organized at the denominational level with members of the educated middle class monopolizing the tops rungs of those hierarchies, they exhibit the same patterns of patron–client relationships, factional alliances, pressure groups, 'vested interests', and preoccupation with short-term advantage over long-term gain that are characteristic of state politics.[191]

The struggle for respect as a religious minority has been primarily an urban Christian struggle. This was due in part to the Christian urban institutional presence, some of whose legal battles concerning minority rights have already been described. Of equal importance was the fact that the primary identifying characteristic of urban Christians in the eyes of others has been their religion, whereas the dominant castes identified rural Christians more by their caste (Dalit) and class (menial labour) than by their religion.[192] As indicated in the previous chapter, urban Christians entered this period not only with a moderate, modernizing, and secular nationalism as well as a good non-communal, nation-building record, but also with considerable apprehension about their continuing religious liberty under the new regime. The provisions in the 1950 constitution

---

[191] The findings and recommendations of a 1990 survey of the Church of North India support this analysis. Despite being 80 per cent rural, the CNI invests virtually all its human and financial resources in the urban churches (pp. 16–17, 21). The authors, therefore, recommended not only that CNI resources be reallocated but also that power in church structures be decentralized and a dialogue with disgruntled dissidents initiated (pp. 50, 84, 85, 87). However, interviews with several CNI bishops and pastors indicate that since then power within the CNI has become even more centralized in the hands of relatively few people and has resulted in a 'People's Synod' in September 2005. Ram Singh (Convener), T.K. Oommen, A.P. Barnabas, T.S. Wilkinson, Ashish K. Mondol, Kuldip N. Thakur Das, *Profile of a Christian Church: Report of the Evaluation Commission to Study the Life and Work of the Church of North India*, Madras: The Institute for Development Education, 1990.

[192] This was quite apparent in the 1973 study of six Punjabi villages. John C.B. Webster, 'Christians and Sikhs in the Punjab: The Village Encounter', p. 24.

guaranteeing religious liberty and prohibiting religious discrimination allayed their worst fears, and the overwhelming majority of Christians in the region faithfully voted the Congress ticket for years to come.[193]

Relations between Christians and members of other religious communities in the north-west have been described for the most part as being very cordial, although, judging from Philip Dayal's study, at the popular level both urban and rural Christians, as well as their neighbours, have tended to confine their social relationships to other members of their own communities.[194] However, at the elite level, Christmas, Christmas music, and Christmas greeting cards have been especially popular, while Diwali—and in some places Holi—are festivals that Christians frequently joined in.[195] The YMCA in New Delhi has hosted a large number of both Christian and interfaith programmes which people of several faiths have either participated in or just attended.[196] The Christian Institute of Sikh Studies in the Punjab initiated interfaith dialogues on a regular basis with the stated aim of gaining a deeper understanding of their neighbours' religious traditions rather than 'scoring points' over an opponent. In turn, the institute's director was regularly invited to give Christian presentations at conferences on religious subjects organized by others.[197] The Commission for Interreligious Dialogue of the Catholic Bishops Conference of India, founded in 1973 and located in New Delhi, as well as Vidyajyoti, have also been active in promoting and participating in interfaith dialogue.

[193] Meeting of Christian political activists at village Shahpur, 27 October 2003.

[194] Philip Dayal did find more inter-community social integration in the town than in the villages he studied. 'Level of Social Integration of Ethnic Minorities', pp. 261–4, 295.

[195] James Massey reported this about both his own village and the institution in Delhi where he worked. I found it true, especially among the residential staff at Baring Union Christian College where I worked. James Massey, 'Religious Solidarity—Some Case Studies', *Bulletin of the Christian Institute of Religious Studies*, pp. 37–42.

[196] Mark S. Clive, *Towards the Mission*, pp. 25–7, 52, 57–68.

[197] Reports of these may be found in the semi-annual bulletins of the institute.

However, all has not been cordiality. Church property in Srinagar was destroyed in 1967 and 1979 while the police stood by.[198] Christians were accused of being spies for Pakistan during the 1965 and 1971 wars, as well as agents of the CIA.[199] The introduction of a national 'Freedom of Religion' Bill in 1978 threatened minority rights and Christians organized protests throughout the country, including the north-west.[200] Militants have broken up public, open-air Christian conventions emphasizing testimony and healing, while the police did nothing to defend the Christians' right to hold such meetings.[201] The best documented of these incidents, because it was investigated by the National Commission on Minorities, took place in Ludhiana in October 1997. Local Christians planned a religious convention from 22 to 26 October featuring a guest speaker and healing of the sick. The magistrate first granted permission for the convention, then withdrew it when others opposed it and were involved in arson at the site, and finally granted it. The police did nothing to disperse the protesters throughout the convention. When the magistrate said he could no longer guarantee its security, even though the largest crowds were expected on the final day, a Sunday, a group of Christian youth sat on the road protesting the premature ending of the convention. They were violently dispersed by the police. Some Christians were taken into police custody and severely tortured there. During the ensuing inquiry it became apparent that the magistrates and police had shown clear partiality to the militant Hindu groups who had opposed the convention and not upheld the Christians' right to hold it.[202] In response to this and the widespread anti-Christian

[198] See footnote 33.

[199] This was certainly true in Batala, where I lived between 1963 and 1968 and again between 1971 and 1976. For Ludhiana, see Kenneth M. Scott, *Around the World in Eighty Years*, p. 209.

[200] K.N. Thakur Das, 'Multi-Ethnic Society and Communal Tension', p. 22.

[201] Freddi Joseph was present at a large religious meeting in Jullundur during 1973 that was broken up by Hindu fundamentalist groups while the police stood by and did nothing. He reported that Sant Fateh Singh had offered to send some Nihangs to protect the meeting, but Pastor Y.C. Mall had declined the offer. Interview with Freddi Joseph, 17 September 2005.

[202] The inquiry report is found in James Massey, *Minorities in a Democracy*, pp. 202–19.

violence throughout India following the Bharatiya Janata Party's coming to power in New Delhi, Freddi Joseph founded a bi-weekly newspaper in Jullundur, the *Masihi Sansar*, to mobilize Christian opinion in protest as well as to affirm their Christian heritage and rights as a minority. He noted in the *Masihi Sansar* that there were forty-two attacks on Christian religious meetings in the Punjab alone during the Akali–BJP regime (1997–2002).[203]

In November 1999, amidst all the anti-Christian violence throughout India and the controversy raging over religious conversion, Pope John Paul II visited New Delhi to promulgate 'Ecclesia in Asia', a document that had emerged from earlier meetings of the Asian bishops. Opposition to his visit was strong. There were demands that he apologize for the Church's past excesses of evangelistic zeal in India and that he tell the Church to stop its proselytizing activities. His effigy was burned and there were threats to blockade his entrance into New Delhi from the airport unless those demands were met. The government, highly embarrassed by these actions from within its own party ranks, took strong measures and the visit passed off politely without incident.[204] In a meeting with religious leaders of eight other religious traditions the Pope sought the common ground of 'shared responsibility for the wellbeing of the human family'[205] and urged dialogue 'to discern and welcome whatever is good and holy in one another'[206] in carrying out that responsibility.

'Ecclesia in Asia', while a public document, was addressed to fellow Catholics. It was inspired by the challenges of evangelization and based on the twin premises of a discerned spiritual hunger in Asia[207] and the Church's desire to 'offer the new life she has found in

---

[203] Interview with Freddi Joseph, 17 September 2005.

[204] 'Father Fixation', *The New Indian Express* (29 October 1999), p. 10; 'Pope Accorded Ceremonial Welcome', 'Pope Concerned over Use of Religion to Divide People', 'Synod Document on Church in Asia Promulgated', *The Hindustan Times* (7 November 1999), p. 5; 'Conversion a Human Rights Issue: Vatican', ibid., p. 8; Amulya Ganguli, 'The Politics of Paranoia', ibid., p. 13.

[205] All the speeches are given in A. Suresh, (ed.), *Holy Father Pope John Pail II Meeting the Religious Leaders in New Delhi*, p. 34.

[206] Ibid., p. 36.

[207] *Post Synodical Apostolic Exhortation Ecclesia in Asia*, p. 25.

Jesus Christ to all the peoples of Asia as they search for fullness of life'.[208] It is to do this in genuine respect both for the rights of conscience and for other religions.[209] While most of the document is devoted to providing theological foundations and practical guidelines for carrying out this evangelistic mission, it did illustrate in its own way a common Christian desire to adhere to their own Christian convictions while at the same time respecting persons and traditions that differed. Both the Pope's visit and this document provoked an intense controversy among Hindus about conversion and, by implication, about the kind of society India was and should become: a hospitable and tolerant pluralistic society or a more homogeneous and homogenizing Hindu society.[210]

The other major struggle in which Christians of the north-west became involved was the Dalit struggle. For them it was a multifaceted struggle because one of the major motivations behind conversion had been to get rid of the stigma and hopefully escape the humiliations of being a Dalit. In 1961, Campbell reported deep divisions among Punjabi Christians about accepting Scheduled Caste and Backward Class benefits. Some rural Christians led by their pastor had strongly protested in 1950 when religious community was made a basis for determining eligibility for these benefits. Given their poverty, rural Christians wanted all the help they could get from such benefits, while urban Christians—including migrant Dalits—considered the benefits available not worth the social stigma of acknowledging one's Dalit background attached to accepting them.[211] In the late 1960s, some small, localized Christian parties contested elections and made alliances, primarily in order to publicize what were in fact largely Dalit Christian demands.[212]

[208] Ibid., p. 28.

[209] Ibid., p. 55.

[210] See the articles both critical of and supporting the Papal visit published in Dominic Emmanuel (ed.), *John Paul II Revisits India*.

[211] Ernest Y. Campbell, *The Church in the Punjab*, pp. 54–6.

[212] These included 'land for landless Christians, reserved places for Christians in government jobs and government schools, protection from intimidation by the upper castes.... [as well as] that Christians be given social welfare benefits similar to those that other lower caste people receive'. Mark Juergensmeyer, *Religion as Social Vision*, p. 191.

The twin problems of social stigma and economic backwardness were addressed directly at a conference of Christians on 'The Gospel for the Punjab' organized by the Christian Institute of Sikh Studies in March 1975. The key paragraph of the conference statement said,

In the Punjabi situation the Gospel is the message of the Cross. In the social sense, acceptance of the Gospel in the present Punjabi situation implies joining an underprivileged and deprived community. It means suffering, humiliation, and loss of status in the eyes of other communities. Yet the message of the Cross is the power of God to transform man and the world. It enables the individual to endure suffering and loss of status but at the same time inspires and enables him to change his lot and the lot of his neighbours. We bear the Cross and discover that it is the power of God.[213]

The statement went on to describe in practical terms how this Gospel of the Cross might best be communicated both to fellow Christians and to others. It was translated into Hindi, Punjabi, as well as Urdu and distributed widely in the Punjab. It also became the basis not only of a larger conference on 'The Self Image of Punjabi Christians' in October 1976 at which the dynamic and life-transforming power of this gospel was emphasized,[214] but also of a Punjabi book which provided the same kind of sociologically informed introduction to Christianity.[215]

The next important event in this struggle was a mass rally organized in New Delhi on 17 August 1990 to demand that Dalit Christians be made eligible for Scheduled Caste benefits along with Dalit Hindus, Sikhs, and Buddhists. Around 100,000 people participated in this All-India Convention for the Rights of Christians of Scheduled Caste Origin; of these an estimated thirty busloads came from Haryana and three to four hundred truckloads from the Punjab. Bishop Joel Mal, who rode in one of the Punjab trucks, reported that both the Congress and the Akali Dal had offered to pay for the transportation, but were refused because the Christians

---

[213] 'The Gospel for the Punjab', *BCISS* (July 1975), p. 14.

[214] Clarence O. McMullen, 'The Self Image of the Christians in the Punjab', pp. 16–23.

[215] James Massey, *Masihiat ik Parichay*.

wanted to make this demonstration on their own. Christian institutions in Delhi and elsewhere closed for the day and many Christian schools there provided hospitality to Christians from outside. A deputation from the rally met with Prime Minister V.P. Singh who assured them that he recognized both the justice of their cause and the widespread support it had within the Christian community, but the rally proved to be no more effective in changing the law than previous efforts had been. However, the rally's impact within the Christian community was quite positive both in raising awareness of the importance and justice of the Dalit cause and in injecting fresh hope, confidence, and determination into the Dalit Christian participants.[216]

Delhi remained the focal point for a concerted effort to persuade the central government to grant the Dalit Christian demand for Scheduled Caste status and benefits. There was a second rally in New Delhi on 1 March 1994 to which about 50,000 Christians came from all of the states in the north-west.[217] The next public step was a two-week relay fast in November 1995, which was inaugurated by Mother Teresa and a host of both Protestant and Catholic Church leaders. This was accompanied by rallies and public meetings, and the closure of Christian institutions in New Delhi as well as in other parts of India (including Amritsar), designed to build up public pressure for the necessary legislation.[218] Meanwhile, Christian deputations contacted prominent politicians and were given all kinds of positive assurances from the United Front government, which in the end decided that it could not take the political risks that the passage of such legislation required.[219] When the BJP, which was strongly

[216] A fuller, eyewitness account of the rally can be found in John C.B. Webster, 'Special Report: A Historic Rally for Dalit Christians', *The Christian Century* (27 February 1991), pp. 236–9.

[217] M.E. Prabhakar, 'National Christian Convention and Mass Rally to Demand Equal Rights for Christian Dalits', *NIC* (April 1994), pp. 9–11.

[218] 'Delhi Declaration on SC Christians', *North India Church Review* (January 1996), p. 5; 'The Church stands with the Dalits', ibid. p. 8; 'Editor's Update', ibid.

[219] 'Present Position of Churches and Christian Community on Dalit Issues', ibid., p. 4; 'National Coordination Committee for Dalit Christians: Memorandum', ibid. (September 1996), p. 4; 'Strong Case for Dalit Christians Prepared by U.F.

opposed to reservations for Dalit Christians, came into power in 1997 the effort was given up as no longer capable of success. However, between 1990 and 1997 the campaign had become a community campaign for minority rights (with significant support from Christians who were not Dalits) as well as a campaign for Dalit human rights.

While not successful in bringing about the desired legislation, the campaign did have two consequences of some importance. It forced the urban elite church leadership to examine their own priorities, especially with regard to their rural Dalit constituents. Dalit concerns found their way into church agendas; the admission and scholarship policies of Christian educational institutions came under closer scrutiny; Christian social service projects were now evaluated with more Dalit-centric criteria; Dalit theology began to find its way into both pastoral training programmes and the public statements of the churches. In short, the Dalit majority within the north Indian churches was making its voice heard and was beginning to affect the churches' ministry and mission. The other important consequence was that members of the educated Dalit Christian elite began to reach out across religious boundaries to other Dalits in an effort to build common Dalit platforms in a shared struggle for dignity, equality, and justice. Perhaps the most ambitious of these efforts was the Dalit Solidarity Programme, formed in 1992 and based in Delhi, which sought to bring together Dalits of all the major religions from all over India to develop a common agenda. Following its second convention in 1997, it became Dalit Solidarity Peoples and worked largely through regional bodies, which have concentrated upon consciousness raising and education/service projects aimed at helping poor Dalits.[220]

Government', ibid. p. 5; 'Bill on Quota for Christians Soon, says Ramoowalia', ibid, p. 6; 'Towards Obtaining Equal Justice for Dalit Christians', ibid; 'News Far and Near: Christians Court Arrest over Quota', ibid. (January 1997), p. 18.

[220] *DSP Report June '93 to June '94* (Dalit Solidarity Programme); *Empowering Dalits for the New Era: DSP Between December 1992 – December 1997 and Future. Report of the Hon. Secretary/Director DSP.*

In May 1990, a few months before the first large rally in Delhi, Alwan Masih, district coordinator of youth in Gurdaspur district, noted that Christian youth in his area were concealing their Christian identities by using names that gave no indication that they were Christians; that the normal Christian salutation, 'salaam', was being used less; and that some Christian young people were wearing steel bangles as though they were Sikhs. This he attributed in part to being ashamed of the public image of Christians as poor Dalits and in part to a desire to acquire Scheduled Caste papers and thus qualify for the reserved benefits other Dalits were entitled to.[221] Masih's observation probably gets very close to the heart of what has motivated these three interrelated struggles over the past fifty years— the same desire for dignity, equality, justice, and respect that led their ancestors to convert to Christianity in the first place. Like the original conversion movements, these more recent struggles have remained localized and sporadic in their more public expressions.

This may be attributed in part to the marginality of the Christian community as well as to its peculiar demographics and social composition, but it has also been a matter of leadership. The Christian leadership has changed since colonial times but its political style has not. Prior to independence the leadership concentrated in Lahore and Delhi was either missionary or drawn from local elites. There were, moreover, recognized community leaders with influence like S.K. Rudra, K.L. Rallia Ram, S.K. Datta, and S.P. Singha. This elite leadership was dispersed at the time of partition and the missionaries gradually disappeared to be replaced either by educated Dalit leaders or by Christians from outside the north-west. These leaders, however, have been ecclesiastical or institutional leaders rather than 'community' or 'movement' leaders as before. Yet they remained committed, as their colonial predecessors had been, to progress through education and individual social mobility rather than through collective political action; to reliance on petitions and personal contacts with people of influence rather than sustained communal

---

[221] Alwan Masih, 'Christians of Punjab–Identity at Crossroads', *NIC* (May 1990), p. 11.

organization (unlike Hindus, Sikhs, and Muslims); and thus to limiting their leadership to the confines of their own ecclesiastical or institutional domains rather than to working together outside their normal domains to push these struggles forward and make them more effective.[222]

RELIGIOUS LIFE

For Christians one of the biggest religious events of the post-independence era in the north-west was the Third Assembly of the World Council of Churches, which met in New Delhi from 19 November to 5 December 1961. The Assembly drew thousands of delegates and observers from churches all over the world. The Assembly theme was 'Jesus Christ The Light of the World' and it issued carefully debated and worded statements on witness, service, and unity which sought to express the meaning of Jesus Christ as The Light of a rapidly changing, highly diverse, and conflicted world. This Assembly, like the Pope's visit to New Delhi in 1999, illustrates the difficulty of describing the inner religious life of the Christians of north-west India since independence. Both the Assembly and the Asian Synod were gatherings of highly trained members of educated urban elites whose official statements used a religious language and reflected a kind of piety that might resonate with people like themselves. Theirs was an important part of the religious culture of the north-west, and especially of New Delhi where the Catholic Bishops Conference of India, the Church of North India, and other national Christian bodies had their headquarters. Their internationally attuned sub-culture was that of what might be termed 'official', or even upper middle-class urban, Christianity. The problem is to determine the continuities and discontinuities between this and other forms of Christian religious life in the north-west during this period.

---

[222] Harish K. Puri observed that Dalits in the Punjab appear to prefer the religious over the political route to identity assertion and emancipation. That would appear to be true of Christian Dalits as well. 'Introduction', in Harish K. Puri (ed.), *Dalits in Regional Context*, pp. 14–15.

There have been two important mediators between these elite, 'great tradition' forms of Christianity and more popular, 'little tradition' Christianities in the north-west. One has been the educated clergy who have been trained in Protestant or Catholic theological colleges similar to Vidyajyoti, but who serve as pastors of non-elite congregations in cities, towns, and even villages. Their mediation occurs primarily through sermons and prayers, Christian instruction and pastoral guidance, as well as through the process of collective decision-making. As Campbell has pointed out, this is not a simple or smooth process; the pastors face inner conflicts between the urban academic culture in which they were trained and the rural culture in which they worked, between the competing expectations of church authorities and local parishioners, between their responsibility for spiritual nurture and guidance on the one hand and community leadership on the other. Many pastors have been overwhelmed by these challenges, while some found creative ways of handling their conflicting roles.[223]

The other important mediator has been the liturgies used in the worship of Roman Catholic and more historic Protestant churches, especially for the sacrament of the Lord's Supper. Both the Catholic mass and the liturgy of the Church of North India, which is a blend of the worship traditions of the uniting churches, have fixed, quite detailed orders of worship that allow for a variety of set prayers and Bible readings according to the season of the church year. While based on very old (Western) Christian liturgies, these present the human condition before God in individualistic terms and as basically the same for all human beings. One could argue that in conveying no sense of external threat to Christian integrity, no sense of conflict with 'the world', they reflect an optimistic, upper middle-class blindness to the particular struggles of Christians in north-west India. In somehow remaining isolated from or seeking to rise above those struggles by not naming them in specific terms, these liturgies offer

---

[223] Ernest Y. Campbell, *The Church in the Punjab*, pp. 49–64. This was confirmed about twelve years later by Clarence O. McMullen et al., *The Amritsar Diocese*, pp. 47–51.

little incentive to engage, and little empowerment to confront, the realities Christians have to face in what is for them a highly competitive and conflicted region.[224] Moreover, the liturgies also represent a more ritualistic, as opposed to a more devotional, form of religious expression that relies heavily on everyone's capacity to read the written word for personal involvement. It is for this reason that their usage is mostly confined to urban congregations, while in the villages and among Pentecostals, 'freer', more spontaneous forms of worship prevail.

There have been no major theological shifts in north-west India from the statements of Vatican II and the New Delhi Assembly of the World Council of Churches. Both had put their stamp of approval on interfaith dialogue and human solidarity with people of other faiths. This did lead to some fresh theological formulations among Christian (academic) participants in those dialogues, but none that captured the imaginations or 'took hold' within the congregations of the region. Only Dalit liberation theology gained some attention in the 1990s, especially among those involved in Christian non-governmental organizations and social service programmes.[225] To date, James Massey and Monodeep Daniel in Delhi and Ayub Daniel in Amritsar have been the best-known Dalit theologians in the region, but the impact which their work has had upon the preaching, teaching, beliefs, and practices in local congregations is difficult to assess.

A major social shift has been the rise of women to positions of religious leadership in at least some of the churches. The Salvation Army has long had women as high-ranking officers. The Church of North India opened up the ranks of the clergy to women in the 1980s and since then there have been women clergy in all three of its

---

[224] See *The Book of Worship of the Church of North India*, Delhi: ISPCK, 1995, pp. 1–17, 105–40 and *Nine Eucharistic Prayers with the Order of Mass*, 12th edition; Bangalore: NBCLC, 2004.

[225] For a brief discussion of the links between liberation theologies and Dalit theology, see my *Religion and Dalit Liberation*, pp. 61–5. For a history of Dalit theology in India as a whole, see John C.B. Webster, *The Dalit Christians: A History*, chapter 5.

dioceses in the north-west. Jane Caleb's survey, undertaken in 1985–6, indicated that women generally supported this and were willing to allow their daughters to train to become clergy.[226] Most urban and many rural Protestant churches of any size have had separate women's organizations, women's representatives on governing bodies, and non-clergy women taking leading roles in worship, including preaching. The large influx of members of the women's religious orders in the Roman Catholic Church, who were both subordinate to the male clergy and largely autonomous, has played such a vital role in expanding and shaping Catholic religious life in the north-west that it would be almost totally different without them.

There have been a number of studies that describe some of the religious beliefs and practices of Christians during this period. Campbell found rural Christians to be rather inarticulate about their faith, drawing largely upon the zaburs (psalms) they sang or catchphrases from sermons they had heard to give expression to it. Campbell described the gospel as being to them 'a declaration of independence'.

It preached a separateness from the old gods, the old beliefs and the old practices and associations. The older Christians spoke often of their 'other worldly home'. The Psalms, which until recently were the major source of Biblical material in illiterate village churches, were admirably suited to expressions of defiance of the world of outside authority. The many references to 'enemies', 'heathen', and 'outsiders' were meaningful in the context of a complete revolt from the conditions of the past.[227]

Alter and Jai Singh, writing at the same time, found the Christians of Delhi to be more articulate about their faith. They noted that for Delhi Christians 'belief in Christ as divine Lord and Saviour is the cornerstone of the Church's faith and marks it off most clearly from all other religious communities'.[228] What this meant for them personally was that he was the crucified saviour, the bestower of

---

[226] Jane R. Caleb, *Women in the CNI Diocese of Delhi*, pp. 52–3.

[227] Ernest Y. Campbell, *The Church in the Punjab*, p. 29.

[228] James P. Alter and Herbert Jai Singh, *The Church in Delhi*, p. 135.

health and strength, and the protector of all who believe in him.[229]
At the same time, they also found a degree of religious relativism
among them. 'They accept Christ's claim to be 'The Way, the Truth
and the Life' but they hesitate to proclaim that without him no man
can come to the Father.[230]

Two subsequent studies sought to discover how Christian faith
helped Christians in the economic, political, and social struggles
described earlier. Both ran into communication problems with
inarticulate respondents. A 1976 study of thirty-three Punjabi, post-
matriculate Christian girls found they had an individualistic and
moralistic faith in which prayer played the most important role. Their
beliefs were conventional. They did not view Jesus Christ as an active
presence nor did they see any difference that their Christian beliefs
had made in their own lives. The study, therefore, concluded that
'the transforming elements have been missing from the kind of
Christianity to which these girls have been exposed'.[231] Dogar's study
of rural Christians some twenty years later found only 19.14 per
cent of the respondents saying that Christian worship was directly
related to their lives, a majority of whom indicated that God helps
them solve their problems.[232] A similar percentage saw Jesus Christ
as a liberating force in the world, but the most widely held views of
Jesus as the bearer of salvation were individualistic and
otherworldly.[233] The respondents' expectations of their pastors
related largely to educational, socio-economic, and political rather
than to spiritual or even community matters.[234] Dogar also rated his
respondents high on his 'self-help thinking' scale.[235] His findings
suggest that the predominant attitude among rural Christians was

[229] Ibid., pp. 129–30.

[230] Ibid., p. 140.

[231] Ellen Purdy Webster, 'Some Aspects of the Religiosity of Punjabi Christian
Girls'.

[232] Vidya Sagar J. Dogar, *Rural Christian Community in Northwest India*,
pp. 180–1.

[233] Ibid., p. 187.

[234] Ibid., pp. 217–8.

[235] Ibid., p. 227.

that in matters of this world one relies primarily on one's own resources (including friends and pastors), but that for eternal life beyond death one relies primarily on Jesus.

Christian religious life in the north-west has been based neither on one-time events like the World Council of Churches meeting or the Pope's visit, nor on periodic religious conventions, nor on such festivals as Christmas and Easter, but on regular services of corporate Sunday worship. In most cases worship is the only religious activity of the congregation.[236] Since relatively few have regular Sunday Schools, women's fellowships, or youth groups, Sunday worship also carries the burden of Christian instruction, fellowship, and pastoral care for everyone.[237] In the north-west, Sunday worship takes a variety of forms according to denominational tradition and local circumstances. Campbell described the Sunday worship of a rural Dalit congregation belonging to the UCNI near Jullundur as very informal. People sat on a cotton rug spread on the ground. Some young men provided music that included a Western hymn, a film tune with Christian words, and a *qawwali* that highlighted events in the life of Christ. As they sang, people gathered and talked with one another until the pastor stood up and formally began the worship. There was a zabur, prayers, a Bible reading, and an offering. The sermon was conversational in style, inviting reflective or emotive comments from the congregation. The service ended with another hymn and a blessing. After worship there was tea and conversation.[238]

A 1973 seminar on 'Popular Religion in the Punjab Today' produced two descriptions of rural Sunday worship. Maqbul Caleb, after visiting a rural Protestant church near Dhariwal on four consecutive Sundays, described worship there in terms similar to Campbell's, except that worship was in a church building and the preacher adopted a more formal style. He presented Jesus as the sole way into God's presence, drawing all his illustrative examples from the Bible and none from village life. Caleb concluded that 'the Church

[236] Clarence O. McMullen *et al.*, *The Amritsar Diocese*, pp. 52, 55.

[237] Ibid., pp. 54–5.

[238] Ernest Y. Campbell, *The Church in the Punjab*, pp. 20–3.

in its Sunday worship is either not taking poverty and its concomitant problems into account in any way or it is simply providing a kind of therapy (*shanti, mukti*) which makes poverty bearable'.[239] Catholic worship centred around the visits of a priest. Like Protestant worship it was more simple and informal than in the 'English style' city churches. Prior to worship, the local catechist instructed the people, confessions were heard, and baptisms performed. There was lots of singing during and after the mass.[240]

A sampling from congregations throughout the region further illustrates the growing diversity of popular Christian worship found in the north-west. The Pentecostal Mission near Dhariwal draws about 1000 people of all ages from urban middle class as well as rural backgrounds. Those who lead are on a platform up front and dressed in white. Worship, conducted in a mixture of English and Punjabi, begins with singing, ecstatic murmurings, and considerable body motion. Then come prayers, testimonies, and a sermon which is not only a proclamation of the presence of God's Spirit within to heal, to empower against external threats, and to help in daily personal struggles, but also a call to firmness of faith. Following two hours of worship there is a langar or common meal.[241]

This, however, should not be seen as representative of all Pentecostal worship. Weekday worship at the Open Door Church begins with singing. Sant Harbhajan Singh delivers a message in a matter-of-fact, conversational style about human sin and Christ's sacrifice that cleanses from sin. There is no murmuring or ecstatic speech, but a few in the congregation are clearly agitated. After a closing prayer those present form two circles—one of men and the other of women—and as Sant Harbhajan Singh prays, others join in murmuring their prayers along with his. Afterwards, people come to him individually with their concerns and, in a few instances, he commands evil spirits to leave them alone. Tea and light refreshments

[239] Maqbul Caleb, 'Christian Sunday Worship in a Punjabi Village', in John C.B. Webster (ed.), *Popular Religion in the Punjab Today*, p. 126.

[240] Fr Timothy, 'Catholicism in the Punjab', in ibid., pp. 74–5.

[241] Visit on Sunday, 26 October 2003, and interview with Pastor Mohan.

are provided to all who stay on to meet one another.[242] At the Church of the Holy Spirit in nearby Kapurthala, an evening prayer service opens with prayers and hallelujahs alternating with songs led by Pastor Mushtaq Masih or by members of the congregation. He then preaches a sermon in a more emotional and emphatic style than Sant Harbhajan Singh used. Worship ends with prayers and singing. People linger to visit afterwards; those with special concerns are prayed for, in some cases with hands placed upon their shoulders.[243]

At the Friends Missionary Prayer Band's Naya Jeevan [New Life] Christ Church in Kotberwal on the outskirts of Jammu, Sunday worship begins with alternating songs and prayers as in the Church of the Holy Spirit. However, individual members of the congregation take a greater share in leading worship by reading the scriptures, singing special songs, and offering their own prayers or testimonies. During a lengthy prayer, the pastor suggests subjects to be prayed about (for example, the nation and the government, peace, those in hospitals or in prison, the church) and all join together in praying the Lord's Prayer together at the end. There is an offering, some announcements, and a sermon. The service ends with a prayer and blessing. Afterwards, some ask the pastor for personal prayers.[244]

At the Salvation Army Hall in Batala, about one-third of the congregation are students from the Salvation Army hostel dressed in white who sit in the front pews; the rest come from the town or nearby villages. From a raised platform in front, officers in uniform lead the worship, the important features of which are congregational singing, special songs, prayers, personal testimonies, and the collective affirmation of Salvation Army doctrines. A special event was the welcoming of the new divisional commander and his wife. The former preached a sermon reminding those present that God has called them to be a light in the world and urging them to listen to God who answers prayers and helps those who ask for it. At the

---

[242] Visit to the Open Door Church, 15 September 2005.

[243] Visit to the Church of the Holy Spirit, 16 September 2005.

[244] Visit to Naya Jeevan Christ Church, 28 August 2005.

end many participants came forward for special prayers and blessings.[245]

Christ Church in Simla has a large historic building in which the British worshipped during colonial times. Today, tourists drop in to take a look, even during Sunday worship. There are two worship services, first in English and then in Hindi, each Sunday morning. At the former, a dozen girls from the Auckland House School sit up front and sing a special song during the service; the rest of the congregation is scattered throughout the sanctuary. At the Hindi service there are more people and they sit closer together. Worship is led by the clergy in their robes and follows the liturgy of the Church of North India. The sermon at the Hindi service is more interactive than at the English service and members of the congregation are invited to pray spontaneously. At both services the hymn singing, to Western tunes, is accompanied by an organ.[246]

Christ Methodist Church in Delhi also has an English followed by a better attended Hindustani Sunday service. Worship is formal but personalized in the prayers for the sick, a recently deceased member, new members joining the church, and a couple celebrating their wedding anniversary. Hymns are sung from a book and accompanied by a harmonium (English service) or electronic organ (Hindustani service). At the English service, the pastor's theologically educated wife preaches from the lectern with her sari covering her head. At the Hindustani service the pastor, wearing a clerical collar and cassock, preaches from a highly elevated pulpit. At the close of the Hindustani service, those who wish to give thanks or make special petitions to God are invited to come forward to the communion rail where the pastor leads in a closing prayer.[247] By way of contrast, at St. Francis Church at Anandgram, also in Delhi, the people remove their shoes before entering, sit on the floor with the men on one side of the church and the women on the other, as is customary except in the larger, more middle-class urban churches. Worship begins with

[245] Visit to the Salvation Army Hall, 4 September 2005.
[246] Visit to Christ Church, 11 September 2005.
[247] Visit to Christ Methodist Church, 25 September 2005.

congregational singing and a silent procession of the pastor and three altar boys. It then follows the Church of North India liturgy with members of the congregation reading the scriptures and the pastor preaching a very interactive sermon. The sick and those with birthdays during the week are prayed for by name. During the Lord's Supper, instead of having everyone drink from the same cup, the pastor first dips the wafer into the cup of wine and then places it in the mouth of each person kneeling at communion rail. This practice of intinction was adopted because of the congregation's history of leprosy.[248]

There are four masses on Sunday mornings at St. Mark's Catholic Church in Punjabi Bagh, New Delhi. The first is a Hindi mass at 6:30 intended primarily for the young tribal women from the Chota Nagpur area who work as domestic servants in the city. Few others attend. They have their own special singing group that presents a special song; other young women read the scriptures, lead the intercessory prayers, and take the offering. Those who attend join in the songs they know as well as in the sung or spoken responses spread throughout the mass. After mass is concluded, some linger to pray in front of a garden shrine. The second (Hindi) and third (English) masses are attended primarily by Roman Catholics living in the vicinity of the church. The music is Indian during the Hindi masses and Western in the English mass. Unlike these three masses that follow the Latin rite, the fourth follows either the Syro-Malabar or the Syro-Malankara rite. The participants are from Kerala and the priest is from outside the parish. The mass is longer, makes greater use of incense, and at the end the people come forward to give their offerings and receive an individual blessing from the priest.[249]

There is only one Latin rite mass at Our Lady of Assumption Catholic Church in the village of Gakhlan on the outskirts of Jullundur, but it is longer than at St. Mark's, is conducted in Punjabi, and is preceded by a rosary and novena for Our Lady of Perpetual Help led by the youth. This is mostly sung with occasional clapping

---

[248] Visit to St. Francis Church, 14 August 2005.
[249] Visit to St. Mark's Church, 21 August 2005.

and raising of hands. While it is going on, the priest hears confessions in the rear of the church and two women place several boxes of sweets as an offering to the side of the altar. (These are blessed by the priest near the end of the mass and are served to everyone, along with a cup of tea, afterwards.) The priest enters in a small procession and mass begins. There is even more congregational participation than in the Delhi masses, largely through song and the recitation of prayers. There is also much more socializing afterwards, as the building does not have to be vacated in time for another mass.[250]

It is difficult to generalize about Christian religious life from this sampling of worship services, as the diversity represented is considerable. That diversity would only be enhanced if house church services, prayer and Bible study groups, and family devotions were added to the sample. This diversity reflects traditions of Christian worship that emphasize spontaneity on the one hand or order and comprehensiveness on the other. Some traditions give special priority to the Spirit's working, others to the proclamation of God's word contained in the scriptures, and yet others to the sacrament of the Lord's Supper as mediating most directly the presence of God to the worshipper. This diversity of Christian worship also reflects varying natural mixtures of the distinctively Indian with the more universally Christian in the culture of worship. However, it does not reflect any correlation between social class and preferred style of worship. There is a mix of social classes in Pentecostal, Church of North India, and Roman Catholic churches. The Christian urban middle classes are even divided in their preferences for English as opposed to Hindi, Hindustani or Punjabi as the language of worship. Nonetheless, worship within each of these traditions and sample congregations comes across as generic in form and standardized in content, largely ignoring the particular social profile and shared struggles of the community.[251] In fact, the problems and issues addressed are generally

[250] Visit to Our Lady of Assumption Church, 18 September 2005.

[251] The distinction between generic and focused ministry is made quite sharply with reference to Dalit Christian women in John C.B. Webster, *et al.*, *From Role to Identity: Dalit Christian Women in Transition*, pp. 112–13.

individual and personal (for example, illness, getting ahead, sin, and forgiveness) on the unstated presumption that Christians are to adjust to and cope with the status quo rather than to change it. If there is a sense of movement undergirding worship it is much more towards personal change than towards social or even community transformation.

Conclusions

The Christianity which entered the post-independence era in north-west India was predominantly that of the older, 'mainline' Protestant churches. Moreover, despite the cleavage between the urban elites and rural Dalits, it was an interconnected and quite cohesive community with prestigious institutions and recognized leaders. The foreign missionary presence, while less dominating than before, was nonetheless conspicuous and influential, contributing through their own remaining structures and networks to the community's cohesiveness. Then came the trauma of partition, which brought out the best of what the community had to offer, but at the same time not only divided and dispersed its leadership but also forced it to reorganize internally. What impetus it had left as a social movement was largely dissipated in the course of this transition.

Since then Christianity has become more denominationally diverse as Roman Catholics, newly formed Indian Evangelical missions, and Pentecostals from elsewhere in India entered the region in significant numbers, and Christians within the north-west started some churches of their own. Christianity has also completed its change of leadership, as foreign missionaries have departed and Indian Christians have taken over. In the Catholic Church, the successors to the foreign missionaries were almost all priests and nuns from outside the north-west, while among Protestants the most noticeable trend has been towards Dalit leadership from within the region. The other major change has been the increased marginalization of the Christian community within north-west Indian society. With the introduction of the adult franchise, the resulting democratization of politics, and increased government responsiveness to large powerful groups, Christians have become even more politically handicapped than they were in the elitist politics of colonial times. Their institutions, which have perhaps saved them from total marginalization, have come under increased competitive and bureaucratic pressure. Their own growing internal fragmentation has added to their political ineffectiveness. It has by no means been clear who speaks for the Christians or that Christian voices have been listened to amidst the clamour of louder, stronger voices in a highly competitive democracy.

What has emerged over the nearly sixty years since independence are three broad streams of Christianity in the north-west. The first and oldest of these can be labelled the historic Protestant stream represented today by the Church of North India which brought together the successor churches of all the original missions in the region, the Methodist Church, and the Salvation Army. Of these the Salvation Army seems to have been faring the best. While the other two have many strong, vibrant congregations, as denominations they appear to be in a kind of holding pattern, devoting an enormous amount of time, energy, and resources to hanging on as best they can to their members, property, and other financial assets in the face of competition from other groups and court cases brought by present or former members. All of these denominations are hierarchically organized and power within them has become increasingly centralized in the hands of top officers who function as patrons of their churches' resources for the benefit of their loudest and most clamorous clients. These churches have been both the most democratic and, at the same time, the most captive to the regional political culture. It is within their denominational structures that clashes of interests and struggles for power within the Christian churches and community have long been most evident.

The Roman Catholic stream in many respects resembles the historic Protestant stream in its earlier stages. It too is hierarchical in structure, with people from outside the region in all the key positions; clergy drawn from the local population are still a rarity. Like earlier generations of Protestants, it not only has been heavily committed to a strong institutional presence through which it can both serve and influence the wider society, but also has had both the human and the financial resources at its command to carry through on that commitment. This combination has given the Catholic Church something of an elite image to go along with the general Dalit image Christianity bears, as well as a profound sense of stability amidst the chaos and conflict among the Protestants. This sense of stability is reinforced by the absence of open politics in Catholic dioceses. The clergy dominate and lay people are appointed to positions from above rather than elected to them from below. Internal conflict thus remains largely hidden.

The third stream consists of the newer Pentecostal and Evangelical churches which have been growing so rapidly in the region. They are the least hierarchical of the churches within the region; some are more loose fellowships of like-minded independent congregations than denominations. Power within them tends to be very decentralized. Their success or failure depends almost entirely upon the evangelistic zeal, initiative, skill, charisma, and entrepreneurship of local pastors. In many cases these pastors not only establish and build their churches, they may even own and run them as well. It is the churches in this stream who are winning by far the most converts from outside the Christian community and are thus giving to Christianity whatever sense of movement it still has in the region. At the same time, they have also been highly vulnerable because, for all their liveliness, they lack the stability and, in many cases, the trained clergy that churches in the other streams provide. In addition, many of their clergy and members are recent converts who, while Christian in religion, still remain within the social nexus provided by their jatis.

There is no one dominant pattern of relationships between representatives and churches in these three streams of Christianity within the region. For example, in Delhi there is the Delhi Christian Pastors Fellowship and its successor, the Delhi Christian Pastors Fraternal, in which clergy from the first two streams have met for worship, reflection, and discussion. Their business items include such matters on which they seek to work together as social issues or maintaining Christian cemeteries, as well as matters which have been a source of tension between them such as inter-church marriages or the admission of Christians from both streams to all Christian educational institutions.[252] On the other hand, in the Punjab, relationships between representatives of these same two streams have long been highly competitive and full of conflict. Those in the third stream seem to have gone their own way quite independently of the other two. However, there have been a lot of people moving back and forth between this and the other two streams. Thus, a family might attend a CNI church for holy communion and retaining community ties on the first Sunday of each month and for major Christian festivals, but go to a Pentecostal house church on the other Sundays or during the week. There are also charismatic Catholics who bridge the gap between the second and third streams.

Christianity in the north-west has thus exhibited two seemingly contradictory tendencies during this post-independence period. One is towards ever-increasing change and complexity. Even at the outset of this period it showed a considerable degree of sub-regional variation. Since then not only have the churches become far more numerous and diverse than they were in 1947, but the Christian community itself has also become more fragile and socially diverse as Christians from within the region have been more mobile and so many from outside the region have moved in. The other tendency has been towards continuity with the past in terms of core beliefs, ecclesiastical and institutional structures, and social base. Their core beliefs in God and in Jesus Christ have not only set Christians apart from other communities but also enabled them to move with relative ease from one stream of Christianity to another. With rare exceptions, their ecclesiastical structures and institutional commitments have been inherited from the past with relatively minor adaptations to changing circumstances. Their social base was really set by the end of the nineteenth century and has remained substantially the same; new additions, except for the migrants, have come from the same backgrounds in roughly the same proportions as in earlier periods. Their struggles and frustrations have continued to help shape both the internal life and external relations of the churches at the local, denominational, and community levels.

[252] Interview with Bishop Anil Couto, the previous president of the Fraternal, 17 September 2005.

7 The North-west in the History of Christianity in India

The history of Christianity in north-west India, recounted in the preceding chapters, is of relatively short duration; its arrival coinciding with that of British rule. This feature of Christianity, shared with north-east and central India, has at times been projected onto Christianity in India as a whole, thus distorting what is in fact a far more complex picture. Christianity in the north-west has also been, until the 1970s, almost exclusively Protestant. This characteristic, also shared with the north-east, further complicates generalized images of Indian Christianity, as Catholics have long outnumbered Protestants. This concluding chapter looks at Christianity's history in the relatively understudied north-west in relation to its history within India as a whole, so as to highlight what is distinctive about Christianity in the north-west and to suggest how its history there might enhance understanding of Christianity within the entire country.

There is a tradition that in AD 52, Thomas, one of the original disciples of Jesus, came to what is now Kerala where he won India's initial converts to Christianity. Whatever the truth underlying that tradition may be, there is more solid evidence of the presence of Christian communities in Kerala by the fourth century. When the Portuguese arrived there at the very end of the fifteenth century they found a large, high-status community of Christians who used a Syrian rite for worship. These 'Syrian Christians' tended to keep aloof from the subsequent converts who came from diverse caste backgrounds and, under Portuguese influence, used the Latin rite. In the late nineteenth and early twentieth centuries, two Dalit caste groups, the Pulayas and Parayas, also converted to Christianity in large numbers. The Christian community in Kerala has thus grown not only in size but also in social diversity. According to the 1991 Census, Kerala's Christians constituted 28.6 per cent of the entire Christian population of India.[1]

[1] *Census of India 1991. Paper 1 of 1995: Religion*, pp. 4–5.

Tamil Nadu has also had a Thomas tradition, but knowledge of the Christian community there is very sketchy until the sixteenth century when the Portuguese arrived. Soon thereafter, first the Paravas and Mukkavas, two fishing communities on the southern tip of India, converted in large numbers. They were followed by higher-caste Vellalars beginning in the seventeenth century, by Shanars or Nadars in southern Tamil Nadu beginning in the late eighteenth century, and then by the Pariahs, the major Dalit caste in northern Tamil Nadu, during the late nineteenth and early twentieth centuries. Thus, like Kerala, Tamil Nadu has had significant numbers of Christians from each of several castes differently placed in local caste hierarchies. In 1991, 16.2 per cent of the Christian population of India lived in Tamil Nadu.[2]

A third major concentration of Christians with a long history may be found in the territories along the western coast of India occupied by the Portuguese during the sixteenth and seventeenth centuries. At the centre of this region, which extended from Mangalore up through Bombay and Salsette, was Goa, which the Portuguese occupied in 1510. There, many influential people, including village headmen, chose to align themselves with the Portuguese against the Muslims by converting to Christianity.[3] As a result, whole villages, and clusters of villages, became entirely Christian. Thus, one of the striking features of Christianity in this region has been that whole social structures and cultural traditions in some locales were transplanted, with modifications, from a Hindu to a Christian religious context. As in Kerala and Tamil Nadu, the Christian population of this region has been predominantly Roman Catholic.

However, the most thoroughly Christian part of India is now the sparsely populated north-east. In 1991 it had 21.9 per cent of India's Christian population, but Christians were very unevenly distributed within the region. In the states of Assam and Tripura, where the process of Sanskritization had preceded the arrival of British administration, only 3.1 per cent of the population is Christian.

---

[2] Ibid., pp. 4, 9.
[3] Rowena Robinson, *Conversion, Continuity and Change*, pp. 47–8.

However, in the five hill states of Arunachal Pradesh, Manipur, Meghalaya, Mizoram, and Nagaland, where it did not, the combined Christian portion of the population is a very high 55.1 per cent.[4] Christianity spread within the hill areas along tribal lines, village by village, rather than among only certain groups as in the more segmented caste society elsewhere in India. It is predominantly Protestant.

These four areas, containing approximately 75 per cent of India's Christian population, have two significant features in common which, from a social history perspective, set them in sharp contrast to the north-west, where only about two per cent of India's Christians live. The first is that in those four areas Christianity made early and significant inroads among locally powerful groups that owned land, were well established in commerce, or were well placed in government service: for example, the Syrian Christians in Kerala, the Vellalars and fisher folk in Tamil Nadu, the village headmen and their caste fellows along the west coast, and entire villages in the north-east where all villagers belonged to the same tribe and often held land in common. This did not happen in the north-west. Thus, whereas in these four other regions the Christian community has had a solid local power and economic base, in the north-west it has had neither. In that respect, Christians in the north-west have more closely resembled those in nearby Uttar Pradesh and in Andhra Pradesh than in the areas of heaviest Christian concentration.

The other important social feature which Christianity in these four areas had in common was that it won converts from several social groups in sufficiently large numbers enabling each to bring into the Christian community not just its own customs and traditions but also its own set of group identities and animosities. In Kerala, Tamil Nadu, and western India these were the caste groups mentioned above, whereas in the north-east they were tribal groups. For them it was possible, and many considered it socially necessary, to retain caste or tribal identities. As a result, in those areas the social and cultural carryovers from Hinduism into Christianity as well as

[4] *Census of India 1991. Paper 1 of 1995: Religion*, pp. 4–5, 8–9, 12–13.

the resulting caste conflicts over status and the criteria of social precedence within the Christian community have been important features of Christianity's social history.[5] Moreover, Christianity there could not be socially identified with any one caste or tribe, or with any distinctive status category of castes or tribes.

In this respect also, north-west India represents a sharply contrasting situation. There, one caste, the Chuhras (or in Delhi the Chamars), completely dominated to the point where caste and caste rivalries have played very minor roles in church life. One obvious consequence of this pattern of conversion has been that throughout the region Christianity has had a Dalit rather than a more complex social image. Another was that social class, one of the key markers of which has been the use of English or Hindustani as the language of worship,[6] rather than caste has been the chief social divide within the churches.

Three other social features of Christianity in north-west India have contributed to its distinctive history. One is the significant roles Christians from other parts of India have played in its history. At the outset, Bengalis like Golaknath, Kali Charan Chatterjee, and later S.K. Rudra provided Indian leadership for the region's emerging Christian community. Since independence, members of Roman Catholic religious orders and Evangelical mission organizations based outside the north-west have spread throughout the region. Secondly, until partition, the north-west was a Muslim-majority region with a very large non-Muslim minority. As indicated in Chapter 4, both internal reform and political mobilization within the region took a clearly communal turn as early as the 1880s. Nowhere else in India was communal rivalry so pronounced and so costly to human life. Christians and Christianity, while politically marginal, have had to contend with these political realities, not just in pronouncements but more importantly in institutional sensitivity and action, as became most obvious during partition when everyone's life was on the line. Finally, the north-west includes New Delhi, the nation's capital city.

[5] See Susan Bayly's *Saints, Goddesses and Kings*, and more recently, Rowena Robinson, *Christians of India*.

[6] See James P. Alter and Herbert Jai Singh, *The Church in Delhi*, pp. 99–100.

It thus has a high proportion of Christians from outside the region and also serves as the headquarters city for many Christian organizations of national importance. This has not only given Christianity there a degree of linguistic and cultural diversity probably unmatched elsewhere in India but also involved it in Christian political activity initiated elsewhere, such as the Dalit Christian agitations of the 1990s.

The preceding emphasis upon regional distinctiveness should not be allowed to hide either what Christianity in the north-west has had in common with Christianity in the rest of India or the important ties connecting Christians in the region to those outside it. One can find a common range of Protestant denominational traditions and Roman Catholic religious orders throughout India. Churches in the Syrian tradition, while based in Kerala, may be found in the north-west, as in most urban centres throughout the country. In like manner, the institutional presence of Christianity has been broadly the same in the north-west as elsewhere in India, and Christians in the north-west have long been connected to Christians in other parts of India through such ecclesiastical structures as the Catholic Bishops Conference of India and the National Council of Churches in India. The influence of some Christian leaders in north-west India has extended beyond the region: Raja Harnam Singh, Sadhu Sundar Singh, S.K. Datta, Rajkumari Amrit Kaur, and more recently, James Massey, the son of a Punjabi village pastor, who was the Christian member of the activist National Commission on Minorities from 1996 to 2001 as well as an intellectual and organizational leader in Dalit circles nationally. Similarly, Christian institutions in the north-west like Christian Medical College in Ludhiana, St. Stephen's College in Delhi, and Vidyajyoti in Delhi have had a significant impact beyond the region.

The history of Christianity in India combines regional distinctiveness with national commonalities, national interconnectedness, and national interdependence. This history illustrates the point that each region has had a distinctive history of Christianity shaped by regional structures, traditions, and conflicts, and that Christians have neither been identically situated nor shared the same image in all parts of India. This has had a profound effect upon the kinds of questions those writing regional histories of it have been led to ask and the kinds of data available to provide answers to those questions. It has also made a generalized Christian social history for India as a whole an extremely difficult task.[7] In concluding this history, therefore, it may be appropriate to sum up by referring to some of the key concepts which have proven to be most helpful when reflecting upon the data used in this study and which, therefore, may be helpful to others as they reflect upon both the history of Christianity in other regions of India and Christian commonalities in India as a whole.

Christianity in north-west India began with evangelism. While often used elsewhere interchangeably with 'proselytism', their root meanings and current overtones differ. To evangelize is to proclaim good news; the emphasis is upon bearing witness, giving testimony, or simply sharing, through both words and actions to news about what God has done through Jesus Christ that is both individual and social in its implications. The consequences or results of this proclamation or sharing are left for God to work out through the minds and hearts of those who see and hear the witness. On the other hand, a proselyte is a stranger, a newcomer, and by implication a convert. Thus the emphasis in this term is upon desired outcomes, that is converts, rather than upon the evangelistic action itself. Moreover, as one analyst has indicated, 'Both the World Council of Churches since the 1960s and the Vatican more recently have accepted the term proselytism to describe any kind of manipulation of another or encroachment upon their personal freedom to choose.'[8] The term 'evangelism' is thus less 'loaded' than 'proselytism' and describes more accurately what Christians have been doing in north-west India. The screening process Christians have put individual and group

---

[7] In her recent sociological study, *Christians in India*, Rowena Robinson found Christian communities to be so immersed in their regional cultures that she avoided making broad generalizations and made inter-regional comparisons instead.

[8] Simon Barrington-Ward, 'Proselytism', in Alan Richardson and John Bowden (eds), *The Westminster Dictionary of Christian Theology*, Philadelphia: The Westminster Press, 1983, p. 476.

inquirers through prior to baptism as well as their persistence in bearing witness despite the outcomes in the region make the term 'proselytism' both inappropriate and pejorative.

A second important concept has been 'alienation'. This history has been based on the observation, stated at the outset, that Christianity is an Indian phenomenon. The concept of alienation proved most helpful in seeking to find out why individuals and groups in Indian society were attracted, and even converted, to Christianity, because it assumes that society is not one harmonious whole, free of inner tensions and conflicts, whether latent or manifest. In the north-west, the overwhelming majority of the converts were already either personally or structurally alienated from their local society before they met up with Christian evangelists. The early converts were orphans, migrants from other parts of India, employees of the Raj or of the missions, or students who had received a Western education which had undermined confidence in their inherited belief systems. Later, it was the Dalits who were alienated because of their inherited status as polluting untouchables under prevailing social custom. In recent years, converts have been individuals with personal problems and Dalits who continue to experience social alienation. Of course not all the alienated converted; most did not, but for some Christianity provided a way of dealing with their alienation.

'Conversion' has been used to refer to a change of religious allegiance and a transfer of membership from one religious community to another. This study suggests that this is a rather minimalist understanding of conversion because it focuses exclusively upon one decisive moment in the total conversion process and largely ignores the rest of it. Conversion, as a process of internal transformation at the core of one's being as well as of external changes in behaviour and relationships, takes time, perhaps even more than one generation. What has been true for the individual has also been true for the community as well. Communal inner transformation has been reflected in changes not just in rites and rituals, but also in the social mores, self-images, and inner spirit of the community. These changes were more apparent in the urban churches, where the community had to be created largely de novo (except in the Chamar bastis of Delhi) and the missionaries exercised more social control, than in the villages where tradition had a stronger hold, a caste biradari to enforce it, and the missionary was only an infrequent visitor.[9]

A fourth important concept in this study has been 'community'. Alter and Jai Singh, in their study of the Church in Delhi, focused on the internal, subjective component of community.

Christians in Delhi tend to conceive of themselves as a distinct community, differing in religion and mores from other communities. The word most commonly used in referring to this corporate existence is *qaum*. . . . In its common usage in North India *qaum* signifies people or community. Every Indian is by birth a member of a *qaum* and, in a society composed of many such communities, owes much of his identity to this membership.[10]

This self-understanding of community is in accord with the more recent Anthropological Survey of India categorization and with popular perceptions of Christians cited in the previous chapter. My own earlier study of the Christian community in north India relied less on accepted Indian usage than on such external criteria as demographic changes, the establishment of community boundaries, and the integration of diverse Christians into a single community through 'the development of a communication network permeating the entire community, the sharing of common beliefs and values, and the growth of functional interdependence, possibly within a common organizational framework'.[11] In this latter view, community is a product not simply of Indian modes of identification, but of a specific historical process as well. Here it has been argued that it was only perhaps in the late 1870s or early 1880s that one can begin to talk meaningfully about the existence of a Christian community, even if the subjective reality of 'qaum' may have existed earlier.

In addition to being a community, Christianity in the north-west has also been a movement, specifically an organized evangelistic movement aimed at changing the religious status quo. While the

[9] Campbell's chapter on 'Church or Community' is a particularly good analysis of this. E.Y. Campbell, *The Church in the Punjab*, pp. 40–8.

[10] James P. Alter and Herbert Jai Singh, *The Church in Delhi*, p. 95.

[11] John C.B. Webster, *The Christian Community and Change*, pp. 246–58.

salvation Christians preached initially was both individualistic and otherworldly, their work as well as their critique of other religions were based on three this-worldly premises. Religion is foundational to any culture or civilization, shaping its values and behavioural norms. The reason why India was suffering under foreign rule was because its religions were providing either false, bad or inadequate (opinions varied) values and norms. Therefore, Indian society needed Christian religion to shape its norms and values in order to awaken to and achieve greatness. When applied to women and Dalits, these premises acquired social and cultural emancipatory dimensions and the Christian movement thus helped lay some foundations for both the women's movement and the Dalit movement in the region. What drove the Christian movement was its capacity to attract and empower adherents from among the alienated sufficiently to challenge traditional orthodoxies and provide justification for other movements for religious, cultural or political change within the region. Christianity subsequently lost its momentum as a social movement and only recently, largely under Evangelical and Pentecostal influence, has shown signs of taking on the characteristics of a movement once again.

'Marginalization' has proven to be yet another useful concept in writing this history. Conversion marginalized from the outset. Missionaries were taken seriously but converts, with rare exceptions, were considered to be of no account by the wider society. This changed somewhat as the Christian movement gained numbers and momentum during the late nineteenth and early twentieth century. After World War I, politics took over completely, while internal religious, social, and cultural issues were largely laid aside. Christians could not compete in the political arena. They did not have the numbers and their leaders were political moderates who chose not to add to the region's communal conflicts by organizing politically as a religious community.[12] Marginalization increased following

---

[12] Chandra Mallampalli found that in the Madras Presidency the Protestants, who did not organize on a communal basis, were less effective politically than were the Roman Catholics, who did. *Christians and Public Life in Colonial South India*, pp. 108–56. The predominantly Protestant north-west followed the Protestant pattern, with similar results.

independence, as others with far greater resources at their command not only threatened Christian minority rights but also moved in large numbers into areas like education and medicine which had been a special Christian 'niche' within the wider society.

Two related concepts used throughout this study have been 'image' and 'identity'. At the outset of this history, Christianity was seen in the north-west both as a novelty and as the religion of the rulers, while anyone who converted was considered to be a scoundrel or worse. These images were defensive in nature, but had a long and useful lifespan. When members of other religious communities were seeking to redefine their own identities and shape their reform agendas, Christians were given grudging respect for their 'selfless service', largely through their educational and medical institutions, and held up as models to be emulated. Twentieth-century politics then reshaped the image of Christians as pro-British, communally neutral, but politically irrelevant. These images have carried over into the post-independence period, but the caste image of Christians as Dalits has become more widely prevalent in the north-west during this period. Christians have sought to forge their own identities through all of these struggles by taking these public images and their own specifically Christian self-images into account. Historically, the three central components of their distinctively Christian self-image in the north-west have been the convictions that all women and men (despite their social status or worldly condition) have been created in God's own image, that God loves them all with a love exceeding what any deserve, and that God has given to the Church a special mission of faith, hope, and love as a witness for individual and social transformation. Although Christians have rejected the scoundrel and foreign images, while perhaps enjoying the flattery of the 'selfless service' image, the Dalit image is the one that has posed the greatest challenge to them and for many remains a source of inner tension. Indeed, the tension between a socially defined Dalit identity and a theologically defined Christian identity is not easily resolved in a caste-based society and within a religious community where, in this particular region, caste is not the primary social marker.

The final concept of special importance to this study has been 'Christianity'. This is not easily or neatly defined. As this social history has shown, Christianity is not a monolithic, homogeneous, and static entity, nor is it an unchanging, self-contained sub-culture or autonomous belief system and way of life. One distinguished historian has noted that it 'continues to be heterogeneous and pluralistic in its forms of organization and worship, belief and life—so much so that it appears difficult or foolhardy or impossible to attempt to identify any characteristics as the distinctive genius or continuing essence of Christianity'.[13] This point needs emphasis here because in India the 'essence' of Christianity has frequently been not only located in its colonial past but also equated with the Christianity of foreign missionaries. While historians in the West have often equated the history of Christianity primarily with the history of the Christian Church as an institution, or of Christian doctrine, in this history the focus has been upon the history of those people who, through baptism and allegiance to Jesus Christ as the bearer of God's salvation for the whole world, are known as Christians. Individually, and especially collectively, they represent and embody Christianity in its 'essence', diversity, and dynamism within north-west Indian society. What Christianity is in north-west India, therefore, has been the product of their history in relation to the history of the people in that region, in India as a whole, and in the wider world.

---

[13] Jaroslav Pelikan, 'Christianity: An Overview', in Lindsay Jones (ed.), *Encyclopedia of Religion*, second edition, Detroit: Thomson Gale, 2005, III, p. 1665. I agree with Euan Cameron's mediating position between the pure relativists and the essentialists that 'all historically visible Christianities are partial manifestations of an essence that is never seen in an unmixed form, and can never be seen in its wholeness and entirety on earth'. Euan Cameron, *Interpreting Christian History*, pp. 6–7.

Glossary

Achhuts	Untouchables
Anand	joy, bliss
Anjuman	society, association
Avatar	incarnation
Baba	an honorific applied to males of wisdom and piety
Barakat	blessing
Basti	neighbourhood
Bhakti	devotion to a personal God
Biradari	caste brotherhood
Catechism	a popular manual of Christian doctrine
Catechist	a person appointed to provide instruction in Christian teachings
Chaudhari	hereditary headman
Communicant Member	church member deemed eligible to receive holy communion
Dai	midwife
Dal	pulses
Dalit	literally 'broken' or oppressed; a name which members of those castes considered untouchable have chosen to give themselves
Darbar	royal court
Dera	abode
Dharam Yudh	a war for the sake of religion
Diocese	the territorial jurisdiction of a bishop
Faqir	Muslim mendicant
Fatwa	a pronouncement by an expert in Muslim law
Gospel	literally 'good news'; a reference to what God has done in Jesus Christ for the salvation of the world

Granthi	professional reader of the Sikh scriptures
Gurdwara	a place for Sikh worship and community gathering
Guru–chela	religious teacher–disciple
Hadith	traditions of Islam
Hartal	an Indian form of general strike
Holy Communion	a sacramental rite of the Christian Church in which bread and wine (or grape juice) are consumed as the substance or symbols of Christ's body and blood in commemoration of his death
Huqqah	a pipe with a long stem often used for communal smoking
Isaai	'Christian', derived from 'Isa' (Christ).
Jagir	the right to revenue from a piece of land, a land assignment
Jagirdar	the one who holds a jagir
Jajmani	hereditary patron–client relationship of a dominant-caste family with a lower-caste family
Jati	caste group based on kinship and lineage
Jihad	a legitimate war waged by Muslims against non-Muslims in the name of God
Khalsa	'the pure'; the religious order instituted by Guru Gobind Singh, the tenth Sikh guru
Kingdom of God	the sovereign reign of God and God's righteousness over the entire universe
Lambardar	village headman
Langar	a free kitchen open to the public
Liturgy	a written text which gives structure and movement to corporate Christian worship
Lord's Supper	see Holy Communion
Madrassa	a school for Islamic learning
Mahdi	the 'rightly guided one' who is to appear at the end of time to establish Islam
Maktab	a primary school

Maulvie	a learned Muslim
Mass	the Roman Catholic sacramental rite similar to Holy Communion
Mela	a fair
Messiah	'the anointed one', the deliverer or saviour
Misldars	acknowledged leaders of bands of Sikh soldiers who join together to occupy or defend territory
Missiology	the study of Christian mission and missions
Mullah	Muslim religious teacher, generally in charge of a village mosque
Murid	a disciple of a Sufi *pir*
Nashin	'one who sits', e.g., one sits in *purdah*
Nihang	a distinct group of Sikhs organized into four 'armies' each with its own commander
Nirankar	formless
Novena	a nine-day public or private devotion, sometimes used as a recurrent devotion
Ordination	a rite through which a person is admitted to the ministry or priesthood of the Church
Panchayat	a council of elders
Panth	a group following a particular teacher or set of doctrines
Pentateuch	the first five books of the Bible
Pir	a Sufi religious guide
Presbytery	a church assembly having jurisdiction over member churches and clergy within a specific geographic territory
Pundit	a Brahmin, learned person
Purdah	a curtain or veil
Roti	bread
Sabbath	seventh day of the Jewish week, a day of rest; Christian Sabbath observance is usually on Sunday as that was the day of Jesus' resurrection
Sabha	assembly or association
Sadhu	a saintly person who is generally an ascetic as well

Salaam	'peace' (a greeting)
Samaj	society
Sampradaya	sect
Sanyasi	a renunciant
Sarkar	government
Sarpanch	head of a *panchayat*
Satyagraha	literally 'truth force'; Gandhian method of non-violent protest
Sepidar	one who renders service in exchange for grain at the end of the harvest
Sepoy	Indian soldier in the British-Indian army
Service (of worship)	a gathering for collective, formal Christian worship
Shakta	a worshipper of the Goddess
Shamiana	canopy
Shastras	scriptures
Shuddhi	purification; a rite used by the Arya Samaj
Swadeshi	'one's own country'
Synod	a governing body made up of representatives of member churches to conduct business affecting them all
Tehsil	an administrative subdivision of a district
Than	deity's abode
Ulama	those learned in Islamic legal and religious studies
Vakil	an attorney or pleader
Varna	literally 'colour'; the broad categories into which *jatis* have been classified
Varnashramadharma	the social order based on people carrying out the sacred moral and religious duties of their respective *varna*s and stages in life
Zabur	psalm
Zamindar	landlord
Zenana	female apartment or section of a house reserved for women

Bibliography

I. Government Sources

The major government sources consulted dealt with the Indian press, education, and the census. Beginning in 1868, the government printed regular confidential reports entitled 'Selections from the Vernacular Newspapers' and from 1902 'Selections from the Native Newspapers'. Selections from the Punjab were combined with those from the North-Western Provinces and Oudh up through 1888 and thereafter were printed separately.

The Punjab Government published an annual report on education which appeared under three different titles: 'Report on Popular Education in the Punjab and its Dependencies' (1860–1 up through 1880–1); 'Report on the State of Education in the Punjab and its Dependencies' (from 1881–2 through 1885–6); and 'Report on Public Instruction in the Punjab and its Dependencies' (from 1886–7 through 1913–14). Reports on education prior to that consulted here were included in the 'General Report on the Administration of the Punjab Territories from 1856–7 to 1857–8 Inclusive Together with a Brief Account of the Administration of the Delhi Territory from the Reoccupation of Delhi up to May 1858'; 'Annual Report on the Administration of the Punjaub Territories from the Year 1858–9; and the 'General Report on the Administration of the Punjab and its Dependencies for 1859–60'. The Punjab government's education proceedings were also consulted. They were variously titled 'Education Consultations' (1862), 'Education Proceedings' (1863–9), Proceedings in the Education, Science and Art Department (1870–1), and from 1872 to 1914 were included in the 'Proceedings of the Home Department'. Another valuable government source on education was 'Report by the Punjab Provincial Committee; with Evidence taken before the Committee, and Memorials Addressed to the Education Commission, Calcutta 1884'.

The first regular decennial Census of India appeared in 1881. Each of those from 1881 through 2001 as well as two prior, less reliable, ones were consulted. 'Selections from the Records of the Government of India (Foreign Department) No. XI Report on the Census taken on the 1st January 1855 of the Population of the Punjab Territories' (Calcutta 1856) and 'Report on the Census of the Punjab Taken on 10th January 1868' (Lahore 1870) revised in 1871.

Other government sources which have been consulted are: *Imperial Gazetteer of India. Provincial Series: Kashmir and Jammu*, Calcutta, 1909; Disorders Inquiry Committee 1919–20, 'Report', Calcutta, 1920; and *Evidence Taken Before the Disorders Inquiry Committee, Vols. IV & V.*

II. Mission, Church, and Institutional Records

These records consist for the most part of correspondence, annual, and occasional reports, as well as minutes of meetings and anniversary volumes. The correspondence, including personal reports, cited in the footnotes belongs to one of four denominational collections. That of the CMS is in their archives at Birmingham University; that of the SPG in their archives in Rhodes House at Oxford University; that of the Presbyterian Church in the USA at the Presbyterian Historical Society in Philadelphia; and that of the Church of England in Canada and its successor Anglican Church of Canada in the General Synod Archives in Toronto. The other records are listed below. Some mission reports from north-west India were incorporated into larger denominational reports and others were issued independently of them. Small handouts, such as an institutional prospectus, calendar, or brochure are referred to only in the footnotes when utilized.

'A Century for Christ in India and Pakistan 1855–1955'
'A Native Church for the Natives: Giving an Account of the Formation of a Native Church Council for the Punjab Missions of the Church Missionary Society and of the Proceedings of their first Meeting at Umritsar, 31st March to 2nd April 1877' [Also 'Accounts of the Second through Seventh Meetings, 1877–82']
'An Advisory Study', New York: Commission on Ecumenical Mission and Relations of the United Presbyterian Church in the United States of America, 1962

'Annual Report of the Board of Foreign Missions of the United Presbyterian Church of North America', 1874–1933

'Annual Report of the Church of England Zenana Missionary Society', 1880–1946

'Annual Report of the Commission on Ecumenical Mission and Relations of the United Presbyterian Church in the U.S.A.', 1958–67

'Annual Report of the Delhi Mission, Branch of the Baptist Missionary Society', 1860–70

'Annual Report of the Forman Christian College', 1933–6

Baptist Missionary Society, 'Indian Report: Bengal, Orissa, Northern India and Ceylon', 1910, 1911, 1914, 1918, 1925–30

Cambridge Mission to Delhi, 'Reports', 1887, 1889, 1891

Cardoza, Fr Paul A., compiler, *Delhi Catholic Directory 2000*

Catholic Diocese of Simla–Chandigarh Directory 2001

Cheruvil, Fr George, ed., *Christward: A Look at the Diocese of Jalandhar on the Occasion of the Dedication of St. Mary's Cathedral 29 October 1989*

Delhi Catholic Directory 2000, compiled by Fr. Paul A. Cardoza

Diocese of Amritsar: A Report for the Period 1986 to 1989 Presented by the Rt. Rev. A.C. Lal to the VII Synod on 5th October 1989

Diocese of Jalandhar Punjab, India: Directory 1999

Diocese of Jammu-Srinagar India Directory 1996, Jammu Cantt: Bishop's House, 1996

Henry Martyn School (of Islamics) Lahore, India, 'Annual Report', 1931–6, 1939–41

Indian Society for the Propagation of Christian Knowledge, 'Triennial Report', 1989–91, 1995–7, 1998–2000

Lodiana Mission of the Presbyterian Church in the USA, 'Annual Reports', 1834–1902

Lodiana Mission of the Presbyterian Church in the USA, 'Minutes of the Annual Meeting', 1857–68, 1871, 1873, 1875–87, 1889–1902

Manual and Constitution of the Punjab Mission of the Presbyterian Church of New Zealand, Lucknow, 1931

Minutes of the Conference of Representatives of the Punjab, North India & Western India Missions of the Presbyterian Church, USA

with Dr. Stanley White, held in Allahabad, 18–20 February 1913, Allahabad, 1913

'Minutes of the General Assembly of the United Presbyterian Church of North America', 1859–78, 1918–58

'Minutes of the Governors, Auckland House'

'Official Minutes of the Delhi Annual Conference of the Methodist Church in Southern Asia' 1944–1948, 1952, 1953, 1955, 1958–1961

New Delhi YMCA, 'Annual Report', 1969–89

North India School of Medicine for Christian Women, Ludhiana, 'Prospectus and Annual Report', 1899–1900, 1901–2, 1904–9

Official Journal of the Indus River Annual Conference and Women's Conference of the Methodist Church in Southern Asia, 1946–55

'Official Minutes of the Delhi Annual Conference of the Methodist Church in Southern Asia', 1944–8, 1952, 1953, 1955, 1958–61

Post Synodical Apostolic Exhortation Ecclesia in Asia of the Holy Father John Paul II to the Bishops Priests and Deacons Men and Women in the Consecrated Life and all the Lay Faithful on Jesus Christ The Saviour and His Mission of Love and Service in Asia "That They May Have Life and Have it Abundantly" (Jn10:10), Vatican City: Libreria Editrice Vaticana, n.d.

'Proceedings of the Annual Meeting of the Punjab Christian Council', 1929, 1930, 1935

'Proceedings of the Church Missionary Society for Africa and the East', 1843–1938

'Proceedings of the General Assembly of the Presbyterian Church of New Zealand', 1919–53

'Proceedings of the Twelfth Conference of Church Missionaries in the Punjab at Lahore, December 13th, 14th, 15th, 16th and 17th, 1873'

'Proceedings of the Thirteenth Conference of Church Missionaries in the Punjab at Umritsar, January 4th, 5th, 6th, 7th, 1875'

Punjab Mission of the Presbyterian Church in the USA, 'Annual Reports', 1902–14, 1931

Punjab Mission of the Presbyterian Church in the USA, 'Minutes of the Annual Meeting', 1903–35

Report of the Second Meeting of the Punjab Presbyterian Conference, held at Lahore in December 1879, Ludhiana, 1880

'Report of Survey Evaluation of Twenty-Eight Schools and Colleges Related to the United Church of Northern India, August 9–November 22, 1962', New York: United Presbyterian Church in the USA, 1963

'Report by the Committee for the Propagation of the Gospel in Foreign Parts, Especially in India to the General Assembly of the Church of Scotland', 1855–1918

'Reports and Minutes of the Women's Foreign Missionary Society of the Indus River Conference', 1922–40, 1944, 1945

Reports and Recommendations of the Deputation of the Board of Foreign Missions of the Presbyterian Church in the USA Modified and Approved by the Final Conference with the India Council and Other Regional Representatives, 22–25 March 1939

Salvation Army Year Book, 1922–49

'Selections from the Proceedings of the Punjab C.M.S. Conferences 1855 to 1872 Inclusive'

'Survey of the Educational Work of the Three India Missions of the Presbyterian Church in the United States of America 1926'

'Survey of the Evangelistic Work of the Punjab Mission of the Presbyterian Church in the USA 1929', Lucknow: The India Council, n.d.

'The Annual Report of the Board of Foreign Missions of the Presbyterian Church in the United States of America', 1920–35, 1947–57

'The Annual Report of the Committee of the Baptist Missionary Society', 1819–86

'The Annual Report of the Diocese of Delhi and the Cambridge Mission to Delhi', 1948–66

The Cambridge Mission to Delhi in connection with S.P.G., 'Annual Reports', 1934–1940

The First Ten Years of the N.M.S. 1905–1916, Salem: The National Missionary Society, n.d.

The General Synod of the Church of England in Canada, *Journal of Proceedings*, 1937–59

The Handbook of Foreign Missions of the United Presbyterian Church of North America, 1910, 1912, 1914–15, 1917, 1919, 1924, 1953

The Indian Christian Association, Punjab, *Eleventh Annual Report, Being the Report for the Years 1909–10 and 1910–11*, Lahore, 1912

The Regional Conference of the Deputation of the Board of Foreign Missions of the Presbyterian Church in the USA, the Punjab Mission, and the Central Board, 14–17 March 1939.

The Punjab Synod of the United Church of Northern India, 'Minutes of the Annual Meeting', 1957, 1958, 1964

'The Report of the All India Conference of Indian Christians', 1914–23, 1926, 1929–1933, 1936, 1937, 1947

'The Report of the Women's Christian Medical College, Ludhiana, Punjab', 1912–13, 1929–36

The S.P.G. and Cambridge Mission in Delhi and the South Punjab, 'Annual Reports', 1917–33

'Triennial Report of Foreign Missions of the United Presbyterian Church of North America', 1916–18, 1919–21, 1926–8, 1929–31

25 Years: Moga Training School for Village Teachers, Lucknow, 1937

'The United Church of Northern India Survey 1968'

Yearbook and Official Minutes of the Indus River Conference of the Methodist Episcopal Church, 1924–42, 1946, 1948

Yearbook and Official Minutes of the North-West India Conference of the Methodist Episcopal Church, 1915–44

III. List of Periodicals

Analecta Ordinis Minorum Capuccinorum (1884–1938, 1959)

Arya Patrika (1885–8)

Church Missionary Intelligencer (1848–1913)

Church Missionary Outlook (1922–50)

Church Missionary Review (1914–27)

CMS Mass Movement Quarterly (1917–47)

Collectanea Lahorensia (1937, 1940)

Collectanea Punjabensia (1942)

Delhi (1920–65)

Delhi Mission News (1895–1918)

Foreign Missionary Chronicle (1833–41)

Home and Foreign Record (1850–67)

India's Women (1881–95)
India's Women and China's Daughters (1896–1918)
Lahore Diocesan Magazine (1919–45)
Lahore Diocesan Record (1908, 1910)
Life and Work
National Christian Council Review
North India Churchman (1871–1994)
North India Church Review (1994–2000)
Other Lands (1930–42)
St. Stephen's College Magazine (1917–34)
The Baptist Magazine (1859–86)
The Church at Home and Abroad (1887–98)
The East and the West (1903–20)
The Folio (1936–41)
The Foreign Missionary (1841–86)
The Forman Christian College Monthly (1906–27)
The Guardian
The Home and Foreign Missionary Record of the Church of Scotland
    (1856–1908)
The Indian Female Evangelist (1881–91)
The Indian Social Reformer
The Indian Standard (1894–1929)
The Indian Witness
The Mission Field (1858–92)
The Missionary Herald (1819–1918)
The Stephanian (1939–48, 1962–3)
The Tribune (January–March 1937, February–March 1946, February–
    July 1947)
The United Presbyterian (1858–86, 1906–9)
United Church Review (1930–53)
Women's Missionary Magazine (1918–48)
Young Men of India

IV. Books

Alexander, Archibald, *Evidences of the Authenticity, Inspiration and Canonical Authority of the Holy Scriptures*, Philadelphia: Presbyterian Board of Publication, 1836

Ali, Imran, *The Punjab under Imperialism 1885–1947*, Princeton: Princeton University Press, 1988

Aloysius, G., *Religion as Emancipatory Identity: A Buddhist Movement among Tamils under Colonialism*, New Delhi: New Age International Publishers, 1998

Alter, James P., and Herbert Jai Singh, *The Church in Delhi*, Lucknow: National Christian Council of India, 1961

Alter, Martha Payne, *Letters from India to America 1916–1951*, edited by Ellen and Bob Alter, Mussoorie, 2006

Anderson, William B., and Charles R. Watson, *Far North in India: A Survey of the Mission Field and Work of the United Presbyterian Church in the Punjab*, revised edition, Philadelphia: Board of Foreign Missions, 1911

Andrews, C.F., *India in Transition*, Delhi: Cambridge Mission to Delhi, 1910

Andrews, C.F., *North India*, London: A.R. Mowbray, 1908

Andrews, C.F., *The Renaissance in India: Its Missionary Aspect*, London: United Council for Missionary Education, 1912

Appasamy, A.J., *Sundar Singh: A Biography*, Madras: Christian Literature Society, 1966

Banga, Indu, *Agrarian System of the Sikhs: Late Eighteenth and Early Nineteenth Century*, Delhi: Manohar, 1978

Banga, Indu (ed.), *Five Punjabi Centuries: Polity, Economy, Society and Culture 1500–1990*, Delhi: Manohar, 1997

Bannerjee, Himadri, *Agrarian Society of the Punjab 1849–1901*, Delhi: Manohar, 1982

Basu, Aparna, and Bharati Ray, *Women's Struggle: A History of the All-India Women's Conference 1927–1990*, New Delhi: Manohar, 1990

Bayly, Susan, *Saints, Goddesses and Kings: Muslims and Christians in South Indian Society 1700–1900*, Cambridge: Cambridge University Press, 1989

Biswas, Niren, *Not Mere Memories: Story of the Community of St. Stephen, Delhi Established in 1886*, Delhi: Community of St. Stephen, 2004

Blondeel, Emmerich, *A Short History of the Catholic Diocese of Lahore*, 1976

Bose, Kheroth Mohini, *The Village of Hope or The History of Asrapur, Punjab*, London: Church of England Zenana Missionary Society, 1914

Brown, Arthur Judson, *One Hundred Years: A History of the Foreign Missionary Work of the Presbyterian Church in the U.S.A., With Some Account of Countries, Peoples and Problems of Modern Missions*, New York: Fleming H. Revell, 1936

Brown, Judith M., and Robert Eric Frykenberg (eds), *Christians, Cultural Interactions, and India's Religions Traditions*, Grand Rapids: William B. Eerdmans, 2002

Brown, William Adams, *Christian Theology in Outline*, New York: Charles Scribner's Sons, 1906

Buck, Edward J., *Simla Past and Present*, second edition, Shimla: Minerva Book House, 1989

Butler, Joseph, *The Analogy of Religion, Natural and Revealed, to the Constitution and Course of Nature, to which are added Two Brief Dissertations on Personal Identity and the Nature of Virtue*, edited by Joseph Cummings, New York: Eaton & Mains, 1903

Caleb, Jane R., *Women in the CNI Diocese of Delhi: A Survey 1985–86*, Delhi: ISPCK, 1987

Caleb, Maqbul, *Count Your Blessings: The Autobiography of Maqbul Caleb, Bishop*, Dalhousie: the author, 2006

Cameron, Euan, *Interpreting Christian History: The Challenge of the Church's Past*, Malden: Blackwell Publishing, 2005

Campbell, Ernest Y., *The Church in the Punjab: Some Aspects of its Life and Growth*, Lucknow: National Christian Council of India, 1961

Celestine, Peter, *North Indian Capuchin Missions 1972–1992*, Sahibabad: Capuchin Publications, 1992

———, *Capuchins in India 1972–1997*, Delhi: Media House, 1998

Chander, Ernest B., *Trishul to Trinity: K.N. Nambudripad and I*, Franklin: Providence House Publishers, 1999

Chandra, Bipin, *Communalism in Modern India*, second revised edition, New Delhi: Vikas, 1987

Charak, Sukhdev Singh, *History and Culture of Himalayan States, Vol. III: Himachal Pradesh, Part III*, New Delhi: Light and Life Publishers, 1979

Clark, Robert, *A Brief Account of Thirty Years of Missionary Work of the Church Missionary Society in the Punjab and Sindh, 1852–1882*, Lahore, 1883

———, *The Punjab and Sindh Missions of the Church Missionary Society, Giving an Account of their Foundation and Progress for Thirty Years, from 1852 to 1884*, second edition, London: Church Missionary Society, 1885

———, *The Missions of the Church Missionary Society and the Church of England Zenana Missionary Society in the Punjab and Sindh*, edited and revised by Robert Maconachie, London: Church Missionary Society, 1904

Clive, Mark S., compiler, *Towards the Mission: A Monograph of New Delhi YMCA's Vision, Commitment & Achievements 1927–1997*, New Delhi: New Delhi YMCA, 1997

Cohn, Bernard S., *Colonialism and Its Forms of Knowledge: The British in India*, Princeton: Princeton University Press, 1996

Cox, Jeffrey, *Imperial Fault Lines: Christianity and Colonial Power in India, 1818–1940*, Stanford: Stanford University Press, 2002

Cunningham, Alexander, *Ladakh, Physical, Statistical and Historical; with Notices of the Surrounding Countries*, London: Wm H. Allen, 1854

Datta, Surendra Kumar, *The Desire of India*, London: Church Missionary Society, 1908

Datta, V.N., ed., *New Light on the Punjab Disturbances in 1919: Volumes VI and VII of Disorders Inquiry Committee Evidence*, Simla: Indian Institute of Advanced Study, 1975

Devanandan, P.D. and M.M. Thomas (eds), *Christian Participation in Nation-Building*, Bangalore: CISRS, 1960

Dickinson, Richard, and Nancy Dickinson, *Directory of Information for Christian Colleges in India*, Madras: Christian Literature Society, 1967

Directory of Christian Missions and Churches in India, Burma and Ceylon 1940–1941, Nagpur: National Christian Council, nd

Dogar, Vidya Sagar J., *Rural Christian Community in Northwest India*, Delhi: ISPCK, 2001

Drew, Frederic, *The Northern Barrier of India: A Popular Account of the Jummoo and Kashmir Territories*, London: Edward Stanford, 1877

D'Souza, Daniel, *Capuchin Missions in India*, Brahmavar: Capuchin Publications, nd

D'Souza, Daniel Anthony, *The Growth and Activities of the Catholic Church in North India, 1757–1858*, Mangalore: St. Anne's Friary, 1982

Early Nineteenth Century Panjab: From Ganesh Das's Char Bagh-i-Panjab (trs and eds), J.S. Grewal and Indu Banga, Amritsar: Guru Nanak University, 1975

Emmanuel, Dominic, ed., *John Paul II Revisits India*, Indore, Satyaprakashan, 2000

Eggleston, Forrest C., *Where is God Not? An American Surgeon in India*, Franklin, Tennessee: Providence House Publishers, 1999

Ewing, J.C.R., *A Prince of the Church in India: Being a Record of the Life of the Rev. Kali Charan Chatterjee, D.D., for Forty-Eight Years a Missionary at Hoshyarpur, Punjab, India*, New York: Fleming H. Revell Company, 1918

Farquhar, J.N., *Modern Religious Movements in India*, New York: The Macmillan Co., 1919

Fernando, Leonard, and G. Gispert-Sauch, *Christianity in India: Two Thousand Years of Faith*, New Delhi: Viking, 2004

Fleming, Daniel Johnson, *Devolution in Mission Administration*, New York: Fleming H. Revell, 1916

Forrester, Duncan B., *Caste and Christianity: Attitudes and Policies on Caste of Anglo-Saxon Protestant Missions in India*, London: Curzon Press, 1980

Frykenberg, R.E. (ed.), *Delhi Through the Ages: Selected Essays in Urban History, Culture and Society*, Delhi: Oxford University Press, 1993

Gibbs, M.E., *The Anglican Church in India 1600–1970*, Delhi: ISPCK, 1972

Golaknath, Henry, *Golak, The Hero*, Bombay: The Times of India Press, 1932

Gordon, Andrew, *Our India Mission: A Thirty Years History of the India Mission of the United Presbyterian Church of North America, Together with Personal Reminiscences*, Philadelphia: Andrew Gordon, 1886

Grewal, J.S., *In the By-Lanes of History: Some Persian Documents from a Punjab Town*, Simla: Indian Institute of Advanced Study, 1975

———, *The Reign of Maharaja Ranjit Singh: Structures of Power, Economy and Society*, Patiala: Punjabi University, 1981

———, *The New Cambridge History of India. I.3: The Sikhs of the Punjab*, Cambridge: Cambridge University Press, 1990

Grewal, J.S., and Indu Banga (eds), *Maharajah Ranjit Singh and His Times*, Amritsar: Guru Nanak Dev University, 1980

Griswold, H.D., *The Religion of the Rigveda*, London: Oxford University Press, 1923.

Gupta, Narayani, *Delhi Between Two Empires 1803–1931: Society, Government and Urban Growth*, Delhi: Oxford University Press, 1981

Hardy, Peter, *The Muslims of British India*, Cambridge: Cambridge University Press, 1972

Hasrat, Bikrama Jit, *Life and Times of Ranjit Singh*, Nabha: The Author, 1977

Heinrich, J.C., *The Psychology of a Suppressed People*, London: George Allen & Unwin, 1937

Hewitt, Gordon, *The Problem of Success: A History of the Church Missionary Society 1910–1942. Volume Two: Asia, Overseas Partners*, London: SCM Press, 1977

Hewlett, S.S., *Daughters of the King*, London: Church of England Zenana Missionary Society, 1886

Historical Sketches of the India Missions of the Presbyterian Church in the United States of America, Allahabad: Allahabad Mission Press, 1886

Hollister, John N., *The Centenary of the Methodist Church in Southern Asia*, Lucknow: Lucknow Publishing House, 1956

Imad-ud-Din, S.J., *Gandhi and Christianity*, Lahore: Northern India Printing and Publishing Co., nd

Indian Christians: Biographical and Critical Sketches of Poets, Educationists, Publicists, Reformers, Ministers of the Church in India, Madras: G.A. Natesan & Co., 1928

Jackson, J. Stuart, *The Delhi Mission of the Society for the Propagation of the Gospel in Four Letters from a Late Missionary to His Successor*, London: Society for the Propagation of the Gospel, 1858

Jacob, Edwin, *A Memoir of Professor Yesudas Ramchandra of Delhi*, Kanpur: Christ Church Mission Press, 1902

Jacob, Mani, compiler and editor, *Directory of Church-Related Colleges in India*, New Delhi: AIACHE, 1995

Jacob, Reny, and Carolyne John, compilers and editors, *Directory of Church-Related Colleges in India*, New Delhi: All India Association for Christian Higher Education, 2001

Jones, Kenneth W., *Arya Dharm: Hindu Consciousness in 19th-Century Punjab*, Berkeley: University of California Press, 1976

Jordens, J.T.F., *Dayanand Saraswati: His Life and Ideas*, Delhi: Oxford University Press, 1978

Judgments on Minority Rights, Volume - I Supreme Court of India 1951–95, New Delhi: Catholic Bishops' Conference of India and All India Association for Christian Higher Education, 1996

Juergensmeyer, Mark, *Religion as Social Vision: The Movement against Untouchability in 20th Century Punjab*, Berkeley: University of California Press, 1982

Kananaikil, Jose, *Scheduled Castes in the Constituent Assembly: Rebirth in a New Nation*, New Delhi: Indian Social Institute, 1982

Kellock, James, *Breakthrough for Church Union in North India and Pakistan*, Madras: Christian Literature Society, 1965

Kent, Eliza F., *Converting Women: Gender and Protestant Christianity in Colonial South India*, New York: Oxford University Press, 2004

Kessinger, Tom G., *Vilyatpur 1848–1968: Social and Economic Change in a North Indian Village*, Berkeley: University of California Press, 1974

Khilnani, N.M., *British Power in the Punjab 1839–1858*, Bombay: Asia Publishing House, 1972

Khiyalie, Vinod K., *Hundred Years of Baring's Mission to Batala: Christian Education and Social Change in a Punjabi Countryside*, Delhi: ISPCK, 1980

Kim, Sebastian C.H., *In Search of Identity: Debates on Religious Conversion in India*, New Delhi: Oxford University Press, 2003

Koilpillai, Victor, *The SPCK in India 1710–1985: An Account of the Work of the Society for Promoting Christian Knowledge, London, and the Indian SPCK*, Delhi: ISPCK, 1985

Korbel, Josef, *Danger in Kashmir*, Princeton: Princeton University Press, 1966

Lavan, Spencer, *The Ahmadiyah Movement: A History and Perspective*, Delhi: Manohar Book Service, 1974

Lefroy, G.A., *The Leather-Workers of Daryaganj: An Occasional Paper of the Cambridge Mission to Delhi*, 1884

Leo, Fr, *The Capuchin Mission in the Punjab with Notes on the History, Geography, Ethnology, and Religions of the Country*, Mangalore: Fr Leo, 1910.

Lucas, E.D., and F. Thakur Das, *The Rural Church in the Punjab: A Study of Social, Economic, Educational and Religious Conditions Prevailing Amongst Certain Village Christian Communities in the Sialkot District*, Lahore, 1938

Maconachie, R., *Rowland Bateman: Nineteenth Century Apostle*, London: Church Missionary Society, 1917

Malhotra, Anshu, *Gender, Caste, and Religious Identities: Restructuring Class in Colonial Punjab*, New Delhi: Oxford University Press, 2002

Mallampalli, Chandra, *Christians and Public Life in Colonial South India, 1863–1937: Contending with Marginality*, London: RutledgeCurzon, 2004

Mangat-Rai, J.N., compiler, *The History and Genealogy of the Goloknath Line*, Boston, 2002

Mathews, James K., *South of the Himalayas: One Hundred Years of the Methodist Church in India and Pakistan*, Nashville: Board of Missions of the Methodist Church, 1955

Massey, James, *Minorities in a Democracy: The Indian Experience*, New Delhi: Manohar, 1999

McKee, William J., *New Schools for Young India: A Survey of Educational, Economic and Social Conditions in India with Special Reference to More Effective Education*, Chapel Hill: University of North Carolina Press, 1930

McLeod, W.H., *Guru Nanak and the Sikh Religion*, Oxford: Clarendon Press, 1969

———, *The Evolution of the Sikh Community: Five Essays*, Delhi: Oxford University Press, 1975

———, *Who is a Sikh? The Problem of Sikh Identity*, Oxford: Clarendon Press, 1989

———, *Historical Dictionary of Sikhism*, Lanham: Scarecrow Press, 1995

Menon, V.P., *The Transfer of Power in India*, Bombay: Orient Longman, 1968

Metcalf, Barbara Daly, *Islamic Revival in British India: Deoband, 1860–1900*, Princeton: Princeton University Press, 1982

Metcalf, Thomas R., *Aftermath of Revolt: India, 1857–1870*, Princeton: Princeton University Press, 1964

Millington, C.M., *"Whether We Be Many Or Few": A History of the Cambridge/Delhi Brotherhood*, Bangalore: Asian Trading Corporation, 1999

Mitra, Alicia, *A History of the Congregation of The Religious of Jesus and Mary in India (1842–1993)*, New Delhi: The Religious of Jesus and Mary, Delhi Province, nd

Mujeeb, M., *The Indian Muslims*, London: George Allen & Unwin, 1967

Nurullah, Syed, and J.P. Naik, *A Students' History of Education in India, 1800–1961*, fourth edition, Bombay: Macmillan and Co., 1962

Oberoi, Harjot, *The Construction of Religious Boundaries: Culture, Identity and Diversity in the Sikh Tradition*, Delhi: Oxford University Press, 1994

O'Connor, Daniel, *Gospel, Raj and Swaraj: The Missionary Years of C.F. Andrews 1904–14*, Frankfurt: Verlag Peter Lang, 1990

Oddie, Geoffrey A., ed., *Religion in South Asia: Religious Conversion and Revival Movements in South Asia in Medieval and Modern Times*, Delhi: Manohar, 1977

——— (ed.), *Religious Conversion Movements in South Asia: Continuities and Change, 1800–1900*, Richmond: Curzon Press, 1997

Pandit, Vijay Laxmi, *Elites and Urban Politics: A Case Study of Delhi*, New Delhi: Inter-India Publications, 1984

Pfander, C.G., *The Mizan ul Haqq: or, Balance of Truth*, translated by R.H. Weakly, London: Church Missionary Society, 1867

Philips, C.H., H.L. Singh, and B.N. Pandey (eds), *The Evolution of India and Pakistan 1858 to 1947: Select Documents*, London: Oxford University Press, 1962

Pickett, J. Waskom, *Christian Mass Movements in India*, New York: The Abingdon Press, 1933

Piggin, Stuart, *Making Evangelical Missionaries 1789–1858: The Social Background, Motives and Training of British Protestant Missionaries to India*, Oxford: The Sutton Courtney Press, 1984

Powell, Avril A., *Muslims and Missionaries in Pre-Mutiny India*, Richmond: Curzon Press, 1993

Prasad, Durga, *Light of Truth: An English Translation of the Satyarth Prakash of Maharishi Swami Dayanand Saraswati*, second edition, New Delhi: Jan Gyan Prakashan, 1970

Prasad, Vijay, *Untouchable Freedom: A Social History of a Dalit Community*, New Delhi: Oxford University Press, 2000

Puri, Harish K., ed., *Dalits in Regional Context*, Jaipur: Rawat Publications, 2004

Puri, Harish K., and Paramjit S. Judge (eds), *Social and Political Movements: Readings on Punjab*, Jaipur: Rawat Publications, 2000

Puri, Harish K., Paramjit Singh Judge, and Jagrup Singh Sekhon, *Terrorism in Punjab: Understanding Grassroots Reality*, New Delhi: Har-Anand, 1999

Rai, Lajpat, *The Arya Samaj: An Account of its Origin, Doctrines and Activities with a Biographic Sketch of the Founder*, London: Longmans, Green and Co., 1915

Rai, Satya M., *Punjab Since Partition*, Delhi: Durga Publications, 1986

Raj, Sebasti L., *Renewal–2000: A Survey of the Archdiocese of Delhi*, New Delhi: Indian Social Institute, 1997

Report of the Commissioners Appointed by the Punjab Sub-Committee of the Indian National Congress. Vol. I: Report, Lahore 1920

Report of the General Missionary Conference held at Allahabad, 1872–73, London: Seeley, Jackson and Halliday, 1873

Report of the Punjab Missionary Conference held at Lahore in December and January 1862–63, Lodiana: American Mission Press, 1863

Richter, Julius, *A History of Missions in India*, trans. by Sydney H. Moore, New York: Fleming H. Revell Co., 1908

Riddle, Douglas Milne, *Life and Light*, Desktop Printed, 2003

Robert, Dana L., *American Women in Mission: A Social History of Their Thought and Practice*, Macon: Mercer University Press, 1996

Robinson, Rowena, *Conversion, Continuity and Change: Lived Christianity in Southern Goa*, New Delhi: Sage Publications, 1998
————, *Christians of India*, New Delhi: Sage Publications, 2003

Robinson, Rowena, and Sathianathan Clarke (eds), *Religious Conversion in India: Modes, Motivations, and Meanings*, New Delhi: Oxford University Press, 2003

Rooney, John, *On Heels of Battles: A History of the Catholic Church in Pakistan 1780–1886*, Rawalpindi: Christian Study Centre, 1986

Saberwal, Satish, *Mobile Men: Limits to Social Change in Urban Punjab*, New Delhi: Vikas, 1976

Sahu, Dhirendra Kumar, *United and Uniting: A Story of the Church of North India*, Delhi: ISPCK, 2001

Said, Edward W., *Orientalism: Western Conceptions of the Orient*, London: Penguin Books, 1995

Scott, Kenneth M., *Around the World in Eighty Years*, Franklin: Providence House Publishers, 1998

Sharma, Dewan Chand, *Kashmir under the Sikhs*, Delhi: Seema Publications, 1983

Sherring, M.A., *The History of the Protestant Missions in India from Their Commencement in 1706 to 1871*, London: Trubner and Co., 1875

Shourie, Arun, *Missionaries in India: Continuities, Changes, Dilemmas*, New Delhi: ASA, 1994

Singh, Bawa Chajju, *A Few Specialities of the Arya Samaj in Relation to Other Reforming Bodies of India*, Lahore, 1904

Singh, K.S., editor, *People of India. Volume XXXVII: Punjab*, New Delhi: Manohar, 2003; *Volume XXIII: Haryana*, New Delhi: Manohar, 1994; *Volume XX: Delhi*, New Delhi: Manohar, 1996; *Volume XXIV: Himachal Pradesh*, New Delhi: Manohar, 1996

Singh, Khushwant Singh, *Ranjit Singh: Maharajah of the Punjab*, London: George Allen & Unwin, 1962

Singh, Ram (Convener), Oommen, T.K., Barnabas, A.P., Wilkinson, T.S., Mondol, Ashish K., Thakur Das, Kuldip N., *Profile of a Christian Church: Report of the Evaluation Commission to Study the Life and Work of the Church of North India*, Madras: The Institute for Development Education, 1990

Singh, Sundar, *The Spiritual World*, Madras: Christian Literature Society, 1967

———, *With and Without Christ*, Madras: Christian Literature Society, 1969.

Singh, S. Thakar, *Comparison of Guru Nanak with Jesus Christ*, Amritsar: Wazir-I-Hind Press, 1906

Smith, Donald Eugene, *India as a Secular State*, Princeton: Princeton University Press, 1963

Smith, Solveig, *By Love Compelled: The Salvation Army's One Hundred Years in India and Adjacent Lands*, London: Salvationist Publishing and Supplies, 1981

Spear, Percival, *Twilight of the Mughals: Studies in Late Mughal Delhi*, Cambridge: Cambridge University Press, 1951

Speer, Robert E. and Carter, Russell, *Report on India and Persia of the Deputation sent by the Board of Foreign Missions of the Presbyterian Church in the USA to Visit These Fields in 1921–22*, New York: Board of Foreign Missions of the Presbyterian Church in the USA, 1922

Stanley, Brian, *The History of the Baptist Missionary Society 1792–1992*, Edinburgh: T & T Clark, 1992

Stewart, Robert, *Life and Work in India: An Account of the Conditions, Methods, Difficulties, Results, Future Prospects and Reflex Influence of Missionary Labor in India, Especially in the Punjab Mission of the United Presbyterian Church of North America*, new edition, Philadelphia: Pearl Publishing Co., 1899

Stock, Eugene, *The History of the Church Missionary Society: Its Environment, its Men and its Work. Volume III*, London: Church Missionary Society, 1899

Stock, Frederick and Margaret, *People Movements in the Punjab, with Special Reference to the United Presbyterian Church*, South Pasadena: William Carey Library, 1975

Suresh, A., ed., *Holy Father Pope John Paul II Meeting the Religious Leaders in New Delhi*, New Delhi: CCI Commission for Ecumenism and Dialogue, 1999

Talbot, Ian, *Punjab and the Raj 1849–1947*, Riverdale MD: The Riverdale Company, 1988

Tanwar, Raghuvendra, *Politics of Sharing Power: The Punjab Unionist Party 1923–1947*, New Delhi: Manohar, 1999

The Christian College in India: The Report of the Commission on Christian Higher Education in India, London: Oxford University Press, 1931

The Social, Economic and Political Problems of the Christian Community in the Punjab: Report of the Findings of a Consultation held at Rajpur, Dehra Dun, 26–30 June 1961, Bangalore: Christian Institute for the Study of Religion and Society, 1961

The New Delhi Report: The Third Assembly of the World Council of Churches 1961, New York: Association Press, 1962

The Story of the Delhi Mission, London: Society for the Propagation of the Gospel in Foreign Parts, 1908

Thirunilath, Dominic, ed., *Christianity in Jammu & Kashmir*, J&K Christian Workers' Conference, 1983

Uppal, Puran Chand, *The Conversion of Puran Chand Uppal: The Story Told by Himelf*, Lodiana, 1903

Vannini, Fulgentius, *Hindustan–Tibet Mission*, New Delhi, 1981

Village Education in India: The Report of a Commission of Inquiry, London: Oxford University Press, 1920

Walji Bhai, *Hari Charitra or Comparison between the Ad Granth and the Bible*, Lodiana: Lodiana Mission Press, 1894

Wallace, Paul, and Surendra Chopra (eds), *Political Dynamics and Crisis in Punjab*, Amritsar: Guru Nanak Dev University, 1988

Webster, John C.B., Premraj, Deborah; Swamidoss, Ida: Udayakumar, Rashilda; and Yesuratnam, Chandra, *From Role to Identity: Dalit Christian Women in Transition*, Delhi: ISPCK, 1997

Webster, John C.B., ed., *Popular Religion in the Punjab Today*, Delhi: ISPCK, 1974

———, *The Christian Community and Change in Nineteenth Century North India*, Delhi: The Macmillan Company, 1976

———, *The Nirankari Sikhs*, Delhi: Macmillan, 1979

———, *The Dalit Christians: A History*, second edition, Delhi: ISPCK, 1994

———, *Religion and Dalit Liberation: An Examination of Perspectives*, second edition, Delhi: Manohar, 2002.

Wherry, E.M., *Islam and Christianity in India and the Far East*, New York: Fleming H. Revell Company, 1907

————, *Our Missions in India 1834–1924*, Boston: The Stratford Company, 1926

Wilkinson, Heber, *Thirst of India: The Story of the Growing Church in the Diocese of Amritsar*, Toronto: The Missionary Society of the Church of England in Canada, 1954

Williams, T., *Exposure of Dayanand Saraswati and his Followers both as to their Deliberate Falsification of the Rgveda and their Immorality*, Delhi, 1889

Yadav, K.C., *The Revolt of 1857 in Haryana*, Delhi: Manohar, 1977

Youngson, J.F.W., *Forty Years of the Panjab Mission of the Church of Scotland*, Edinburgh: R.& R. Clark, 1896

V. Articles

Baago, Kaj, 'The First Independence Movement among Indian Christians', *Indian Church History Review*, 1 (June 1967), pp. 65–78

Baker, David, 'St. Stephen's College, Delhi, 1881–1997: An "Alexandria on the Banks of the Jamuna"?' in Mushirul Hasan (ed.), *Knowledge, Power and Politics: Educational Institutions in India*, New Delhi: Lotus Collection, Roli Books, 1998, pp. 66–113

Barrier, Norman G., 'The Arya Samaj and Congress Politics in the Punjab, 1894–1908', *The Journal of Asian Studies*, XXVI (May 1967), pp. 363–79

————, 'The Punjab Disturbances of 1907: the Response of the British Government in India to Agrarian Unrest', *The Panjab Past and Present*, VIII (October 1974), pp. 444–76

————, 'The Punjab Government and Communal Politics, 1870–1908', *Journal of Asian Studies*, XXVII (May 1968), pp. 523–39

Bray, John, 'A History of the Moravian Church in India', in *The Himalayan Mission: Moravian Church Centenary 1885–1985*, Leh, 1985, 28–33

Dalmia, Vasudha and Heinrich von Stietencron, 'Introduction', in Vasudha Dalmia and Heinrich von Stietencron (eds), *Representing Hinduism: The Construction of Religious Traditions and National Identity*, New Delhi: Sage Publications, 1995, pp. 17–32

Daniel, Monodeep, 'The People Who Believe that God is Faithful: The Story of the People of the Turkman Darwazah (Holy Trinity

Church), Delhi', in George Oommen and John C.B. Webster (eds), *Local Dalit Christian History*, Delhi: ISPCK, 2002, pp. 110–29

Dushkin, Lelah, 'Scheduled Caste Politics', in J. Michael Mahar (ed.), *The Untouchables in Contemporary India*, Tuscon: University of Arizona Press, 1972, pp. 165–226

Fitzgerald, Rosemary, 'Rescue and Redemption: The Rise of Female Medical Missions in Colonial India during the late Nineteenth and early Twentieth Centuries', in A.M. Rafferty, J. Robinson, and R. Elkan (eds), *Nursing History and the Politics of Welfare*, London: Routledge, 1996, pp. 64–79

Frykenberg, R.E., 'The Emergence of Modern "Hinduism" as a Concept and as an Institution: A Reappraisal with Special Reference to South India', in Gunthur D. Southeimer and Herman Kokle (eds), *Hinduism Reconsidered*, New Delhi: Manohar, 1989. pp. 29–49

Gibbs, M.E., 'The Anglican Church in India and Independence', *Bulletin of the Church History Association of India* (February 1967), pp. 43–57.

Howard, J.E., 'Is the Baptism of a Minor Legal?', *The Indian Evangelical Review*, XVII (July 1890), pp. 56–77

'India', *Seventh Day Adventist Encyclopedia*, revised edition, Washington: Review and Herald Publishing Association, 1976, pp. 622–33

'Indian Social Institute through the Fifty Years', *Indian Social Institute Golden Jubilee*, pp. 35–54.

Jodhka, Surinder S., 'Caste and Untouchability in Rural Punjab', *Economic and Political Weekly* (11 May 2002), pp. 1813–23

Johal, Daljinder Singh, 'Literary Evidence on Social Structure in the Punjab (1750–1850)', *Journal of Regional History*, I (1980), pp. 51–69

Judge, Paramjit S., 'Emerging Trends in the Caste Structure of Punjab', *The Administrator*, XLII (January–March, 1997), pp. 55–65

Kennedy, D.M., 'The CNI History', *Indian Church History Review*, VI (December 1972), pp. 101–45

———, 'Work in Progress: The CNI History', *Indian Church History Review*, VII (June 1973), pp. 1–27

Khanna, Chander Mani and Webster, John C.B., 'Views of Christianity and Christians in the Sikh Press, 1897–1930', *Bulletin of the Christian Institute of Sikh Studies*, 5 (January 1976), pp. 5–12

Martin, S., 'Work among the Depressed Classes', *Report of the Third Decennial Missionary Conference Held at Bombay, 1892–93*, Bombay, 1893, I, pp. 18–26

Masih, Alwan, 'Christian Youth Issues in Punjab: A Challenge', *Religion and Society*, XXXVIII (June 1991), pp. 51–3

Masih, Nazir, 'Education and Development of Punjabi Christians', *Religion and Society*, XXXVIII (June 1991), pp. 47–50

Maskiell, Michelle, 'Social Change and Social Control: College-Educated Punjabi Women 1913 to 1960', *Modern Asian Studies*, 19:1 (1985), pp. 55–83

Massey, James, 'Presbyterian Missionaries and the Development of Punjabi Language and Literature', *Journal of Presbyterian History*, 62 (Fall 1984), pp. 258–61

———, 'Religious Solidarity—Some Case Studies', *Bulletin of the Christian Institute of Religious Studies*, 24 (July 1995), pp. 37–42

McMullen, Clarence O., 'A Survey of the Christian Community in North West India: A Preliminary Report', *Bulletin of the Christian Institute of Religious Studies*, 22 (January 1993), pp. 20–8

———, 'The Self Image of the Christians in the Punjab', *Bulletin of the Christian Institute of Sikh Studies*, 6 (January 1977), pp. 16–23

Parker, Kenneth Lawrence, 'The Development of the United Church of Northern India', *Journal of the Department of History of the Presbyterian Church in the USA*, XVII (September–December 1936), pp. 113–202

Powell, Avril A., 'Processes of Conversion to Christianity in Nineteenth Century North-Western India', in Geoffrey A. Oddie (ed), *Religious Conversion Movements in South Asia: Continuities and Change, 1800–1900*, Richmond: Curzon Press, 1997, pp. 15–55.

Powell, Avril A., '"Pillar of a New Faith": Christianity in Late Nineteenth-century Punjab from the Perspective of a Convert from Islam', in Robert Eric Frykenberg (ed.), *Christians and Missionaries in India: Cross-Cultural Communication since 1500*, Grand Rapids: William B. Eerdmans, 2003, pp. 223–55

Puri, Harish K., 'Scheduled Castes in Sikh Community: A Historical Perspective', *Economic and Political Weekly* (28 June 2003), pp. 2693–701

Rai, Satya M., 'Agrarian Movement in the Punjab 1906–09: The Role of Lala Lajpat Rai and Sardar Ajit Singh', *Punjab History Conference English Session 15–16 December 1973 Proceedings*, Patiala: Punjabi University, 1975, pp. 132–47

Sagar, Anil, 'Problems of Christian Youth in Punjab', *Religion and Society*, XXXVIII (June 1991), pp. 65–8

Sagar, Vidya, 'The Christian Community in the Punjab: An Analogy', *Religion and Society*, XXXVIII (June 1991), pp. 13–18

Thakur Das, K.N., 'Multi-Ethnic Society and Communal Tension', *Bulletin of the Christian Institute of Sikh Studies*, 16 (January & July 1987), pp. 20–8

Thapar, Romila, 'Syndicated Moksa', *Seminar 313* (September 1985), pp. 14–22

'The Gospel for the Punjab', *Bulletin of the Christian Institute of Sikh Studies*, 4 (July, 1975), pp. 14–16

Velte, H.C., 'Mission Work Among the Low Caste Tribes of the Punjab', *Indian Evangelical Review*, 69 (July 1891), p. 11

Webster, Ellen Purdy, 'Some Aspects of the Religiosity of Punjabi Christian Girls: A Sociological Inquiry', *Bulletin of the Christian Institute of Sikh Studies*, 5 (July 1976), pp. 2–23

Webster, John C.B., 'A Quest for the Historical Ditt', *Indian Church History Review*, XXXVII (June 2003), pp. 53–68

———, 'Mission Sources of Nineteenth-Century Punjab History', in W. Eric Gustafson and Kenneth W. Jones (eds), *Sources on Punjab History*, Delhi: Manohar Book Service, 1975, pp. 171–218

———, 'Christians and Sikhs in the Punjab: The Village Encounter', *Bulletin of the Christian Institute of Sikh Studies*, 6 (December 1977), pp. 2–27

———, '"Arya Evidences"—A Study of Christian Influence', *ICHR* XII (June 1978), pp. 1–19

———, 'The History of Christianity in India: Aims and Methods', *Indian Church History Review* XIII (December 1979), pp. 87–122

————, 'Punjabi Christians and the Indian Nationalist Movement, 1919–1947', *Indian Church History Review*, XIV (December 1980), pp. 66–89

————, 'British Missions in India', in Torben Christiansen and William R. Hutchison (eds), *Missionary Ideologies in the Imperialist Era: 1880–1920*, Struer: Aros, 1982, pp. 38–47

————, 'Presbyterian Missionaries and Gandhian Politics, 1919–1922', *Journal of Presbyterian History*, 62 (Fall 1984), pp. 246–57

————, 'American Presbyterian Missionaries and Nationalist Politics in the Punjab', *Indian Church History Review*, XXXIV (June 2000), pp. 51–73

————, 'The Christian Movement in the Punjab', in Harish K. Puri and Paramjit S. Judge (eds), *Social and Political Movements: Readings on Punjab*, Jaipur: Rawat Publications, 2000, pp. 111–34

————, 'Dalits and Christianity in Colonial Punjab: Cultural Interactions', in Judith M. Brown and Robert Eric Frykenberg (eds), *Christians, Cultural Interactions, and India's Religious Traditions*, Grand Rapids: William B. Eerdmans, 2002, pp. 92–118

————, 'Missionary Strategy and the Development of the Christian Community: Delhi 1859–1884', in Selva J. Raj and Corinne C. Dempsey (eds), *Popular Christianity in India: Riting Between the Lines*, Albany: State University Press of New York, 2002, pp. 211–32

————, 'Christian Conversion in the Punjab: What Has Changed?', in Rowena Robinson and Sathianathan Clarke (eds), *Religious Conversion in India: Modes, Motivations and Meanings*, New Delhi: Oxford University Press, 2003, pp. 351–80

————, 'The Women of Amritsar through Missionary Eyes', in Reeta Grewal and Sheena Paul (eds), *Precolonial and Colonial Punjab: Society, Economy, Politics and Culture. Essays for Indu Banga*, New Delhi: Manohar, 2005, pp. 265–88

Wherry, E.M., 'Islam in North India', in *The Mohammedan World of Today, Being Papers Read at the First Missionary Conference on Behalf of the Mohammedan World held at Cairo April 4th–9th, 1906*, second edition; New York: Fleming H. Revell Company, 1906, pp. 147–71

―――, 'Some Unfounded Muslim Claims', *North India Conference of Christian Workers 1911*, pp. 36–49

―――, 'The Sinless Prophet of Islam', *The Indian Evangelical Review*, VI (April 1897)

VI. Unpublished Works

Anikuzhikattil, Michael, 'The Punjabi Century (1846–1947): Evangelization and Mass Movement, Licentiate in Church History', Paper: Pontifica Universitas Gregoriana, 1996

Brush, Stanley Elwood, 'Protestants in the Punjab: Religious and Social Change in an Indian Province in the Nineteenth Century', Unpublished PhD Dissertation: University of California, Berkeley, 1971

Dayal, Philip, 'Level of Social Integration of Ethnic Minorities: A Case Study of the Christians of Gurdaspur District in the Punjab', Unpublished PhD Dissertation: Panjab University, Chandigarh, 1982

Fernandes, Archbishop Angelo, 'Delhi in the Sixties and Seventies: Church in Action', Mimeographed, 1975

Ferrell, Donald W., 'Delhi, 1911–1922: Society and Politics in the New Imperial Capital of India', Unpublished PhD Dissertation: Australian National University Canberra, 1969

Gilmartin, David Paul, 'Tribe, Land and Religion in the Punjab: Muslim Politics and the Making of Pakistan', Unpublished PhD Dissertation: University of California, Berkeley, 1979

Griswold, H.D., 'Review of the Last Decade in the History of the Punjab Mission (1901–1910)', Typewritten in H.D.G., Letters and Articles

Harding, Christopher, 'The Dynamics of Low-Caste Conversion Movements: Rural Punjab, c. 1880–1935', Unpublished D. Phil. Dissertation: Oxford University, 2004

Jyoti, Kanchan, 'The City of Jullundur: A Study in Urban History, 1846–1947', Unpublished PhD Dissertation: Guru Nanak Dev University, 1988

Jennings, E., 'Memoir of My Father, The Rev. M.J. Jennings, M.A.', Typewritten manuscript, Dorset, nd

'Mission History of Delhi', Typewritten manuscript prepared by English Capuchins in possession of Fr Benedict Santos, Secretary, Archdiocese of Delhi

Ponnan, Joseman, and Savari Muthu Y., 'A Brief History of the Archdiocese of Delhi: A Seminar Paper Written under the Guidance of Fr Leonard Fernando SJ', Delhi: Vidyajyoti, 2003

Report on Mission Work in Delhi: Report of Revs John Aldis and Wm. Sampson, Deputation appointed to visit North-Western Provinces, 1878

Singh, Kanwar Raghbir, 'The Causes Preventing the Young Educated Indian Christians from Taking up Mission Service', A Paper Read at Jullundur City in a Conference connected with the Spring Meeting of the Lahore Presbytery, 29 March 1914 (typewritten)

Strickler, H.J., 'The Religion and Customs of the Chuhra in the Punjab Province, India', Unpublished MA Thesis, University of Kansas, 1926

Thakur Das, K.N., 'Himalayan Mission of C.M.S. And Spiritual Movements in Simla Hills 1840–1947', Unpublished cyclostyled manuscript, nd

Thakur Dass, G.L., 'Things Commendable and not Commendable in the Thought and Practice of the Arya Samaj', Handwritten ms.

Western, F.J., 'The Early Years of the Cambridge Mission to Delhi', Typewritten manuscript, 1950

Index